THE LIFE OF ROBERT BROWNING

ROBERT BROWNING
1889

THE LIFE OF
ROBERT BROWNING

WITH NOTICES OF HIS WRITINGS
HIS FAMILY, & HIS FRIENDS

BY

W. HALL GRIFFIN

COMPLETED AND EDITED BY

HARRY CHRISTOPHER MINCHIN

ARCHON BOOKS
HAMDEN, CONNECTICUT
1966

FIRST PUBLISHED 1910
METHUEN & CO., LTD.

REPRINTED 1966 WITH PERMISSION
FROM THE THIRD EDITION,
REVISED AND ENLARGED, 1938

LIBRARY OF CONGRESS CATALOG CARD NUMBER: 66-15388
PRINTED IN THE UNITED STATES OF AMERICA

PREFACE TO THIS RE-ISSUE

THE indulgence of the reading public carried this book to a second edition in 1911. To-day it is almost impossible to procure a second-hand copy ; and, a new generation of readers having arisen, the Publishers have thought it opportune to re-issue the work with corrections and additions, and at a popular price.

Since 1911 research, both in England and America, has brought to light fresh biographical materials, which have been carefully scrutinized and weighed. Browning's devoted care for old and young in their need can be seen at work in *The Last Days, Letters, and Conversations of Walter Savage Landor*, 1934, and in *The Letters of Owen Meredith to R. and E. B. Browning*, 1936, the latter admirably edited by Mr. and Mrs. J. Lee Harlan, publication in each case being made possible by the kindness of Dr. A. J. Armstrong, of Baylor University, Waco, Texas, who owns the originals. Mr. Bertram Dobell discovered in 1915 two poems from the unpublished " Incondita," supposed to have been destroyed, which will be found in Sir F. G. Kenyon's *New Poems by R. and E. B. Browning*. In her *Recollections* Mrs. Fannie Barrett Browning recalls her father-in-law's last days ; how he read to her from the proof sheets of *Asolando* " Reverie " and, with emotion, " Imperante Augusto natus est."

Certain facts have been taken, suggestions adopted, and inferences drawn from the *Correspondence of Robert Browning with Isa Blagden*, edited by Dr. A. J. Armstrong, 1923 ; from (same date) *Shelley and Browning, a Myth and some Facts*, by Professor F. A. Pottle, of Yale ; from *Browning's Parleyings : the autobiography of a mind*, by Professor W. Clyde De Vane, also of that University, 1927 ; from two valuable articles in *Modern Language Notes* by Professor W. Raymond, of Bishop's University, Lennoxville, Quebec, "New light on the genesis of *The Ring and the Book*" and "Browning's Dark Mood, a study of *Fifine at the Fair*," 1928 ; from Dean T. L. Hood's *Letters of Robert Browning*, the late Mr. Thomas A. Wise's collection, 1933 ; and from Professor De Vane's *A Browning Handbook*, 1936. The two last-named works are indispensable to the study of Browning. I have also, thanks to Dr. Armstrong, had access to an account of the poet's last illness, written by one who was staying at the Palazzo Rezzonico at the time. To all these works I am indebted ; and I desire to express my acknowledgments and thanks to their authors and editors ; also to Sir John Murray, K.C.V.O., D.S.O., for kind permission to quote from Mr. Hood's edition of the *Letters*.

It is natural, perhaps, to speculate on the number and quality of Browning's readers at the present time. He is certainly studied by many of the rising generation in America, where in many universities courses in his poetry form a part of the curriculum. In the absence of any such incentive among ourselves it is hazardous to attempt an estimate. Poetry of late has passed, and is passing, through strange phases, and in their clamour and even cacophony his nobler numbers may have lacked the attention they merit. It is my best hope for this book that it may bring him new readers. But be his admirers few or many, his fame is assured. As Mrs. Browning wrote long ago, " Robert *is*." He " has his corner at ' the Mermaid ' " ; from which nothing, short of the destruction of this planet, can, I am very sure, dislodge him.

H. C. MINCHIN

PREFACE

NO apology is expected from the author of a work of imagination, but a biographer must show cause why he has undertaken his task. Unhappily, in the present case, this duty cannot be carried out by him with whom the design originated. Professor Hall Griffin had amassed much material for a biography of Robert Browning, whose career and writings had been for many years a principal subject of his thought and study. He had been at great pains to identify the sites of his early homes in South London; thence he had followed him to Asolo and to Florence, and had gone on pilgrimage to the various cities and regions of Italy which were visited by the poet and his wife during their summer wanderings, or were the scene of their winter sojourns. Nor had he neglected spots which were closely connected with his later years; La Saisiaz, for instance, and, above all, Venice. He had enjoyed the friendship of Browning's son and sister, who gave him ungrudging help; Miss Browning's wonderful memory, in particular, throwing light upon many obscure points in her brother's early history; while he had made, with Mr. Barrett Browning's sanction, an extensive examination of the books in the Palazzo Rezzonico, those "wisest, ancient books," amid which the future poet passed his childhood. The recollections of surviving friends had been also put at his disposal; those, for example, of the late Sir Theodore Martin and of Mr. W. C. Cartwright, of Aynhoe, who was on terms of close intimacy with Browning in Florence and in Rome. At last he was ready to begin; and rather more than half his projected work was written, when an acute attack of illness obliged him to lay aside his pen, as it proved for ever.

Should this mass of material and this partial achievement be left to gather dust, unseen and useless? Or should another hand, following the author's design as closely as might be practicable, seek to complete the unfinished fabric? These were questions which Professor Griffin's executor was presently called upon to decide. After consultation with those acquainted with his plans, especially with Professor Churton Collins, whose loss also we have since had to deplore, the verdict was that the attempt, though difficult, should at least be made. The present volume is the result of that decision.

As Professor Griffin's collaborator (if the term may pass) read through the manuscript and notes entrusted to him the author's purpose became apparent. Something more complete and more exact than what his predecessors had achieved was evidently intended. Without the least desire to depreciate the interest of earlier *Lives*, certain errors— errors both of fact and of inference—were to be rectified. For the attainment of this end new material was available, to which Mrs. Orr, for example—whose work must always possess a peculiar attraction, inasmuch as she had the advantage of a close friendship with Browning—had not access ; chiefly the *Letters of Robert Browning and Elizabeth Barrett Barrett*, the four volumes of the poet's letters privately printed by Mr. Wise, and Alfred Domett's unpublished diary, of which last Professor Griffin was practically the discoverer. Again, as to the poems, no systematic interpretation of them was contemplated, such as is included in Professor Dowden's *Robert Browning*, nor any detailed criticism ; but, on the other hand, everything that could be discovered as to their origins, their growth and their reception by the public was to be included. Such was the impression which the manuscript conveyed, and it is on these lines that the task of completion has been attempted. In the result, what is now offered is not a study of the life of Robert Browning seen through a temperament, but a record based upon a sympathetic review and interpretation of accepted facts.

In the forefront of works which have been consulted, or from which brief citations have been made, are to be placed

the *Life and Letters of Robert Browning*, by Mrs. Sutherland
Orr, and her *Handbook;* and the biographical studies of the
poet by the late Mr. W. Sharp and by Professor Dowden.
To these must be added T. A. Trollope's *What I Remember;*
Miss Frances Power Cobbe's autobiography and her *Italics;*
Macready's *Reminiscences;* Forster's *Life of Dickens* and
his *Walter Savage Landor, a Biography;* Ruskin's *Modern
Painters;* Gavan Duffy's *Conversations with Carlyle* and
My Life in Two Hemispheres; Miss Martineau's *Auto-
biography;* Mrs. Andrew Crosse's *Red Letter Days;* Fanny
Kemble's *Further Records;* Dr. Moncure Conway's *Memorials
of South Place;* Nathaniel Hawthorne's *Notebooks;* Sir T.
Wemyss Reid's *Life of Lord Houghton;* Margaret Fuller's
Memoirs; The Life and Letters of Sir J. E. Millais; Connop
Thirlwall's *Letters to a Friend;* the Abbé J. Dominique's
Le poète Robert Browning à Ste. Marie de Pornic; and several
more. Some valuable information has been gleaned from
periodicals, particularly from Mrs. Bronson's papers, *Brown-
ing in Venice* (*Cornhill* and *Century*, Feb. 1902) and *Browning
in Asolo* (*Century*, 1900); those by Kate Field on Mrs. Browning
and on *The Last Days of Walter Savage Landor* (*Atlantic
Monthly*, September, 1861 and April, 1866); Miss Masson's
Robert Browning in Edinburgh (*Cornhill*, February, 1909, by
kind permission of Editor and Author); Th. Bentzon's *A
French Friend of Browning* (*Scribner*, July, 1896); and Mr.
Edmund Gosse's *Swinburne: Personal Recollections* (*Fortnightly Review*, June, 1909).

It is my duty and pleasure as collaborator to thank those
who by conversation or letter have helped me to form a
clearer conception of Browning's character and bearing;
especially Mr. Edmund Gosse, Mr. and Mrs. Sidney Colvin,
and Mrs. R. Courtenay Bell; Mr. W. M. Rossetti, Lord
Tennyson, the Master of Balliol, Mr. and Mrs. Arthur
Sidgwick, Mr. A. L. Smith, Mr. R. C. Lehmann, Mr. Comyns
Carr, and Mr. Percy Fitzgerald. I am also indebted to
several of the above for leave to derive information from
their published works; from Mr. Gosse's *Robert Browning:
Personalia* and his article *Robert Browning* in the Supplement to the *Dictionary of National Biography;* from Mr.

Rossetti's *Some Reminiscences* and *Ruskin, Rossetti, Pre-raphaelitism;* from Mr. Lehmann's *Memories of Half a Century;* from Mr. Comyns Carr's *Some Eminent Victorians;* from Mr. Percy Fitzgerald's *John Forster;* and from *Tennyson: a Memoir.* I also desire to express my acknowledgment of permission to make use of some passages in Mr. Henry James's *William Wetmore Story and his Friends,* Lady Ritchie's *Records of Tennyson, Ruskin and the Brownings,* and Mr. Marcus B. Huish's *Happy England.* My thanks are due to Messrs. F. Warne and Co. for leave to cite a passage from a preface by Mrs. Ogilvy, prefixed to their edition of Mrs. Browning's poems; to Balliol College for a similar sanction in the case of *The Life and Letters of Benjamin Jowett;* to the late Dr. F. J. Furnivall for the loan of an annotated copy of his *Browning Bibliography* and for some valuable suggestions; to Mr. Thomas J. Wise for access granted to Browning's privately printed *Letters,* and to the publications of the Browning Society; and to Mr. Alfred Nelson Domett, who put his father's diary at Professor Griffin's disposal. Above all, Mr. Barrett Browning is to be thanked, both for his assent to the scheme and for his permission, granted in conjunction with his representatives, Messrs. Smith and Elder, to utilize copyright matter, whether in the shape of letters or poems. If any other acknowledgment remain unpaid, the omission is inadvertent, and may, I trust, be pardoned.

In conclusion, I have to tender my sincere thanks to Mrs. Hall Griffin for entrusting me with a delicate and honourable task, of whose responsibilities I have been fully sensible, and to express the hope that she and Professor Griffin's friends, as well as readers of this book in general, may not be wholly dissatisfied with the result.

H. C. M.

CONTENTS

Frontispiece : PORTRAIT OF ROBERT BROWNING TAKEN IN 1889
(Photo: W. H. Grove & Son)

THE LIFE OF
ROBERT BROWNING

CHAPTER I

PARENTAGE AND EARLY HOME INFLUENCES

Robert Browning's inheritance from his grandfather—His father's early manhood in the West Indies, return to England, mode of life and marriage—His mother's parentage—His grandfather and father reconciled—His favourite uncle, Reuben—Reuben's gifts to him—Reuben's estimate of his half-brother, the poet's father—Influence of Browning's home upon his mental growth—Early reading in his father's library—His love of pictures—Gérard de Lairesse and the Dulwich Gallery—His love of music—" The Bandsman Avison "—His masters, Abel and John Relfe—His taste for out-of-the-way learning—Bernard de Mandeville and "putting a case"—His acquaintance with Daniel Bartoli's *Simboli*—His debt to Wanley's *Wonders of the Little World*, and to the *Biographie Universelle*.

ON the fly-leaf of a large, old-fashioned, illustrated family Bible there stands written in a bold, clear hand :—

"Robert Browning married to Sarah Anna Wiedemann at
Camberwell Feb 19 1811.
Robert Browning born 7th May 1812.
Sarah Anna Browning born 7th Jan 1814."

The handwriting is that of the poet's father, and these names are those of the four who composed the household at Southampton Street, Camberwell, where, wrote one who knew them well,[1] "father, mother, only son, and only

[1] Alfred Domett.

B

daughter, formed a most united, harmonious, and intellectual family."

Browning has recorded two facts connected with his own birth; that he was born with light yellow hair, and that he was born "supremely passionate." As, according to the same authority, his father was "tender-hearted to a fault," and as his mother was equally gentle, we must doubtless look to his grandfather, the first really recognizable figure in the family history, for the origin of this passionate element in the poet's nature. Robert Browning, the grandfather, was a handsome, vigorous, capable business man, first a clerk, and subsequently head of a department in the Bank of England. Evidences of his possession of a hasty and irascible temper are to be found in his dealings with his eldest son, Robert, who was to become, in course of time, the poet's father.

He was twice married, first to Margaret Tittle, a West Indian lady. They settled at Battersea, then a quiet river-side village, where, in 1782, their eldest son was born. Two years later the little family moved to Camberwell, then also a village, whose square embattled church tower was visible across the fields from Battersea, as it was from the river bridges and the cross roads of the Strand. It stood at the base of the pretty, tree-clad slopes of Denmark Hill, Herne Hill, and Champion Hill, amid hedgerows and oak trees, surrounded by well-stocked pastures and their overshadowing willows, amid flowers and fruit trees, which were the haunt of the butterfly. Was not the "Camberwell Beauty" famous? Indeed, when the Browning household moved to Camberwell the parish authorities had just been busy "apprehending" the too numerous caterpillars, and in a single season had secured some four hundred bushels! A generation later, in 1810, Dame Priscilla Wakefield[1] in her *Perambulations* described Camberwell as "a pleasant retreat for those who have a taste for the country, while their avocations still call them daily to London, as it is only three miles from that city;" and as Margaret Tittle's husband was a clerk in the Bank, Dame Priscilla's description may well apply to him.

[1] Grandmother of the famous colonizer of New Zealand, Edmund Gibbon Wakefield.

Two other children [1] were born at Camberwell, and five years after the removal from Battersea, in the spring of the year in which the Bastille fell, Margaret Tittle was laid to rest beside her youngest boy in the churchyard of the old parish church of St. Giles, not far from the village green, famous then and for more than fifty years afterwards for its boisterous annual Fair. Her sole surviving son, Robert, was but a child of seven, too young to appreciate the stirring events then taking place in the French capital where he was to pass the closing years of his life, and too young to take interest in the resolutions just submitted by Wilberforce to Parliament for the abolition of the slave trade. But some thirteen years later, when he found himself among the slaves at St. Kitt's, in a lucrative position on his late mother's sugar plantation, " he conceived such a hatred of the slave system . . . that he relinquished every prospect—supported himself, while there, in some other capacity, and came back while yet a boy, to his father's profound astonishment and rage." He had actually tried to teach a negro to read ! His father was no longer a widower ; five years after his first wife's death, when his son was twelve and he a man of forty-five, he had married a bride of twenty-three. Margaret Tittle's portrait was promptly relegated to the garret, and Margaret Tittle's son was before long allotted a definite career on his mother's West Indian estate. The " profound astonishment and rage " of the passionate man of fifty-three at his son's return are not inexplicable. Parson Adams, we are told, was " a little encumbered with a wife and six children ; " Mr. Browning's second marriage involved provision for nine. It is true that the "handsome income of twenty-three pounds a year" assigned by Fielding to the good parson did not represent that of the poet's grandfather ; but a salary of less than £500 a year is perhaps not so ample a provision for thirteen people as to lead a practical man to look with complacency upon the renunciation by his eldest son of a lucrative position, for conscientious scruples which he evidently did not share. He doubtless regarded this act very much as Sir Timothy Shelley regarded some of the acts of his incomprehensible

---

[1] Margaret Morris, died unmarried in 1857, and William, died 1784, in infancy.

son. " My father," wrote Browning in regard to this matter,
" on his return, had the intention of devoting himself to art,
for which he had many qualifications and abundant love ;
but the quarrel with his father, who married again and continued to hate him till a few years before his death, induced
him to go at once and consume his life after a fashion he
always detested." [1] This fashion was to follow in the paternal
footsteps by becoming a clerk in the Bank of England. He
took the decisive step in November, 1803, four months after
attaining his majority. Nearly fifty years later Browning's
father doubtless welcomed his release as heartily as Charles
Lamb welcomed his, when he quitted his desk in Leadenhall
Street some thirty years before. " Here am I," wrote Lamb
to Wordsworth in 1825, " after thirty-three years' slavery,
sitting in my own room at eleven o'clock, this finest of April
mornings, a freed man, with £441 a year for the remainder
of my life." The " slavery " of the poet's father had lasted
seventeen years longer than that of Lamb, but his retiring
pension amounted to not quite half that assigned to the
author of *Elia* by the directors of the East India Company.

Sarah Anna Wiedemann, the poet's mother, who was of
German parentage, though born in Scotland, had in her
girlhood also lived at Camberwell, where she and her sister
Christiana had their residence with an uncle. Christiana,
whose eldest son James became one of Browning's early
intimates, was the aunt who generously paid for the publication of *Pauline* in 1833. She had married a well-to-do
local brewer, Mr. John Silverthorne, and when Browning's
grandfather, eight years after the West Indian crisis, heard
that his eldest son was a suitor for the remaining Miss
Wiedemann, " he benevolently waited upon her uncle," wrote
the poet to Miss Barrett in 1846, " to assure him that his
niece would be thrown away on a man so evidently born to
be hanged !—these were his words." Their very violence, in
all probability, militated against the effect they were intended
to produce. The marriage took place, although without his
sanction.

Passionate and self-willed as he was, Robert Browning's
grandfather seems to have been of a far more placable nature

---

[1] *Letters of Robert Browning and Elizabeth Barrett Barrett*, vol. ii. p. 477.

than his future father-in-law, Mr. Barrett, who never forgave the marriage of his eldest daughter Elizabeth, of his second daughter Henrietta, or of his son Alfred. Son or daughter, the offence was the same; mention of them must never again be made in his presence, and their names were at once struck from his will. But, in 1819, two years before Robert Browning, the grandfather, retired from the Bank on a pension of £421 a year, he made his will, and in it he wrote :—

"As my son Robert Browning and daughter Margaret Morris Browning have had by their Uncle Tittle and Aunt Mill a much greater proportion than can be left to my [nine] other dear children, I trust they will not think I am deficient in love and regard to them : I give to my said dear children Robert and Margaret Morris Browning, ten pounds each for a ring. I give to my dear wife Jane Browning, all the rest I shall die possessed of, trusting in her love and prudence she will to the best in her power, take care of our dear children." [1]

As the irascible grandparent lived to see the publication of *Pauline* in 1833,[2] it would seem that the duration of the quarrel has been somewhat exaggerated, and that friendly intercourse may probably be regarded as having been resumed by the date of the not unkindly worded will, when the poet was a child of seven. Collateral evidence is found in the family tradition that the old man stood in dread of the proximity of his lively grandchild to his gouty foot. However this may be, it is certain that, after his death at the age of eighty-four, his widow, who was but eleven years older than her stepson, the poet's father, moved from Islington, where her husband had died, and settled once more on the south side of the river, just beyond the toll-bar at New Cross, in one of the five houses of Albert Terrace, about a hundred yards from the farmhouse cottage in which her stepson and his family came to dwell in December, 1840. It is also certain that cordial relations existed between the two households. Margaret Tittle's portrait had ere this emerged from the garret, and was

---

[1] Browning Soc. Papers, lviii., *Robert Browning's Ancestors*, by Dr. F. J. Furnivall, p. 14.

[2] *Pauline* appeared in March, 1833 ; the grandfather died in September.

hanging in her son's dining-room. At New Cross the widow's second son, Reuben, the poet's favourite uncle and but nine years his senior, stabled his horse at " The Cottage," as there was no stable at Albert Terrace on the opposite side of the high-road ; and the poet, a skilful rider from boyhood, had free use of the horse, a gallop upon whose back inspired the anapæstic lines, *As I ride, as I ride*, in which he commemorates the Arab chieftain, Abd el Kadr. But there are clear indications of pleasant intercourse even during the lifetime of the Irascible, one of which has a special suggestiveness. Reuben Browning, an excellent classical scholar, evidently took an early and kindly interest in the studies of his nephew, for on the flyleaf of a translation of Horace— whose *Odes* Browning's father is said to have known by heart—is written in Reuben's clear handwriting, " Robert Browning, July, 1824, the gift of his Uncle, Reuben Browning." This gift to the boy of twelve, who was then writing his first volume of Byronic verse, was to bear unexpected fruit ; for the translation was that of Christopher Smart, whose sad life-story Browning doubtless soon learnt from his book-loving father, and with whose *Song to David* he was not long in becoming familiar. Sixty-three years later, Smart, " who translated Horace," was hailed by the poet of seventy-five, in his *Parleyings with Certain People of Importance in their Day*, as one who had sung

> " A song where flute-breath silvers trumpet-clang,
> And stations you for once on either hand
> With Milton and with Keats."

Of Smart's long-neglected poem, termed by Rossetti " a masterpiece of rich imagery, exhaustive resources and reverberant sound," Browning became the great champion. In later days he loved to recite its fervid stanzas to his friends, and in earlier days it was not without influence upon the evolution of his own noble *Saul ;* but ten years before the date of *Saul* the sad fate of the author of the *Song to David*—Smart's only real poem—which was composed in Bedlam, had inspired some of the most striking lines in *Paracelsus* (1835) :—

"One man shall crawl
Through life surrounded with all stirring things,
Unmoved ; and he goes mad : and from the wreck
Of what he was, by his wild talk alone,
You first collect how great a spirit he hid." [1]

One other gift from his Uncle Reuben is worth mention. Its date is six years later than that of the *Horace*, but still three years before the death of the grandfather. It was not a translation this time, but an original ; an exquisite edition of the *Encheiridion* of Epictetus, printed by the scholarly and unfortunate Robert Foulis, whom Gray ranked with the Etiennes and Elzevirs, and of whose *Homer* Gibbon declared that it made even that "poet's sense appear more beautiful and transparent." Gray and Gibbon, moreover, were speaking of the ordinary editions of the Glasgow printer : every page of Browning's *Encheiridion* was a page of pure white silk.

Robert Browning, the grandfather, is said to have mainly confined his reading to the Bible and *Tom Jones*, but he certainly gave all three of his sons an excellent education. The poet's father "was a scholar and knew Greek" as well as Latin, French, Spanish, Italian, and Hebrew. The exact Latin scholarship of Reuben Browning drew words of praise from the lips of Lord Beaconsfield ; [2] and William Shergold Browning, the eldest son by the second marriage, contributed essays to the *Gentleman's Magazine*, and wrote, as well as some forgotten historical novels, a very acceptable *History of the Huguenots*. The practical father, who had placed his firstborn in the Bank of England, secured for the two younger sons positions with Messrs. Rothschild ; Reuben was in the London office, and William Shergold—of whom the households at New Cross, therefore, saw but little—was in Paris from 1824 till October, 1845. Reuben was twenty-one years younger than his half-brother Robert, the poet's father, of whom he said that "one could not know him without being

---

[1] "Depend upon it," he wrote in 1887, "no goody-goody writer ever conceived or executed the stanzas I could repeat—as I did, with all the effect I supposed would follow—to people of authority enough : Tennyson, the present Bishop of London, and, last year, to Wendell Holmes, who had asked me innocently at Oxford ' whether I knew the wonderful poem.' "

[2] See Mrs. Orr's *Life*, p. 81.

inspired with regard and admiration." He cordially admired his "extraordinary talents, profound intelligence, and pre-eminent good nature, his facetious epigrams, and fugitive poems"—the words are his own—and regretted that, owing to a most unassuming, reticent, and retiring nature, "of all his acquaintance few were cognisant of his intrinsic worth." Reuben placed on record his impressions, and this is his description :—

" His wonderful store of information might really be compared to an inexhaustible mine. It comprised not merely a thorough scholastic outline of the world, but the critical points of ancient and modern history, the lore of the Middle Ages, all political combina-tions of parties, their description and consequences ; and especially the lives of the poets and painters, concerning whom he ever had to communicate some interesting anecdote not generally known. In short, he was a living encyclopædia. The love of reading attracted him by sympathy to books ; old books were his delight, and by his continual search after them he not only knew all the old book-stalls in London, but their contents, and if any scarce work were spoken of, he could tell forthwith where a copy of it could be had. Nay, he would even describe in what part of the shop it was placed, and the price likely to be asked for it. Thus his own library became his treasure. His books, however, were confessedly not remarkable for costly binding, but for their rarity or for interesting remarks he had to make on most of them ; and his memory was so good that not infrequently, when a conversation at his table had reference to any particular subject, has he quietly left the room and in the dark, from a thousand volumes in his library, brought two or three illustrations of the point under discussion." [1]

The well-knit, rather undersized, blue-eyed, bright-com-plexioned book-lover, who had "the scent of a hound and the snap of a bull-dog" for an old or rare volume, eagerly visiting the bookstalls of London or, in later days, those on the Quais of Paris, recalls the tall, quick-eyed, rapid-striding Southey bent on similar quests ; and the home at South-ampton Street resembled Greta Hall in that it was lite-rally overflowing with books. "Why, Montesinos," remarks

[1] Introductory notes by Reuben Browning, prefixed to a small volume of sketches by Robert Browning, senior. The sale of this work in an auction room is recorded in the *Art Journal*, 1896, p. 55.

Southey, at the beginning of his Colloquy on the Library,
" with these books, and the delight you take in their constant
society, what have you to covet or desire ? " " Nothing," was
the reply—" except more books."

Such a book-lover, then, was the poet's father ; and
rightly to understand the poet's own development it is
absolutely essential to understand his home, for there to
all intents and purposes he received his whole early education ; consideration of what more conventional training he
had may fitly, for the moment, be postponed. His school
life counts for very little ; of college life he had practically
none ; but among his father's books he read voraciously.
" It was in this way," said his sister, "that Robert became
very early familiar with subjects generally unknown to boys."

The *Parleyings with Certain People of Importance in their
Day,* published in 1887, towards the close of his life, has, no
less than *Pauline* at the beginning of his career, a distinctly
autobiographical importance, and affords an éxcellent example of the peculiar home influences exerted upon Browning
during his early life. Reference has already been made to
Christopher Smart, but he is only one of the seven people
with whom the poet of seventy-five supposes himself to be
holding converse in his *Parleyings.* To most readers, perhaps, Gérard de Lairesse, Charles Avison, George Bubb
Dodington, Bernard de Mandeville, and Daniel Bartoli are
little more than names ; but with Browning the Flemish
painter, the Newcastle musician, the eighteenth-century
politician, the anglicized Dutchman, and the Italian Jesuit
historian, were all " men whose works connected themselves
with the intellectual sympathies and the imaginative pleasures
of his very earliest youth." [1] For example, Browning's father,
as has been mentioned, had desired to be an artist, and among
his books was the second English edition, that of 1778, of *The
Art of Painting in all its Branches,* by Gérard de Lairesse.
On the fly-leaf of this volume Browning made the following
note :—

" I read this book more often and with greater delight when I
was a child than any other : and still remember the main of it most

---

[1] Mrs. Orr in her *Handbook,* p. 339, stated on Browning's authority.

gratefully for the good I seem to have got from the prints and wonderful text."

This note was made in 1874, thirteen years before the appearance of the *Parleyings*, in which he speaks of de Lairesse as

> "the man I loved
> Because of that prodigious book he wrote
> On Artistry's Ideal."

The English translation of the *Groot Schilderboek* of the Flemish artist may reasonably be called a "prodigious book" with its two substantial quarto volumes, its five hundred pages of solid technical matter, and its seventy purely technical illustrations. Is it not significant that this, the accepted text-book[1] of two or three generations of art students in Europe, should be the favourite reading in childhood of the future poet of *Andrea del Sarto* and *Fra Lippo Lippi?* It became, indeed, sadly true in regard to this volume, as to much else, that

> "Bearded experience bears not to be duped
> Like boyish fancy,"

yet the memorable "Walk" which de Lairesse described with so much elaboration in his two closing chapters on Landscape[2]—

> "'Walk,' come what come may,
> No measurer of steps on this our globe
> Shall ever match for marvels,"

not only delighted Browning as a boy, but so far retained its fascination for "bearded experience" that the poet of seventy-five matched it in his *Parleyings* with his own splendid description of another imaginary walk. But to the student of Browning it is of far greater interest to connect the boy's delight in the imaginary walk in the company

[1] As late as 1817 W. M. Craig, a painter to the Queen, in editing a new edition, wrote, "I have repeatedly recommended it in my lectures at the Royal Institution as the best work on art that my auditors could consult."

[2] Book VI. deals with Landscape. Chapter XVI. is of the "Painter-like Beauty in the Open Air"; Chapter XVII., "Of things Deformed and Broken, falsely called 'Painter-like.'" These are illustrated by a walk in which appropriate objects are supposed to be seen.

of de Lairesse among tombs, temples, monuments, and other
paraphernalia of the pseudo-classical school, with the oft-
repeated "green half-hour's walk" across the meadows
between Camberwell and Dulwich in company with his
father, past hedges and stiles, ivy-covered cottages, and the
homely but genuine village pound and stocks. For Browning,
it must be remembered, was "a young wonder" at drawing,
and it is a significant coincidence that the very year in which
his father proudly wrote " R. B. ætat. two years and three
months" beneath a little picture of a "certain cottage and
rocks in lead pencil and black currant-juice—paint being
rank poison, as they said when I sucked my brushes"—was
the year in which the Dulwich Picture Gallery was opened.

It is difficult, after nearly a century has passed, to realize
the importance of thus making accessible to the Londoner of
1814 the gift of Sir Francis Bourgeois. The National
Gallery did not exist ; Trafalgar Square itself was undreamt
of. Mr. Angerstein's collection of thirty-eight pictures, the
nucleus of the present national collection, was not bought by
the nation until ten years later, and for fourteen years after
its purchase it still remained in the ill-lighted rooms of the
collector's private house in Pall Mall ; not till April, 1838—
i.e. twenty-four years after the opening of the Dulwich collection—was the present National Gallery thrown open.
Dulwich was thus, during the early years of the nineteenth
century, the chief English public picture gallery. Not only
was it a novelty to view pictures in a building specially constructed for their reception, but the Dulwich collection
attracted attention by reason of the representative character
of the three hundred and fifty paintings it contained ; for
these included examples of the Dutch, French, Spanish,
Italian, and English schools. The Brownings lived but two
miles from Dulwich: what wonder that the art-loving father
of the poet was always well supplied with the tickets then
necessary for admission ? What wonder that Browning
wrote of Dulwich as the " gallery I so love and am so grateful
to, having been used to going there when a child far under
the age [fourteen] allowed by the regulations" ? And is it
not noticeable in connection with his subsequent sympathetic
interpretation of pictures and painters, that he added, " I

have sate before one, some *one* of those pictures I had pre-determined to see, a good hour, and then gone away"? If, therefore, for the general public the importance of the Dulwich Gallery has diminished, as certainly, for the student of Browning, its importance remains. It was this gallery, in conjunction with the work of de Lairesse, which bred and nurtured in the future poet his intense interest in the sister-art of painting.

Rossetti described Browning's father as having "a real genius for drawing—but caring for nothing in the least except Dutch boors," and as late as 1842 Mrs. Jameson could speak of the Dulwich Gallery as "the only collection freely accessible to the public which affords an opportunity of studying the Dutch masters." The landscapes of Cuyp and others did not attract the father: his favourite English artist was Hogarth, of whose works he had a capital collection of prints; and, among Dutch artists, he admired "Brouwer, Ostade, Teniers—he would turn from the Sistine altar-piece to these," said his son. And even to-day these artists are represented at Dulwich as they are represented in no other English public gallery; indeed, the "Interior of an Ale-house" (No. 108), by the hard-drinking Adrian Brouwer, is said to be unsurpassed in any of our public galleries. Of Adrian Ostade there are four examples; of the Teniers, father and son, twenty-two. Browning himself is said, during his school days, to have been fond of "making pen-and-ink caricatures, which he did very cleverly," and when reminded of the fact in later years he remembered it, and remarked that he "had always envied the life of an artist."[1] This temporary tendency to caricature would seem to have been due to the influence of his father, of whom Reuben Browning wrote :—

"His caricatures were of so amusing a nature that it is surprising and to be regretted that so few of them were made public. Their extraordinary merit is enhanced by the manner and rapidity with which they were produced. Generally speaking, they were the work of a moment: at a party, perhaps, when any public or private topic

[1] With this remark, however, it is well to compare the passage from *Pauline* quoted in the next chapter, p. 30.

of the day engrossed attention, forthwith with slips of paper and pencil at hand he issued scores of sketches illustrative of the subject, to which his never-failing satire attached some witty explanation, sure to excite the admiration and risible faculties of the company."

These hasty sketches, hundreds of which still remain, are usually heads, but more rarely full-length figures ; as a rule they are mere graphic outlines, but occasionally they are cleverly filled in with washes of sepia or indian ink. In almost all cases they are grotesque : Browning's father could not draw a pretty face. If, however, Browning himself ever came under the influence of the Dutch school, even for caricatures, it was but for a time ; and one would imagine him even as a boy marching resolutely past the Dutch pictures in the first two rooms of the Dulwich gallery to sit down before the paintings he mentioned to Miss Barrett in 1846—"those two Guidos, the wonderful Rembrandt's ' Jacob's Vision,' such a Watteau, the triumphant three Murillo pictures, a Giorgione music-lesson group, all the Poussins with the 'Armida' and ' Jupiter's nursing.'" In this list there is but one Dutch picture, and that is not of the school of Ostade and Teniers. Modern critics look coldly and more than sceptically upon the so-called Rembrandt,with its dimly lighted figure of the patriarch below and the "bird-like" angels in the glow of light above, but in earlier days it was indeed held to be "wonderful." Hazlitt spoke of it with rapture, and Mrs. Jameson knew "nothing more wild, visionary, and poetical." [1] The "Fête Champètre" (No. 167)—"such a Watteau"— remains an excellent example of the peculiar style of that French painter ; and although, in the days when Hazlitt was teaching the public that "no one ever told a story half so well" on canvas as Poussin, the sixteen paintings by that master attracted more attention than they now do, yet it is true even to-day that one can study Poussin to better advantage at Dulwich than at Trafalgar Square, and that the "Rinaldo and Armida" (No. 238) and its pendant, "The infant Jupiter suckled by the goat Amalthea" (No. 234), are,

---

[1] It may be hazardous, but one can hardly resist the temptation of regarding this once famous picture as having consciously or unconsciously played a part in the evolution of Browning's well-known lines on the "Lyric love."—W. H. G.

as they were to Browning, pictures of note. But, from the very first, three Murillo pictures out of the ten by that painter were acknowledged to be "triumphant"—the gems of the gallery; not the much retouched "Madonna del Rosario" (No. 281) of the fifth room, but the "Spanish Flower-girl" (No. 199), with its mellow browns and yellows, and the two splendid groups of Spanish peasant boys, Nos. 222 and 224, the latter of which Hazlitt declared to be not only the "triumph of the collection," but "almost of painting." Of Italian pictures, with which he was to become so familiar in middle life, Browning alludes to the " St. John " (No. 262) and to the " St. Sebastian " (No. 268) of Guido Reni, which faced one in the distance on entering the gallery ninety years ago as they do to-day, and to the Giorgione "Music Lesson," now no longer attributed to that painter.

But, apart from all questions of merit or authenticity, the fact remains that it was at Dulwich that Browning first learnt to study and interpret painters and pictures. For example, after reading in his loved de Lairesse that artist's description of the ideal of landscape as a setting for

"flying shapes, earth stocked with brood
Of monsters—centaurs bestial, satyrs lewd,—
Not without much Olympian glory, shapes
Of god or goddess in their gay escapes,"

he himself has told how his youthful piety obtained somewhat dubious satisfaction by making acquaintance with the artist-work of this unfortunate painter; and such acquaintance began with the " Pan and Syrinx " (No. 179) and the "Apollo and Daphne " (No. 176) at Dulwich. It was at Dulwich that the Raphael of Browning's *One Word More* first became to him, if only through the figures of two saints from a predella,[1] something more than a name among painters. At Dulwich he first became acquainted with the Guercino of his *Guardian Angel*, and with the Tizian and Giorgione who appear in his *In a Gondola ;* nay, that the name of a painter so rare and so little known as Bartolomeo Schedone is introduced

[1] No. 241.

into the latter poem is simply due to the fact that Browning had seen it as a boy beneath two pictures at Dulwich. Here, too, Browning first saw a Madonna by Andrea del Sarto ; and even " florid old rogue Albano " and the Carlo " Maratta who paints Virgins so," of whom he was to make such effective and dramatic use fifty years later in *The Ring and the Book*, became familiar to him in his teens in the collection of Sir Francis Bourgeois.

The volumes of de Lairesse abound in references to painters, and by way of commentary Browning had Vasari's *Lives* and Pilkington's *Dictionary of Painters*—from the latter of which most of his early knowledge of the history of art was gained [1]—as well as the abundant learning of his father, who, as we have seen, " had ever to communicate some interesting fact not generally known " about both poets and painters. With the *Notizie* of Filippo Baldinucci it does not seem that Browning became familiar until his residence in Florence : its influence certainly is not marked until the appearance of *Fra Lippo Lippi* in 1855, and not avowed until the *Filippo Baldinucci on the Privilege of Burial* in the *Pacchiarotto* volume of 1876.

If the name of Gérard de Lairesse is thus to be associated with Browning's early education in art, that of " Charles Avison, organist in Newcastle," with whom he also held an imaginary parleying in 1887, may be associated with his life-long interest in music. Avison is doubtless now re-membered, if remembered at all, by the familiar air adapted from one of his old-fashioned concertos by Thomas Moore for his well-known *Sacred Song*, " Sound the loud timbrel." And it was not from the *Essay on Musical Expression* referred to in his poem that Browning first came in touch with " the bandsman Avison," although two copies of this little book were on his father's shelves. His love of music, which was marked even from earliest childhood, came to him from his mother, a sympathetic and accomplished musician who loved to sit at the piano in the gloaming when, perhaps, amid the gathering darkness, the spell of music is most subtle and most potent : and one of his earliest memories was of her

---

[1] Browning used the 1805 edition, revised by Henry Fuseli. The influence of Pilkington is plainly traceable in his work.

playing Avison's once popular Grand March in C Major, which

> " timed in Georgian years
> The step precise of British Grenadiers."

This was in the days ere his little "hand could stretch an octave ;" and seventy years later the memory of his early love led him to print the music of this simple march from an old manuscript copy, at the end of his *Parleying*.

Avison, however, was but one and not at all the most important of the early musical influences upon Browning. Abel, a pupil of Moscheles, was his instructor in technique,[1] and he was also, as he mentions in his *Parleying*, "an all-unworthy pupil" of

> " Great John Relfe,
> Master of mine, learned, redoubtable."

John Relfe, musician in ordinary to his Majesty, was the son of one who for fifty years had officiated as organist at Greenwich Hospital, and was himself reputed to be among the best teachers of the pianoforte in London. He was, moreover, a composer and a writer upon musical theory, and as he lived in Church Row, Camberwell—close to St. Giles' Church—it was all the more natural that Browning should be among his pupils.

It was from the learned author of the *Principles of Harmony*, of *Lucidus Ordo*—"an attempt to divest thorough-bass and composition of their intricacies"—and other works, that Browning gained that knowledge of musical theory which helped him to set songs to music, to compose fugues, and emboldened him, before he was twenty-one, to contemplate writing an opera! "I was studying the grammar of music," said Browning, in later life, "when most children are learning the multiplication table, and I know what I am talking about when I speak of music."[2]

It was John Relfe with his "Mu-schedula" or music

---

[1] It was of him that Browning, in later life, told the following story : "Yes," Abel said to him, "I am in love; it destroys my appetite, interferes with my sleep, and considerably breaks in upon my practising!" (Wise, *Letters from R. B.*, vol. ii. p. 72).

[2] From the record of a conversation with Mrs. Ireland, communicated by her to the *Manchester Examiner and Times* of 18 December, 1889.

scroll who claimed to teach Browning and his other pupils "not only Thorough Bass, but the whole arcana of the science, so as completely to analyze any regular composition." And the influence of this learned, redoubtable contrapuntist is seen combined with that of "the bandsman Avison," the writer on musical expression, in lines so technical as those which describe the emotion of the lovers as they listen in Venice to Galuppi playing upon the harpsichord :—

"What?   Those lesser thirds so plaintive, sixths diminished, sigh
     on sigh,
Told them something?   Those suspensions, those solutions—
   'must we die?'
Those commiserating sevenths—'Life might last! we can but try!'"

From the days when as a mere child he stole downstairs from bed to listen to his mother at the piano, and, as she ceased, flung himself into her arms, whispering, amid sobs, "Play, play," until the days when he drew music from the organ at Vallombrosa, or charmed his intimate friends with his improvisations on the piano, or wrote *Abt Vogler, Master Hugues of Saxe-Gotha* and *A Toccata of Galuppi,* and became the friend of Joachim and Clara Schumann, Browning remained a music-lover. At Asolo, during the last months of his life, he would sit in the little *loggia* of his friend Mrs. Bronson, and in the gathering twilight would discourse old-time melodies upon the little tinkling spinet which his hostess had provided for his pleasure ; with perchance a thought of the days when his loved mother used to play in the gloaming among the trees and flowers of Camberwell, in the land where the thrush sings "at the bent spray's edge."

That Browning in early life read the *Diary* of that now-forgotten, self-seeking eighteenth-century time-server, George Bubb Dodington, is in itself of slight importance. What is of importance is that the two copies of this work which stood on the bookshelves of Southampton Street may be accepted as an indication of the fact that those shelves were crowded with historical works. Browning's father was an intense student of history, and even when he was an old man of nearly eighty-five, his son declared: "The other day, when I wanted some information about a point of mediæval

c

history "—it was in connexion with *The Ring and the Book*—
" he wrote a regular bookful of notes and extracts thereabout."
This inquiry and the ready response with which it met are
typical both of the father and of the son. It was from his
encyclopædic father that Browning inherited a taste for
out-of-the-way learning and out-of-the-way people, and that
bias which led him instinctively to deal with a real Paracelsus
or Sordello, and with a real " Roman murder case."   Indeed,
when he came to define the creative power of the poet, he
declared

> " That, although nothing which had never life
> Shall get life from him, be, not having been,
> Yet, something dead may get to live again."

It would, however, be an utter mistake to conceive of
Browning at any period of his life as a literary or historical
antiquary ; his varied knowledge came to him in the most
natural way. He read extensively among the historical works
in his father's library, and thus unconsciously developed that
tendency toward historical accuracy which is so singularly
combined in him with imaginative power.   Yet it is not
without significance that through the influence of the French
friend who is said to have suggested *Paracelsus* Browning
was made, in the very year in which that poem was published,
a member of the *Institut Historique* of France : and that
within six months of the appearance of this poem he was
helping his new friend, John Forster, to complete his prose
Life of Strafford.[1] Not to speak of *Sordello* and its well-
known familiarity with what George Eliot happily terms
" those hidden lakelets of knowledge in the high mountains
far removed from the vulgar eye, only visited by the soaring
birds of love," there is manifest in *The Ring and the Book*
a wide knowledge of the social, political, religious, and
artistic history of the period to which the story refers ; and
Browning's father was not the only one whom he consulted
as to the accuracy of the details of his poem. He actually
communicated with the Astronomer Royal concerning the
phases of the moon in the year 1697 before he would insert

---

[1] Information from Miss Browning puts this matter beyond dispute ; none the
less, the completed work is Forster's, not Browning's.

the words of Caponsacchi to Pompilia with regard to their flight on April 22 of that year :—

> "Leave this house in the dark to-morrow night,
> Just before daybreak :—there's new moon this eve—
> It sets, and then begins the solid black."[1]

The *Fable of the Bees*, by Bernard de Mandeville, that daring, outspoken contemporary of Swift and Addison, was condemned by the Grand Jury of Westminster in 1723 as "having a direct tendency to the subversion of all religion and civil government, our duty to the Almighty, our love to our country, and regard to our oaths " ; and yet, this so-called " dangerous and immoral " book, the title-page of which boldly declared "private vices public benefits" was presented to Browning by his father on Friday, 1 February, 1833—three months before his majority. As the influences of Browning's home were strongly religious, this is the more suggestive. His father had, after his custom, annotated the volume, and he evidently had scant sympathy with the views of the Westminster Jury; so had Browning. Mandeville forthwith became "my fine fellow" ; and when, in 1887, Browning wrote his *Parleying*, he actually so far identified himself with the much abused author, that he made him the mouthpiece of his own views in an argument on speculative matters with one who represents Carlyle. Browning evidently accepted Mandeville's various *Vindications* of his work—these were included in the copy given him by his father—and it would seem probable that these *Vindications* were not without influence upon the evolution of his own later defences of a Blougram and a Sludge : while his avowed admiration for Mandeville's power of making "a case" can hardly be dissociated from that striking example of his own powers in the same direction which is furnished in *Fifine at the Fair*.

Yet another name connected with the *Parleyings* is that of Daniel Bartoli. Browning himself felt that this name at least would be so unfamiliar to his readers that he added a footnote to explain that Bartoli was a "Jesuit and the historian of that Order." To this footnote, which is in Italian, is affixed the name of Angelo Cerutti ; and it was

---

[1] So he informed Lord Courtney of Penwith, in a letter dated 14 May, 1881.

he who brought the works of Bartoli to Browning's notice. Born in the Milanese, Angelo Cerutti became, like so many of his countrymen, an Italian in England; he gave lessons in his native tongue in London, and his dwelling was at Camberwell. Having returned to Italy, he published an autobiography, in which he mentions that while teaching at the school of the Misses Goodson at Camberwell he had as a pupil a young lady named Browning "ben fornito d'intelletto," with black eyes and hair and a complexion so dark that she seemed Italian rather than English.[1] For his English pupils, among whom was Browning as well as his sister, Cerutti prepared an Italian grammar; and as, during the early part of the nineteenth century, Daniel Bartoli was being proclaimed by the poet Monti and others, "the purest and one of the greatest prose writers of Italy," Cerutti also prepared for his pupils an edition of the *Simboli*[2] which he considered one of the three best works by Bartoli. In the list of subscribers for this reprint appear the names of "Robert Browning, Esquire," then aged eighteen, and of his sister; and it was from the preface to this book that Browning selected the footnote for his *Parleying*. For years the *Simboli* formed his favourite reading, and partly on account of its contents, partly on account of the purity of its style, he took it with him to Italy in 1838; and thus it happened that upon the cover of this octavo volume he wrote in pencil during the voyage his *Good News from Ghent* and *Home Thoughts from the Sea*.

The books and writers of the *Parleyings* of 1887 are, therefore, indicative of much in the early life and training of Browning; but perhaps no single volume in his father's collection played such an important part in stimulating his early love for the odds and ends of learning as that fascinating storehouse of fact and fancy, *The Wonders of the Little World*, by the seventeenth-century Coventry divine, Nathaniel Wanley, father of the well-known antiquary.[3] This book,

---

[1] *Vita da lui scritta*, 1846, vol. i. p. 332. "Con occhi e capelli neri e color bruno, ella pareva piu presto italiana che inglese."

[2] De' Simboli Transportati al morale dal P. Danielo Bartoli edizione coretta e emendata da Angelo Cerutti. Londra [1830?].

[3] Wanley, it is clear, remained a life-long favourite with the poet. "See how prettily," he writes to Frederick Lehmann in 1873, "the story is told in the

with its thousands of anecdotes illustrating the prodigies of
human nature, shows omnivorous reading, and upon its
treasures the father of the poet often drew for the amusement of his children. In its pages and in those of the ever-
delightful *Epistolæ Ho-Elianæ* of Ben Jonson's friend, the
much-travelled James Howell—one of Thackeray's "bedside
books"—Browning first read of the Pied Piper of Hamelin.
The story, however, was familiar to him even before he had
learned to read, for it was a favourite with his legend-loving
father, who, devoted as he was to children, versified and
illustrated the tale with pen and pencil for other small folk
than those of his own family. One house which he often
visited was at Hackney, the home of Mr. Earles, who, like
himself, was in the Bank of England, and the following
extract from a version of the Pied Piper by Browning's father
leaves little room for speculation as to whence came the poet's
tendency to odd rhymes and humorous verse :—

"There is at a moderate distance from Hanover—
      A town on the Weser of singular fame :
A place which the French and the rats often ran over—
      But though my tale varies
      Yet sage antiquaries
Are all in one story concerning its name—
'Tis Hammelin (but you had better perhaps
Turn over your atlas and look at the maps)—
      Which, without flattery,
      Seem'd one vast rattery ;
Where the rats came from no mortal could say—
      But for one put to flight
      There were ten the next night ;—
And for ten over night, there were twenty next day :—
      With double the number perhaps the next morning—
      In vain did the lodgers and tenants give warning—
And declared that unless they were driven away—
      The rats and taxation
      Would bring on starvation—
And they wouldn't stay to be famished—not they !"[1]

good old style of Wanley, 1677." The story is the familiar one of the young man
who bore a striking resemblance to Augustus.

[1] This version ends abruptly, after about sixty lines, with the following note :
"I began this not knowing that Robert had written on this subject ; having heard

Browning, it will be remembered, called his own poem "a child's story," for it was written for a boy of ten, little Willie Macready, the son of the actor. It was natural, when asked for some verses for the sick child to illustrate, that he should instinctively think of the legend he himself had enjoyed since childhood, a legend, moreover, which his own father's sketches had taught him was so well suited for varied and graphic illustration.

But the influence of Nathaniel Wanley is by no means confined to the *Pied Piper ;* it can be traced from the *Pauline* of 1833 to the *Asolando* volume of 1889. It seems strange, for instance, to the ordinary reader, to encounter at the beginning of a poem by a youth of twenty a long extract in Latin from a work by so unfamiliar a person as that German occult philosopher of the sixteenth century, Heinrich Cornelius Agrippa. But Browning had had his youthful imagination stimulated by reading in Wanley how the magician Agrippa could cause an evil spirit to enter into the body of a dead man and make it seem alive ;[1] and how Agrippa himself " was ever accompanied with a devil in the shape of a black dog which on his death-bed he dismissed with the words, *Abi, perdita bestia, quæ me perdidisti :* ' Begone thou wretched beast which hast utterly undone me. ' "[2]   When, therefore, he found among his father's books a little octavo volume lettered *H. Corn. Agrippa. Opera,*[3] he doubtless pounced upon it eagerly ; nor would his interest be lessened by the fact that his father had made a note on the fly-leaf to say that the book had once formed part of the library of so attractive an occult philosopher as Sir Kenelm Digby. From this volume, then, he borrowed his preface to *Pauline.* Paracelsus, again, seems an odd subject for a young man of three-and-twenty to select for his first acknowledged poem ; but the anecdotes

him mention it, I stopped short. I never saw his manuscript till some weeks afterward.   R. B., 2nd March, 1843." This note was evidently added some time after the lines were written, for Browning's poem was published in November, 1842 ; possibly this publication suggested the note.   At a later date the father was bold enough to complete his version by the addition of some two hundred lines, so that it assumed about the same proportions as that of his son.

[1] *Wonders of the Little World,* ed. 1806, vol. ii. p. 270, § 18.

[2] *Ibid.*

[3] The first volume, at least, was there ; and doubtless the others also.

in Wanley had made the name of the Swiss physician familiar to Browning almost from the days of the nursery, and his father "was completely versed in mediæval legend and seemed to have known Paracelsus, Faustus, and even Talmudic personages, personally."[1] Added to which, Browning, as he glanced at the bookshelves, would see beside the folio edition of Fuller and the 1692 folio of Bunyan, three folio volumes, upon the title-page of which he would read, *Aur. Philip. Theoph. Paracelsi Bombast. ab Hohenheim medici et philosophi celeberrimi, Chemicorumque Principis, Opera omnia;*[2] and opposite the title-page of the first volume he would be confronted with the face of Paracelsus himself—an engraving from the portrait which Tintoretto had painted *ad vivum* the year before Paracelsus died.

It was in Wanley, too, that Browning met with odd names, such as Schafnaburgensis,[3] which he used in 1842 in the title of one of his two poems called *Garden Fancies ;* and it was in Wanley that he read of the "prestigious feats almost incredible" of "Johannes Teutonicus, a Canon of Halberstadt in Germany," who reappears in *Transcendentalism* among the *Men and Women* of 1855 as the "stout mage" John of Halberstadt who "vents a brace of rhymes," and forthwith the roses spring up "over us, under, round us every side." It was in Wanley[4] that he read as a boy how "Pope Stephen the Seventh, having been hindered from the Popedom by Formosus, his predecessor, when after his death he was made Pope, caused his fingers to be cut off, and to be cast into the river for the fish to devour"; and this incident, which Browning's father used to relate to his children as they sat upon his knee, afterwards became the theme of the first hundred and fifty lines of the Pope's noble speech in *The Ring and the Book*. Nor does the influence of Wanley cease in 1869 with *The Ring and the Book ;* twenty years later in *Asolando*, the last volume Browning published, appeared the lines called *The Cardinal and the Dog*, which tell how, at

---

[1] W. Sharp's *Browning*, p. 19.
[2] This was the 1658 Geneva edition, the best, by F. Bitiskius, from whom Browning quotes so freely in the notes to his poem.
[3] That is, a native of Aschafenburg.
[4] Wanley, *Wonders of the Little World*, vol. ii. p. 37, § 9, ed. 1806.

the Council of Trent, Cardinal Crescentio sat writing letters, when

> "A black dog of vast bigness, eyes flaming, ears that hung
> Down to the very ground almost, into the chamber sprung
> And made directly for him, and laid himself right under
> The table where Crescentio wrote—who called in fear and wonder
> His servants in the ante-room, commanded everyone
> To look for and find out the beast ; but, looking, they found none."

In regard to which incident Browning declares, "I give mine Author's very words : he penned, I reindite." How far this is the case may be judged from the following from "mine Author," Wanley :—

> "Crescentius the Pope's Legate at the Council of Trent 1552, March 25, was busie writing of Letters to the Pope till it was far in the night, whence rising to refresh himself, he saw a black dog of a vast bigness, flaming eyes, ears that hung down almost to the ground enter the room, which came directly towards him, and laid himself down under the table. Frightened at the sight, he called his Servants in the Anti-chamber [*sic*], commanded them to look for the Dog, but they could find none. The Cardinal fell melancholy, thence sick, and died at Verona : on his death-bed he cryed out to drive away the Dog that leaped upon his bed." [1]

These lines, however, although not published till 1889, were written in 1842 for little Willie Macready, at the same time as the *Pied Piper ;* but there is a later example of the survival of the influence of Wanley to be mentioned. In 1883 Browning's *Jocoseria* appeared, the name being taken from "such rubbish as Melander's *Jocoseria*," as that volume had been termed in a note to *Paracelsus ;* for, like the works of Cornelius Agrippa and Paracelsus, Otto Melander's dumpy little Latin volume of eleven hundred pages of seventeenth-century jest and anecdote was on the bookshelves at Southampton Street. Browning, having been taken to task for his literary shortcomings, replied to his critics at the close of his volume of 1883, and the reply was in the form of a metrical version of an anecdote from Wanley :—

> "Pambo came to a learned man, and desired him to teach him

---

[1] *Wanley*, p. 611, ed. 1678. Browning, by mistake, gives the date of the Council of Trent as 1522 instead of 1552.

some Psalm : he began to read to him the thirty-ninth, and the first verse, which is : ' I said I will look to my ways, that I offend not with my tongue.' Pambo shut the book, and took his leave, saying, ' he would learn that point.' And having absented himself some months, he was demanded by his teacher, 'When he would go forward?' He answered, ' That he had not yet learned his old lesson—to speak in such a manner as not to offend with his tongue.' " [1]

Browning in 1883 genially saluted his forerunner as a brother—"*Arcades ambo sumus*" ; for fifty years he said, in substance, I have done my best—

> " Yet much the same
> *Offend with my tongue*—like Pambo ! "

It is singular, therefore, that Wanley's curious book has been consistently neglected by students of Browning. They have also overlooked the *Biographie Universelle* which he so freely consulted. Browning quotes from its pages in his Note to *Paracelsus*, he used it for *Sordello*, he took from it the subject of his proposed tragedy of *Narses*, it helped him to *King Victor and King Charles*, and it suggested the idea of *The Return of the Druses*. One would almost surmise that he had read its fifty volumes through.

Such are some of the influences of the Camberwell home upon Browning. As an infant he was hushed to sleep by his father to the words of an ode by Anacreon,[2] hummed to the tune of *The Cottage in the Wood*. As a child of five he was interested in the Tale of Troy[3] by a father who, as a schoolboy, had learnt by heart the first book of the *Iliad*, and had waged Homeric battles in the playground at Cheshunt with his schoolfellow, John Kenyon. And in a copy of an early eighteenth-century edition of Dryden's translation of the satires of Juvenal, Browning made the following note : " My

---

[1] *Wanley*, bk. iii., ch. iv., § 10, p. 227, ed. 1806, vol. i.

[2] Five months after his father's death Browning wrote on the title-page of a 1783 Glasgow edition of *Anacreontis et Sapphonis carmina*, the words " My father's schoolbook. Robert Browning, Nov. 5, 1866." He himself had used it, for it also bears his signature dated 1826.

[3] Cf. his lines *Development*, in the *Asolando* volume, the details of which, however, must not be taken literally. " The description in the Troy poem was entirely fanciful." [Note by Miss Browning, 1902.]

father read the whole of the Dedicatory Preface aloud to me as we took a walk together up Nunhead Hill, Surrey, when I was a boy." Verily, the hundred pages of the *Essay on Satire* formed substantial reading for a boy during a country walk!

Browning, in early manhood, declared that he could "forget nothing—but names and the date of the battle of Waterloo." Thus gifted, and with influences such as have been here indicated around him from his childhood, what wonder that John Kenyon should speak of his "inexhaustible knowledge;" or that the historian Kinglake, after spending a few days with him in a country house with a large library, should come away "quite astounded" at the versatility of his learning?

CHAPTER II

BOYHOOD AND SCHOOLDAYS

Browning's home at Camberwell—Changes in the locality—His schooldays at Peckham—Lisping in numbers—Dislike of Mr. Ready's school—A "poet-biography"—Browning's dramatic instinct—Inherits his mother's love of animals, birds and flowers—The lion of the Surrey Gardens—"A principle of restlessness."

A HUNDRED years ago Dowlas Lane wound snake-like through the fields from the Walworth Road to that which united Camberwell Green and the village of Peckham. Walworth, now one of the most densely populated districts of London, then had its Manor House with spacious and lordly grounds—ere long to be transformed into the Surrey Gardens. At the familiar "Elephant and Castle," where the Walworth Road begins, one listened to the note of the coach-horn as the horses cantered along the New Kent Road on their way from the "Golden Cross," of Pickwickian fame, towards Dover. Walworth Road had then its trim grass plots and well-kept houses, and its toll-bar at Camberwell Gate, whence were visible the whirring sails of a windmill among the trees toward Camberwell Green: and midway between the turnpike gate and the village green was the entrance to Dowlas Lane.

Halfway along this lane was the little Dowlas Common with its trees and shrubs ; close at hand was Dowlas Farm ; further on, towards the Peckham Road, overhung by trees, was the quaint old wooden inn, the "Rosemary Branch," whose swinging sign and ample grounds were known for miles around by all lovers of cricket and field sports. But almost with the opening of the century ungainly two-storied little terraces, happily half hidden by trees, began to creep like devouring caterpillars along the lane, and comely little detached and semi-detached houses, with flower gardens in front and strawberry-beds and fruit trees in the rear, sprang up to take the place of hedges, until in the days of Browning's boyhood the little Common, or Cottage Green as it came to be called, was nearly all that remained to break the continuity of the homesteads, and Dowlas Lane became transformed into Southampton Street.

It was in Southampton Street, near the little Common, that Robert Browning was born,[1] and in Southampton Street he lived for eight and twenty years. But this was in the days when he could still watch the white-throat and the swallow building their nests; when he could still listen, like Keats at Hampstead, to the song of the nightingale and to the note of "the wise thrush" as it sang "each song twice over," and when he could still look out across fields "rough with hoary dew" or gay with buttercups, and see

> "That the lowest bough and the brush-wood sheaf
> Round the elm-tree bole are in tiny leaf,
> While the chaffinch sings on the orchard bough."

The Southampton Street of to-day is for the most part a much-decayed or cheaply rebuilt, poverty-stricken street in an overcrowded district. The birthplace of the poet has vanished. A second home has also vanished. Hanover Cottage, his home for sixteen years, has likewise perished. It may, however, afford a dubious satisfaction to the student of Browning to know that if he will but take his stand at the corner of Sedgmoor Place and look across Southampton Street toward Coleman Road, the houses or shops now numbered 173 and 175 occupy approximately the site of the home in which Browning was first thrilled by the poetry of Keats and Shelley, and in which he wrote *Pauline, Paracelsus*, and *Pippa Passes*, as well as *Sordello, King Victor and King Charles* and *The Return of the Druses*.[2]

---

[1] "R. B. was born in a house in Southampton Street, pulled down long ago. I was an infant when we went to another house, also in Southampton Street, where we lived till we moved to Hanover Cottage. I do not remember the precise date ; I was then about ten years old. Hanover Cottage, just built, was a semi-detached house with a garden behind and trees in front of it." [Note by Miss Browning, born 1814, aged ten in 1824.]

[2] The Cottage Green, or Common, which adjoined Wells Street on the north side of Southampton Street, has now been built upon, but the name still remains ;

Some aspects of the influence of this home upon the development of Browning have already been traced, and it has been stated that it is thither that one must look for his early education, and not to his school. Browning's school-days with the Rev. Thomas Ready at Peckham, about a mile from his home, do not seem to have been either happy or profitable. As a man of sixty he talked them over, in a reminiscent mood, with his old friend Alfred Domett, who was also Camberwell born, and Domett forthwith made the following entry in his Diary [7 February, 1873] :—

"He says they taught him nothing there, and that he was bullied by the big boys. When first there, at eight or nine years of age, he says he made a copy of verses which he remembered to this day—and "great bosh they were!"—intended to ingratiate himself with the master, a Mr. Ready. He quoted the two concluding lines, which ran thus :—

"We boys are privates in our Regiment's ranks—
'Tis to our Captain that we all owe thanks."

—a compliment to the master, which got him favoured in his school exercises for some time, and enabled him to play with impunity little impudent tricks, such as shutting the master's lexicon when his head was turned away while hearing his class, to give him the trouble of hunting up a word again, which would have immediately procured any other boy a box on the ear."

Mr. Ready's school was, it would seem, the descendant of that of Dr. Milner,[1] in which Goldsmith had been usher,

all the property between this and Coleman Street—formerly called Grove Lane— has been rebuilt and two new streets made. Hanover Cottage had a large garden running back to Grove Lane, in which the stable was situated, beyond this were other gardens and fields. The neighbouring church of St. George, in Wells Street, then stood in the midst of fields.

[1] The site, No. 77, Queen's Road, Peckham, is now occupied by a bank. The old house, a large roomy place, was pulled down in 1877 ; it stood just opposite Rye Lane and Hanover Chapel, where the Rev. John Milner, D.D., whose usher Goldsmith was, preached till his death in 1757. In Browning's days the popular Dr. Bengo Collyer occupied the pulpit, and for him the chapel was rebuilt. What was called "Goldsmith's house" (pulled down in 1876), was in Goldsmith Street close by. Whatever its possible connection with Goldsmith, it was far too small to have been occupied by Dr. Milner's school, and inquiries have only served to confirm the tradition that Browning's school was that associated with Goldsmith. The school garden and orchard have now been transformed into a yard for Messrs. Tilling's omnibuses.

and where he met the bookseller Griffith. Two of Domett's brothers were schoolfellows of Browning, but not Domett himself ; John Domett, the elder of these, was six years Browning's senior, and therefore probably left school soon after the little boy came, nevertheless he distinctly remembered

"young Browning in a pinafore of brown Holland, such as small boys used to wear in those days, for he was always neat in his dress ; and how they used to pit him against much older and bigger boys in a chaffing match to amuse themselves with the little bright-eyed fellow's readiness and acuteness of repartee."

For Browning, even as a child, "was made up of an intensest life," and was, as he himself long afterwards confessed, "unluckily precocious." He was, as has been stated, "a young wonder at drawing" at the age of two, and was known among his schoolfellows for his powers as a caricaturist ; his father, for a time at least, seems to have had serious hopes that his son would develop into an artist, but, as Browning has declared in *Pauline*—

"I had
No wish to paint, no yearning ; but I sang."

The doggerel lines on Mr. Ready may serve to recall this tendency to "song," as well as the fact that Browning, like Pope, Elizabeth Barrett, Ruskin, and scores of children unknown to fame, composed verses before he could read. His first dose of "nasty" physic is said to have been accompanied by the impromptu :

"Good people all who wish to see
A boy take physic, look at me."

Before he was five he could read and write, and although he was not, like Ruskin at that age, sending to the Circulating Library for second volumes, he was reading books which contained scraps from Ossian, which he so enjoyed that he set to work to imitate them in the first "composition" of which he was ever guilty. His previous efforts he knew were nonsense, but this he thought exceedingly well of, and

laid up for posterity under the cushion of a great armchair.[1]
"I could not have been five years old," he said. Even
before that age he had been removed from a neighbouring
dame's school because his proficiency in reading and spelling
had roused the jealousy of the parents of other pupils ; and
before he entered, at the age of eight or nine, the preparatory
school presided over by the Misses Ready—those good
ladies who used to brush and oil the children's hair once a
week to the accompaniment of the hymns of Isaac Watts—
he knew by heart much of Pope's *Homer.* He remained at
the Peckham school as a weekly boarder under these sisters,
and then under their brother, until he was fourteen ; and as
the years passed, the quick-witted precocious child and, later,
the growing, rather agressive lad, who was by no means
deficient in self-confidence, could hardly avoid coming to the
conclusion that his father was considerably more learned
than the schoolmaster. The juvenile reader of Wanley,
De Lairesse and Quarles' *Emblems*—his "childhood's pet
book"—would speedily become more than sceptical as to
whether the library of Mr. Ready contained six thousand
volumes like that across the fields in Southampton Street,
and might be quite certain that the reverend gentleman's
collection of Bibles did not compare favourably with that of
his father, who could take from his bookshelf a rare 1568
Biblia Sacra, which was lacking even from the famous
collection of eleven hundred editions of the scriptures in the
library of the Duke of Sussex. Browning's interest therefore continued to centre in his home ; he made few school
friends, he became intolerant of school ways and of his
schoolmaster. Seven years after he left school he heard that
the Rev. Thomas Ready had preached a heavy sermon :
his instant comment was,

"A *heavy* sermon—sure the error's great
For not a word Tom utters has its weight."

This impromptu was written in March, 1833, the month,
that is, in which Browning's first published poem, *Pauline,*

<hr>
[1] *Letters of R. B. and E. B. B.*

appeared, and the account given in *Pauline* of his school-
days and of their effect upon him is not flattering :—

> " Long constraint chained down
> My soul till it was changed.   I lost myself;
> And were it not that I so loathe that time,
> I could recall how first I learned to turn
> My mind against itself; and the effects
> In deeds for which remorse were vain as for
> The wanderings of delirious dream ; yet thence
> Came cunning, envy, falsehood."

There is obvious danger in seeking to interpret the
details of poetry too literally ; readers of *Manfred* went
somewhat astray when they reckoned Byron among mur-
derers ; *Julian and Maddalo* presents some interesting pitfalls
for the literal interpreter of Shelley ; and Tennyson has
taken care to warn his readers that *In Memoriam*, full as it
is of personal history, is, nevertheless, "a *poem* and not an
actual biography."   What justification Browning had for his
self-accusation, and how far this is to be taken literally,
cannot be exactly determined ; but it would be a great
mistake to dismiss his avowal as wholly due to the play of
fancy.   Did Mr. Ready object to "cribs," and had not Uncle
Reuben given his nephew Smart's translation of Horace ?
Might not some measure of "cunning" be advisable when
the young caricaturist and writer of epigrams was at work ;
for what schoolboy would spare his masters ?   Were all
Browning's early verses written out of school hours ?   Was
Mr. Ready, as scholastic Lord Chamberlain, made aware of
the various plays little Browning wrote, and did he sanction
the theatrical troupe the boy organized for their production ?
Was he, or were those at home, informed of a certain visit
after sundown to the loved elms on the Camberwell hilltop,
when the boy was spellbound as he first saw London by night
with its recently installed gas-lamps ; or was this, the first of
many nocturnal rambles, like Wordsworth's moonlight row
on Esthwaite Water, "an act of stealth and troubled
pleasure ? "   However this may be, there is no doubt as to
Browning's attitude toward his school.   Seven or eight
years after the production of *Pauline*, as he was passing the

old playground and orchard with his friend Domett, Browning spoke of the "disgust with which he always thought of the place," and quoted an epigram he had made years before expressive of the "undiluted misery" of the "hapless childhood" he had spent there. Nor was this because the school was a Dotheboys Hall and Mr. Thomas Ready a Kentish Wackford Squeers. The exact opposite was the case. "I know he always disliked being at Mr. Ready's," wrote Miss Browning in 1902, "but that was not the fault of the school, which was a very good one. He always acknowledged that the boys were most liberally and kindly treated." Apart from considerations such as have been already suggested, there was another and perhaps still more potent influence at work; this was the restraint put upon his imaginative faculties, for Browning was, as a boy, possessed of an imagination which

> "Has been an angel to me, coming not
> In fitful visions but beside me ever
> And never failing me."

This avowal is from *Pauline*; and, in spite of his warning that this poem was his earliest attempt at poetry, "always dramatic in principle, and so many utterances of so many imaginary persons, not mine," it may be accepted in its main outlines as distinctly autobiographical, and, if read aright, as the most authentic record of his early life. His intimate friend Joseph Arnould at any rate described *Pauline*, in 1847, as a

"strange, wild, and in parts singularly magnificent poet-biography: his own early life as it presented itself to his own soul: in fact, psychologically speaking, his *Sartor Resartus*."[1]

In *Sartor* it is possible in all essentials to replace the name of Teufelsdröckh by that of Carlyle; Hinterschlag Gymnasium is but a name for Annan school; Blumine represents a real Margaret Gordon, and the incident of the "Everlasting No" becomes none the less real when the reader is aware that it is to be associated with Leith walk, and not with "the dirty little Rue St. Thomas de l'Enfer" in Paris. And so it is with *Pauline*.

[1] *Sartor*, oddly enough, was, like *Pauline*, printed in 1833.

D

When, for instance, Browning speaks of

> "My first dawn of life
> Which passed alone with wisest ancient books,"

he is really speaking of the library at Southampton Street; and when he tells how the unnamed boy of the poem entered heart and soul with a child's vivid imagination into the legends of which he read, he is also writing autobiography. What is related of Walter Scott at the age of six might be applied, with one significant alteration, to Browning.   Mrs. Cockburn described Scott as

"the most extraordinary genius of a boy I ever saw. He was reading a poem to his mother when I went in.   I made him read on: it was the description of a shipwreck.   His passion rose with the storm.   He lifted his eyes and hands—'There's the mast gone!' says he, 'crash it goes!—they will all perish!'   After his agitation, he turns to me,—'That's too melancholy,' says he, 'I had better read you something more amusing.'   I preferred a little chat, and asked him his opinion of Milton and other books he was reading, which he gave me wonderfully."

Both in regard to the perusal of books not usually read by boys, and to vividness of imagination, this might have been written of Browning as well as of Scott, but whereas Scott, the future novelist, saw the scene *ab extra*, and exclaimed, "*They* will all perish," Browning, the future dramatic poet, would have identified himself with those of whom he was speaking, and his instinctive cry would have been, " *We* shall all perish."   It was by reason of such imaginative sympathy that the Greek legends he so early loved—"those old times and scenes where all that's beautiful had birth for me" —became

> "All halo-girt with fancies of my own:
> And *I myself went with the tale.*"

Vivid imagination is so much the rule among children that it would call for no comment in the case of Browning were it not for its dramatic intensity and for its duration.

With him the dramatic impulse, imperfect as it undoubtedly was, remained lifelong.   The *Dramatic Lyrics* of 1842

were followed by the *Dramatic Romances* of 1845, and these
again by the *Dramatis Personæ* of 1864 and by the *Dramatic
Idylls* of 1878 and 1880 ; and these poems are not dramatic
in name only, but in fact.   *Pauline*, his first published poem,
was a dramatic monologue ; *Paracelsus*, his next, he called a
" dramatic poem " ;   *Strafford*, the third, was an acted
drama ;   in his fourth, *Sordello*, he reluctantly adopted a
narrative form, for which, after a dozen lines, he was forced
to apologize :—

> " Never, I should warn you first,
> Of my own choice had this, if not the worst
> Yet not the best expedient, served to tell
> A story I could body forth so well
> By making speak, myself kept out of view,
> The very man as he was wont to do."

And, even after having thus adopted the narrative form, he
could not keep to it, but repeatedly drifted into dramatic
monologue.   Also, when he came to trace the mental history
of Sordello, a poet like himself, it was to describe him as
dramatically identifying himself now with an Este, now with
an Ecelin ;   at one time he is the Emperor Frederick, at
another a crusader, or even an Apollo.   This is evidently but
a reflex of Browning's own experiences.   Nay, so instinctive
was the dramatic impulse, that in *Pippa Passes*, the publication of which immediately followed that of *Sordello*, little
Pippa is represented as finding her greatest joy in spending
her only holiday in the whole year in imagining herself to
be several other people in turn.

> " I may fancy all day—and it shall be so,
> That I taste of the pleasures, am called by the names
> Of the happiest four in our Asolo."

At the same time it may be admitted that Browning
rather overworked the adjective " dramatic."   " Dramatic
Idyll " is not a very happy phrase.   Gerard Manley Hopkins,
in his correspondence with R. W. Dixon, styles it " a mon-
strous name."   Browning's addiction to the term is probably
due to his fear of people regarding the opinions and feelings

ascribed to his characters as necessarily his own. But of course they often were. How could a man so vigorous, copious and emphatic suppress his personality in his poetry ? As well might an eagle try to pass itself off as a jack-daw.

Nor was Browning's early dramatic sympathy limited to human beings : it extended even to animal life. From his mother he inherited that love of birds and animals for which he was remarkable throughout life, just as he inherited from her his highly nervous nature, his love of music and of flowers. Mrs. Browning we are told, had that

"extraordinary power over animals of which we hear sometimes, but of which I have never known a case so perfect as hers. She would lure the butterflies in the garden to her, and domestic animals obeyed her as if they reasoned.'" [1]

Browning inherited something of this power, and even in the closing months of his life his soft, low whistle would entice the lizards as they basked by the roadside in the Italian sunshine, and his keen eye could still detect the tiniest inhabitant of the hedges. His pet owl was not un-known to visitors at Warwick Crescent ; less familiar were his pet geese. These would follow him about like dogs and would come and nestle lovingly in his arms ; nor was the humour of the situation lost upon Browning, for, after having suffered much from the cackle of reviewers, he genially gave to his hissing companions the suggestive names of the *Edinburgh* and the *Quarterly*. As a boy he rode his pony, played with his dogs, had his numerous pets—monkeys, magpies, and even an eagle ; his pockets were frequently full of the uncanny "portable creatures" for which he had such a fancy, frogs, toads, and efts. Possibly, the occasional visits of a favourite snake or hedgehog to Mr. Ready's may have contributed to the evolution of that schoolboy "cunning" to which reference has been made. His half-holidays were often spent lying under the elm-trees on the hilltop at Camberwell above the village church [2] whence he

---

[1] W. J. Stillman, *Autobiography of a Journalist*, vol. i. p. 279.
[2] This hill was that on which Camberwell Grove is now built. In Browning's

could look down upon London and beyond to its northern heights—to the Hampstead of Keats and the Highgate of Coleridge, and to the more distant spire beside which another schoolboy, his then much-loved Byron, used to lie on the flat tombstone beneath the Harrow elms.   Browning would lie "beside a hedge or deep in meadow grasses, or under a tree . . . and there give himself up so absolutely to the life of the moment that even the shy birds would alight close by and sometimes venture-somely poise themselves on suspicious wings for a brief space upon his recumbent body.   I have heard him say that his faculty of observation at that time would not have appeared despicable to a Seminole or an Iroquois : he saw and watched everything." [1]

Pippa Passes was conceived and largely composed beneath the trees of Dulwich Wood, a favourite haunt of Browning from early youth ; and the words of Pippa's song are as true of their writer as of the little silk-winder of Asolo.

> " Overhead the tree-tops meet
> Flowers and grass spring 'neath one's feet ;
> There was nought above me, and nought below
> My childhood had not learned to know !
> For what are the voices of birds
> —Ay, and of beasts—but words, our words,
> Only so much more sweet !
> The knowledge of that with my life began."

But Browning's imaginative communion with the birds and beasts extended at times much further than this would imply, as is indicated by some suggestive lines in *Pauline* :—

> " I have gone in thought
> Thro' all conjuncture, I have lived all life
> When it is most alive. . . .
>
> .   .   .   .
>
> . . . I can mount with the bird
> Leaping airily his pyramid of leaves
> And twisted boughs of some tall mountain-tree,
> Or rise cheerfully springing to the heavens ;
> Or like a fish breathe-in the morning air
> In the misty sun-warm water."

childhood the houses were confined to the Peckham Road end, where Browning's friend, Alfred Domett, lived ; gradually the houses crept upward—in one, near the middle of the Grove, Joseph Chamberlain was born.

[1] William Sharp's *Robert Browning*, p. 96.

This is simply a more extreme, less permanent, but far from rare,[1] example of the dramatic impulse ; and Browning, in *The Glove*, which appeared among the *Dramatic Lyrics* of 1845, has given a more mature and strikingly artistic example of the same tendency. During the poet's boyhood foot-passengers along the Strand found their path suddenly blocked by a projecting building beneath which the pavement passed, and as they glanced upward on entering the arcade below it was to see on the wall above pictures of monsters and wild beasts, and to read in large letters— "Exeter Change. Royal Menagerie. Edwd. Cross, dealer in foreign birds and beasts." This famous menagerie, with its little rooms painted with exotic scenes, and its dens and cages wherein were lions and tigers whose roar alarmed the horses in the Strand below, was much beloved of "country cousins," and was likewise beloved of the boy Browning. Some years later, when the grounds of the Walworth Manor House were transformed into the Surrey Gardens, Cross's popular menagerie was moved south of the Thames, and was thus within easy access of Southampton Street; and the pride of the collection at the Surrey Gardens was the magnificent lion so graphically described by Browning in *The Glove*—a huge creature with black mane, stiffening tail, and glowing eyes. But what is really significant in the description is the way in which Browning dramatically associates himself with the feelings of the lion as it issues from its den :—

> "The lion at last was delivered.
> Ay, that was the open sky o'erhead !
> And you saw by the flash on his forehead,
> By the hope in those eyes wide and steady,
> He was leagues in the desert already,
> Driving the flocks up the mountain ;
> Or cat-like crouched hard by the fountain
> To waylay the date-gathering negress."

Yet the indications of this dramatic tendency in Browning do not cease even here. Among the "wild fancies" poured

---

[1] It is by no means uncommon among children. I have known a child, whose imagination had been stimulated by a picture and a long name, imagine himself for weeks to be a *duck-billed platypus !*—W. H. G.

into the ear of Pauline is not only that of gazing "drowsily on the bees that flit and play," but the certainty that he—

> " Can live all the life of plants . . .
>   . . . . or with flowers
> And trees can smile in light at the sinking sun
> Just as the storm comes, as a girl would look
> On a departing lover."

It matters little whether this is a record of Browning's own early imaginative life; it is sufficient that he should even have imagined such an experience. But it becomes additionally significant when one notices that the same tendency is described not only in connection with the poet of *Pauline* but with the poet whose history is traced in *Sordello*; for the Mantuan poet " partook the poppy's red effrontery," and in imagination was "transferred to flower or tree." It was only after having passed through this stage that he finally came to live in an imaginative world of *men*—

> "as he used to blend
> With tree and flower—nay more entirely, else
> 'Twere mockery."

Browning's strong love for flowers came to him from his mother. " How I remember the flowers—even grasses—of places I have seen!" he wrote to Miss Haworth in 1838. "Some flower or weed, I should say, that gets somehow connected with them." A snowdrop transported him to Prussia, because he had seen those flowers at Tilsit on his way to Russia in the spring of 1834; flowering willows brought back visions of the flat meadows, the canals, and early morning mists of Holland; almost the only souvenir he brought from Rome in 1844 was a few seeds from the Fountain of Egeria to plant in the garden at Hatcham; the sole fact he cared to glean from one Latin book which he read for *Paracelsus* was that the Swiss physician loved pansies.[1] In later life, when he was asked, "You have not a great love for Nature, have you?" he replied, "Yes, I have, but I love men and women better." In earlier life no one

---

[1] He mentioned the flower in *Paracelsus*, book iii., and added the note, " Citrinula (flammula) herba Paracelso multum familiaris.—Dorn."

would have dreamed of the necessity of asking such a question ; and Frances Power Cobbe, who saw much of the poet in Florence, has recorded that

"when we drove out in parties he would discuss every tree and weed and get excited about the difference between eglantine and eglatere (if there be any), and between either of them and honey-suckle." [1]

The garden at Hatcham was his mother's delight, and in it mother and son had culled the flowers he continually carried to Miss Barrett during the days of his courtship :—

> " Beloved, thou hast brought me many flowers
> Plucked in the garden, all the summer through
> And winter."

When, therefore, in 1849, the news reached Florence of the death of his mother, it was of her garden that Browning instinctively thought. " He says it would break his heart to see his mother's roses over the wall, and the place where she used to lay her scissors and gloves." [2] If Browning, like Sordello, ceased early in life to desire to "blend with tree and flower," after the fashion described in *Pauline*, he seems to have retained in another and characteristic manner some-what of the same longing, for, in the letter of 1838, from which quotation has already been made, he declared, " I have, you are to know, such a love for flowers and leaves— some leaves—that I every now and then, in an impatience at being able to possess myself of them thoroughly, to see them quite, satiate myself with their scent—bite them to bits." It is the poet of *Pauline* over again possessed by

> " a principle of restlessness
> Which would be all, have, see, know, taste, feel, all."

---

[1] *Life of Frances Power Cobbe*, vol. ii. p. 15 (1894 ed.).
[2] E. B. B. to Miss Mitford, April 30, 1849. *Letters of Mrs. Browning*, vol. i. p. 399.

CHAPTER III

" PAULINE "

Byronic influence—*Incondita*—W. J. Fox's approbation—Browning's friendship with Eliza and Sarah Flower—He leaves school at fourteen—Entered at London University—His brief attendance there—A period of revolt—Influence of Shelley—" Growing pains "—Chooses poetry as his vocation—Attends lectures at Guy's hospital—His studies and relaxations—His young ambitions—*Pauline* published—Fox's encouragement—John Stuart Mill's strictures—" Autumn in everything."

EARLY in 1824, one name was on every lip : Europe had been thunderstruck by the news from Missolonghi. Tennyson, a boy of fifteen, rushed forth to carve on the rocks near Somersby the words " Byron is dead." Carlyle wrote to his wife, " Alas ! poor Byron ! The news of his death came upon my heart like a mass of lead . . . as if I had lost a brother." " I was told it," says another, " all alone in a room full of people. If they had said the sun or the moon was gone out of the heavens, it could not have struck me with the idea of a more awful or dreary blank in the creation than the words 'Byron is dead.'" It is no wonder that when Browning, as a schoolboy of twelve, began in this same year, a little volume of verse, his muse bore strong evidence of the influence of Byron.

Browning humbly called his little volume *Incondita*, possibly in allusion to the fact that " in the beginning " even the earth itself was " without form." These early efforts were inevitably imitative, though his parents thought so highly of them that they made serious but futile attempts to find a publisher. Upon his father's bookselves were the sixty-two volumes of the 1807 edition of Bagster's English poets, and in these the boy had read freely with the result recorded in *Pauline* :—

> " I had done nothing, so I sought to know
> What mind had yet achieved.   No fear was mine
> As I gazed on the works of mighty bards,
> In the first joy at finding my own thoughts
> Recorded and my powers exemplified,
> And feeling their aspirings were my own."

But, adds he,

> " I rather sought
> To rival what I wondered at, than form
> Creations of my own."

Even apart from Byron's death it is probable that his influence would have been marked ; but the tragedy of 1824 would tend to accentuate this influence.   Twenty years later Browning wrote to Miss Barrett, " I always retained my first feeling for Byron in many respects, I would at any time have gone to Finchley to see a curl of his hair or one of his gloves, I am sure—while Heaven knows that I could not get up enthusiasm enough to cross the room if at the other end of it all Wordsworth, Coleridge, and Southey were condensed into the little china bottle yonder, after the Rosicrucian fashion." [1] And in 1878, thirty years after the date of this letter, in spite of his grief at the sudden death of his friend, Miss Egerton Smith, he could not leave Geneva and La Saisiaz without first visiting the Villa Diodati, where Byron had lived, to pluck a leaf as a memorial—" ivy, plucked for Byron's sake."

Miss Eliza Flower, a lady of twenty-two, whose acquaintance the boy had recently made at Hackney, saw these unpublished poems and admired them so much that she made a copy, which she showed to the Rev. W. Johnson Fox, then fast becoming one of the notabilities of the day—" which verses," says Browning, " he praised not a little, which praise comforted me not a little."   Browning himself confessed that in his youth he wrote only musically, and Fox afterwards remarked to the poet that his impression of *Incondita* was that it showed " too great splendour of language and too little

[1] *Letters of R. B. and E. B. B.*, vol. ii. p. 455, 22 August, 1846. The reference to Finchley is due to the fact that two days previously Miss Barrett had written that she had driven as far as that spot.

wealth of thought." Browning wisely destroyed his manuscript, as he also in later years destroyed the copy made by Miss Flower, when it fell into his hands.[1] The only things memorable in connection with the childish volume are the influence of Byron and the introduction to Mr. Fox, who became, as he said, his " literary father."

Fox, " the Norwich Weaver Boy," as he signed himself during his vigorous labours against the Corn Laws, was twenty-six years older than Browning and but four years younger than the poet's father. From the loom at Norwich, where his mother had read to him as he worked, he had passed to the Homerton Congregational College, and in 1810 became pastor of a Congregational Chapel at Fareham, in Hampshire. Brought up on what he termed the " sour milk of Calvinism," he had even at that date moved rapidly towards Unitarianism, and by 1812, the year of Browning's birth, the renunciation of his belief in the doctrines in which he had been trained was practically complete. When Browning, as a child of five, was writing Ossianic poems, Fox was called to London as minister of the chapel in Parliament Court, and speedily became the acknowledged leader of the Unitarians. Keenly interested in all public questions, he became known not only as an eloquent preacher, but as a social and educational reformer, a writer, and an able platform speaker, whose presence was eagerly sought by many who did not share his religious views. In 1824, when *Incondita* was begun, his new chapel in South Place, Finsbury, was opened, and he himself was writing the first article for the *Westminster Review*, which he helped Mill's father to found. When Fox came to London, in 1817, he had settled at Hackney, not far from his old college at Homerton, where his friend the Rev. Robert Aspland had among the members of his congregation the family of Mr. Earles, for whose children Browning's father wrote the version of the *Pied Piper*, from which quotation has been made. Thus Camberwell came in touch with Hackney, for Mr. Browning was a frequent visitor at the cottage of Mr. Earles.

Fox, an advanced Liberal and Reformer, had long known and revered Benjamin Flower, thirty years his senior, who as

---

[1] Two poems, however, have survived, *The First-born of Egypt* and the *Dance of Death*. Rediscovered by Mr. Bertram Dobell, they are included in Sir F. G. Kenyon's New Poems of R. and E. B. Browning (1914).

editor for seven years of the *Cambridge Intelligencer* [1] had made that paper a power among advocates of political and religious liberty. Imprisoned for alleged libel, Flower was visited in prison by an admiring lady whom he afterwards married; the paper was given up, and after settling as a printer at Harlow, in Essex, he retired to Dalston, close to Hackney, where he died. At his death, in 1829, some three years before the publication of *Pauline*, Eliza and Sarah, his two beautiful and intellectual daughters, who were intimately associated with the early life of Browning, were left under Fox's guardianship. Browning's intimacy with these ladies dates from the period of their visits to Hackney some three or four years before 1827, the date at which Flower finally removed from Harlow. As is evident from the following extract from a letter written by Sarah Flower to a cousin at Stratford-on-Avon in June, 1833, two months after the publication of *Pauline*, there had been a lull in the intimacy :—

"Have you seen anything of *Pauline*? I will send you down one of the first copies. We have renewed an old acquaintance with the author, who is the 'poet boy' we used to know years ago. He is yet unmatured, and will do much better things. He is very interesting from his great power of conversation and thorough originality, to say nothing of his personal appearance, which would be exceptionally poetical if nature had not served him an unkind trick in giving him an ugly nose." [2]

Eliza Flower was nine, and Sarah Flower seven, years Browning's senior, and of the elder sister Mrs. Orr has truly said that, "if in spite of his denials, any woman inspired *Pauline*, it can be no other than she." In his early teens he wrote her boyish letters and verses, all of which he destroyed when they fell into his hands, after Fox's death in 1864. His boyish love is said to have subsided into a "warm and very loyal friendship," yet his admiration and tenderness "had so deep a root that he never in latest life mentioned her name

---

[1] To this Coleridge had sent his "Ode to the Departing Year," published 31 December, 1796. When Coleridge closed his *Watchman* (June, 1796), he advised his readers to transfer their interest to the *Cambridge Intelligencer*.

[2] Letter of June, 1833, to Mrs. E. F. Flower. *Centenary of South Place*, by Moncure D. Conway, 1894, p. 88. Dr. Conway wittily suggests that "the nose must have improved along with the poetry."

with indifference." Her affection for him seems to have lasted to the end: she died, unmarried, at the age of forty-three, in 1846, the year of Browning's marriage, and not long before her death from consumption he wrote—" of your health I shall not trust myself to speak : you must know what is unspoken."

Browning's intimacy with the two sisters was largely due to community of interests. Eliza was very musical : so was he. She composed, played, and sang: so did he. In 1846 he wrote, " I never had another feeling than entire admiration for your music—entire admiration," and he added words which, considering his own acknowledged musical knowledge and attainments, are sufficiently striking :—" I put it apart from all other English music I know, and fully believe in it as the music we all waited for." Sarah Flower was passionately fond of the stage ; so, in early days, was Browning. She had even desired to take a place among actors : this too, for a time, was among Browning's dreams. He would walk all the way from Camberwell to Richmond to see Edmund Kean perform during his last days, and would return on foot through the country lanes in the early morning hours with his cousin, James Silverthorne. At the end of *Pauline* are the words " Richmond, 22 October, 1832," which have led the unwary to declare that Browning was then living at Richmond ; but he never even passed a night there. A note which he made in his own copy of the first edition of *Pauline* explains how he came to date his poem from that spot :—

" Kean was acting there; I saw him in Richard III that night and conceived the childish scheme already mentioned [*i.e.* of writing *Pauline* and other works]. There is an allusion to Kean, page 47. I don't know whether I had not made up my mind to *act* as well as to make verses, music, and God knows what,—*que de châteaux en Espagne !* "

Kean died in the following May, so "sunk by error" and intemperance that the vigour of his last representations of the youthful Richard was the more remarkable. The following lines from *Pauline* are those which refer to the great tragedian at the little theatre on Richmond Green, beside which he lived and died—a theatre which saw not only the last performances of Kean, but the first performance of Helen Faucit, who, not long afterwards, was to take the heroine's part in Browning's *Strafford* and in his *Blot in the 'Scutcheon* :—

> " I will be gifted with a wondrous soul,
> Yet sunk by error to men's sympathy,
> And in the wane of life ; yet only so
> As to call up their fears ; and then shall come
> A time requiring youth's best energies ;—
> And straight I fling age, sorrow, sickness off,
> And I rise triumphing over my decay."

But there were still other bonds between Browning and the two sisters, both of whom had literary tastes. Eliza Flower's critical judgment was allowed to be excellent, and Sarah wrote poetry. Her long dramatic poem *Vivia Perpetua* (1841), named after the martyr, is doubtless not known to one in a hundred thousand of those who are familiar with her *Nearer, my God, to Thee,* a hymn first sung by the two sisters at Mr. Fox's chapel at South Place, where they led the singing.

Robert Browning may reasonably be said to have contributed to the evolution of this famous hymn : he certainly had his share in creating those " stony griefs " out of which his friend, in the year in which his own *Sordello* appeared, raised her " Bethel," as is clear from the following extract from a pathetic letter written by Sarah Flower to Fox in November, 1827, when Browning was a lad between fifteen and sixteen :—

" My mind has been wandering a long time, and now it seems to have lost sight of that only invulnerable hold against the assaults of this warring world, a firm belief in the genuineness of the Scriptures. . . . The cloud has come over me gradually, and I did not discover the darkness in which my soul was shrouded until, in seeking to give light to others, my own gloomy state became too settled to admit of doubt. It was in answering Robert Browning that my mind refused to bring forward argument, turned recreant, and sided with the enemy. . . . And now, as I sit and look up to the room in which I first had existence [*i.e.* at Harlow] and think of the mother who gave it, and watch the window of the chamber in which she yielded hers, in death as in life a fervent Christian, that thought links itself with another—how much rather would she I had never been, than to be what I now am." [1]

This letter indicates something of that spirit of revolt and restlessness which had taken possession of Browning—an experience destined ere long to contribute to the dramatic intensity of portions of *Paracelsus*. This period of *Sturm und Drang*, to employ the somewhat hackneyed phrase, began not long after the "oddish sort of boy"—so he termed himself—finished his school life at the age of fourteen.

Regret has been expressed that Browning did not proceed to a public school. But the experience at Mr. Ready's was hardly encouraging. Undoubtedly an Arnold or a Thring might have exerted a helpful influence upon Browning; but in 1826, Arnold was still the unknown private tutor of Laleham; and Thring was a child of five. Nor were public schools in good odour: "a complete reformation or a complete destruction of the whole system seemed to many persons sooner or later to be inevitable." [2] Browning, therefore, for two years after leaving Mr. Ready, studied under a French tutor, Loradoux by name, who spent the mornings at Southampton Street, the boy's soul being left free to "seek its old delights" for the rest of the day among the book-shelves and in music. He read widely in history and in literature, and soon came in touch with the poet Donne, whose *Go and Catch a Falling Star* he set to music and was fond of singing. It was not, however, till later that the poetry of Donne became a potent literary influence upon him. He continued of course to write verse—even French verse, in which he made false quantities in Greek names so as to avoid offending the not too scholarly susceptibilities of his French *Professeur des Langues*.[3] These two years were really a period of waiting and preparation for what proved in his case to be an unsuccessful experiment. Carlyle described Browning's parents as "people of respectable position among the dissenters, but not rich neither"; the proposals set forth

---

[1] *Centenary of South Place*, 1894, p. 46.
[2] Stanley's *Life of Arnold*, chap. iii.
[3] *Letters of R. B. and E. B. B.*, vol. i. p. 420. "My father," says Mr. R. Barrett Browning, "could then write French verse as easily as English. He and his sister were much interested in French literature, and took in the *Siècle*."

therefore in March, 1825—a year before Browning left school—for the foundation of a University in London would very naturally arouse their interest and attention. Oxford and Cambridge were then closed to the conscientious dissenter ; indeed, until 1854 no dissenter could take a degree at Cambridge, and no dissenter could even become a student at Oxford. But in 1825 it was proposed to found a new University in London, the objects being threefold :—it was to be wholly unsectarian, the education was to be far less costly than at the older universities, and home life and home influence could coexist with the higher education given. All three objects appealed to the household at Camberwell, so that Mr. Browning was among the early shareholders or " proprietors " who subscribed £100 toward the new venture.

The letter in which he applied for his son's admission has been preserved among the university archives. It throws a valuable light on the boy's progress in education. " I can answer," wrote his father, " for his unwearied application for the last six years to the Greek, Latin, and French languages." He adds that his son is most anxious to be admitted.

In October the lectures and classes began, but, three months before that date and within less than three weeks after the first entry, Browning's name was placed on the Register thus : " No. 16, June 30, 1828. Robert Browning : age 16 : Hanover Cottage, Southampton Street, Camberwell, nominated by Robert Browning, senior." The classes arranged for were Greek, German and Latin, and as the work began early—the German class was held at eight in the morning— lodgings were taken for Browning with a Mr. Hughes in Bedford Square. After one week, however, Browning, who had gone home for the Sunday, decided not to return to Bedford Square, so that the German class, apparently, knew him no more. With similar abruptness, during the second term " the bright handsome youth with long black hair falling over his shoulders " quitted the university altogether. Perhaps, like the poet in *Pauline*, he

> " was lonely, far from woods and fields
> And amid dullest sights, who should be loose
> As a stag."

So that to his home-sickness, his dislike of the bricks and mortar of Bloomsbury, and his sense of restraint is to be attributed his father's loss of nearly £100.[1] Surely Browning only stated the truth when he wrote of his parents some twenty years later, " I have been 'spoiled' in this world ";[2] "Since I was a child I never looked for the least or greatest thing within the compass of their means to give, but given it was—nor for liberty but it was conceded;"[3] "I know as certainly as I know anything that if I could bring myself to ask them to give up everything in the world they would do it and cheerfully;"[4] and Carlyle, after a visit to Browning at Hatcham, remarked that "the little room in which he kept his books was in that sort of trim that showed he was the very apple of their eyes." It is not surprising that Browning became self-centred and for a time selfish, and that his first three poems contain studies of self-centred natures. Born "supremely passionate," it was natural that " during this time of growth he should have been not only more restless but less amiable than at any other. The always impatient temper assumed a quality of aggressiveness. He behaved as a youth will who knows himself to be clever, and believes he is not appreciated. . . . He set the judgments of those about him at defiance, and gratuitously proclaimed himself everything that he was and some things that he was not."[5] The influence of Shelley accentuated although it did not create this mood.

Browning's mother, "a divine woman " he called her, was deeply religious. Six years before his birth she had joined the Congregational Church which met at York Street, Walworth, and until her death, forty-three years later, she might have been seen Sunday after Sunday walking thither

---

[1] Subscribers were to receive four per cent. interest ; this could not be paid. Moreover, free education was granted to their nominee, and Browning's fees for the first session amounted to £22. Latin, £7 10s. ; Greek, £7 10s. ; [Italian scratched out and replaced by] German, £6 ; Library, £1. At this rate, therefore, Mr. Browning may be said to have prepaid five sessions, of which his son completed about half the first.

[2] *Letters of R. B. and E. B. B.*, vol. i. p. 34. 1845.

[3] *Ibid.* vol. ii. p. 228. 1846.

[4] *Ibid.* vol. ii. p. 230. 1846.

[5] Orr, *Life of Browning*, pp. 45, 46.

E

even from Hatcham, after the family had left Camberwell. Not even the acutest neuralgia could keep her from her place. Her children were both christened at York Street ; and in 1820, under her influence, her husband, who had been brought up as an Episcopalian and is said to have been more than liberal in doctrinal matters, also joined the Congregational body. Browning, of whom Hiram Powers, the American sculptor in Florence, said that he had " the biggest bump of reverence " he ever saw, adored his mother, and was, in early days, to use his own words, " passionately religious " ;[1] but neither the bump of reverence nor his mother's influence served to restrain him during this period of revolt. Seated with his parents in the front of the gallery on the right of the pulpit, he " did not care to conceal his something more than indifference to the ministrations to which he listened weekly, and which once brought down upon him a rebuke from the Pastor in open church."   The Rev. George Clayton, however, was one of the old school, who is said to have " stiffened and starched " those who sat under him,[2] as his more outspoken and fiery neighbour the Rev. Joseph Irons, of Camberwell Grove, is said to have " ironed " them ;[3] even the Rev. Edward White, brother of the writer of this account of Browning, felt impelled as a boy to gnaw the pew-top during Mr. Clayton's lengthy prayers—" prayers which were newspapers, entering into every particular of births, marriages, and deaths, and foreign travel of deacons and the like."   The sermons of good Mr. Clayton, moreover, did not reveal either the intellect of a Pascal or the eloquence of a Jeremy Taylor. But, in addition to this, Browning, while reading with his French tutor, had come in touch not only with Marot, who was to supply a motto for *Pauline* and to re-appear later on in *The*

[1] Orr, *Life of Browning*, p. 26.

[2] Mr. Clayton—the Rev. *Georgius* Clayton he was often called—is described in the *British Weekly* of 20 December, 1889, from which these references to him are taken, as one who " combined the character of a saint, a dancing master, and an orthodox eighteenth-century theologian in about equal proportions."

[3] Domett (in his *Diary*) recalls going up Camberwell Grove one Sunday evening with a friend, to try how far off they could hear Mr. Irons " bawling out his sermon " ; and how they stood outside at a little distance and clearly overheard : " I am very sorry to say it, beloved brethren, but it is an undoubted fact that Roman Catholic and midnight assassin are synonymous terms."

Glove, but with Voltaire, all of whose works were on the bookshelves. These works the boy set himself to read, and it was as a juvenile student of the Philosopher of Ferney that he posed Miss Sarah Flower, as narrated in her letter of November, 1827.

Voltaire's influence on Browning's development, however, was transient ; that of Shelley was more lasting and significant. To his temporary profession of atheism, a phase which had vanished before *Pauline* was written, both may have contributed ; but it is reasonable, in default of any other recorded cause or motive, to ascribe to Shelley his conversion to vegetarianism, for Shelley had set forth its physical and moral advantages in a voluminous footnote to *Queen Mab*. Browning adhered to a vegetarian diet for two years, and only gave it up on finding that his eyesight was weakening.

He had read *Queen Mab*, then, at this period ? Presumably. But it is a curious fact that while the names of most of Shelley's other works occur in his correspondence, that of *Queen Mab* does not. Yet Browning's first biographer, William Sharp (who also wrote as Fiona Macleod), states categorically that *The Dæmon of the World*, a name given by Shelley to a revised version of *Queen Mab*, was his first introduction to Shelley's poetry. Here is Sharp's account of what occurred : " Passing a bookstall one day, he saw, in a box of second-hand volumes, a little book advertised as ' Mr. Shelley's atheistical poem, very scarce.' He had never heard of Shelley." The boy's interest was aroused, however, and he bought it.

Finding Sharp's anecdote plausible and attractive, Browning's later biographers, one after another, adopted it, either word for word or with variations. It seemed to fit into the picture so appropriately. But, as Professor Pottle has proved in his *Shelley and Browning : a Myth and some Facts*, the story is devoid of truth. Browning's first acquaintance with Shelley was not made in the pages of *Queen Mab*, but in those of a far more inspiring volume. For what he acquired, by gift not purchase, was a collection of the best of Shelley's lyrics ; and it was these that counted for so much in the poetical development of their youthful possessor.

Here is the book's title : *Miscellaneous Poems*. By Percy

Bysshe Shelley. London. William Benbow, 252 High Holborn. 1826. It is " a little duodecimo volume bound in light drab boards " ; and the inside of the cover bears the following note in Browning's hand.

This book was given to me, probably as soon as published, by my cousin, J. S. The foolish markings and still more foolish scribblings show the impression made on a boy by this first specimen of Shelley's poetry. Robert Browning, June 2, 1878. " O World, O Life, O Time."

The cousin was James Silverthorne. *This first specimen of Shelley's poetry* disposes of the Sharp fable once for all. The book itself was a literary piracy. It was sold in May, 1913, when Robert Browning's library was dispersed on the death of his son. It passed, as rare books do, through several hands, and Professor Pottle re-discovered it in America.

Years afterwards Browning wrote of Shelley that men would not

" persist in confounding, any more than God confounds, with genuine infidelity and an atheism of the heart those passionate impatient struggles of a boy towards truth and love. . . . Crude convictions of boyhood, conveyed in imperfect and unapt forms of speech,—for such things all boys have been pardoned. They are growing pains, accompanied by temporary distortion of soul also." [1]

It is impossible not to see in this a memory of his own experience ; he never forgot the sorrow his own " growing pains " had caused his mother, nor her patience and love—" it distressed his mother, the one being in the world he truly loved, and deserves remembering in the tender sorrow with which he himself remembered it." [2]

But Shelley's influence was not confined to *Queen Mab* and atheism and vegetarianism. Inspired by what he had read, Browning eagerly set himself the " sweet task to gather every breathing " of the almost unknown poet. From the editor of the *Literary Gazette*—the *Athenæum* was but a few months old—he finally learnt what the booksellers could not

[1] Browning's preface to the *Letters of Shelley* (afterwards found to be spurious), 1852.
[2] Mrs. Orr, p. 46.

tell him, that Shelley's poems could be obtained from Charles Ollier of Vere Street, and, as May was drawing near, he asked for them as a birthday present. By the irony of fate it was his devout mother who was the purchaser. Presently, perhaps on his birthday, and while the nightingales were singing in the gardens behind Southampton Street, he sat turning the leaves of *Rosalind and Helen*—afterwards lent to Fox and lost in the Barnet woods by Eliza Flower ; of the *Cenci* ; of the Pisa edition of *Adonais*—borrowed and sold by Thomas Powell ; [1] of the *Epipsychidion*, of the *Prometheus Unbound* and the *Hellas*. Cowley has told how, as a boy, he read the *Faerie Queene* and was thus made a poet on the spot ; Wordsworth has described his own dedication as a poet during the memorable walk along the hills of Cumberland, when mountains, sea, and misty valleys were glorified by the rising sun ; and Browning as he read the *Prometheus* and the *Hellas* realized that he had become subject to a spell such as had never yet been laid upon him.

> " I was vowed to liberty,
> Men were to be as gods and earth a heaven,
> And I—ah, what a life was mine to be !
> My whole soul rose to meet it."

The formal classes in Gower Street, which began five months later, not unnaturally proved repugnant to this enthusiastic mood.

Shelley did not come unattended. The *Adonais* spoke of another poet who had become

> "a portion of the loveliness
> Which once he made more lovely ; "

and Shelley proved an introduction to Keats, whose works were soon procured. Nor were minor singers neglected, for, in a letter of 1841, Browning narrates how he had run—" real running, for I was a boy, to Bond Street from Camberwell, and came back with a small book brimful of the sweetest, truest things in the world "—the now forgotten *Lyric Offerings* of Laman Blanchard, which appeared in the summer of 1828.

---

[1] An admitted scamp, by whom Browning and some of his early friends were taken in.

The spring of 1829, when Browning abruptly left College, no long time after these experiences, marks his definite choice of poetry as his vocation. "He appealed to his father, whether it would not be better for him to see life in its best sense, and cultivate the powers of his mind, than to shackle himself in the very outset of his career by a laborious training foreign to that aim." These words are simply the prose equivalent of what is stated in *Pauline* immediately after the reference to his college days :—

> "'Twas in my plan to look on real life,
> The life all new to me : my theories
> Were firm, so them I left to look and learn
> Mankind, its cares, hopes, fears, its woes and joys."

One experience in this "plan to look on real life" is interesting. Keats as a medical student walked the hospitals ; Coleridge, fascinated by his brother's studies, "became wild to be apprenticed to a surgeon" ; and Browning, eager to "see, know, taste, feel, all," attended the well-known Dr. Blundell's lectures at Guy's Hospital. It was "dear old Pritchard," a brisk, dapper, little, grey-haired sea-captain, with a squint and a delightful fund of tales of adventure, who brought this about, for he was Dr. Blundell's cousin. Captain Pritchard, a memorable figure in the poet's early life, lived at Battersea, where Browning's father was born : he is mentioned in the earliest existing letter written by Browning, and when he died he left the poet's sister £1000. Dr. Blundell's lectures are said to have aroused in Browning "considerable interest in the sciences connected with medicine," and as Coleridge, in describing his own period of medical enthusiasm, says, "English, Latin, yea, Greek books of medicine read I incessantly, Blanchard's Latin *Medical Dictionary* I had nearly by heart,"[1] so may it have been with Browning ; a possibility, or probability, not without interest for the evolution of *Paracelsus*.

Browning's chief companions during these early days were his cousins, James, John, and George Silverthorne, who lived in Portland Place, Peckham Road, adjoining their father's brewery and within a few minutes' walk of Hanover

---

[1] J. Gillman, *Life of S. T. Coleridge*, 1838, pp. 22, 23.

Cottage. All three brothers were musical, and have been described as "wild youths." Browning's chosen friend was James, the eldest, who ultimately succeeded for a short time to the brewery. On his death, in May, 1852, Browning wrote the tender lines *May and Death*, in which he refers to the "warm moon-births and long evening ends" when they had walked home together arm-in-arm from theatre or opera—simple pleasures like those described in Lamb's essay on *Old China*—or had rambled in a "certain wood," the favourite Dulwich Wood, where grew the spotted Persicaria which he so touchingly introduces into this poem. James Silverthorne was the only friend present at Browning's marriage in 1846, and his name stands in the register of Marylebone Church as one of the two witnesses.

That Browning continued his music, that he studied, that he wrote—and destroyed what he had written—that he danced, rode, fenced and boxed, during this period of preparation, is well known.[1] Mrs. Orr, however, seemed more than doubtful as to whether he sought experience of "real life" among the gipsies and at fairs. He was certainly not without experience of both; for from the days when Pepys recorded that he and his wife "and Mercer and Deb went to see the gipsies at Lambeth" until the days of Byron and of Browning, these wanderers were familiar to those who dwelt south of the Thames. The very name of Gipsy Hill commemorates Margaret Finch, the famous Gipsy Queen of Norwood, who, like the old crone in *The Flight of the Duchess*, was "the oldest Gypsy then above ground," for when she died in 1740 she was a hundred and nine. When, not long before Browning's birth, the gipsies quitted Norwood, it was to establish themselves in Dulwich Wood: here Byron, when a schoolboy at Dr. Glennie's in Lordship Lane,

---

[1] Some lines in *A Likeness* (1864) recall—

> " the spoils
> Of youth,—masks, gloves, and foils,
> And pipe-sticks, rose, cherry-tree, jasmine,
> And the long whip, the tandem-lasher,
> And the cast from a fist ('not, alas! mine,
> 'But my master's, the Tipton slasher'),
> And the cards where pistol-balls mark ace,
> And a satin shoe used for cigar-case,"

with other miscellaneous treasures.

used to visit them, and here Browning, who walked the wood by day and after nightfall, must frequently have met them. At the age of fifty years he learnt to swim at Pornic, but he had no need to wait for his visit to that little Breton seaside village to behold a handsome gipsy Fifine at the Fair. For three days each summer the Walworth Road from Camberwell Gate to the village green—a goodly mile—was aglow after sunset with candles beneath coloured shades on the road-side stalls : on the Green itself, besides the inevitable boats and swings and merry-go-rounds, there was the canvas-covered avenue with its gingerbread booths, there was music and dancing, and best of all, there was the ever-popular Richardson's Theatre—appreciated, it is said, by the poet in his younger days. Peckham also had its fair, which was held just opposite Mr. Ready's school ; and Greenwich, noisiest and most boisterous of fairs, was close at hand.

In writing to Miss Barrett early in 1846, Browning remarked :

"my sympathies are very wide and general,—always have been —and the natural problem has been the giving unity to their object, concentrating them instead of dispersing."

This remained true throughout his life. In Rome, in 1860 and 1861, for instance, this tendency temporarily revealed itself in an absorbing passion for modelling in the studio of his friend William Story ; and nearly thirty years previously it had led him with youthful self-confidence to outline a vast scheme by which he hoped to give expression to the many-sidedness of his nature. *Pauline*, which appeared in March, 1833, was to be the first portion of this huge scheme, the details of which he duly set forth in a note inserted at the beginning of his own copy :—

"The following Poem was written in pursuance of a foolish plan which occupied me mightily for a time, and which had for its object the enabling me to assume and realize I know not how many different characters :—meanwhile the world was never to guess that 'Brown, Smith, Jones and Robinson' (as the spelling books have it) the respective authors of this poem, the other novel, such an opera, such a speech, etc., etc., were no other than one and the same individual. The present abortion was the first work of the *Poet* of the batch, who would have been more legitimately *myself* than most of the others : but I surrounded him with all manner of (to my then notion) poetical accessories, and had planned quite a delightful life for him.

Only this crab remains of the shapely Tree of Life in this Fool's paradise of mine.—R.B."

This plan was conceived on the October evening of 1832, on which he had seen Kean at Richmond in *Richard III ;* and as the preface to *Pauline* indicates, that poem was completed by January, 1833. Like all Browning's early poetry, except *Strafford,* it was published at the expense of the family. His aunt, Mrs. Silverthorne, with whom he was a great favourite, paid the twenty-six pounds five shillings [1] to Saunders and Otley for *Pauline :* his father bore the expense of *Paracelsus, Sordello,* and the eight parts of *Bells and Pomegranates.* In March, when *Pauline* was ready, Browning bethought himself of the Rev. W. J. Fox, whom he had not seen since the days of *Incondita.* Fox had recently added to his many labours the duties of editor of the *Monthly Repository,* which he had purchased and transformed : it had been the chief Unitarian theological organ ; he made it a social and literary review. In January of this year he had devoted ten pages to the recently published *Poems* of Tennyson : in April he devoted the same space to the anonymous volume of Browning.[2] He had felt confident of Tennyson, he felt " no less certain of the author of *Pauline,*" whom he emphatically pronounced a poet and a genius. *Pauline* was evidently a " hasty and imperfect sketch," said Fox, but

" in recognizing a poet we cannot stand upon trifles, nor fret ourselves about such matters. Time enough for that afterwards, when larger works come before us. Archimedes in the bath had many particulars to settle about specific gravities and Hiero's crown ; but he first gave a glorious leap and shouted *Eureka !* "

Seldom has a young poet received such a welcome. Browning was filled with "inexpressible delight " ;[3] and

---

[1] She gave him £30, the rest of which was spent in advertising, Browning told Mr. Wise.

[2] *Monthly Repository,* New Series, vol. vii. Tennyson, pp. 30–41 ; *Pauline,* pp. 252–262.

[3] Orr, p. 102 ; letter of 1837 to Miss Haworth.

this, "the most timely piece of kindness in the way of literary help that ever befell me," [1] as he termed it half a century later, laid the foundations of a friendship which lasted for thirty years, till Fox's death in 1864. He lost no time in thanking his "Master," as Fox now became.

"I can only say," he wrote, "that I am very proud to feel as grateful as I do. . . . I shall never write a line without thinking of the source of my first praise." [2]

Nor did this welcome stand alone, for, a week later, Allan Cunningham wrote in the *Athenæum*,

"We open the book at random; but fine things abound; there is no difficulty in finding passages to vindicate our praise. . . . To one who sings so naturally, poetry must be as easy as music is to a bird."

Why did Browning speak of a poem thus praised as an "abortion"? Why did he refuse to reprint it for nearly five and thirty years?—"I acknowledge and retain" it, he ultimately said in 1867, "with extreme repugnance and indeed purely of necessity." Not solely, it may be surmised, because he felt that "good draughtmanship" and "right handling were far beyond the artist" in 1833, but also because he had come to realize—and to realize very speedily—that, dramatic as he had intended his poem to be, there was only too much of self-revelation in its pages. John Stuart Mill seems to have been the unconscious instrument of this reaction. Six years the senior of Browning, whose very name was unknown to him, Mill, then unknown to fame, was Fox's friend and helper. The January number of the *Monthly Repository*, which contained the editor's article on Tennyson also contained a paper by Mill on "What is poetry?" Fox, therefore, naturally sent Mill one of the twelve copies of *Pauline* which had been forwarded from Camberwell, as Mill was also a contributor to the *Examiner* and to *Tait's Edinburgh Magazine*. The *Examiner* refused to insert Mill's notice. During the summer of 1833, the editor of *Tait's* found himself so overwhelmed with verse that in July he even had

---

[1] Unpublished letter to J. Dykes Campbell, January 26, 1887 (Wise).
[2] Orr, p. 57. Mrs. Orr printed four letters to Fox about *Pauline*, pp. 55-57.

to apologize for being in arrears; it happened therefore that in August *Pauline*, an anonymous poem, was dismissed at the end of two pages in which a dozen volumes had been criticized with the words—"a piece of pure bewilderment." Meanwhile Mill had read the poem four times, and whether Browning really suffered or gained by the overcrowded condition of the magazine may be judged from the note which he made at the end of the volume sent to him by Fox :—

"With considerable poetic powers, the writer seems to me possessed with a more intense and morbid self-consciousness than I ever knew in any sane human being. I should think it a sincere confession, though of a most unlovable state, if the 'Pauline' were not evidently a mere phantom. All about her is full of inconsistency —he neither loves her nor fancies he loves her, yet insists upon *talking* love to her. If she *existed* and loved him, he treats her most ungenerously and unfeelingly. All his aspirings and yearnings and regrets point to other things, never to her; then he *pays her off* toward the end by a piece of flummery, amounting to the modest request that she will love him and live with him and give herself up to him *without* his *loving her—moyennant quoi* he will think her and call her everything that is handsome, and he promises her that she shall find it mighty pleasant. Then he leaves off by saying he knows he shall have changed his mind by to-morrow, and despite 'these intents which seem so fair,' but that having been thus visited once no doubt he will be again—and is therefore 'in perfect joy,' bad luck to him! as the Irish say. A cento of most beautiful passages might be made from this poem, and the psychological history of himself is powerful and truthful—*truth-like* certainly, all but the last stage. *That*, he evidently has not yet got into. The self-seeking and self-worshipping state is well described—beyond that, I should think the writer had made, as yet, only the next step, viz. into despising his own state. I even question whether part even of that self-disdain is not *assumed*. He is evidently *dissatisfied*, and feels part of the badness of his state; he does not write as if it were purged out of him. If he once could muster a hearty hatred of his selfishness it would *go;* as it is, he feels only the *lack* of *good*, not the positive evil. He feels not remorse, but only disappointment; a mind in that state can only be regenerated by some new passion, and I know not what to wish for him but that he may meet with a *real* Pauline.

"Meanwhile he should not attempt to show how a person may be *recovered* from this morbid state,—for *he* is hardly convalescent, and ' what should we speak of but that which we know ? ' "

Browning, we are told, " was always ready to say he had been worth little in his young days. 'I am better now,' he has said more than once, when its reminiscences have been invoked." [1]   How far then was " John Mill, the metaphysical head," correct in his diagnosis of the spiritual condition of the author of *Pauline,* and when did Browning become convalescent ?   Did Mill's closing words strike home, and is their influence to be traced in the soul-histories of Paracelsus and Sordello ?   It would seem possible.

In October, 1832, Browning had walked the ten miles from Richmond to Camberwell confident in heart and with his mind aglow with his vast plans : a year later he was reading Mill's words and was writing on the fly-leaf of the little volume which had been returned to him by Fox :— " Robert Browning, October 30, 1833."   Mill's note was at the end : did Browning write his own note at the beginning of the volume by way of supplement ?   Not a single copy of his poem had been sold ; and a bale of unbound sheets was destined to be sent home from the publishers.   The " inexpressible delight " of spring had vanished : autumn had come—" autumn in everything," as Andrea del Sarto sadly exclaims,—when Browning wrote on a blank page of his first published work, " Only this crab remains of the shapely Tree of Life in this Fool's paradise of mine." [2]

[1] Mrs. Orr's *Life,* p. 46.

[2] This fateful copy of *Pauline* is now in the Dyce and Forster Library at South Kensington.

CHAPTER IV

"PARACELSUS"

Journey to St. Petersburg—Acquaintance with de Ripert-Monclar—Sources of *Paracelsus*—Shelley's influence discernible—Browning's own experiences reflected—Antecedent study—*Paracelsus*, coldly received in general, is praised by John Forster—Wins its way among literary men—Browning's first meeting with Macready—He meets Forster at Macready's house—The *Ion* supper—" The author of *Paracelsus* " and " the poets of England."

BROWNING'S "plan to look on real life " would seem to have had a somewhat unexpected fulfilment in the spring of 1834, for on Saturday, 1 March, when Chevalier George de Benkhausen, the Russian consul general, set forth on a special mission to Russia, he was accompanied by the youthful poet whose *Pauline* had appeared a year before. The origin of the acquaintance has not been traced.

The first sight of foreign countries is a unique experience to the least imaginative ; to Browning's ardent and enthusiastic temperament the idea and its fulfilment must have afforded the keenest satisfaction.

The General Steam Navigation Company already had poor little packets—which, according to that indefatigable maker of books, Mrs. Trollope, formed a painful contrast with those she had seen in America—running from London to Ostend and Rotterdam : but beyond this steam was not available, for even Belgium had, as yet, no railways. For fifteen hundred miles, therefore, the travellers journeyed day and night as fast as horses could take them. Four years later Browning told in stirring lines how three steeds and their riders had dashed into the darkness to gallop through the night, and how Roland, the "horse without peer," had alone survived to stagger into distant Aix bearing "the good news from Ghent." It was from his two journeys through the Low Countries, in 1834, that he acquired the knowledge of localities shown in his spirited poem; and, in 1838, three months after his first voyage to Italy—during which he had written it—he once more passed from Aix to the sea-coast on his homeward journey by way of the Rhine.   After leaving Rotterdam, on his outward journey, 1834, he passed by the home of the heroine of his *Colombe's Birthday* :—

> " Castle Ravestein—
> That sleeps out trustfully its extreme age
> On the Meuse' quiet bank, where she lived queen
> Over the water-buds,"

and then through "ancient famous happy Cleves," whence came Colombe's lover, the advocate Valence ; while the " thriving little burgh " of Juliers, now Germanized as Julich, which he makes the scene of his drama, lies not far to the east of Aix.   At Aix, in the Council-hall of the Rath-haus, he saw the famous and oldest portrait of Charlemagne, a description of which he introduced into the fifth book of his *Sordello*.   Of his journeys through the sandy flats of Prussia his poems bear no impress, but at Tilsit, on the eastern border, where, twenty-seven years before, Napoleon and the Tsar had met on a raft in mid-stream, he saw the snowdrops in blossom. Then began his experiences of the still ice-bound Russia :— the Cossacks at the *douane*, the huge inns with their double-windowed, stove-heated dining-rooms festooned with ivy and other climbing plants, which grew as if in a hot-house, the peasants in their sheepskin coats, the scattered and scanty villages with gabled wooden houses, the interminable pine forests of Courland, Riga with its walls, narrow streets and interesting fair beside the frozen Dwina, the hills and valleys of Livonia, and the lonely level shores of Lake Peipus, the sandy soil and pine woods of Esthonia, and then St. Petersburg.

About 1843, Browning wrote an unpublished play, *Only a Player-girl*, and laid the scene in the Russian capital—"it was Russian," he told Miss Barrett, " and about a fair on the Neva, and booths and droshkies and fish-pies and so forth, with Palaces in the background."   It was also the fruit of observation, for, when he reached the city, the Neva was still frozen. Before he left, however, he could see crowds of bushy-bearded, long-booted workmen in their sheepskin tunics and gaily coloured shirts, kept back by the pole-axes of the coarsely clad police, as they gathered to watch the huge ice-field gradually sink in mid-stream, split and crack in all directions, and then whirl in broken fragments, grating and grinding as they were swept along. A few days later he heard the booming of the guns, as the governor crossed the open stream to bear to the Tsar a goblet of the sparkling Neva water: then followed the rush of boats and boatmen : St. Petersburg, no longer three isolated portions, was once more united, as the floating wooden bridges swung into place across the mighty stream, and the city was *en fête*.

It was in Russia that Browning met a king's messenger called Waring, a name to be employed eight years later for a fancy portrait of his loved friend, Alfred Domett, whom, among other imaginary experiences, he supposes to visit that wintry land :—

> " Waring in Moscow, to those rough
> Cold northern natures borne, perhaps."

Among the pictures at the Hermitage he saw " florid old rogue Albano's masterpiece," to which he makes Guido refer in *The Ring and the Book*, as " bouncing Europa on the back o' the bull," [1] a subject to become more familiar to him in middle life from the *replica* in the Uffizi at Florence. The huge pine forests, however, through which he had driven day after day, " wall and wall of pine," impressed him more than anything he saw.[2] In 1837, when he acted as godfather to the child of a friend, and was desirous of appropriately commemorating the occasion, his mind recurred to the " parent firs" he had seen three years before " in far Esthonian solitudes " and to the little seedlings which grew up beneath their sheltering shade ; and his musings resulted

---

[1] *Guido*, lines 270-275.

[2] A traveller who followed Browning in 1835 describes the monotonous beauty of these forests in the spring sunlight—the pines and birches with an undergrowth of juniper and a rich green carpet of blae-berries. " The fable of the magician's garden seemed realized, every leaf was hung with sapphires, rubies, and emeralds."

in *A Forest Thought*.[1]   Forty years later, in 1878, while staying on the Splügen pass, the snow and the pine-trees of Switzerland conjured up memories of the snow and the pine woods of Russia, and he wrote *Iván Ivánovitch*, a poem in which there figures so tragically the useful two-headed axe he had seen at the girdle of every Russian workman—" 'Tis a hammer and saw and plane and chisel and—what know I else?"   One other thing interested the music-loving poet— the melancholy strains chanted by the Russian peasants. Half a century afterwards he met in Venice the Russian Prince Gagarin.   For an hour they talked of Russian folk-songs and music, while Browning sang in a low voice the national airs he had picked up by ear during his brief visit of 1834, till the Prince exclaimed in wonder that Browning's musical memory was "better than my own, on which I have hitherto piqued myself not a little."[2]

After an absence of about three months Browning was again in London; and the middle of 1834 is marked by an intimacy with a talented young Frenchman, Comte Amédée de Ripert-Monclar, who for several years spent the summer in England.   Whatever may be the case with Chevalier de Benkhausen, there is, fortunately, no doubt as to the origin of this friendship.   Devoted as he was to the cause of the dethroned Bourbons, Monclar in his annual visits acted as a means of communication between the Royalists in France and the refugees of the revolution of 1830; but his friendship with the Brownings was quite unconnected with political considerations.   Monclar's uncle, the Marquis of Fortia, member of many academies, widely known for his generous interest in literature, and himself a busy writer, was acquainted with William Shergold Browning, to whose literary work reference has already been made.   Also, Monclar belonged to a branch of the family which had been ennobled by Louis XV. on account of the skill of Jean Pierre François, first Marquis of Monclar,[3] in matters of finance: and Count

[1] See *Country Life*, 10 June, 1905. "An unpublished poem by Robert Browning"; fifty-two lines, written November, 1837.

[2] *Century Magazine*, vol. lxiii. pp. 578–9, an article by Mrs. Bronson, "Browning in Venice," also printed in *Cornhill*, 1902.

[3] Created Marquis 1769. He wrote wisely and well on fiscal matters, so that

Amédée, afterwards Marquis, also developed an interest in financial affairs, so that there was special appropriateness in the fact that he was introduced to the cheery Reuben Browning, and thus to the household at Camberwell, by the brother who was engaged in the Paris banking house of the Rothschilds. As Browning was a good French scholar, and as, among other gifts, the Count was something of an artist and a student of history, it is evident that there was much that would be congenial to him at Southampton Street. It was he who drew the first existing portrait of Browning, and it was to him that Browning dedicated, in 1835, his first acknowledged poem, *Paracelsus*.

To the young Frenchman of twenty-seven Browning, we are told, was indebted for the suggestion of the subject of his poem.[1] This, however, seems of minor importance compared with the facts already indicated—that Browning's father was as familiar with *Paracelsus* as if that interesting empiric had been present in the flesh in the library at Camberwell instead of being represented by three goodly folios, that he himself had already dabbled in medicine and kindred studies, and that *Pauline* had been prefaced by a quotation from the *Occult Philosophy* of Cornelius Agrippa, a work dedicated to that Abbot Tritheim who appears in the poem of 1835 as the teacher of Paracelsus. Moreover, it is evident from Browning's confession to Miss Barrett concerning the difficulties arising from the many-sidedness of his own nature that it would be natural for him to look with interest upon a character such as he conceives Paracelsus to have been. Indeed, in *Pauline* he had confessed—

" I envy—how I envy him whose soul
Turns its whole energies to some one end.

. . . .

. . . I would have one joy,
But one in life, so it were wholly mine,
One rapture all my soul could fill."

Louis XV. invited him to be Comptroller of Finance, a position he refused. Count Amédée also wrote on financial questions ; his little *Catéchisme financier* (1848) was several times reprinted. He published an account of his uncle, who died in 1843. De Fortia wrote much on history, but none of his too abundant work has any real value.

[1] Mrs. Orr is the authority. See the *Life*, p. 72.

F

Paracelsus, as represented by Browning, is emphatically a man of one idea—he "aspired to KNOW." And it is noticeable that in *Pauline* Browning had already set forth the danger which besets the path of such a man :—

> "This restlessness of passion meets in me
> A craving after knowledge : the sole proof
> Of yet commanding will is in that power
> Repressed; for I beheld it in its dawn,
> The sleepless harpy with just-budding wings,
> And I considered whether to forego
> All happy ignorant hopes and fears, to live,
> Finding a recompense in its wild eyes;
> *And when I found that I should perish so,*
> I bade its wild eyes close from me for ever."

Two years after writing these lines Browning represented Festus as pleading with the youthful Paracelsus in the garden of Würzburg not to seek his recompense in the wild eyes of this sleepless harpy ; and to his pleadings Michal added her prophecy—so bitterly recalled fourteen years later by Paracelsus—which repeats the very words of *Pauline* :—

> "You will find all you seek, and *perish so !*"

Miss Barrett was indignant that *Paracelsus* should be termed "an imitation of Shelley, when if *Paracelsus* was anything, it was the expression of a new mind, as all might see, as *I* saw."[1] Miss Barrett was perfectly right : yet Emerson was not wholly wrong when he wrote that "the greatest genius is the most indebted man." "Ah, *that was* a poet !" exclaimed Browning enthusiastically to Domett, as they passed on the staircase at Camberwell a bust of Shelley, which Mrs. Leigh Hunt had executed and presented to him. *Pauline*, as Joseph Arnould, another of Browning's early friends, emphatically declared, was written "when Shelley was his god" ; and *Paracelsus* was begun but eighteen months after *Pauline* was published. The influence of *Alastor* upon *Pauline* is evident; is it absent from *Paracelsus* ? In his preface to *Alastor* Shelley speaks of "one who drinks deep of the fountain of knowledge and is still

---

[1] *Letters of R. B. and E. B. B.*, vol. i. p. 327

insatiate," of one who experiences a sudden awakening as
to the need of Love, the ideal of which he vainly seeks ere
he "descends into an untimely grave." Further, at the close
of his preface, he even points the moral that those "who
keep aloof from sympathies with their kind, rejoicing neither
in human joy nor mourning with human grief; these and
such as they have their appointed curse. . . . Those who love
not their fellow-beings live unfruitful lives." Similar to this
is the language of Festus in Browning's poem :—

> " How can that course be safe which from the first
>   Produces carelessness of human love ? "

Browning did not imitate Shelley, but he could not fail to
read and interpret the life of the historical Paracelsus in the
light of the poetic creations which so filled and coloured his
own imagination. This is true with regard to his general
conception, for the Paracelsus of history was by no means as
indifferent to the love of human kind as, for poetic purposes,
Browning has chosen to represent him. It is also true, at
times, in regard to details. The "grey hair, faded hands, and
furrowed brow"[1] ascribed to the Paracelsus of eight-and-
twenty, are not derived from history, but from the "scattered
hair, sered by the autumn of strange suffering," and the
"listless hands" of *Alastor ;* nor can one doubt that the glitter-
ing eye, "brighter than ever" as the end draws near, had its
origin in the lustre of the dark eyes "as in a furnace burning"
of the same poem.

Nor are the echoes of Shelley confined to his *Alastor.*
From some elements in the myth of Prometheus Browning
unmistakably evolved the conception of his Aprile as
not only the lover and the poet,[2] but as the potential
sculptor, painter, orator, and musician. Browning was so
fascinated by the Prometheus legend that among his early
dreams was that of endeavouring to "restore the Prometheus
πυρφόρος as Shelley did the Λυόμενος."[3] This dream, like
the combination in Aprile of the spirit of Love with the spirit

---

[1] Cf. Part II. of the poem.

[2] As will be pointed out in its place, the influence of the story of Sordello is
doubtless also to be traced in the evolution of Aprile.

[3] *Letters of R. B. and E. B. B.*, vol. i. p. 38.

of the artist, is due to Shelley, whose Prometheus when unbound not only listens to " the low voice of Love . . . and Music" but sees in vision

> " the progeny immortal
> Of painting, sculpture, and rapt Poesy."

But other things contributed to the evolution of *Paracelsus* : certain aspects of Browning's character, and various mental experiences of his own.   He is described at the time of the appearance of this poem as " full of ambition, eager for success, eager for fame—and what's more, determined to conquer fame and to achieve success." [1]   Ten years later he himself wrote, " I have never been frightened of the world, nor mistrustful of my power to deal with it, and get my purpose out of it, if once I thought it worth while," and he spoke of " meaning, on the whole, to be a poet, if not *the* poet . . . for I am vain and ambitious some nights."   Is this wholly unlike the mood of the Swiss student at Würzburg, as the autumn sun is setting behind St. Saviour's church ? The Paracelsus of nineteen is represented as breaking away from the routine of Abbot Tritheim and refusing to study in " one of Learning's many palaces, after approved example," as he preferred to study among men.   The English student of seventeen had in the same way found the shackles of Gower Street intolerable.   Paracelsus, again, is depicted as a youth of " wondrous plans and dreams and hopes," many of which were doomed to failure ; he who drew the picture, after indulging in " plans and dreams and hopes," had recently termed the dwelling-place of his soul a " fool's paradise," and had proclaimed the first-fruits of his genius a bitter " crab " apple.   When, therefore, Monclar suggested for poetic treatment the life of Paracelsus, such experiences must have tended to reveal to Browning the potentialities of the subject, and must to some extent have coloured the manner of its dramatic presentation.

" The liberties I have taken with my subject are very trifling," said Browning in a note at the end of his poem, " and the reader may slip the foregoing scenes between the leaves of any memoir of Paracelsus he pleases, by way of

---

[1] Mrs. Bridell-Fox wrote thus to a correspondent.   Mrs. Orr, *Life*, p. 93.

commentary." And, for proof, he proceeded to translate a brief biography. But in this memoir one finds no faithful Festus, and one finds no Michal—maid, wife, and mother—the earliest figure, and but lightly sketched, in his great gallery of women ; these, like the shadowy Italian poet Aprile, are wholly his creation. For the opening scene he had, at least, but a few scattered hints, and his own experiences would count for far more than any hints he had. The incidents of the second scene have no historical basis whatever, and the influence of Shelley is manifest. The third and fourth parts are more historical in outline : but not even Æschylus himself could be more amazed, were he summoned from the grave to listen to the lyric strains of *Prometheus Unbound* in place of his own lost drama, than Paracelsus would be, were he called forth and confronted with the splendid vision of his death-bed with which the poem closes. By this, Leigh Hunt, who somewhat sharply criticized portions of Browning's poem, was so moved that he called it

> " An Orphic song indeed,
> A song divine of high and passionate thoughts
> To their own music chanted ! " [1]

Browning, therefore, in his note is speaking not as an historian, but as a poet: *Paracelsus* is a poetic "commentary" upon the facts of a life which he had sympathetically studied.

It is, however, quite a mistake to imagine that he engaged in "vast research among contemporary records," or that before his poem appeared there had been nothing written on Paracelsus save a "caricature drawn by bitter enemies." Browning's research was not vast : the erudition, seen especially in his notes, is more apparent than real ; nor did he undertake his subject in the spirit of a Ruskin when writing *Modern Painters*.[2] He opened his father's volumes and he found in the first five pages of the preface by Bitiskius a defence of the life and work of Paracelsus, the main outlines

---

[1] Quoted by Hunt in his review of *Paracelsus* from Coleridge's lines on Wordsworth's *Prelude*.

[2] Browning's enthusiasm would doubtless grow as he proceeded, as was the case with a more modern student :—" Au fur et à mesure que j'avançais dans l'étude de ses œuvres, à la défiance initiale succéda un curieux interêt, puis à la fin une quasi-admiration." *La médicine occulte de Paracelse*, L. Durey, Paris, 1900, p. 54.

of which he adopted, poetically developed and idealized. Paracelsus had died in 1541, and, if it is true that both before and after death he had lacked neither foes nor detractors, it is equally true that he had wanted neither disciples nor defenders. His secretary, John Oporinus the "arch-knave," who appears but to disappear in the opening lines of the fourth part of the poem, had lifted up his heel against his master by circulating evil tales, but had lived to repent and recant. During the days when Shakespeare was a schoolboy at Stratford, Thomas Erastus, long Professor at Heidelberg, had given currency to the bitter words of Oporinus in his two lengthy Latin *Disputationes*. In the next century the learned Hermann Conring, whose epitaph describes him as a counsellor of kings and princes, learned in the law of nations, skilled in the practice and theory of all philosophy, a philologist of distinction, an orator, a poet, a physician, and a theologian, was another opponent of what was long termed the "New Medicine." But Conring, in turn, was vigorously opposed by a sturdy disciple of Paracelsus, the able Professor of Chemistry at the University of Copenhagen, Olaus Borrichius.

It was in 1658, during the lifetime of these two distinguished scholars, in the year when the September winds were howling round the deathbed of the great Protector, that Frederick Bitiskius published at Geneva the three folio volumes of the works of Paracelsus which Browning used for his poem. Bitiskius, in his preface, stood forth to defend Paracelsus and his works from the fouler aspersions of his detractors, yet he was not blind—nor was Browning who followed him—to faults: he would not speak of the "divine" Paracelsus, nor would he represent him as an Achilles made invulnerable to evil by being plunged in the waters of a moral Styx, rather, he apologetically pleaded, had be been immersed in the stream of Original Sin. To Bitiskius, Paracelsus was *Chemicorum facile princeps* and gifted with "an inexhaustible desire to probe the secrets of nature," but one might as well search his volumes for the lyrics of Browning's poem as for the thoughts which it contains. The record of aspiration, defeat and attainment—all that really constitutes the spiritual history of the poem—is of Browning's creation, it is his "commentary," just as the main thought of the poem, the need of the union of Power and Love, is Browning's life-long creed ; first expounded in his first acknowledged work *Paracelsus*, reiterated again and again, till it found final expression in the *Reverie* of the aged poet of seventy-seven, published on the very day he died, in the *Asolando* volume of 1889.

To return, for a moment, to the assertion that the extreme erudition of Browning's notes is often more apparent than real. As few readers ever trouble to consult these notes, this may seem hardly worth emphasizing. Yet the matter is not devoid of interest as supplying a further indication of the obvious manner in which much of his very wide and varied learning was acquired. For example, when Browning mentions that " it appears from his treatise *de Phlebotomia* and elsewhere" that Paracelsus had discovered the circulation of the blood and the sanguification of the heart," this statement undoubtedly seems to savour of "vast research." But in reality Browning is merely copying from Bitiskius two marginal headings which state, *Paracel. nouit circulationem sanguinis—et sanguificationem cordis*, and incorporating a few words from the text where mention is made of the *Tractatio de Phlebotomia* and other works. To take but one further example : when he speaks of " Franciscus the servant of Paracelsus who describes in a letter to Neander a successful projection at which he was present," this does not really indicate any intimate knowledge of the household of Paracelsus or of the correspondence of the now-forgotten sixteenth-century schoolmaster, Michael Neander. It simply indicates that he had read the preface of Bitiskius, to whom he so frequently and so frankly refers. That Browning should have to study his subject is obvious—just as Shakespeare read Holinshed's *Chronicles*, and Tennyson worked "hard and unceasingly during two years at *Queen Mary* and consulted some twenty works." [1] But *Paracelsus*, a poem of over four thousand lines, as its author wrote in a discarded preface, "had not been imagined six months" before it was completed ; and although he faithfully consulted the works referred to or cited by Bitiskius and others, yet, it

[1] *Memoir*, by his son, vol. ii. p. 176.

might fairly be said that the so-called "sources" of his poem are practically contained in a few pages of Bitiskius, sundry passages in the works of Paracelsus himself, and in that interesting little octavo of 1620, the *Vitae Germanorum Medicorum* [1] of Melchior Adam.   But the most important source of all is Robert Browning.

The preface to *Paracelsus* is dated 15 March, 1835 : a month later Browning obtained through Fox an introduction to Moxon the poet-publisher of Dover Street, Piccadilly, whose *Sonnets* had appeared about the same time as *Pauline*. But "it was a flat time," says Sir Henry Taylor in his *Autobiography* ; "publishers would have nothing to say to poets, regarding them as unprofitable people."   In spite of favourable reviews and of a second edition within six months, his own *Artevelde* had not paid expenses ; after two and a half years, only three hundred copies of Tennyson's last volume had been sold ; and Moxon had published both.   So Moxon declined *Paracelsus :* and the publisher of *Pauline* declined *Paracelsus.*   Fox, however, eventually secured a publisher. In April Browning had written of his poem "there are a few precious bold bits here and there, and the drift and scope are awfully radical" ; this commended it the more to the ultra-liberal Effingham Wilson, whose name was familiar until recent years at the Royal Exchange.   But the poem had to be published at the expense of Browning's father. A second time, therefore, Fox had proved himself a " literary father " ; but as a reviewer he was silent till November.

When Browning returned from Russia in the summer of 1834, about a month before the death of Coleridge—to be followed ere the year closed by that of his friend and schoolfellow Lamb—he had found that the literary event of the day was the appearance of *Philip van Artevelde* by Henry Taylor. Lockhart, Taylor's friend, welcomed the new "dramatic romance" in twenty pages of the June *Quarterly ;* the July

---

[1] This prints in full the epitaph of Paracelsus to which Browning thus refers in note (6), " his epitaph which affirms, 'Bona sua in pauperes distribuenda collocandaque erogavit,' *honoravit,* or *ordinavit,* for accounts differ."   Did Browning then carefully compare even the versions of an epitaph?   Melchior Adam supplies the answer ; to the word " erogavit " he adds a marginal note, *Alii, honoravit vel ordinavit.*

Edinburgh followed with the same generous space; fifteen columns did not suffice for the *Athenæum* reviewer to utter all he would.

Paracelsus, the "dramatic poem" of 1835, was very differently received. The *Quarterly* was silent—Browning knew no Lockhart; the *Edinburgh* was as mute as *Blackwood*, wherein Christopher North, the self-proclaimed patron of young poets, would neither then nor at any time deign to worry his readers with the name of Browning. In 1833, the *Athenæum* had devoted a hundred lines to the anonymous *Pauline;* in 1835 its reviewer found relief for what mind and soul he had in seventy-three words :—

" PARACELSUS, by Robert Browning. There is talent in this dramatic poem (in which is attempted a picture of the mind of this noted character), but it is dreamy and obscure. Writers would do well to remember (by way of example) that though it is not difficult to imitate the mysticism and vagueness of Shelley, we love him and have taken him to our hearts as a poet, not *because* of these characteristics—but *in spite* of them [22 Aug., 1835]."

This, wrote Browning in 1845, "is a most flattering sample of what the 'craft' had in store for me"; elsewhere he speaks of "the reviews and newspapers that laughed my *Paracelsus* to scorn." "Every journal that thought worth while to allude to the poem at all, treated it with entire contempt . . . out of a long string of notices one vied with its predecessor in disgust at my 'rubbish,' as their word went."[1] There was, however, as he explains, one notable exception, in the pages of the *Examiner*.

Fox's silence was due to his absorption in political journalism. He had recently been appointed leader-writer on the *New Sun*. Browning had kept in touch with him ; he had contributed a sonnet to the *Monthly Repository* in 1834,[2] and speaks of having shown Fox other poems— probably *Johannes Agricola* and *Porphyria's Lover*, written in St. Petersburg, and both first printed in the *Repository* of 1836.

Another champion, however, had in the meantime entered the lists. Two weeks after the *Athenæum* notice there appeared in the *Examiner* a review of three columns which

---

[1] *Letters of R. B. and E. B. B.*, vol. i. pp. 208 and 323.
[2] See Appendix A.

began, "Since the publication of *Philip van Artevelde* we have met with no such evidences of poetical genius and general intellectual power as are contained in this volume." And the closing words were:—

"It is some time since we read a work of more unequivocal power than this. We conclude that its author is a young man, as we do not recollect his having published before. If so, we may safely predict for him a brilliant career, if he continues true to the present promise of his genius. He possesses all the elements of a fine poet."

This notice was from the pen of John Forster,[1] an able, pushing, rising young critic and journalist of three and twenty—one month older than Browning. Unknown to each other they had been fellow-students at Gower Street in 1828: unknown to each other they had been among those who gathered at the grave of Edmund Kean at Richmond in May, 1833.[2] Three months after the *Examiner* review they became acquainted at the house of Macready the actor, and remained, for many years at least, firm friends.

Browning's introduction to Macready, and thus indirectly to Forster, was due to Fox, who, after having moved from Hackney to Dalston, had now settled at Bayswater, in Craven Hill, next door to the Novellos, whose eldest daughter had become Mary Cowden Clarke.[3] In his little old-fashioned sitting-room, with its chintzes and black-framed engravings, Browning read aloud the manuscript of *Paracelsus;* thither he came, "with a quick light step," a few weeks later, when concerned about that momentous question, a publisher—"slim and dark and very handsome," writes

---

[1] Forster was born 2 April, 1812, at Newcastle. He, also, was precocious. When he was sixteen a two-act play by him was performed at Newcastle. He came to London in 1828, studied law at Gower Street, and entered the Inner Temple. He at once made literary friends, among them Leigh Hunt and Lamb. In 1833 he was writing for four journals, and was soon appointed chief literary and dramatic critic of the *Examiner*. In 1834 he moved to "his well-known chambers," 58, Lincoln's Inn Fields—afterwards the haunt of his numerous circle. This house, in the middle of the west side of the square, is recognizable at once by the large semicircular portico which extends over the entrances to two houses.

[2] A tablet within the parish church—where Thomson of the *Seasons* is also buried—commemorates Kean.

[3] Cowden Clarke introduced Browning to Moxon.

Fox's daughter—"and may I hint it? just a trifle of a dandy, addicted to lemon-coloured kid gloves and such things : quite 'the glass of fashion and the mould of form.'"[1] But the day of this visit, it should be remarked, was his birthday. Six months later, on 27 November—the month in which *Paracelsus* was reviewed (at last) by Fox and by Leigh Hunt—in the same little sitting-room Browning met Macready.

For Browning the interview was epoch-making. His love of the drama was strong; he felt proud to have shaken the hand of Edmund Kean, whose little green silk purse it was afterwards his joy to possess;[2] he now met another great actor whom for years he had admired. On Wednesday, 21 October, 1830, he had seen the Hamlet of Macready, to whom he afterwards described it as "one of the most vivid recollections I had meant to keep as a joy for ever." During seven years Macready and he were to be close friends, and for Macready he was to write three—perhaps four—plays, two of which were to be represented. Macready, always sensitive and eager for appreciation, was in low spirits and despondent; he felt slighted and shelved; all the more therefore, would he appreciate the "simple and enthusiastic manner" of one whom he described as looking and speaking "more like a youthful poet than any man I ever saw." The entry in his Diary reads: "I took Mr. Browning on and requested to be allowed to improve my acquaintance with him. He expressed himself warmly, as gratified by the proposal." Ten days later Macready, deep in *Paracelsus*, wrote : "the writer can scarcely fail to be a leading spirit of his time." So quickly did the friendship ripen that, one month after their first meeting, Browning was rumbling along in Billing's coach from the "Blue Posts" in Holborn, past the Welsh Harp and Edgware, to the pretty little village of Elstree, to spend the last night of the old year in Macready's dearly loved country home. Here among other guests he first met John Forster, whose greeting

---

[1] Mrs. Orr, *Life*, p. 92.

[2] Sold at the Irving sale.

[3] See *Macready's Reminiscences and Selections from his Diary and Letters*, vol. i. p. 474.

was, "Did you see a little notice of you I wrote in the
Examiner ? " [1]

With the appearance of *Paracelsus* Browning thus began
to take a place in the literary world. Few copies of his
poem were sold: no second edition was called for ; he even
considered "that he was not acknowledged much by the
public till the generation succeeding ours," wrote Domett
in his Diary in 1872 ; and added, "I suppose he knows
best, but I should have thought his reputation had grown
gradually from 1835, or the time of the publication of
Paracelsus, the genius of which was most cordially recognized
and welcomed by a good many of his own contemporaries, to
say the least." Both Browning and Domett were right.
Public acknowledgment Browning had not ; nor did *Paracelsus* open to him the doors of Holland House and Lansdowne House, as was the case with the author of *Artevelde*.
"If I had continued to be as much liked and sought in
society as I was in 1834–5," wrote Henry Taylor, "my
time and strength would have been wasted and I might have
become good for little else." But Browning had an audience
"fit though few." He was happy in his quiet visits to Fox
and Eliza Flower at Craven Hill, where he first met Richard
Hengist Horne, soon to succeed Fox as editor of the
Repository ; in his visits to Elstree, where was no lack of
pleasant and intellectual society ; and in his more frequent
visits to the "well-known chambers" of John Forster, whose
intimate he at once became. It was in Forster's rooms that
he met in the early part of 1836 the precocious Bulwer ;
Laman Blanchard, "a dear-tempered genial friend of everybody," for whose *Lyric Offerings* he had run to Bond Street
eight years before ; artists like Clarkson Stanfield and
Maclise—for one of whose pictures he was to write, in those
very rooms, the lines which developed into his *In a Gondola ;*
Talfourd, Lamb's friend and biographer and Macready's
staunch supporter, who was at once lawyer, poet, essayist
and dramatist—to him Browning, a few years later, "affectionately" dedicated *Pippa Passes*—and that more delightful
lawyer-poet, Procter, of whom, using the pseudonym by
which he was best known, the dedication of *Colombe's*

---

[1] *Robert Browning, Personalia*, by Edmund Gosse, p. 39.

Birthday speaks :—" no one loves and honours Barry Cornwall more than does Robert Browning." Forster, Talfourd and Procter formed the triumvirate of friends who were then helping Leigh Hunt with the *Examiner*. Hunt was at that time living in Cheyne Row, where he had Carlyle, with whom he had been several years acquainted, as a neighbour. Among his treasured possessions was a lock of Milton's hair ; and this, in token of appreciation, he now shared with Browning.[1]

One incident reveals the position which was at once taken among such men by the author of *Paracelsus*. At the famous *Ion* supper, in May, 1836, when Talfourd's home was thronged with lawyers, artists, actors, and authors, Browning found himself remaining seated while the other guests rose with one accord at the call of their host to drink to the " Poets of England," a toast which Talfourd associated with the name of the author of *Paracelsus*. Among those who rose to lift a glass to the youthful poet was a man of sixty, over whose declining years Browning was to watch with filial devotion, and one to whom he " always said that he owed more than to any contemporary "—Walter Savage Landor. Another guest, five years Landor's senior, leaned across the table and remarked, " I am proud to drink to your health, Mr. Browning ! " It was William Wordsworth, who may or may not have been aware that Leigh Hunt had recently classed *Paracelsus* with the still unpublished *Prelude*, and that two months before the night on which he raised his glass to the youth of four-and-twenty who " looked still younger than he was," John Forster had written thus :—

" Without the slightest hesitation we name Mr. Browning at once with Shelley, Coleridge, and Wordsworth. He has entitled himself to a place among the acknowledged poets of the age. This opinion will possibly startle many persons, but it is most sincere. . . . Mr.

[1] The lock was given to Hunt by Dr. Batty, the physician, "a man of excellent character." Batty had it from Hoole, the translator of *Tasso*, "and Hoole, though a bad translator, was a very honest man." Hoole had it from Dr. Johnson, "whose scrupulous veracity as to matters of fact is well known," and Johnson from some unknown person who had it from Addison. (Letter from Leigh Hunt to Robert Browning, 31 December, 1856, on the occasion of the publication of *Aurora Leigh*, printed in the *Cornhill Magazine*.)

Browning is a man of genius, he has in himself all the elements of a great poet, philosophical as well as dramatic . . . he has written a book that will live."

Browning never sought to disown the child of 1835 as he would fain have done with that of 1833: for eleven years the title-page of each successive work bore the words " By the author of *Paracelsus*."

CHAPTER V

EARLY FRIENDS

" The set "—Captain Pritchard, of Battersea—William Curling Young
—The Dowsons—Joseph Arnould, his career and correspondence—Alfred
Domett—His acquaintance with Browning traced—Their close friendship
—Domett the original of *Waring*—His departure for New Zealand—
Mention of him in *The Guardian Angel*—His return foreshadowed.

BROWNING'S increasing acquaintance among literary
people was in every way advantageous to him,
making easier the path of his honourable ambition
and widening his intellectual horizon. But he brought no
starved heart or mind to Macready's house or Forster's
chambers. He had already formed, nearer home, a
fellowship of some half-dozen comrades like-minded with
himself, in whose company he spent many hours of
discussion, many hours of relaxation. They resembled in
some degree that other group of young enthusiasts who in
Cambridge, a little earlier,

> " held debate, a band
> Of youthful friends, on mind and art,
> And labour, and the changing mart,
> And all the framework of the land." [1]

The bonds which united the members of this London
fellowship were in each case severed only by death. Almost
the latest to join its ranks was the one who beyond all other
men was to Browning in his earlier manhood what Arthur
Hallam was to Tennyson, the " friend of his bosom," the
" more than a brother "—Alfred Domett, who was, in
essential characteristics, the prototype of *Waring*.

[1] *In Memoriam*, stanza 87.

The oldest member, and in a sense the originator of " the set," as the friends called themselves, was Captain Pritchard, of Battersea, who, as we have seen, put Browning in the way of attending lectures at Guy's Hospital. His elasticity of mind bade defiance to advancing years, and enabled him to associate unconstrainedly with those who were very considerably his juniors. He could have said, as Dr. Johnson did to Langton aud Beauclerk, " Come, my lads, I'll have a frisk with you," without any sense of incongruity being suggested. One peculiarity he had, " he never let anyone know where he lived." Even when seriously ill he would not forego the secrecy of his abode. For women he had a chivalrous regard, and he left his money between two maiden ladies, " for," said he, " women should be provided for, as they cannot earn their living." The date of this sentiment— 1859—is instructive.

Captain Pritchard had, as was natural, friends connected with ships and ship-building, George Frederick Young and Christopher Dowson by name ; and he was, it appears, the means of introducing Browning to their circle. Between Browning and the sons of these two men an intimacy speedily arose. It is convenient to give at once a list of " the set," otherwise " The Colloquials," as put on record by one of themselves. The names are Pritchard, Christopher and Joseph Dowson, William Curling Young, Alfred Domett —these two were cousins—Joseph Arnould, and Robert Browning. The " Colloquials," whose palmy days seem to have been from about 1835 to 1840, used to meet at the Youngs' home at Limehouse, then a river-side village. They lived in a detached square house, at the corner of Church Row, close to St. Anne's Church, with big bow-windows looking northward and eastward across fields to the River Lea. Mr. Young was Member of Parliament for Tynemouth from 1832 to 1837, and one of the first directors of the New Zealand Company. A portrait of his son William, which has been preserved, depicts him as tall, handsome, and intellectual-looking. He emigrated to New Zealand, but unhappily lost his life by drowning in the river Wairoa. His death in 1842 caused the first gap in the ranks of " the set." Many years later Browning, then in Italy, was asked, " Do you remember William Young?" His emphatic answer was in the form of another question, "Who that knew William Young could ever forget him?"

The Dowsons were near neighbours of the Youngs. They also lived in Church Row, and the eldest son, Browning's "dear Chris. Dowson," was a constant intimate of the poet's early manhood. In 1836 he married Mary Domett, Alfred's sister. He was of a nervous and mercurial temperament, devoted to the theatre, and fond of entertaining his friends. After his marriage he lived in Albion Terrace, Limehouse, as near to his old home as possible. Here and at his summer retreat, a cottage at Woodford in Epping Forest, Browning was a frequent visitor. Dowson's life, however, was not a long one, for he died at Blackheath, in 1848, of consumption. His brother, Joseph, seems to have been an equally amiable character—"the unvaryingly happy Joe, that is Joe who tries to be unvaryingly happy," as he once described himself. Browning, it is recorded, would drop in upon him at his office and find him intent upon a contribution to *Olla Podrida*, the magazine of the "Colloquials," rather than on the rise and fall of the price of copper. Occasional visitors to the debates, though not of the inner circle, were Field Talfourd, brother of the author of *Ion*, two cousins of Domett, Oldfield by name, and, it has been suggested, Benjamin Jowett. But the inclusion of the future Master of Balliol would seem to be more than doubtful, and to have arisen, possibly, from the fact that like the three most important members of "the set"—Browning, Arnould, and Domett—he, too, was a native of Camberwell. At any rate, if he ever was present it must have been on an occasion when Browning was away; for, writing to a friend on 12 June, 1865, he speaks of making a new friend in "Mr. Browning, the poet," in terms which preclude the idea of an earlier acquaintance.[1] The later meetings of "the set" were held in a room hired at the "British Coffee Tavern" in Cockspur Street, W.C., and the severity of the debates was tempered by a half-yearly dinner either at "the old 'Artichoke' at

[1] See *Life and Letters of Benjamin Jowett*, by Evelyn Abbot and Lewis Campbell, vol. i. p. 400.

G

Blackwall, with a bow-window projecting over the Thames, a forest of masts in the foreground and Shooter's Hill for the background," [1] or at the " Star and Garter " at Richmond. The " British Coffee Tavern " and the " Artichoke " have alike disappeared.

To Joseph Arnould and Alfred Domett, quite apart from their interest as individuals and the poet's friends, students of the life of Browning are greatly indebted, to the one for his admirable letters, to the other for the diary, with its embodied reminiscences, which he kept on his return from his thirty years' absence in New Zealand. Both men, when Browning first knew them, were studying for the Bar ; but whereas Arnould had the law in his bones, Domett's spirit was chafed by its laborious and wordy technicalities. Both men had had what Browning missed, an University training. Both were ambitious, in their several ways, and each attained to eminence in his chosen calling.

Joseph Arnould, son of a doctor living in the Peckham Road, was described by Browning to Miss Barrett as " an Oxford Prize Poet, and an admirable dear good fellow." Educated at Charterhouse and at Wadham College (where he afterwards became a Fellow) he gained the Newdigate in 1834, and had the honour of reciting his *Hospice of St. Bernard* in the Sheldonian theatre amid thunders of applause begotten of a timely reference to Waterloo and the Iron Duke, who was present as Chancellor of the University. Later he worked hard at his profession, produced genial verse as the Poet Laureate of his circuit, wrote for the reviews, and was so successful as a journalist that he was offered the editorship of the *Daily News*, founded by Dickens and Forster. About his verse he had no illusions. He had, as he assured Domett in 1843, too just an appreciation of poetry to " add another to the metrical prosers of the day." He had married happily in 1841 ; and sticking to his proper last became, in 1848, "Arnould on Marine Insurance," [2] and, in 1859, " Sir Joseph " as a Judge of the High Court at Bombay. After ten years of successful work in India—one

---

[1] Letter of Arnould to Domett, November, 1845.
[2] A work now (1938) in its eleventh edition.

of his judgments was so much admired by the people of
Bombay that it was printed on a leaflet in letters of gold and
widely circulated—he retired, to live first at Naples, and
then at Florence, where he died in 1886.   His graphic letters
to Domett contain many glimpses of Browning and "the
set."   Here, for example, are his words as to Browning,
written in July, 1844 :—

" At Browning's especially you are a constant topic ; nothing can
exceed the kindness with which he speaks of you, in fact he is a
true friend—he has an energy of kindness about him which never
slumbers—in me he seems to take a thoroughly friendly interest,
and it is solely by his means that I have obtained an entrance at
last into Periodical Literature, which I have so long been endeavouring through less zealous friends to procure.   He is a noble fellow.
His life so pure, so energetic, so simple, so laborious, so loftily
enthusiastic.   It is impossible to know and not to love him."

This outburst is followed by a brief description of the
poet's sister, the truth of which will be cordially acknowledged
by all who had the privilege of knowing her.

" Sarianna, as my wife now always calls her, we are both very
much attached to—she is marvellously clever, such fine, clear animal
spirits, talks much and well, and yet withal is so simply and deeply
good hearted that it is a real pleasure to be with her."

We are now come to the last, and, if words mean anything, the closest of these earlier friends.   Alfred Domett,
who was born in 1811, and lived in Camberwell Grove, had a
strain of adventure in his blood.   His father ran away to sea
as a boy, served as a middy under Parker against the Dutch
at the battle of the Dogger Bank, in 1781 ; then forsook the
navy for the merchant service, and, marrying, became a ship
owner.[1]   He retained, however, a passion for the sea, and
kept his own yacht.   One of his connections, his son's diary
records, was Admiral Sir William Domett, K.C.B., " one of
Nelson's captains, and the friend and familiar of that famous
man."

Alfred Domett attended a school at Stockwell.   " The
place," he wrote in 1875, " was like an old country house,

---

[1] He and Mr. Young both married into the family of the Curlings of Denmark
Hill.

with a park." The description is pleasant, yet equally with Browning (and, it may be added, with Tennyson) he looked back to this period of his life with anything but satisfaction. "I loathe the recollection of my earlier school years there, though we used to have some fun, too, now and then." He went up to St. John's College, Cambridge, in 1829, but after four years' residence left the university without taking a degree. Instead, he published a volume of *Poems*, which made no great stir ; and had his headquarters at his father's house, described by a correspondent—a sister of Sir Frederick Young—as a "bright, unconventional, if somewhat rough house, where there was always such a lively atmosphere of freedom, interest and gay fun." Facilities for travel, too, were granted him, considerable for those days. He wandered to Canada in 1834, visited Italy and the Tyrol, and printed in 1839 *Venice*, a small volume of poetical impressions. *Venice* had, it seems, something to do with his friendship with Browning ; but a more potent factor, in all probability, was his admiration for Browning's early poetry:

> "It all grew out of the books I write;
> They find such favour in his sight
> That he slaughters you with savage looks
> Because you don't admire my books." [1]

How, we shall presently be able to infer. But the admiration is borne out by one of Browning's letters. "I shall certainly," he writes to his friend (22 May, 1842), "never be quite wanting in affection for essays that have got me your love, as you say and I believe." Exactly when the two first met, it is not possible to say. Domett mentions in his diary (1883) some remarks made to him by Browning "somewhere between 1835 and 1840." There are, however, at least two indications in the diary which show that he was rather indefinite as to dates. The earliest actual evidence of acquaintance is Browning's letter of 7 March, 1840, accompanying a copy of *Sordello*, which he asks Domett to accept—"Pray accept the book, and do not reject me." The gift is somewhat formally inscribed, "Alfred Domett, Esq., with R. B.'s best regards"; whence it is reasonable to suppose that the

[1] *Time's Revenges.*

intimacy was at an early stage.   Be that as it may, intimacy
rapidly ripened into friendship.   The glimpses that we get of
this time are mainly retrospective, when Domett had exchanged London for the antipodes.   "The 7th of May last
was my birthday," writes Browning on 22 May, 1842, "and
on that day I dined with dear Chris. Dowson and your sister.
We were alone, and talked of you and little else."   Again on
13 July of the same year he recalls the talks they used to
enjoy " over here or at Limehouse " ; and on 13 December

" I could easily fancy," he writes, " you were no farther off than
Brighton—not to say Exeter—all this while, so much of you is here,
and there, and wherever I have been used to see or think about you.
I have wished myself with you less often than I expected—and no
doubt the reason is, that you are not so surely away, after all."

Again, on 15 May, 1843 :—

" I wish I had seen more of you, for I forget nothing I did see,
and so should be richer and better able to bear dull evenings—but
the time will come yet."

And on 8 November, when there was some idea of Domett
coming home :—

" There you walk past our pond-rail (picking up one of the
fallen horse-chestnuts), and now our gate-latch clicks, and now—
. . . 'Tis worth while running away to be so wished for again."

On 23 February, 1845, a similar thought is expressed.

" You will find no change . . . in this room, where I remember
you so well.   I turned my head, last line, to see if it was you come
up, with hat above the holly hedge."

Two features emerge most prominently from these letters;
the first, Browning's deep affection for his friend ; the second,
his intense belief in that friend's intellectual powers.   He
felt for Domett " a real love—better love than I had supposed
I was fit for."   And as to the second, " I do," he writes
(5 March, 1843), " most truly, look for great works from
you."   He hopes for " a 'rousing word' (as the old Puritans
phrase it) from New Zealand."   "Write more," he says,
" and justify my prophecy then and now."   There emerges,
too, the picture of a true and noble friendship, marked by

generosity and unselfishness on either side. We do well to
imagine the repeated interchange of helpful counsel, the long
talks and discussions at whose end the two would "see truth
dawn together," the sympathy of heart as well as of mind.
Domett could criticize his friend's work on occasion, but grew
very irate at what he considered unfair treatment of it by
other people.   Thus, in 1841, he sent Browning some lines in
manuscript " on a certain critique on *Pippa Passes*." These
lines began with an expression of scorn for the small-
mindedness of the unnamed critic, who is compared to a
black squat beetle which

> " Has knocked himself full-butt with blundering trouble
> Against a mountain he can neither double
> Nor ever hope to scale.   So, like a free,
> Pert, self-complacent scarabæus, he
> Takes it into his horny head to swear
> There's no such thing as any mountain there ! "

The care with which this enthusiastic champion cherished
Browning's letters, as well as the copies of his works which
the poet sent to him from time to time, speaks for itself.
Among the reminiscences in his diary there is a glimpse of
the home life of the Brownings at this period. He recalls
Mrs. Browning's pride in her son, and how affectionate he
was towards her.

"On one occasion, in the act of tossing a little roll of music from
the table to the piano, he thought it had touched her head in passing
her, and I remember how he ran to her to apologize and caress her,
though I think she had not felt it.   His father used to speak of his
son as 'beyond him,' alluding to his *Paracelsuses* and *Sordellos ;*
though I fancy he altered his tone very much on this subject at
a later period."

The whole family were at one in their liking for Domett, and
their regret at losing him.

It is probable that a variety of motives influenced Domett
in forming what seems to have been rather a sudden determination to leave England ; a growing distaste for the law,
disappointment at the little recognition which his writings
won, and that instinctive desire for expansion which has
made colonists in every age.   The decision, at any rate, was

as stoutly maintained as it was quickly formed. "To have asked you *not to go*," wrote Arnould later, "would have been as wild and hopeless as to request the spring tide with compliments to defer its daily flow." Something of this determination one seems to read in Domett's face, as it appears in Lance's drawing. The eyes are downcast, under heavy lids, which is always something of a disguise ; power is discernible in the features, though qualified by a certain indolence. The head- and neck-gear are suggestive of Waring's

> "great grass hat and kerchief black,"

and in conjunction with a loose and ample cloak lend an air of mystery to the whole. In such guise may Domett have parted with his comrades, after a last "Colloquial" dinner, late in the April of 1842, bound for New Zealand, whither his cousin William Young had already preceded him.

It is as certain that Domett inspired Browning's *Waring* as that he is not to be *identified* with the hero of that poem. We have Browning's own word for it. "Waring came back the other day," he wrote to Miss Blagden in 1872, "after thirty years' absence, the same as ever,—nearly."[1] Domett himself did not disclaim the likeness, while pointing out that most of the setting was imaginary. Arnould wrote to New Zealand that the poem "delighted us all very much, for we recognized in it a fancy portrait of a very dear friend." Fact and fancy, indeed, are freely mingled. The secrecy of Waring's departure, for example, had no counterpart in reality, nor was the time "the snowiest in all December." But the beautiful and touching lines which attest the poet's devotion to his friend are but a poetical version of what he expressed with equal directness in his letters.

> "Meantime, how much I loved him,
> I find out now I've lost him.
> I who cared not if I moved him,
> Who could so carelessly accost him,
> Henceforth never shall get free
> Of his ghostly company."

[1] Mrs. Orr, *Life*, p. 293.

Of how many hearts is not that the cry! There is no more human touch in Browning's poetry.

His letters to the exiled Domett were numerous, as we have seen, during several years. With the poet's marriage, however, they ceased. But his friend was not forgotten. Messages were sent to him repeatedly through Arnould, and there were more direct assurances. There is certainly something of *Waring* in the "friend, over the sea" of *Time's Revenges* (1845). Three years later Browning's visit to Fano with his wife inspired *The Guardian Angel*, with its explicit references to Domett, and its note of wistful inquiry :—

> " My love is here.   Where are you, dear old friend?
> How rolls the Wairoa at your world's far end?"

The colonist, meanwhile, was hewing out his career, "subduing," like Clough's hero, "the earth and his spirit." He was to return at last, and pick up the threads of the old friendship ; but the Wairoa was to roll its waters seaward for four-and-twenty years, ere that should happen.

CHAPTER VI

"SORDELLO"

"Sordello's story"—Publication long delayed—Sordello in Dante—His name preserved at Mantua—Aliprandi's poem in his honour—"Another Richmond in the field"—Browning's poem consequently modified—The historical element accentuated—Browning's first Italian journey—He invests Sordello with a passion for humanity—Reason for this—His father's sketch of Sordello's life—Points of resemblance—Extent of the fictitious element in the poem.

I N tracing the growth of Browning's friendship with Domett incidental mention has been made of the publication of *Sordello*.

Since the days when its author wrote "Who wills may hear Sordello's story told" so much has been written in aid of those whom this poem has perplexed that no reader need now lose his way in the maze of a confessedly difficult work: but, strange to say, the story of the evolution of the poem itself, and of the circumstances attending its production, still remains not only untold but almost unattempted. Yet none of Browning's poems has a more interesting history.

The *Sordello* of 1840 has its roots in the *Pauline* of 1833. There can be little doubt, indeed, that it was not only conceived but actually begun before the rapidly-written *Paracelsus* was undertaken ; nor can there be much doubt that the introduction into the latter work of the imaginary poet-lover, Aprile, was due to an already existing interest in the real Italian poet-lover, Sordello. In April, 1835, in writing to Fox about the publication of *Paracelsus*, Browning remarked, " I have another affair on hand rather of a more popular nature, I conceive ; but not so decisive and explicit on a point or two, so I decide on trying the question with this." This is the first known allusion to *Sordello*, the possibly "popular" character of which will presently appear.   Almost exactly a year later, when asked by Macready to write him a tragedy, Browning, in spite of his eagerness to respond to the invitation, was so occupied with his poem that two months elapsed before he could even decide upon a subject.   " I was engaged on other work," he explained in 1888, "whence the delay in determining on a subject fit for Macready" ; while in a discarded preface to *Strafford*, the play produced in May, 1837, he wrote, " I had for some time been engaged in a poem of a very different nature when induced [*i.e.* in the previous May, 1836] to make the present attempt " ; and that his labours had been severe is evident from the fact that he added that he was not without apprehension lest his "eagerness to freshen a jaded mind by diverting it to the healthy natures of a grand epoch may have operated unfavourably on the represented play."   Three months later *Sordello* was spoken of as "announced " ; and in August, probably on the first of that month, Browning could write to his friend Miss Haworth that he was about to begin finishing it.   Eight months elapsed, but in April, 1838, this purpose was still unaccomplished when Browning started for Italy, hoping to complete the work "among the scenes it describes."   On 31 July, just after his return, the end once more seemed near —"You will see *Sordello* in a trice, if the fagging fit holds," he wrote : and yet the poem was not published for nineteen months, that is, for more than two years and a half after the first mention of its anticipated completion.

The subject of *Sordello* is remote and apparently unattractive ; yet Browning's choice of it arose, like everything else in his life, in the most natural way.   In 1828, at the age of sixteen, twelve years before the appearance of the poem, Browning was entered among the students of Italian at London University, Gower Street ; but since Angelo Cerutti was available for private lessons at Camberwell, Italian was replaced upon the college books by German.   To study Italian was to study Dante ; and as Browning read the *Divina Commedia* with Angelo Cerutti, and became familiar with the striking description of the meeting of Virgil and Sordello upon the lower slopes of the Hill of Virtue, Dante's picture suggested to him the idea of a poem which should set forth the spiritual awakening of a poetic nature, such as he had attempted in *Pauline,* and in regard to which John Stuart Mill had declared that he had failed. This poem had been anonymous: not a copy had been sold: it was practically non-existent. *Sordello* was intended to replace *Pauline.* Information upon the subject of the projected work was not far to seek. The praise accorded by Coleridge in his lectures of 1818 to Cary's translation of Dante had at once led to the disposal of one edition of this work and to the speedy issue of another, so that the book was in the hands of all English students of the Florentine. In a lengthy note on *Purgatorio VI.* Cary referred his readers to some of the leading authorities upon the " fabulous narrative " which had grown up around the name of the once famous Sordello. These and other works connected with Troubadour literature Browning consulted in the old reading-room of the British Museum.

Mantua boasts of two poetic names—Virgil and Sordello. The name of Virgil—" degli altri Poeti onore e lume "—is a household word ; that of Sordello is, comparatively speaking, unknown, and his thirty-four poems unheard of. And yet, when one crosses the lagoon which washes the walls of Mantua and, after threading its quiet streets, enters the central piazza, one finds that this spot—once the city forum and now overlooked by Duomo, mediæval Castello and ducal Palazzo—bears not the name of Virgil, but that of the almost unknown Sordello. Aliprandi, the earliest of Mantuan chroniclers, may explain this anomaly. Hundreds of years before Browning was born, Aliprandi had composed three thousand lines of *terza rima* to celebrate the exploits of the " famous Sordello," the poet hero of Mantua.

> " Wise, bold and valiant man was he,
> A better warrior ne'er was seen,
> Of stature huge, a heart of fire,
> A man all grace, of splendid mien."

Sordello, said Aliprandi—probably in the very piazza which now bears his name—fought and overcame Leonello, one of the doughtiest knights of the thirteenth century. Cunizza, the sister of Ezzelin the Tyrant, became so enamoured of him that she disguised herself as a man to win her way to him and gain his love.   The French king, hearing of his renown, invited him to France, where Sordello still further advanced his reputation for gallantry and valour.   On his return, people flocked from far and near to welcome him, and to the sound of the trumpet proclaimed him the greatest warrior of his age.   Mantua honoured him with an eight days' feast, and he became her Prince, defender and saviour.   Such are the legends which the historian Platina, best known for his *History of the Popes*, afterwards embodied in sober Latin prose, and it is to such legends that Browning refers when he declares that

> " The Chroniclers of Mantua tired their pen
> Telling how *Sordello Prince Visconti* saved
> Mantua, and elsewhere notably behaved.
>
> .   .   .   .
>
> As knight, bard, gallant, men were never dumb
> In praise of him."

Nor was the renown of this poet-hero confined to Mantua and the Middle Ages.   In 1844, when Browning landed at Naples, among the first sights that met his view were advertisements of the performance of an opera on Sordello ; and to-day, in the windows of Italian bookshops, one may see paper-covered volumes on the legend of Sordello and of the Ezzelini family who figure so prominently in Browning's poem.   Even in England Browning was not the only writer who had found interest in these legends.   A Mrs. W. Busk had turned to them, and having been filled with regret that a poet once so celebrated should have become forgotten, she also determined "to sketch his adventures, fictitious or real." Accordingly, in the summer of 1837, just when Browning was talking of finishing his poem, there appeared two volumes of *Plays and Poems* with regard to which the *Athenæum* of 22 July, 1837, wrote: "the authoress's fugitive poems are collected and headed by a longer poem *Sordello*.   Is this founded upon the same subject as that chosen by the author of *Paracelsus*, for his announced poem ? "

The work of Mrs. Busk demands attention for two reasons.   First, it reveals the popular (one might almost say the normal) treatment of the Sordello legend, which

Browning deliberately rejected ; and, further, its appearance in 1837 without doubt supplies a reason for some of the most peculiar features of Browning's poem of 1840. Mrs. Busk was a disciple of Scott, and her *Sordello*, consisting of some 2000 lines of rhyming dimeters, is, like that of Browning, divided into the six cantos which Scott had made fashionable. In the Chronicle of Aliprandi Sordello may be said to appear as the poet-warrior ; in the work of Mrs. Busk, of which the following is a brief summary, he is essentially the poet-lover :—

"Sordello, a famous warrior and poet had sung many a martial lay, but love had hitherto been to him a subject for scorn. Suddenly summoned to Verona by his native lord, Ezzelin the Tyrant, he speedily assumes a first place as courtier, warrior, and counsellor : here, too, he sees Cunizza, the sister of Ezzelin, and forgetting his cold disdain he at once loves and pines. Declaring his love, he is at first rejected, but ultimately accepted. Ezzelin, however, being desirous of marrying his sister to Count Richard of St. Boniface, plots with his brother Alberic to send Sordello to the wars, and Cunizza is forced to wed Count Richard. Sordello, hearing this amid his victories, renounces war and wanders far and wide as a minstrel, till Ezzelin is driven to seek his aid in withdrawing Cunizza from the court of his brother-in-law, with whom he has quarrelled. Sordello, as a Troubadour, visits Count Richard, and Cunizza, disguised as a page, flies with him from her husband. Thereupon the Count is attacked and slain, and the poem closes with the marriage of Sordello and Cunizza."

"There were many singular incidents attending my work," wrote Browning some years later to Miss Barrett, and surely the most singular was the unexpected appearance in the summer of 1837 of this poem. *Strafford* had just been acted, and the *Edinburgh Review* of July had gone out of its way to devote twenty pages to that drama ; his own *Sordello* was nearing completion, and Browning, who was full of ambition, must have been eager to retain and increase his hold upon the public, when he found himself thus suddenly forestalled. Two courses were open to him. He might wholly discard his work, exactly as at that very time he was discarding the "splendid subject" he had chosen for a tragedy, because Richard Hengist Horne was publishing a play upon the same theme : or he might so modify his poem that it should differ radically from the received Sordello tradition. The latter was the course adopted. During the autumn and winter of 1837 the poem was probably laid aside, for Browning was engrossed in theatrical matters. When he returned to it, it would seem to have occurred to him that one means of differentiating his work from that of others would be to accentuate the historical element.

Several circumstances inclined him to adopt this plan. Thus there was the fact, already noticed, that he had strong historical leanings, which had been amply encouraged by his father. In *Paracelsus*, indeed, he had made no serious attempt to create an historical background. But six months after its appearance history laid claim upon his thoughts by reason of his interest in Forster's *Life of Strafford*—an interest which presently suggested to him the subject of his own first acted drama. Nor was the impulse exhausted by the completion of his *Strafford*, for within two months he was meditating another historical play, *King Victor and King Charles*. Again, the appearance, in 1837, of Carlyle's *French Revolution* was something of a revelation to those occupied in the study of history, discovering as it did the value of elaborate detail and of acquaintance with locality : a fact not without significance, in view of Browning's known admiration of Carlyle. It is true, indeed, that in 1863 he wrote of *Sordello* that his "stress lay on the incidents in the development of a soul," and declared that the "historical decoration was purposely of no more importance than a background requires"; yet the evidence is conclusive that in the early months of 1838 this historical background had become, for the time at least, of absorbing interest. Browning had been studying the three volumes of G. B. Verci's *Storia degli Ecelini*—a scholarly work wholly overlooked by students of the poet—from which he borrowed most of those recondite historical details which have added to the confusion of his readers; and inspired by this work he sailed for North Italy, intending, as has been said, to finish his poem "among the scenes it describes."

Leaving St. Katharine's docks in the afternoon of Good Friday, 13 April, 1838, he arrived nearly seven weeks later at Trieste, whence he at once proceeded to Venice.[1] His visit

[1] This was Browning's first Italian visit ; he did *not*, as has been repeatedly

in Italy lasted but a month, yet so fascinating did the island city prove that, although it had no direct connection with the purpose of his journey, he lingered there for more than a fortnight.

On leaving Venice he passed through Treviso, where he saw the Titian to which he refers in *Pippa Passes*, and then walked westward across the plain through Giorgione's Castelfranco to the prettily situated Bassano, with its river, its quaint wooden bridge, its castle and its memories of the Ezzelini family. The neighbouring "delicious Asolo" which he had found mentioned in Verci, next became his headquarters for four days ; and thence he rambled northward to Possagno, the birthplace of Canova, and westward to Romano, the ancestral home of the Ezzelini family, which Dante had long since made familiar to him. Here, standing beside the church tower which now rises on the site of the huge quadrangular fortress of olden days, he looked southward across the valley to San Zenone degli Ezzelini, the last stronghold of the hated family. Fifty years later, in 1889, during his third visit to Asolo, just before his death, this tragic spot still retained its fascination for him, and from the *loggia* of his friend and hostess he would watch the sun sinking behind San Zenone's tower-crowned hill-top, and would relate the doom of Alberic, brother of the tyrant Ezzelin, who there

> "Saw his exasperated captors burn
> Seven children and their mother, then, regaled
> So far, tied on to a wild horse, was trailed
> To death through raunce and bramble-bush." [1]

stated, visit Italy in 1834. He sailed at 4 p.m., in the *Norham Castle*, Captain Matthew Davidson. Owing to gales and snow, a week elapsed before they reached Start Point, Devon. On 26 April he was off Lisbon ; on the 27th Cape St. Vincent was sixteen miles to the north-west [cf. *Home Thoughts from the Sea*]; on Sunday, the 29th, he passed the Straits of Gibraltar, and entered "burning heat." At 5 a.m. on the following Sunday, 6 May, the capsized smuggler, so graphically described in the letter to Miss Haworth, printed by Mrs. Orr [*Life*, pp. 96-100], was sighted off the coast of Algiers in lat. 37° 3' N., long. 33° 9' E. Next Sunday, 13 May, he was seven miles from Valetta : on Monday, close to Syracuse, and during a calm on 16 May Mount Etna was in sight all day [cf. *Sordello*, book iii. ll. 951-960]. Another fourteen days passed before he reached Trieste, on 30 May, at 4 p.m. ; he left the next evening by steamer for Venice, where he arrived at 7 a.m. on Wednesday, 1 June. While coasting along North Africa he wrote *How they Brought the Good News from Ghent*.

[1] *Sordello*, book vi., *ad fin.*

Moving again to Bassano he walked northward along the Brenta to the convent at Oliero to which Ezzelin the Monk retired, and crossed the stream to visit his reputed grave at Solagno. From these little-known spots he passed to Vicenza and Padua, whence he returned (26 June) to Venice. He journeyed homeward by way of Verona, the Tyrol, and the Rhine.

Such are the spots—"all my places and castles" as he termed them—to see which Browning made a special visit to Italy; and yet not one of these places except Verona has anything whatever to do with Sordello or with the development of his soul; they have everything to do with the historical background, with Verci and his *History of the Ecelini Family*.

Nor is this all. Venice, though unconnected with the subject of his poem except for a few and quite unimportant details, laid such a spell upon Browning that the fortnight he spent there was destined to lead to a revolution in his work. The main purpose of *Sordello* was, as has been said, to trace the development of a human soul, and the first half of the poem is almost wholly devoted to the story, elaborately psychological in character, of the spiritual and mental growth of the Mantuan poet. Dante, from whom Browning had received the first stimulus for his work, and whose influence upon it is manifest from beginning to end, had represented Sordello as a lonely spirit standing aloof from the other shades upon the mountain slopes of the Ante-Purgatorio, because, explains Benvenuto da Imola, the earliest of Dante commentators, Sordello loved solitude. Mrs. Busk retained this conception :—

> " The empty praises of the crowd
>   Shunning, he oft in museful mood,
>   Sought the recesses of the wood.
>
>   .   .   .   .   .
>
> 'Twas there Sordello loved to stray
>   And sometimes dream a sultry day
>   In balmy listlessness away."

Browning represented Sordello not only as thus spending a brief period, but as passing almost the whole of his life in the isolation of Goito, his reputed birthplace :—

"beyond the glades
Of the fir-forest border, and the rim
Of the low range of mountains, was for him
No other world : but this appeared his own
To wander through at pleasure and alone."

But Dante not only described Sordello as a solitary figure, he placed him among the spirits of those who had died violent deaths and had delayed repentance to the last. Yet Dante gave no hint as to how Sordello had sinned. Tradition, however, depicted him as a lover of the type of Launcelot and Tristram ; and Cunizza, his beloved, as being as passionate and guilty as Guinevere or Iseult. Mrs. Busk had made the advent of love the means of effecting a sudden transformation in her Sordello ; yet in deference to contemporary opinion she had purified the old story by putting Sordello's union with Cunizza after and not before the death of her husband. Similarly, Browning, bearing in mind that Dante had placed the five-times-married Cunizza not in the *Inferno* but in the "swooning sphere" of the *Paradiso*, represented his heroine[1] as being simply betrothed, and betrothed unwillingly, to Count Richard of St. Boniface, when, in order to save herself from marriage, she sends for Sordello and, suddenly confessing her love, invites him to fly with her to Ferrara. Yet the love element in the poem of 1840, it must be confessed, is disappointingly vague and subordinate ; but had it appeared in the summer of 1837 there seems to be no doubt that *Sordello* might have been fairly described in the words of Tennyson with regard to *Maud* as " the history of a morbid poetic soul . . . raised to sanity by a pure and holy love which elevates his whole nature." How the change came about Browning himself has related in one of the least-understood portions of his poem.

Before leaving for Italy in April, 1838, he had conceived

---

[1] Palma is Browning's name, as he explains, for the one

" Dante spoke with in the clear
Amorous silence of the swooning sphere—
Cunizza, as he called her." . . .

It was really the name of a half-sister of Cunizza. *Sordello*, Book V., *ad fin.*

of Palma as just such a woman as might fire the heart of
Sordello—fair-haired, blue-eyed, a vision of beauty :—

> " How the tresses curled
> Into a sumptuous swell of gold, and waved
> About her like a glory ! even the ground
> Was bright, as with spilt sunbeams."

But, six days after his arrival in Venice, when he mingled
with the crowds that thronged the vast Piazza of San Marco
during the festival of Corpus Christi, or as he sat upon some
" ruined palace-step " quietly watching the simple peasant
girls in their gondolas bearing fruit and flowers to market, he
realized afresh what he had learned " years ago " and " leagues
at distance " when, as a boy at Camberwell, he had been
thrilled by the verse of Shelley—that it was not needful for
Humanity to be " dizened out as chiefs and bards " to form
a fit theme for the poet ; and the outcome of these musings
was seen in the fact that queen-like Palma

> " Whose early foot was set
> Forth as she'd plant it on a pedestal,
> Now, i' the silent city, seems to fall."

For thus wrote Browning in describing how the idea flashed
upon him of modifying the received Sordello legend, by
superseding the passion for a beautiful high-born woman by
that love for the " warped souls and bodies " of suffering
Humanity which he decided to represent as being developed
in the mediæval poet.[1]

That he underestimated the labour which the introduction
of this new motive would involve is evident from the long
interval which was still to precede the completion of the
poem. The work, indeed, had to be thoroughly recast ; and
that the possibility of a *Sordello* of a vastly different character
was contemplated by at least one member of the Camberwell
household is somewhat amusingly illustrated by one of the
curiosities of Browning literature, in the form of a rough draft
in the handwriting of the poet's father, who, among his other
gifts, was somewhat of a novelist. Of this the following is a
brief summary :—

---

[1] *Sordello*, Book III., towards the close.

"Sordello, nephew of Ezzelin the Tyrant, is invited by his uncle [1] to his court at Vicenza; but on account of a feud between the two branches of the family, he is advised not to go. He therefore flees to France, where he becomes a Troubadour. Returning to Italy, he seeks the court of his uncle, to whom he is personally unknown—for Sordello had been carried away as an infant [2] and educated at Pisa—and he enters the household as tutor to Alfonzo and Bertha, two prisoners, children of Count Julian of Visconti whom Ezzelin had murdered. Discovering that Ezzelin desires to wed Bertha, Sordello, who loves her, proposes flight, whereupon Ezzelin at once orders the arrest of the poet. The lovers, however, escape to Genoa and embark for Alexandria; but off the coast of Sicily they are captured by pirates, taken to Algiers, purchased by the wealthy Mustapha and carried to his estate. Ezzelin, in pursuit, reaches Genoa; here, his life being in danger, he vows to visit the Holy Land. On his recovery he sets out, but off Crete he also is captured by the corsairs, borne to Algiers, and purchased by Mustapha. Finding that Sordello, who had risen in favour, is about to wed Bertha, Ezzelin makes himself known and claims his bride; Mustapha decides that she shall be given to the one who shall turn Mohammedan. This Sordello indignantly refuses, but Ezzelin accepts; and the marriage is arranged for the following day.

"Meanwhile, Alfonzo having escaped from Vicenza by means of a pirate with whom he was acquainted, accidentally lands at Tunis, and hearing of the proposed marriage of his sister seeks the aid of his pirate friend in rescuing her. By the help of a slave he gains access to the garden of Mustapha, slays Ezzelin and retires. Mustapha, on discovering the deed, accuses Sordello and has him strangled with a bow-string; whereupon the slave, falling at his master's feet, declares how the murder had been committed. In order to make all possible amends Mustapha offers Bertha his hand! This she reluctantly accepts, and the poem concludes with a description of the magnificent wedding."

Dominie Sampson's "Prodigious!" may seem to anyone

---

[1] *Cf.* Rolandino, *De factis in Marchia Tarvisana*, Book V. ch. 3. The expression "de *ipsius* familia," there given, is sometimes accepted as referring to the household of Count Richard of St. Boniface. Both Browning and his father take it as referring to Ezzelin : Browning, understanding by "familia" the *household* of Ezzelin, makes Sordello a page ; his father, taking "familia" in the sense of family, makes Sordello a nephew.

[2] This detail, which appears in an altered form in Browning's poem, is found in none of the old accounts.

familiar with Browning's poem the only word adequate for this fantastic sketch ; and yet a little reflection shows that in spite of the remarkable changes he has effected, Browning's father has most ingeniously contrived to retain the essential motives of the original story, and moreover—and this is the remarkable fact—has introduced certain wholly new elements which are to be found nowhere except in his son's poem. For example, Sordello still remains the traditional poet-lover, but the lady of his love is as yet unmarried, and the purpose of her flight is to escape from a union with one to whom she is betrothed and betrothed unwillingly—modifications which are only to be found in the poem of the son. Then, Sordello is represented as having been stolen away in infancy and as being unrecognized by his family on his return. These conceptions, common enough in romances from the days of *Amadis* downward, are wholly unknown to the Sordello legend except in this sketch and in Browning's poem. Again, the refusal of Sordello to accept the hand of Bertha at the price of his religious faith, creates a situation involving a struggle between love and duty exactly comparable to that which closes the poem of 1840 ; while the subsequent violent death of Sordello under the bow-string is an ingenious adaptation of Dante's words with regard to the group of which Sordello was a member —"we all by violence died"—which Browning, under the influence of Shelley, preferred to interpret by causing Sordello to "evaporate" under the violence of his conflicting emotions.

One important consideration remains. This *fantasie* really departs, in many respects, no further from the recognized Sordello legend than the poem of Browning, which in spite of its wealth of historial detail is as much of a fiction as *Marmion* or *The Lady of the Lake.* The main action of Browning's poem is assigned to the year 1224, soon after the death at Goito of Adelaide of Tuscany, a reputed dealer in the black arts of whom various legends are related. In the father's sketch, her son, Ezzelin the Tyrant, at least retains his traditional rôle, that of the villain of the piece, assigned to him from the time of Benvenuto da Imola. Browning, however, has displaced the son by the mother, whom he supposes to confess upon her death-bed that thirty years before she had stolen from Vicenza and hidden at Goito the infant child of her husband's dearest friend and henchman, the splendid warrior Salinguerra, on account of her jealous fear that the son of so distinguished a father should eventually prove the rival of her own child. This event, upon which the whole of Browning's poem turns, and upon which he has built a whole series of imaginary crises, has, however, no foundation in fact. Upon hearing the avowal of Adelaide, her husband at once resigns his worldly power and retires to the lonely convent at Oliero, to be known henceforth as Ezzelin the Monk. This creates a second crisis, for Salinguerra, receiving the news of this withdrawal just as he is about to sail with the Emperor Frederick II. to the Crusades, at once hastens northward from Naples. His return to his native Ferrara brings about a crisis in the affairs of that city, where he is promptly attacked by his foes, among whom is Count Richard of St. Boniface, to whom Palma has just been betrothed by her wily father, Ezzelin the Monk, in order to patch up peace between the rival Guelphs and Ghibellines. This warfare produces, in turn, a crisis in the life of Count Richard, who is taken prisoner by Salinguerra as described at the beginning of Browning's poem. This, again, produces a crisis in the life of Palma, who, having learnt the secret of the birth of Sordello, whom she loves, sends for him to Verona, and confessing her love hastens with him to Ferrara in order to make the great revelation to Salinguerra. The making known of Sordello to his father, who for thirty years has thought him dead, gives rise to one of the most dramatic scenes in the poem, and brings about the catastrophe, in which Sordello, discovering himself to be the son of the greatest warrior of the day, and possessor, if he please, of the hand of the beauteous Palma and of the lordship of Northern Italy, dies broken-hearted, in the conflict between ambition and love, on the one hand, and the claims of the "warped bodies and souls" of suffering Humanity, on the other.

Now, except that Browning was dealing with real people and places, and—somewhat freely—with historical events, this story is as fictitious as that of Aladdin. That the castle of Goito, to take but one example, was built for Adelaide of Tuscany, and was ever her resort or that of the lovely Palma, is as mythical as the existence of the Goito described in the poem, for that castle with its maple-panelled room, its arabesques, its palm-like pillars, its vault and beautiful font, belongs to the realm of the vision of Kubla Khan : while the surrounding scenery with its "few low mountains," the fir trees and larches, the maples, oaks, ilexes, and myrtles, had their origin in Virgil, who first created in his Pastorals ideal scenery for the "smooth sliding Mincio, crown'd with vocal reeds," upon the banks of which Goito stands.   But Goito, at least, is traditionally connected with Sordello as his birth-place : just as Ferrara is historically connected with Salinguerra.   Between Sordello and Salinguerra, however, there is no link at all, except the golden one forged by the imagination of Browning.   The real Sordello, also, was quite unconnected with Ferrara : he did not die there, nor did he die at the age of thirty : he is said to have lived to nearly three times that age.

The introduction of this Salinguerra element was evidently not present to the mind of Browning when he went to Italy in 1838, for among all his "places and castles" Ferrara, it seems, was unvisited : yet in 1840 it had become the scene of half his poem.   Its introduction was obviously due to the Vision of Humanity which had come to him in Venice, for, on his return, he discovered how he could combine Dante's description of Sordello with what had come to him through Shelley.   Dante, after describing the welcome accorded by Sordello to his fellow-Mantuan, Virgil, immediately proceeds to contrast with it the bitter civil strife which in his own day was tearing Italy asunder.

> "This gentle spirit,
> Even from the pleasant sound of this dear land
> Was prompt to greet a fellow-citizen
> With such glad cheer; while *now* thy loving ones
> In thee abide not without war; and one
> Malicious gnaws another : ay of those
> Whom the same wall and the same moat contains." [1]

Now in the *Parva Chronica Ferrariensis*, which Browning had consulted at the British Museum, he had read of the

---

[1] *Purgatorio*, Canto vi. 79–85.

horrors of civil strife at Ferrara, and this strife, he had learnt, was most fierce in the days of Salinguerra. He saw that he could associate the sudden awakening of the self-centred Sordello to the claims of Humanity with the sight of the horrors of the besieged city. He had read of thirty-two towers within the city walls being laid low, and of forty years of discord, during which one or other of the rival factions was driven out ten times, and on each occasion the homes of the vanquished were laid waste. Hence sprang that description, Dantesque in its intensity, of the horrors of the siege with which his fourth book opens.

The influence of Dante upon Browning's poem is, as has been said, traceable from beginning to end. Some years later, indeed, he distinctly applied to his own creation the description of the final repentance of Sordello in the *Purgatorio*. He had been re-reading this portion of Dante, and thereupon wrote to Miss Barrett—"the first speech of the group of which Sordello makes one, struck me with a new significance as well describing the man and his purpose and fate in my own poem." He therefore translated the passage " off hand ":—

> " And sinners were we to the extreme hour :
> *Then* light from heaven fell, making us aware,
> So that, repenting us and pardoned, out
> Of life we passed to God, at peace with Him
> Who fills the heart with yearning Him to see."

"Which," remarked Browning, " is just my Sordello's story."

CHAPTER VII

BROWNING AND THE DRAMA

THE story of Browning's active connection with the stage is a story of seven or eight years of his life, the beginning of which takes us back to a period four years before the publication of *Sordello*, when, in February, 1836, he proposed to Macready a tragedy on Narses, the victorious general of Justinian.[1] Macready forthwith wrote in his diary, " It would indeed be some recompense for the miseries, the humiliations, the heart-sickening disgusts which I have endured in my profession, if by its exercise I had awakened a spirit of poetry whose influence would elevate, ennoble and adorn our degraded drama. May it be ! "[2] For the English stage was at this date, in the words of a contemporary critic, " a byword of contempt." This cry was not wholly new, for nearly thirty years had elapsed since Byron wrote—

> " Now to the Drama turn—oh ! motley sight,
> What precious scenes the wondering eyes invite."

---

[1] " A passing fancy : one difficulty in the subject was insuperable, I soon saw."
[*Notes by R. B. to Mr. William Archer*, June, 1888.]
[2] *Macready's Reminiscences and Selections from his Diaries and Letters*, vol. ii. p. 8.

But Byron did not live to see the days when Covent Garden, "the home of the Kembles," the play-house built and managed by the brother of Sarah Siddons, had passed beneath the sway of Mr. Osbaldiston, late of the Surrey Theatre.

Drury Lane and Covent Garden were still the two National theatres, which, together with the Haymarket, had an exclusive monopoly of the representation of the "regular" drama; yet the managers of these theatres in their, often vain, endeavours to avoid bankruptcy were pandering to the public taste for melodrama, spectacular displays, or even circus performances and wild-beast shows. In the year of *Paracelsus*, Byron might have seen upon the stage of John Philip Kemble a coach and six horses, and a highwayman who was advertised to take the leap upon a Blood Steed, "as described so beautifully in the celebrated novel by E. L. Bulwer, Esq., M.P." In 1836, instead of the Lady Macbeth of Mrs. Siddons, he might have beheld pretty Miss Vincent from the Surrey Theatre—soon to be acting Queen Henrietta in Browning's *Strafford,*—as Thalaba the Destroyer, in a Burmese chariot, drawn by Burmese bulls, and followed by elephants, ostriches, and other zoological accompaniments from the Surrey Gardens. One of the chief attractions of Covent Garden in this same year was

"the Splendid Pageantry, Grotesque, Unique Effects and the Total Novelty of the Magnificent, Serio-Comic, Musical, Grand Easter Romance and Extravaganza, *Za-Ze-Zi-Zo-Zu*, or Dominoes ! Chess ! ! and Cards ! ! !" [1]

These adaptations of *Paul Clifford*, of Southey's poem and of a French burlesque were three of the many works of Mr. Edward Fitzball, also late of the Surrey Theatre, now specially retained as salaried dramatist by Osbaldiston of Covent Garden, and installed in an apartment in the Theatre. Mr. Fitzball's views upon the dignity of the drama have been

---

[1] "A city built of dominoes, another of cards, and a railway, then not only new to the stage, but to the world. A game of dominoes was played by the characters as dominoes in a most remarkable way"; it made "a remarkable hit : nearly all the aristocracy came to see it." [Fitzball's *Thirty-five Years of a Dramatic Author's Life*, 1859, vol. ii. p. 46.]

preserved. "Everything dramatic," said he, "that is *moral*, interesting, and *amusing to the public, is* the legitimate drama, whether it be illuminated with blue fire, or in one act or in twenty."[1] It was a blue-fire drama by this writer that cut short the brief career of Browning's first play : and when the poet's name first appeared upon a play-bill it was to announce that his tragedy was to be acted " for the last time this season," for the benefit of Mr. Edward Fitzball.[2]

But these attractions of Covent Garden were far surpassed by the "peculiar novelties " of Drury Lane under the " poet " manager Alfred Bunn, with whom Macready had that memorable quarrel in April, 1836, by reason of which he suddenly became a popular favourite and the champion of the legitimate drama. It was Bunn who introduced into his *Charlemagne* the circus-rider Ducrow with his "double stud of highly trained Palfreys," together with Mr. Van Amburgh and his celebrated lions. Six times within as many weeks did the youthful Queen Victoria visit the lions. This was in 1838, when Macready, who had succeeded Osbaldiston as manager of Covent Garden, was struggling to restore and uphold the dignity of the drama. His stage-manager thus records the result :—" we were all sick at Covent Garden,— men, women and children. We saw the drama dead, starvation staring us in the face, while over the way at Drury Lane, Bunn and his lions were fat and flourishing." Macready's regular drama was producing £200, often, indeed, less than £100 a night ; Bunn and the lions realized, on the occasion of the royal visit of January, 1839, over £700.

So fallen was the drama in 1836 that the appearance of the last three volumes of the now-forgotten *Plays* of Joanna Baillie was gravely compared to the advent of a new comet ! In January the *Athenæum* longed to see them acted : in March, after two of them had been performed, it ruefully confessed that "they are for the closet and not for the stage." Sheridan Knowles "alone can write stage plays," remarked *Blackwood,* and Knowles, actor, schoolmaster, dramatist, and

---

[1] Fitzball's *Thirty-five Years of a Dramatic Author's Life,* 1859, vol. ii. p. 107.

[2] Fitzball is, perhaps, best remembered by his song " My Pretty Jane," made popular by the rendering of Sims Reeves. He also wrote, for his friend Michael Balfe, the libretto of *Maritana.*

ultimately Baptist minister, had remained since his *Virginius*
of 1820 what Hazlitt had termed him—"the first tragic
writer of his time." Yet Knowles was not quite alone.
The other generally recognized dramatists of 1836 were
Mr. Jerrold, Mr. Planché, Mr. Peeke, Mr. Buckstone, and
Mr. Fitzball—"there are a few others," added the compiler
of this list of celebrities, with unconscious humour, "but their
productions are of so inferior a character that we may well
be excused for forgetting their names." *Paracelsus* seemed
to herald a change. In March, 1836, there appeared in the
New Monthly Magazine an article by John Forster, headed
"Evidences of a new genius for Dramatic Poetry," which
boldly proclaimed that "Mr. Browning has the powers of
a great dramatic poet," and that his genius "waits only the
proper opportunity to redeem the drama and elevate the
literary repute of England."

Such an opportunity was offered to Browning by Macready
on the evening of 26 May, 1836, after the first representation
of Talfourd's classical drama *Ion.* It was Macready's first
benefit night at Covent Garden—he had just quitted Drury
Lane, where he had acted for thirteen years, on account
of his quarrel with Bunn—and the theatre was crowded
from floor to ceiling. In one box sat Wordsworth, heartily
applauding, and beside him was Landor, recently returned
from Italy: Miss Mitford was there from her pretty cottage
near Reading: John Forster was taking notes for a friendly
notice in the *Examiner,* and with him was his new friend
Robert Browning. After the excitement of the theatre came
the supper at 56 Russell Square, with the toasts to Macready
the actor, to Ellen Tree the actress, to Talfourd the host and
dramatist—whose birthday it happened to be—and as we
have seen, to the youthful poet, Robert Browning. As the
guests were dispersing, Macready turned to the young poet
of twenty-four and said, "with an affectionate gesture, 'Will
you not write me a tragedy, and save me from going to
America?'"[1] Browning was willing enough, but he was
already so deep in *Sordello,* that two months elapsed before
Forster, Macready's neighbour in Lincoln's Inn Fields, called
to say that the subject decided upon was *Strafford.* "He

[1] *Robert Browning, Personalia,* by Edmund Gosse, p. 43.

could not have hit on one which I could have more readily concurred in," was the comment of Macready.[1] Decided upon slowly, *Strafford* was slowly written. The *Blot in the 'Scutcheon* and *The Return of the Druses* are each said to have been written in five days: nearly eight months passed before *Strafford* was completed. In March, 1837, when Macready read the play, he at once feared that it was "too historical: it is," he said, "the policy of the man and its consequences upon him—not the heart, temper, feelings that work on this policy, which Browning has portrayed—and how admirably." Osbaldiston, the manager of Covent Garden, however, caught at the play with avidity, agreed to produce it as soon as possible, and promised the author £12 a night for twenty-five nights, and £10 for each of ten subsequent nights should the play have such a run. A month later, on the evening of 1 May, 1837, at a quarter before seven, the largest theatre in London was once more, as for *Ion*, crammed from floor to ceiling, for Macready's benefit night. It was the first of five representations of *Strafford*.

If the legitimate drama as a whole had a hard struggle for existence, it must be confessed that *Strafford*, in particular, had more than its share of misfortunes. Osbaldiston was on the verge of bankruptcy: six weeks later he had to close his theatre abruptly. Not "one rag" could be afforded for the new piece. Macready, indeed, whose reputation was at stake, did his utmost and looked like a Vandyke portrait. He was ably seconded by Helen Faucit as Lady Carlisle: but Helen Faucit was then but a girl of twenty, with less than twenty months' experience of the stage. Pym, the real hero of the play, was represented by Vandenhoff: praised by some, he was more commonly described as "a mixture of good and very indifferent," "sadly prosy," "rather croaky" and even "positively nauseous with his whining and drawling and slouching." As for the King Charles of Mr. Dale, it was pronounced to be "awfully bad," "as bad as could be," "utterly imbecile," "nothing short of execrable," "some one should have stepped out of the pit and thrust Mr. Dale from the stage. Anything should have been done rather than such

---

[1] *Macready's Reminiscences and Selections from his Diaries and Letters*, vol. ii. p. 43.

exhibitions should be allowed to disgrace the stage of a 'national' theatre." The Queen, it would seem, was "a shade better," but "quite out of place"—"Miss Vincent plays Queen Henrietta—only think of that, gentle readers," remarked one critic, for pretty Miss Vincent was associated with Burmese bulls and light comedy. Others among the actors needed to be informed that "impeachment" did not mean "poaching." What wonder then, apart from the peculiar character of the play, that the green-room forecast was "doubtful"? What wonder that Browning was so annoyed at the "go" of things behind the scenes, that he vowed he would never write a play again as long as he lived? " Perfect gallows" was his description of the situation to Fox a few hours before the curtain rose : and that the curtain should fall without considerable disapproval being manifested was more than Macready dared hope.

And yet *Strafford* proved a success! The fall of the curtain was accompanied by the "vehement cry" and the "unmerciful vociferation" of the galleries, as first Macready, then Vandenhoff, and Miss Faucit were summoned to bow their acknowledgments. There were also loud cries of "Author," "Author," doubtless from the little group of friendly claqueurs in the pit—of whom Sir Frederick Young still remembers forming one ; and Webster, the stage-manager, "had some difficulty in silencing the rioters by the assurance that the author was not in the house." The play was announced for repetition amid further signs of approval, and on the following morning the *Constitutional*—that short-lived journal so tragically connected with the fortunes of Thackeray —contained the following notice, probably from the pen of Douglas Jerrold :—

" Such a reception as was given to this play last night gives the lie to any twaddling assertion that there is no taste or no patronage left in England for the real drama. The house in compliment to Mr. Macready—and likewise to the noble tragedy in which he was called to act the principal part—was thronged at a very early hour, and it was only through a sea of waving heads and bonnets that we were able to catch an occasional glimpse of the actor and the piece. . . .

" At every concluding act the house rang with plaudits. It would be a poor compliment to the public, and a vain task at so short a notice, to attempt an analysis of the play or its beauties: we shall take an early opportunity of examining the work itself: to-night we can only testify to its signal and deserved success.

"Some very keen critics have predicted for Mr. Browning that he is to rise to such an eminence as a dramatic poet as has not been attained by any in our time. We have not had the opportunity to study sufficiently the book before us to pronounce so confidently upon his merits, but certainly, if success be a criterion of desert, there are few poets who can rank more highly."

On the second night [3 May] *Strafford* is described as being " received with applause, warm indeed, but not so much as it deserved," and the play was pronounced " *by far* the best tragedy that has been produced at this, or any other of our great theatres for many years." On this occasion Browning sat muffled up in the pit to feel the pulse of the audience : and four years later in the preface to *Pippa Passes* (1841) he declared " that a Pit-full of good-natured people applauded it." On the fourth night we hear of the " fervid applause " of an " admirably filled house," while the play-bill for that evening, Tuesday, 9 May, announced that

"The New Tragedy of STRAFFORD, continuing to be received with the same marks of approbation as attended its first representation, will be repeated this evening (Tuesday) and on Thursday next."

Thursday came, but there was no *Strafford*, for there was no Pym. Vandenhoff, as Macready records, had taken scant interest in his part. Moreover, though in 1835 he had accepted what Macready had refused, the part of Eleazar in the popular melodrama *The Jewess*, he took offence on finding himself, in 1837, advertised to take the chief part in *Walter Tyrrel*, a melodramatic " scarecrow tragedy " by Edward Fitzball, of which the *Times* remarked that " such a tissue of absurdities has rarely been brought together." Offered, at this juncture, an engagement in America, he at once accepted it ; and not only refused to act in Fitzball's play, but withdrew from *Strafford* also. *Walter Tyrrel*, however, with its forest scenes, its blue fire and moonlight effects, was rapturously applauded and replaced *Strafford* upon the bills for the only two available nights before a series of benefits began. Among these benefits was that of Mr. Edward Fitzball, who among the varied attractions of 30 May, 1837, chose "the highly popular Historical Tragedy written by — Browning, Esq., entitled *Strafford*," because, he remarks in his Memoirs, it had been "uncommonly well received."

Such is the history of the production of *Strafford*, a drama whose shortcomings are so obvious that some of the critics of 1837 did not fail to point them out : but what is most important is, that all united in acknowledging the promise which the play afforded. The dramatic critic of *John Bull*, for instance, the most fearless and discriminating of the day, praised the opening scene as spirited, found the end of act III a veritable *coup de theâtre* worthy of the French stage, and pronounced act IV touching and poetically devised. Yet he condemned the play as a whole; but in so doing wrote as follows :—

"Now, unfavourable as is our judgment on the tragedy, it has been given in no intolerant spirit. . . . It is for the promise which the effort betokens that we speak. . . . The very faults of the drama are proofs of talent. . . . The very plainness of the language, too, evinces strength, and is a good augury for the future. . . . In his next attempt, let him bring on the scene character in action, and we will answer for it that he triumphs." [1]

Yet in spite of this encouragement and in spite of the fact that Browning declared in the preface to his play—which was published by Messrs Longman, at their own expense, on the day of representation—that even failure would not discourage him from another effort, "Robert Browning, writer of plays," did not re-appear as an acted dramatist for nearly six years : and this is the more remarkable inasmuch as events seemed distinctly to favour him. Within five months of the acting of *Strafford* Macready had become the manager of Covent Garden theatre, with a splendid troupe of actors, all pledged to uphold the better traditions of the stage. This position he retained for two years, during which Browning was in constant attendance, from the night of 30 September, 1837,

---

[1] *Strafford* was revived by the Oxford University Dramatic Society in the year following its author's death, and proved a great success. The part of Strafford was played by Mr. H. B. Irving, of New College.

when Macready recited the opening address of his friend Talfourd, until that of 16 July, 1839, when he stood amid piles of bouquets, wreaths and laurel branches, to bid farewell to his enthusiastic audience.   In April, 1838, a week before Browning sailed for Italy, he was sharing in the enthusiasm with which the *Two Foscari* was represented for Macready's benefit at Covent Garden, and immediately after his return, three months later, he was at the Haymarket, admiring the actor's Kitely.   Day after day, during rehearsals, Browning might have been seen seated on the stage by the prompter's table, together with men like W. J. Fox, Dickens, Bulwer, Forster and Maclise.   On 16 December, 1838, he was one of a select committee invited to listen to the first reading of Bulwer's *Richelieu*, and long afterwards it gave him satisfaction to recall that he had pronounced the first verdict in its favour when he silently wrote down his opinion—"a great play." Nay, so full was his mind of the theatre that he apologized at the beginning of *Sordello* for adopting the narrative form rather than the dramatic : and although during his Italian trip he wrote hardly a line of the poem for which he had undertaken his journey to Italy, yet he could not resist jotting down a scene for a play in passing through the Straits of Gibraltar. Not only so, but within two months of the representation of *Strafford,* Browning with a brain full of "half conceptions, floating fancies" had no fewer than three new plays in view. He had definitely selected one "splendid subject," and wrote —dispensing with the formality of an introduction—to Mr. Payne Collier to state that

" Mr. Browning is desirous of obtaining Mr. Collier's permission to look over the MS. ballad of *The Atheist's Tragedy* "—which had been quoted in the *New Particulars* of 1836—" as it would be of essential service to him in a work he is about to begin."

This subject, however, was promptly discarded owing to the appearance in the *Monthly Repository* of August, 1837, of his friend R. H. Horne's one-act tragedy *The Death of Marlowe.* But in the letter to Miss Haworth in which Browning mentions this, he also mentions that he is eager to begin two more plays, one of which he " meant to have ready in a short time." This was *King Victor and King Charles.* For the other, he was still in search of "a subject of the most wild and passionate love," involving "self-devotement, self-forgetting": this became, how soon it cannot be said, *The Return of the Druses*. Both plays were designed for the stage, and with a view to economy of production both plays have but one scene ; both, it seems, were submitted to Macready, and both were refused by him. Rightly or wrongly they were, in his judgment, rather suited—to borrow the *Athenæum's* phraseology—for the closet than for the stage. Further, it seems that the actor's criticism upon the conception of self-forgetting love as embodied in the Anael of the *Druses* led Browning to produce in hot haste his other picture of self-forgetting devotion, *A Blot in the 'Scutcheon*, the completion of which was announced to Macready in the following rather apologetic note:—

> " Hanover Cottage,
> " Southampton [St.]
> " Monday morning.
>
> " MY DEAR MACREADY,
> " 'The luck of the third adventure' is proverbial. I have written a spick and span new Tragedy (a sort of compromise between my own notion [*i.e.* in the *Druses*] and yours—as I understand it at least) and will send it to you if you care to be bothered so far. There is *action* in it, drabbing, stabbing, et autres gentillesses,—who knows but the Gods may make me good even yet? Only, make no scruple of saying flatly that you cannot spare the time, if engagements of which I know nothing, but fancy a great deal, should claim every couple of hours in the course of this week.
> " Yours ever truly,
> " ROBERT BROWNING "[1]

This letter—undated as is usual with the poet's early letters—must have been written before the end of December, 1840, for in that month the Brownings left Southampton Street: but the play was not accepted by Macready until the autumn of 1841, toward the close of his third Haymarket engagement under Webster [3 July to 7 December, 1841], and it was not produced till February, 1843, more than two

---

[1] *Letters from Robert Browning to Various Correspondents*, vol. i. p. 6, edited by Thomas J. Wise.

years after it was offered to him. Its production led, unhappily, to a complete breach between the friends.

In justice to Macready some facts must be borne in mind.
His first management at Covent Garden [30 September, 1837
to 16 July, 1839] had not resulted in the material success he
had anticipated; at its close, therefore, he adopted the safer
course of acting for two and a half years under Webster at
the Haymarket, until, in December, 1841, he ventured once
more to undertake management, this time at Drury Lane.
Strafford, as even Browning's friends allowed, was not a
popular play: its success had really been the success of
Macready the actor, and not of Browning the inexperienced
dramatist. Moreover, in 1840, Browning had seriously
damaged his position by the enigmatical *Sordello*; and,
meanwhile, Macready had discovered in the popular, versatile
Bulwer a dramatist who was both able and willing to meet
his requirements. Bulwer's first play the *Duchess de la
Vallière*, produced by Osbaldiston a few months before
Strafford, had been a failure: his *Cromwell*, Macready
had refused: but his *Lady of Lyons* [15 February, 1838],
after trembling in the balance, proved a decided success and
was acted thirty-three times. His *Richelieu*, altered and
rewritten as Macready dictated, proved the greatest triumph
of that actor's Covent Garden management [7 March, 1839]:
"the vast pit seemed to rock with enthusiasm as it volleyed
its admiration in rounds of thunder," so that for three months
Macready had no need to make any new effort of importance.
When *Money* was produced at the Haymarket it ran for
eighty consecutive nights, and a special licence from the Lord
Chamberlain had to be obtained to extend the theatrical
season for a couple of months.

Such had been Macready's experiences when he began his
second management on 27 December, 1841, having already
promised to produce the *Blot*. On 4 April, 1842, "a new
play" was advertised as being in active preparation: three
days later the name was announced. It was *Plighted Troth*
by a brother of George Darley, which was acted on
20 April. Macready was confident of success; yet the play
proved an utter failure. "The piece should never have been
produced," said the *Times*. "Produced and damned," was

the comment of *John Bull*. It was one of the bitterest disappointments of Macready's life. On Sunday, 1 May, he
frankly wrote to Browning that this unforeseen event had
" smashed his arrangements altogether," and three weeks
later, on 23 May, he prematurely closed his theatre. The
next season opened on 1 October, and by the end of the
month the speedy production of another new play began to
be announced daily. Four weeks elapsed, and the bills
disclosed that this was the *Patrician's Daughter*, a published
play by J. Westland Marston, a youth of twenty-two, and
already a friend of Browning. Marston had heard Macready
speak in high terms of Browning's tragedy, and the question
of its representation had evidently been under consideration.
Doubts, however, had arisen as to how the public might
regard the situation upon which the play turns—a situation
due to the direct suggestion of Macready himself. Macready
consulted Forster, to whom he handed the manuscript.
Forster seems to have shared, if, indeed, he did not originate,
these doubts. He passed the play on to Dickens, who was
at that moment, at Macready's desire, writing the prologue
for the *Patrician's Daughter*. On 25 November, 1842, as the
following passage from a letter to Forster shows, Dickens
gave emphatic expression to his utter dissent from the views
of his friends :—

" Browning's play has thrown me into a perfect passion of sorrow.
To say that there is anything in its subject save what is lovely, true,
deeply affecting, full of the best emotion, the most earnest feeling,
and the most true and tender source of interest, is to say that there
is no light in the sun, and no heat in the blood. It is full of genius,
natural and great thoughts, profound and yet simple and beautiful in
its vigour. I know nothing that is so affecting, nothing in any book
I have ever read, as Mildred's recurrence to that ' I was so young—
I had no mother.' I know no love like it, no passion like it, no
moulding of a splendid thing after its conception, like it. And I
swear it is a tragedy that MUST be played : and must be played,
moreover, by Macready. . . . And if you tell Browning that I have
seen it, tell him that I believe from my soul there is no man living
(and not many dead) who could produce such a work." [Forster's
Dickens, ed. 1873, vol. ii. p. 25.]

Forster did *not* tell Browning, who remained unaware of

the existence of this letter, until its appearance thirty years
later, in the *Life of Dickens !* This fact, taken in connexion
with certain words used by Forster next year with regard to
Colombe's Birthday, seems to point to the probability of
Forster's having had more to do with the unhappy fate of
the *Blot* than has hitherto been imagined.

The story of the production of the play has been several
times told with various degrees of accuracy; but the only
contemporary account is that of Browning's friend Joseph
Arnould, who in May, 1843, thus wrote to Alfred Domett
in New Zealand :—

"Well, on the 11th of February his play *A Blot in the 'Scutcheon*
(three acts) was brought out at Drury Lane. That was all the public
knew about the facts ; but those who knew Browning were also aware
of a little history of bad feeling, intrigue and petty resentment, which,
I fancy, making all allowance for both sides, amounts just to this :
Macready had the usual amount of plays on hand and promises
to authors unperformed when you and I witnessed the 'deep
damnation' of the bringing forth of *Plighted Troth.* That shook
him a good deal. He might possibly, remembering *Strafford*, have
looked doubtfully at Browning's chance of writing a play that would
take ; and he brought out two new plays, one of which (*The Patrician's
Daughter*) had a decent success, while still nothing was heard of
Browning's play. Meanwhile judicious friends, as judicious friends
will, had a habit of asking Browning when the play was coming out.
You can fancy how sensitively Browning would chafe at this. At
length the paramount object with him became to have the play acted,
no matter how, so that it was *at once.* With these feelings he forced
Macready to name an early day for playing it. The day was named :
Macready was to take the part of Austin Tresham, which was *made* for
him ;[1] and everything was going on swimmingly, when lo ! a week or
so before the day of representation, Macready declines altogether his
part, unless the play can be postponed till after Easter. Browning
naturally 'in a sultry chafe' at this, declines postponement : with
haughty coolness indicates that, if Mr. Phelps will take the part he
shall be perfectly satisfied, and under this new arrangement, Mr.
Phelps having zealously laboured his part, comes the last rehearsal
day. Macready then again appears, hints that he has studied the
character—will act the first night. Upon this our Robert does not

---

[1] An obvious slip : Thorold, Lord Tresham, is meant.

fall prone at his feet and worship him for his condescending goodness: not that at all does our Robert do, but quite other than that.
With laconic brevity he positively declines taking the part from
Phelps—dispenses with Macready's aid, etc. And all this in the
face of a whole green room! You imagine the fury and whirlwind
of our managerial wrath—silent fury—a compressed whirlwind—
volcano-fires burning white in our pent heart. We *say* nothing, of
course; but we *do* our spiteful uttermost; we give no orders [*i.e.* free
orders for admission to the theatre; even Browning himself did not
receive any]; we provide paltry machinery; we issue mandates to
all our dependent pen-wielders—to all tribes of men who rejoice in
suppers and distinguished society, under penalty of our managerial
frown that they are to be up and doing in their dirty work. The
results of their admirable labours I have enclosed for your inspection,
and now may proceed to give you an exacter notion of the real
reception the piece met with."

Among these "admirable labours" was the notice in the
Times, which after declaring that the play was "one of the
most faulty dramas we ever beheld," allowed that a "moderate
success" had been achieved. But the criticism which Browning most deeply resented was that of the one whom forty years
later he wrote of as Macready's "Athaneum upholder":—

"If to pain and perplex were the end and aim of tragedy, Mr.
Browning's poetic melodrama called *A Blot in the 'Scutcheon* would
be worthy of admiration, for it is a very puzzling and unpleasant
piece of business. The plot is plain enough, but the acts and
feelings of the characters are inscrutable and abhorrent, and the
lauguage is as strange as their proceedings. . . . A few of the
audience laughed, others were shocked, and many applauded; but it
is impossible that such a drama should live even if it were artfully
constructed, which this is not. . . . The farce [which followed the
Blot] was the more amusing for the foregone horrors. [*Athenæum,*
18 February, 1843, p. 166.]

Arnould's letter, which, as being the only known account
of the three representations of the *Blot,* has a quite unique
value, continues:—

"The first night was magnificent (I assume that Browning has
sent you the play). Poor Phelps did his utmost, Helen Faucit
very fairly, and there could be no mistake at all about the honest
enthusiasm of the audience. The gallery—and of course this was

very gratifying, because not to be expected at a play of Browning's— *took* all the points as quickly as the pit, and entered into the general feeling and interest of the action far more than the boxes, some of whom took it upon themselves to be shocked at being betrayed into so much interest in a young woman who had behaved so improperly as Mildred. Altogether the first night was a triumph. The second night was evidently presided over by the spirit of the manager. I was one of about sixty or seventy in the pit, and we yet seemed crowded compared to the desolate emptiness of the boxes. The gallery was again full, and again, among all who were there, were the same decided impressions of pity and horror produced. The *third* night I took my wife again to the boxes : it was evident at a glance that it was to be the *last*. My own delight and hers, too, in the play, was increased at this third representation, and would have gone on increasing to a thirtieth ; but the miserable great chilly house, with its apathy and emptiness, produced on us both the painful sensation which made her exclaim that ' she could cry with vexation ' at seeing so noble a play so basely marred. Now there can be no doubt whatever that the absence of Macready's name from the list of performers of the new play was the means of keeping away numbers from the house. Whether, if he had played and they had come, the play would have been permanently popular is another question. I don't myself think it would. With some of the grandest situations and the finest passages you can conceive, it does un-doubtedly want a sustained interest to the end of the third act ; in fact, the whole of that act on the stage is a falling off from the second act, which I need not tell you is for all purposes of performance the unpardonable fault. Still it will no doubt have— nay it must have done this—viz. produced a higher opinion than ever of Browning's genius and the great things he is yet to do in the minds not only of a clique, but of the general world of readers. No one now would shake his head if you said of our Robert Browning, ' This man will go far yet.' "

Arnould's account is substantially in agreement with Browning's own version of the affair, as communicated long afterwards to Mr. Frank Hill, editor of the *Daily News ;* whom he further informed that Macready had proposed to cut down the text of the play considerably, and to mitigate its tragic ending by making Tresham not swallow poison, but announce his intention of withdrawing to a monastery.[1]

Browning at the time was justly angry: "Macready has used me vilely," he wrote to Domett. The truth was that Macready wished to be released from his engagement, and instead of saying so plainly, chose the unpleasant course of putting every sort of difficulty in the way. Browning had not sufficient experience of the theatre to see through these manœuvres. "One friendly straightforward word," he said to Mr. William Archer forty-five years later, "to the effect that what was intended for an advantage, would, under circumstances of which I was altogether ignorant, prove the reverse; how easy to have spoken it, and what regret it would have spared us both!"

Their friendship was at an end. Some twenty years afterwards they met, each saddened by the loss of his wife, and it was to shake hands and forgive. "I found Macready as I left him—and happily after a long interval resumed him," wrote Browning the year before he died—

"one of the most admirable, and, indeed, fascinating characters I have ever known: somewhat too sensitive for his own happiness, and much too impulsive for invariable consistency with his nobler moods." [1]

One other of Browning's dramas led to a quarrel with a friend. The play was *Colombe's Birthday*, and the friend John Forster.

During Macready's management at Drury Lane, Charles Kean—son of the Edmund Kean at whose shrine Browning had worshipped some ten years before—was performing at Covent Garden. Kean was anxious to perform in new parts, and after the quarrel with Macready he opened negotiations with Browning, to whom he was disposed to offer £500 for a suitable play. Within three months Browning had written, though not actually completed, *Colombe's Birthday*: for reasons unknown, the drama was not finished until March, 1844. The circumstances in which it was then read to Kean and

---

123. Mr. Gosse, in *Robert Browning, Personalia*, has embalmed Macready's emendation :—

"Within a monastery's solitude,
    Penance and prayer shall wear my life away."

[1] *Eminent Actors*, edited by William Archer, p. 214.

his wife are set forth in the following letter to Christopher
Dowson :—

> "New Cross,
> "March 10 [1844].

"MY DEAR DOWSON,

"You may remember I told you my appointment with
C. Kean had been for that morning (Monday, *i.e.* March 4), and
then stood over for the next Saturday (yesterday)—but that, having
made an effort and ended work the evening I saw you, I meant to
call on Kean the following morning. I did so, but in consequence
of my letter, received the day before, his arrangements were made
for the week, so that till Saturday the business had to wait. Yesterday
I read my play to him, and his charming wife [Ellen Tree]—who is
to take the principal part. All went off *au mieux*—but—he wants
to keep it till 'Easter next year,' and unpublished all the time !   His
engagement at the Haymarket, next May, is merely for twelve nights,
he says. He leaves London for Scotland to-morrow, or next day,
and will be occupied for ten hours a day till he returns. My play
will take him two months at least to study, he being a special slow
head, and after the Haymarket engagement nothing is to be done
till this time next year. Of all which notable pieces of information
I was apprised for the first time after the play was read and approved
of—for it certainly never entered into my mind that anybody, even
an actor, could need a couple of months to study a part, only, in
a piece, which I could match with such another in less time by a
good deal.

"But though I could do such a thing, I have a head—that aches
oftener now than of old—to take care of; and, therefore, will do no
such thing as let this new work lie stifled for a year and odd, and
work double tides to bring out something as likely to be popular
this present season. For something I must print, or risk the hold,
such as it is, I have at present on my public—and, on consideration
of the two or three other productions[1] I have by me in a state of
forwardness, neither seems nearly so proper for the requirements of
the moment as this play; and two or three hundred pounds will pay
me but indifferently for hazarding the good fortune which appears
slowly but unmistakeably settling in upon me, just now. You will
not wonder, therefore, that—though I was so far taken by surprise
as to promise Kean a copy for Scotland and a fortnight's grace to
come to terms in, before I either published this play or accepted any
other party's offer—I say, you will not wonder if I have determined

---

[1] *Luria* and *A Soul's Tragedy.*

to print it directly. Acting on the best advice, I sent it to press yesterday, and merely put the right of the acting at his disposal—if he will purchase it with such a drawback as Macready would; for I fear the only alternative I shall allow—that of his getting up the part for next May—is quite beyond his power. The poorest man of letters (if really of letters) I ever knew is of far higher talent than the best actor I ever expect to know; nor is there one spangle too many, one rouge-smutch too much on their outside man, for the inward. Can't study a speech in a month! God help them, and bless you, my dear Dowson, says and prays

" Yours,

" R. BROWNING

" I will communicate the end of the matter when I have it." [1]

Never again did Browning write for the stage. *Colombe's Birthday* remained unacted till 1853, when the faithful Phelps successfully produced it at the Haymarket, with Helen Faucit as the heroine. But in 1844 the "end of the matter" was a quarrel, certainly not of Browning's seeking, with Forster, who reviewed the printed play in the *Examiner* of 22 June. His closing words were as follows :—

"There can be no question as to the nerve and vigour of this writing, or of its grasp of thought. Whether the present generation of readers will take note of it or leave it to the uncertain mercies of the future, still rests with Mr. Browning himself. As far as he has gone, we abominate his tastes as much as we respect his genius."

It was these words which led Browning in September, 1845, to speak of Forster to Miss Barrett as his "old foe." [2] A month later, however, one is glad to add, Forster called and was "very profuse of graciocities," so, declared Browning, "we will go on again with the friendship as the snail repairs his battered shell" [3]; and he accepted an invitation to go and see the amateur representation of *Every Man in his Humour*, wherein Forster acted Bobadil to the Kitely of Charles Dickens. The days were yet far off when the "battered shell" could no longer be repaired.

---

[1] *Letters from Robert Browning to Various Correspondents*, edited by Thomas J. Wise, privately printed, vol. i. pp. 7-11.

[2] *R. B. to E. B. B.*, vol. i. p. 212 (postmark, 18 September, 1845).

[3] *Ibid.*, vol. i. p. 245 (postmark, 15 October, 1845)

CHAPTER VIII

"BELLS AND POMEGRANATES"

The Brownings' removal to Hatcham—*Bells and Pomegranates*—The title explained—*Pippa Passes*—Sources of some *Dramatic Lyrics* and *Romances*—Browning's second Italian journey—Ruskin's praise—Politics of the time—*The Lost Leader*—Browning's delineations of love—His use of the dramatic monologue—His gradual advance in favour—Appreciated by Landor and Carlyle—His literary friendships—Carlyle—Miss Martineau—Miss Martineau and *Sordello*—Chorley—" Barry Cornwall " —Miss Haworth's admiration—The fateful meeting with John Kenyon— " R. B., a poem."

OUR endeavour to present a continuous narrative of Browning's active connection with the theatre has entailed the momentary displacement of other matters, both literary and domestic, to which return must now be made.

In December, 1840, rather more than three years before the publication of *Colombe's Birthday*, the Browning family, desirous of greater space within doors and without, left Camberwell for a larger house at Hatcham. To reach it, as the poet wrote to Laman Blanchard, one had to "conquer the interminable Kent Road, pass the turnpike at New Cross, and take the first lane with a quickset hedge to the right. We have a garden," he adds, "and trees, and little green hills of a sort to go out on." [1]

The new home at Hatcham is associated with the eight parts of *Bells and Pomegranates*, with the courtship of Robert Browning, and with the death of his mother. The builder's hand has swept away the old-fashioned three-storeyed

---

[1] The letter is printed in the memoir, by Blanchard Jerrold, prefixed to *The Poetical Works of Laman Blanchard*, London, 1876.

cottage, once a farmhouse ; the pond is filled up, the holly
hedges, the shrubs, the rose bushes, the chestnut-tree and
the orchard have vanished : the neighbouring mansion, with
its large grounds and stately cedar of Lebanon, is gone :
the stile, the open fields and the elm trees behind have
disappeared.   And though one can still look northwards
over London from the adjoining Telegraph Hill—which
Wordsworth, when told that Browning "lived over there,"
termed, in the language of the Lakes, a "rise"—it is from
amid a mass of bricks and mortar.   But in the forties one
might have climbed the staircase, as " Waring " did, past the
bust of Shelley and the drawing-room where Browning loved
to play Beethoven or Handel, to the large, low upper room
crammed with books, and to the adjacent study where was
the little desk and russet portfolio, containing poems yet
unpublished.   There, upon the wall above, hung the precious
" Andromeda " of Caravaggio, rescued years since from
among the father's prints and the desecrating neighbourhood
of a group of Ostade's boors ; there, too, was the skull, in the
jaws of which a spider was allowed to spin his web.[1]   In this
room Browning worked, clad in blue shirt and blue blouse ;
and here were written the letters to Miss Barrett, only to be
discontinued when the unbroken companionship of marriage
did away with the need for them.

Colombe's Birthday, when published in 1844, formed the
sixth of the eight parts of what its author quaintly named
Bells and Pomegranates.   In a note prefixed to the concluding number he declared himself surprised that this title
should have perplexed his readers, and explained that it was
intended to express "something like an alternation, or
mixture, of music with discoursing, sound with sense, poetry
with thought."   The symbolism is certainly not so obvious
as he supposed it to be, though it becomes rather clearer on
reference to a passage in the Book of Exodus :—

"And beneath upon the hem of it (the High Priest's ephod)
thou shalt make pomegranates of blue, and of purple, and of scarlet ;
and bells of gold between them round about : a golden bell and a
pomegranate, upon the hem of the robe round about." [2]

---

[1] *Letters of R. B. and E. B. B.*, vol. i. p. 28.
[2] Exodus, ch. xxviii. verses 33 and 34.

Diction of this sort, instinct as it is with chiming sound and vivid colour, would instantly captivate Browning's imagination, while the meaning which he read into the passage may well have been, although unconsciously, not the primary cause of its appeal. Be this as it may, it is characteristic of him that he expects his reader to be as clear-sighted as himself; and for the title, when its significance is perceived, it needs no justification as applied to a series which includes *Pippa Passes*, *My Last Duchess*, *The Lost Mistress* and the first part of *Saul*.

Bells and Pomegranates appeared at intervals between 1841 and 1846. The successive numbers were issued at the expense of the author's father by Edward Moxon, whose connection with Browning had begun with *Sordello*. Moxon, the poet-publisher, eleven years Browning's senior, had married Lamb's adopted daughter, and was the friend to whom the Essayist had bequeathed his books; he was also the friend and publisher of Wordsworth and of Rogers, and brought out books for Tennyson, Sir Henry Taylor and Coventry Patmore. He was well known to Talfourd, whose privately printed *Ion* he had circulated, and to Forster, so that it was easy for Browning through them to come in touch with 44, Dover Street, where until his marriage he was a frequent visitor, listening to the gossip about Tennyson's sensitiveness to criticism, or his isolation at Mablethorpe, where his letters were delivered by the muffin man : hearing how Wordsworth had gone to Court in Rogers' suit, or seeing poor Campbell dozing unnoticed over the fire.

At the end of *Sordello*, Moxon had advertised as "nearly ready" *Pippa Passes*, *King Victor and King Charles*, and *Mansour the Hierophant*, afterwards renamed *The Return of the Druses ;* and as Browning had failed to secure a place for the two latter on the stage, and as Dickens in his *Pickwick Papers* had made the issue of parts popular, Moxon suggested that these other plays might be brought out in cheap little yellow, paper-covered, double-columned volumes, printed in the small type he was then using for his reprints of Elizabethan dramatists : the cost of each pamphlet being about £16. In a discarded preface Browning explained his reason for adopting this mode of publication. Ever since "a pit-full of good-natured people" had applauded *Strafford*, he had been "desirous of doing something in the same way that should better reward their attention"; and, added he, with rather a pathetic reference to his rejected dramas,

"what follows I mean for the first of a series of Dramatical Pieces to come out at intervals, and I amuse myself by fancying that the cheap mode in which they appear will for once help me to a sort of Pit audience again."

At first, it seems, the design was to confine the series to plays, and a revised text of *Strafford* was to be included;[1] but, possibly because the first two parts had no great sale, Moxon suggested that it might be advisable "for popularity's sake"[2] to issue a collection of small poems. The *Dramatic Lyrics* of 1842 and *Romances* of 1845 are the outcome of this advice.

The series opened with *Pippa Passes*, which Miss Barrett could find it in her heart to envy, and which Browning in 1845 declared he liked better than anything he had so far produced.[3] *Pippa* was written after Browning returned from Italy, and while he was finishing *Sordello*. It may, indeed, be described as an indirect product of *Sordello*, for it is no mere chance that *Sordello* closes with a barefoot child climbing the dewy Asoloan hillside in the early morning and singing "to beat the lark, God's poet, swooning at his feet"; and that *Pippa Passes* should begin with the barefoot maiden climbing the same slopes and singing that

> "Morning's at seven;
> The hill-side's dew-pearled;
> The lark's on the wing."

Pippa, indeed, seems to have been conceived as a direct contrast to *Sordello*. The circumstances of the origin of *Pippa* have been recorded. Browning was indulging in one of his frequent solitary walks in the Dulwich wood, doubtless thinking of the changes to be made in *Sordello*, when

[1] Kenyon's *Robert Browning and Alfred Domett*, p. 38.
[2] *Ibid.* p. 36.
[3] *Letters of R. B. and E. B. B.*, vol. i. p. 28.

"the image flashed upon him of one walking thus alone through life; one apparently too obscure to leave a trace of his or her passage, yet exercising a lasting though unconscious influence at every step of it; and the image shaped itself into the little silk-winder of Asolo, Felippa, or Pippa." [1]

Pippa therefore, like Sordello, is solitary, but the life of the solitary self-conscious Sordello, (of whom Browning had evidently come to weary, or he could not have described that life as a "sorry farce"), accomplishes nothing, and his song is of no avail, while the lonely little Pippa is utterly unconscious of self, yet her songs affect the lives of all with whom she comes in contact—the beautiful Ottima and her lover Sebald, the sculptor Jules and his bride Phene, Luigi and his mother, Monsignor the Bishop—and through him, it is suggested, the destiny of the singer herself. As if to accentuate the contrast Browning has given them this in common, that both are stolen children, Sordello brought up as a dependent, Pippa in poverty, while each is ultimately revealed as the only child of wealthy parents; and both works deal, to a degree unknown elsewhere even in Browning, with a series of crises. Moreover, the "light from heaven" which finally falls upon Sordello is but a gleam which brightens his death : the light of God shines about Pippa from the outset—"God's in his heaven, all's right with the world." Not without reason, therefore, was the scene of *Pippa Passes* laid in Venetian territory and in the lovely district of Asolo, for Pippa is the triumph of that vision of Humanity which had come to Browning in the island city. Palma has once more fallen from her pedestal, to be replaced as Queen by one of the contadini from "delicious Asolo," whom Browning describes himself as watching as they "bind June lilies into sheaves to deck the bridge-side chapel." [2]

Part II. of the *Bells*, published in the spring of 1842, consisted of *King Victor and King Charles*, a drama modelled on the simple lines of Alfieri, whose works Browning had been studying very closely. In November, or early in December, there appeared as Part III. the *Dramatic Lyrics*.

---

[1] Mrs. Orr, *Handbook to the Works of Robert Browning*, p. 55, 6th edition.
[2] *Sordello*, iii. line 684.

A month or so later, in January, 1843, Part IV. contained *The Return of the Druses ;* while Part V., which appeared on February 11, the day on which *A Blot in the 'Scutcheon* was produced, contained the text of this play, hastily printed in twenty-four hours by Moxon, in order to prevent Macready's attempt to mutilate it. Thus three parts of the *Bells* had appeared in a little over three months, and the delay of a year before *Colombe's Birthday* was sent to the printer (9 March, 1844) quite explains Browning's inability to accede to Kean's request for a further delay of still another twelve months. Twenty months more elapsed before the *Dramatic Romances and Lyrics* could be put together (Nov. 1845) for many of these were new poems. Part VIII., containing two plays, *A Soul's Tragedy* and *Luria,* closed the series : this appeared on 13 April, 1846. Neither play was written for the stage. "I have lost of late interest in dramatic writing, as you know, and perhaps occasion," was the explanation giving by Browning to Miss Barrett. We have seen the reason.

The *Dramatic Lyrics* and *Romances* of 1842 and 1845, consisting of about forty poems, afford further evidence, if such be needed, of the perfectly natural manner in which their author found subjects for his verse. In 1836, for example, Leigh Hunt's *The Glove and the Lion* appeared in the *New Monthly Magazine,* a review in which Browning was particularly interested. Adopting quite a different view of the episode, and as a kind of criticism upon that of Hunt, he produced his own version of it, *The Glove,* in which he makes out a good case for the lady who dares her lover to brave the lion. The vigorous *Cavalier Tunes* are a later fruit of studies which went to the composition of *Strafford.* The first four lines of *Home Thoughts from the Sea* are an exact transcript of the scene which he beheld from the deck of the *Norham Castle* on the evening of Friday, 27 April, 1838, on his first voyage to Italy :—

" Nobly, nobly Cape St. Vincent to the north-west died away ;
  Sunset ran, one glorious blood-red, reeking into Cadiz Bay ;
  Bluish 'mid the burning water, full in face Trafalgar lay ;
  In the dimmest north-east distance dawned Gibraltar, grand and
      gray."

And then follows the reflection, memorable among the patriotic utterances of our literature, which such a sight naturally inspired in such a gazer :—

"'Here and here did England help me : how can I help England'—
　　say,
　Whoso turns as I, this evening, turn to God to praise and pray,
　While Jove's planet rises yonder, silent over Africa."

A few days later, while they coasted along the northern shores of Africa, the confinement of a sailing vessel aroused memories of many a delightful gallop upon the good horse " York,"then in the stables at Camberwell, and *Good News from Ghent* was written. Glimpses of the Algerian coast made more real and vivid to the traveller the struggle with the French maintained for fifteen years by the resourceful Arab chieftain Abd-el-Kadr, so that, on his return home, to the beat of his horse's hoofs he one day composed his anapæstic verses, " As I ride, as I ride." Again, the contrast between an Italian June and the English April which had witnessed his departure suggested the *Home Thoughts from Abroad.* This lyric should be dear to all who love England, and may serve to allay any rising jealousy which the later *De Gustibus* might otherwise occasion, since it shows that the poet's heart was not entirely given to Italy ! *Rudel to the Lady of Tripoli* is hewn from the quarry of Troubadour literature from which *Sordello* had already emerged. The seven lines which now stand at the beginning of *In a Gondola* were at first a separate entity. Browning wrote them towards the close of 1841 by Forster's request, and in his chambers at Lincoln's Inn, by way of illustration of *The Serenade,* a picture by their friend Maclise, exhibited at the British Institution next year. Forster described the picture to Browning, and " pressed me," says the latter, " into committing verse on the instant."[1] The seven lines were expanded into two hundred after he had seen the painting. The origins of *Waring* and of *The Pied Piper,* both written in 1842, have already been traced. During the same year, inspired by the recollection of a song which as a child he had heard sung by a woman one Guy Fawkes' day, " Following

[1] Letter to Miss Haworth, quoted in Mrs. Orr's *Life,* p. 134.

the Queen of the Gipsies, O," he began *The Flight of the
Duchess*, but, being interrupted by a friend's call, put the
poem aside for a while. Some months later, in September,
when he was staying with Sir John Hanmer at Bethsfield
Park, in Flint, the chance remark of Kinglake, a fellow-guest,
that the "deer had already to break the ice in the pond,"
acted as a spur to lagging imagination ; and on his return to
town he resumed his work with an embodiment of the incident
which Kinglake had observed :—

> "Well, early in autumn, at first winter-warning,
> When the stag had to break with his foot, of a morning,
> A drinking-hole out of the fresh tender ice
> That covered the pond till the sun, in a trice
> Loosening it, let out a ripple of gold,
> And another and another, and faster and faster,
> Till dimpling to blindness the wide water rolled." [1]

A few more examples may be cited. The story of Saul
and David might well attract any poet, but Browning in
particular ; for, as we have seen, Christopher Smart's *Song to
David* was with him an old favourite, and he was familiar
with Alfieri's drama on the same subject. Further travel,
too, was the occasion of other numbers. The year 1844 saw
his second voyage to Italy. Landing at Naples, he wandered
over the Piano di Sorrento, and climbed Vico Alvano, whence
he looked down upon the Isles of the Sirens—experiences
embodied along with others in his *Englishman in Italy*.
Now, too, was suggested its companion poem, *The Italian in
England*, which Mazzini read aloud to his fellow-exiles, to
show them how an Englishman could sympathize with their
struggles for liberty and their sorrows.[2] From Naples
Browning journeyed northward, and beheld Rome for the
first time. No exhaustive record remains of what he saw or
felt. But he paid homage at the grave of Shelley; he
followed Byron to the grotto of Egeria, where he gathered
hemlock in mistake for fennel ; and he wandered one day
into the little church of Saint Prassede, hard by Saint Maria
Maggiore—Saint Praxed's, obviously, where the sixteenth-
century Bishop "ordered his tomb." Memorable would this

---

[1] Wise, *ut supra*, vol. ii. pp. 17-19.
[2] Mrs. Orr's *Handbook*, p. 306.   He translated it into Italian.

K

first stay in Rome have been, had it produced nothing but the dying Bishop's monologue, in which the paganism underlying the thin veneer of Renaissance religiosity is pitilessly exposed. It would be harder to find any one more capable of criticizing this poem than Ruskin, whose opinion of it was thus set on record :—

" Robert Browning is unerring in every sentence he writes about the Middle Ages, always vital, right, and profound. . . . I know no other piece of modern English, prose or poetry, in which there is so much told, as in these lines, of the Renaissance spirit. . . . It is nearly all that I said of the Central Renaissance, in thirty pages of *The Stones of Venice*, put into as many lines, Browning's also being the antecedent work." [1]

" Not deep the poet sees, but wide," wrote Matthew Arnold ; Browning's work, at any rate as exemplified in the contents of *Bells and Pomegranates*, cannot be cited in support of Arnold's theory. No thinking mind, quite apart from Ruskin's appreciation, will deny depth of insight to *The Bishop orders his Tomb*, to *Pippa Passes*, or to *Saul*; while numbers III. and VII. in particular, containing the *Dramatic Lyrics* and *Dramatic Romances*, bear witness to the wide expanse of subjects which his vision traversed, as lightning plays over some broad and varied landscape. *Artemis Prologizes*, admired by so discerning a critic as Matthew Arnold, shows that he had familiarized himself to some purpose with the Greek tragedians, especially with Euripides ; it shows, too, that he could on occasion write as lucidly and with as perfect choice of phrase as even his critic could desire. The lines were to have served as prologue to a play with Hippolytus for subject, but the idea was abandoned, the poet contenting himself with translating, many years afterwards, two dramas of Euripides, instead of seeking to imitate or, conceivably, to rival him. *Artemis Prologizes* remains a fragment, but a flawless one. Again, Browning had, as we know, loved pictures from his boyhood, and in the *Dramatic Romances* the dawn of his meditations upon art is visible. The pale, thinly-drawn figure of *Pictor Ignotus* is the first of his portrait studies of artists, and foreshadows, if but

[1] *Modern Painters*, vol. iv. pp. 377-9.

dimly, the clearer outlines and deeper analysis of the later *Andrea del Sarto* and *Fra Lippo Lippi ;* while parts of *Waring, In a Gondola,* and *My Last Duchess* already afford ample evidence of his knowledge of the art of painting and his great feeling for it. He touches upon music, too, and upon the political issues and temper of the day. Had he been asked what poetry has to do with politics, particularly current politics, he would probably have replied, not a great deal. But it would be a mistake to infer from their rare intrusion on his verse that he was indifferent to them. As a man he had political opinions of a very definite kind ; as a poet he seldom transgressed what seems to have been with him an unwritten canon, that they were out of place ir his verse. The few exceptions to this rule are consequently the more worthy of remark. Certain lines in *Waring* show that to him, as to Carlyle, the political life of England in the Chartist days seemed painfully lacking in seriousness :—

> "Our men scarce seem in earnest now.
> Distinguished names !—but 'tis, somehow,
> As if they played at being names
> Still more distinguished, like the games
> Of children."

In the same year in which these lines were published he rejoices, in a letter to Domett, over Sir John Hanmer's con- version to anti-Corn-Law principles. To him the Corn Laws were so unmitigated an evil that he could hardly tolerate discussion of them ; and his scorn of those who opposed their repeal breaks out in the closing lines of *The Englishman in Italy.* As well might one debate, he avers,

> "If 'twere proper Scirocco should vanish
> In black from the skies !"

The Lost Leader, too, is a leader lost to liberalism. But what leader ? Browning has himself supplied the answer. "I *did* in my hasty youth presume to use the great and venerable personality of Wordsworth as a sort of painter's model ; one from which this or the other particular feature may be selected and turned to account ; had I intended more, above all, such a boldness as portraying the entire man, I should not have talked about 'handfuls of silver and bits of ribbon.' These never influenced the change of policy in the great poet ; whose defection, nevertheless, accompanied as it was by a regular face-about of his special party, was to my juvenile apprehension and even mature consideration an event to deplore.   But just as in the tapestry on my wall I can recognize figures which have *struck out* a fancy, on occasion, that though truly enough thus derived yet would be pre-posterous as a copy, so, though I dare not deny the original of my little poem, I altogether refuse to have it considered as the 'vera effigies' of such a moral and intellectual superiority." [1]   The details, in short, are not to be pressed, any more than in the case of *Waring, Bishop Blougram's Apology,* or *Mr. Sludge, the " Medium."*   Yet the idea of a *Lost Leader,* however small the underlying element of fact, cannot be divorced from pain ; and it was probably a relief to Browning to turn to foreign scenes and bygone periods—to the sardonic humour of the cloister in Spain, or to Gallic heroism on the field of battle.

Viewed collectively, these shorter poems, whether "lyrics" or "romances," are a glass reflecting many passions ; but love's image dwarfs the rest.   It is no surprise to find the love-interest prominent in the dramas of this series—witness the stories of Mertoun and Mildred, Anael and Djabal, Valence and Colombe—because a modern play without such interest is a rarity.   But with the shorter poems it is the same.   The portrait-gallery of men and women whose natures are glorified or degraded by this passion now begins.   A note is struck to which the poet will be found returning again and again.   Browning plumbed the depths of the love of man for woman and woman for man more impressively and more repeatedly than any English poet since Shakespeare. The insight which these poems display is the more remark-able if, as appears to be the case, his own experiences in this field had hitherto been of a purely fugitive description.   The explanation is to be found in that keen dramatic sense which

[1] Letter to the Rev. A. B. Grosart, Wise, vol. i. pp. 28-29.   Another of a very similar purport, and written in the same year, 1875, is given in Mrs. Orr's *Life,* p. 132.   Wordsworth, it will be remembered, was opposed to Catholic Emancipation and the Reform Bill.   A suggestion furnished by the tapestry on the poet's wall will be noted later.

made him feel not for but with his characters, and in the gift
of sympathetic imagination which revealed to him the nature
of their emotions.   Let any one attempt to mend the issue of
any one of the love poems, if he wishes to be convinced
that in these matters Browning's instinct is unerring.   Each
shade of feeling is interpreted with an admirable delicacy.
Love crowned with happiness in *Count Gismond;* love hopeless yet triumphant in *Cristina;* love's inadequacy, that
"cannot praise, it loves so much" ; its dainty fancifulness in
The Flower's Name; its humiliation in *Time's Revenges* ; how
perfectly are they each and all expressed !

In the dramatic monologue, so freely used in the shorter
pieces of *Bells and Pomegranates,* Browning had hit upon
the poetic form which was henceforth to be peculiarly his
own.   No unessential details are admitted, and the effect is
commonly won by concentration and a sparing use of ornament.   It is impossible to dissociate these merits from his
experience as a writer for the stage and his observation of
theatrical exigencies ; while it must also be remembered that
the dramatic instinct was deeply rooted in his nature, and
grew with his intellectual growth.   *My Last Duchess, The
Confessional* and *The Laboratory* (the last named, by the way,
being the subject of Rossetti's first water colour) are typical
examples of his method.

The Glove, admirable in spite of a metre which occasionally
jars, is more ambitious.   It has more background ; more
pains are spent in suggesting the atmosphere of King Francis'
court, but only in order to bring out in clearer relief the
character of the king himself, of Ronsard, the narrator, and
chiefly of de Lorge and the unnamed lady.   Leigh Hunt,
following Schiller, had in his version confined himself to the
simple incident of the lady throwing her glove among the
lions, her challenge to de Lorge to recover it, his acceptance
and her repudiation.   But this is not enough for Browning :—

"Human nature—behoves that I know it ! "

He elicits, as Ronsard, the lady's motive ; what is more,
follows her and de Lorge into their future lives, and (in a
second act, so to say) shows us the harvest which honesty
and insincerity are apt, respectively, to reap.

His own harvest was as yet deferred.   Only one number of *Bells and Pomegranates*, that containing *A Blot in the 'Scutcheon*, reached a second impression.[1]   At the same time there is evidence that the series steadily advanced his fame. The larger reviews began to take more notice of him, and in 1844 one of their articles was reprinted in R. H. Horne's *New Spirit of the Age*.   But informal expressions of opinion from private sources are of greater interest.   Walter Savage Landor, to whom the last *Bell* was dedicated, wrote to Forster that Browning was

"a great poet, a very great poet indeed, as the world will have to agree with us in thinking. . . . God grant he may live to be much greater than he is: high as he stands above most of the living, *latis humeris et toto vertice.*"

To Browning himself he sent some appreciative lines, of which the father was so proud that he had them printed for circulation among his friends.   *Laudari a laudato viro*—he might well be pleased at Landor's judgment.

"Since Chaucer was alive and hale
No man has walked along our road with step
So active, so enquiring eye, and tongue
So varied in discourse."

Among the younger men of the day, too, he had his devotees.   Ebenezer Jones, a young poet, "full," in D. G. Rossetti's words, "of vivid, disorderly power," used to thrust one of the *Bells* into his pocket as a companion on a country walk.[2]   W. M. Rossetti foretold that in twenty years' time their author would be the first of living poets.   Arnould wrote to Domett, in 1847,

---

[1] It was probably sold at the theatre, when the piece was played.

[2] Jones, who died at the age of forty in the year 1860, published one volume only, *Studies of Sensation and Event*.   Of this book, Browning wrote to Mr. Gosse in 1878, "It was lent to me for a somewhat hurried reading.   I remember speaking about it to W. J. Fox, who told me he knew the writer personally, and shared in my opinion of his power ; and, I *almost* think, it may have been from one of those roughly-printed blue-paper books that Eliot Warburton, at breakfast once, declaimed to me an impassioned Chartist *tirade* in blank verse—the speech of an orator addressing a crowd."   Wise, *ut supra*, second series, vol. ii. p. 7.

" I find myself reading *Paracelsus* and the *Dramatic Lyrics* more often than anything else in verse. Browning and Carlyle are my two crowning men amongst the highest English minds of the day."

What Carlyle thought of the poet, seventeen years his junior, whose name was thus coupled with his own, is clearly stated in one of his talks with Gavan Duffy, whom he met in Ireland in 1849. " I begged him," writes Duffy,

" to tell me something of the author of a serial I had come across lately, called *Bells and Pomegranates*, printed in painfully small type, on inferior paper, but in which I took great delight. There were ballads to make the heart beat fast, and one little tragedy, *A Blot in the 'Scutcheon*, which, though not over-disposed to what he called sentimentality, I could not read without tears. Carlyle's answer was, that ' Browning had a powerful intellect, and among the men engaged in England in literature just now was one of the few from whom it was possible to expect something.' "

And when Duffy, quoting Coleridge's *Suicide's Argument*, suggested the possibility of Browning having imitated its manner, Carlyle replied that

" Browning was an original man, and by no means a person who would consciously imitate any one. . . . It would be seen by and bye that he was the stronger man of the two, and had no need to go marauding in that quarter." [1]

The appearance of the last number of *Bells and Pomegranates*, just five months before its author's marriage and departure from London, where in the next fourteen years he was only to be an occasional sojourner, may fitly be regarded as the close of that literary epoch in his life which began eleven years earlier with the publication of *Paracelsus*. A new era, for him superlatively important, is about to begin ; but before we seek to tell its story a backward glance may be permitted. Something more must be said of the friends and acquaintances whom his verse had gained him in the earlier time, and of the houses and neighbourhoods where his visits, now of necessity to be interrupted, were most frequent.

When, and at whose introduction, he first met Carlyle, we

---

[1] Gavan Duffy's *Conversations with Carlyle*, 1892, pp. 56–57.

have no certain knowledge.   The intimacy was certainly ten years old at the date of the conversation recorded by Gavan Duffy, for Browning and Carlyle are found dining at Macready's early in 1839, together with Harriet Martineau and the Bullers.   Browning soon became a familiar figure at Cheyne Row, and received, presumably with amusement, the sage's advice to give up poetry.   He had a great and growing regard for Carlyle.

"I dined with dear Carlyle and his wife," he writes to a friend,[1] "(catch me calling people 'dear' in a hurry, except in letter-beginnings !), yesterday.   I don't know any people like them."

On the occasion of the dinner at which Miss Martineau was present, a son of Burns was also there, who sang some of his father's songs.   We have glimpses of Browning listening to Carlyle crooning " Charlie is my darling " and wishing that he could write a song ; lending the historian of Cromwell a copy of the first edition of *Killing No Murder*, or procuring from an uwilling possessor the loan of a coveted letter. Carlyle was sarcastic at the expense of *Sordello*, declaring that his wife had read it through without being able to make out whether Sordello was a man, or a city, or a book.   The remark, like others said to have been made about this poem, savours of humorous exaggeration.   *Sordello* was, in truth, a disappointment to many who had taken delight in *Paracelsus*. There is nothing apocryphal about Miss Martineau's opinion. Admiration of *Paracelsus* had led her to seek its author's acquaintance, through Fox, their common friend.

"It was a wonderful event to me," she writes, "my first acquaintance with his poetry.   Mr. Macready put *Paracelsus* into my hand when I was staying at his house [at Elstree], and I read a canto before going to bed. . . . The unbounded expectation I formed from that poem was sadly disappointed when *Sordello* came out.   I was so wholly unable to understand it that I supposed myself ill."[2]

In 1837 Browning had spent a day with Miss Martineau at Ascot, and later visited her at Elstree.   The prophetess of Economics and the Poor Law graciously undertook to advise him as to his worldly concerns, and unquestionably enjoyed

---

[1] Miss Haworth.   [2] *Autobiography*, vol. i. p. 417.

his society. "In conversation," thus she follows up her remarks upon *Sordello*,

"no speaker could be more absolutely clear and purpose-like. He was full of good sense and fine feeling, amidst occasional irritability, full also of fun and harmless satire, with some little affectations which were as droll as anything could be. A real genius was Robert Browning assuredly." [1]

Dining at her house in Westminster in 1838, he met John Robertson, assistant editor of the *Westminster Review*, for which Miss Martineau wrote, who might have proved a useful friend. But Browning alienated him by declining to send him an advance copy of *Sordello* for review purposes, considering that such preferential treatment would have been unfair to other journals. Another guest that evening was Henry Chorley, musical critic of the *Athenæum*, or as Arnould described him, " Annual-Athenæum-Review-Novel-and-Opera writer, also a very pleasant clever fellow." In 1833 Chorley had recognized from Fox's review of *Pauline* "the print of a man's foot in the sand," and when Miss Barrett's *Romaunt of Margaret* appeared in the *New Monthly* in 1836, he had learnt it by heart, and talked of it "in season and out of season." He was Arnould's neighbour in Victoria Square, Pimlico, and later he and Arnould were trustees for Browning's marriage. His bachelor abode was noted for the good music heard there—" Mendelssohn, Moscheles, Liszt, Ernst, David, Batta, and almost all the great instrumentalists of the day performed there at various times." But music was not everything, there was talk as well. " I am just returned from dining at Chorley's with Barry Cornwall and Browning," writes Arnould to Domett,

" and have been enjoying a great treat. Glorious Robert Browning is as ever—but more genial, more brilliant, and more anecdotical than when we knew him four years ago." [2]

Here, too, Browning met Charlotte **Cushman**, and Adelaide Kemble, afterwards Mrs. Sartoris. Many **of Mrs.** Browning's letters are addressed to Chorley, who dedicated to her his last novel, *Roccabella*.

---

[1] *Ibid.*   [2] Dated 24 November, 1845.

The home of Bryan Waller Procter ("Barry Cornwall"),
now 114, Harley Street,[1] where all the leading literary people
of the day were to be met from time to time, was also one of
Browning's constant resorts.   Procter, "quiet, unaffected,
natural, but with a vast deal of hidden fire which breaks
through his grey tranquil eyes and his placid, simple phrases
in rather startling flashes"—the description is Joseph
Arnould's—was two and twenty years Browning's senior.
He gave him his *Poems*, also an Italian guide-book when
Browning set out for Naples in 1844.   Mrs. Procter, "one of
the cleverest and at the same time most sarcastic women in
London society," was said to be "our Lady of Bitterness'
of the preface to Kinglake's *Eothen*.[2]   Kinglake came to
know her through being, as was also Eliot Warburton of
Crescent and Cross fame, one of her husband's law pupils.
Mrs. Procter and Browning were good friends—he used
regularly to go and see her every Sunday evening during the
later years of her widowhood [3]—but she thought it a pity he
"had not seven or eight hours a day of occupation," as her
husband had, who yet found time to write poetry; and her
father, "dear, foolish old Basil Montagu,"[4] was of the same
opinion.   Indeed, he went so far as to invite Browning to
read law with him, with no expense incurred.   By precisely
the same offer, in as kind a spirit, and with as litttle success,
Arnould tried to lure Domett back from the antipodes.
Birds of that feather are not snared so easily.

Browning's earliest visit to Macready's house at Elstree,
which has been already mentioned, was the first of many.
Those who frequented it—Forster, the artist Cattermole, Talfourd, and the rest—came mostly, like himself, from London;
but there was at least one of the actor's country neighbours
with whom he struck up a great friendship.   This was Miss
Euphrasia Fanny Haworth, a lady eleven years his senior,
who lived with her mother at the Manor House, Barham
Wood, an Elizabethan dwelling pulled down rather more than
half a century since.   Her temperament was romantic,

[1] It was then, says Lady Ritchie, 13, Upper Harley Street.
[2] Mrs. Crosse's *Red Letter Days*, vol. ii. p. 177.
[3] Procter died in 1874.
[4] *Letters of R. B. and E. B. B.*, vol. i. p. 199.

as may be inferred from a volume of stories she had published in 1827, *The Pine Tree Dell and Other Tales*. She corresponded with Browning and is addressed by him at the close of the third book of *Sordello* as "My English Eyebright," her first name being the Greek equivalent for that little flower supposed long since (it would seem by Milton amongst others [1]) to "make old eyes young again." Two "Sonnets to the author of *Paracelsus*," which appeared in the *New Monthly Magazine* of September, 1836, are from her pen. The first of these, regarded as a contemporary's impression of the poet, has a certain value.

> " He hath the quiet calm and look of one
> Who is assur'd in genius too intense
> For doubt of its own power ; yet with the sense
> Of youth, not weakness,—like green fruits in spring,
> Telling rich autumn's promise—tempering
> All thought of pride ; he knows what he hath done
> Compar'd with the dim thrill of what shall be,
> When glorious visions find reality,
> Is like an echo gone before,—a tone
> When instruments would prove their harmony
> Before the strain begins."

The future is his, in fact. The second closes in a very deprecating fashion.

> " Then, poet, give to me
> No splendour, but one feeling true and kind
> That, if unskill'd wholly to comprehend
> Thy scope of genius—I may call thee *friend*."

Eleven years later Miss Haworth published a volume of verse, *St. Sylvester's Day and Other Poems*, in which both these sonnets, with slightly altered titles (*The Young Poet*, 1836, and *To a Poet*), are included. A third, *To Miss Barrett, on hearing of her Secluded Life from Illness*, was certainly rather jejune in 1847, when Miss Barrett had become Mrs. Browning. The press was not kind to *St. Sylvester's Day*, and something in the book, perhaps the sonnet to Miss Barrett, seems to have offended Browning. "I quite took your view," Mrs. Browning writes to her sister-in-law,

---

[1] *Paradise Lost*, book xi. l. 414.

" of the proposed ingratitude to poor Miss Haworth—it would have been worse than the sins of *Examiner* and *Athenæum*. If authors won't feel for one another, there's an end of the world of writing." [1]

But Browning's irritation was momentary. His " proposed ingratitude," whatever it may have been, never took material form ; he made his wife known to Miss Haworth on the first opportunity, and the two became great friends.

It was at Talfourd's house, 56, Russell Square, three years after the *Ion* supper, that Browning first met Mr. John Kenyon, a man who was to exercise a remarkable influence upon his future. Kenyon, now a widower, was for thirty years a prominent figure in London society. He was spoken of by Southey as "one of the best and pleasantest men whom I have ever known, one whom everybody likes at first sight, and likes better the longer he is known." [2] Drawing his chair beside Browning's, at the close of dinner, he asked him whether he were not the son of a Robert Browning with whom he had been at school at Cheshunt. Finding this to be the case, he conceived a great liking for the son of his old school-fellow, and speedily took out a license for praising him, though with reservations. He praised his " inexhaustible knowledge and general reasonableness," and contrasted his common-sense with his " muddy metaphysical poetry " ! [3] His best praise was to declare that Browning "deserved to be a poet, being one in heart and life " ; [4] his best and most precious gift the introduction to his second cousin, Miss Elizabeth Barrett.

We may think of Browning, then, during this period, as seeing a great deal of society, and sharing its lighter pleasures as well as its intellectual interests. How far he cared about it, is another matter. Writing to Miss Barrett in 1845, he assures her that he "always hated it." " I have put up with it these six or seven years past," he tells her,

" lest by foregoing it I should let some unknown good escape me, in the true time of it, and only discover my fault when too late." [5]

---

[1] *Letters of Elizabeth Barrett Browning*, vol. i. p. 322.
[2] *Red Letter Days*, vol. i. p. 122.
[3] *Letters of R. B. and E. B. B.*, vol. i. p. 79.
[4] *Ibid.* p. 267.
[5] *Ibid.* p. 41.

The obvious comment is, that if he had shunned society he would not have met Kenyon, and so would have probably missed the "unknown good." The quest of some such felicity leads other men besides poets to mingle with their kind, and it is a happy ordinance of nature which impels them. But it is an old story that the poet is torn by conflicting impulses, "one drives him to the world without, and one to solitude." Browning was no exception to the rule. It was his social activity which struck Miss Barrett, when first he came into her life, in its almost painful contrast to her own loneliness and isolation :—

> " Thou, bethink thee, art
> A guest for queens to social pageantries,
> With gages from a hundred brighter eyes
> Than tears even can make mine, to play thy part
> Of chief musician." [1]

As for him, he had perhaps had enough of society to make him desire something more intimate, more satisfying. "What I have printed," he wrote to Miss Barrett in the early days of their correspondence,

" gives *no* knowledge of me—it evidences abilities of various kinds, if you will—and a dramatic sympathy with certain modifications of passion . . . But I have never begun, even, what I hope I was born to begin and end—' R. B., a poem.'" [2]

That poem, however, was already begun—and we may suspect he knew it.

[1] *Sonnets from the Portuguese*, No. III.
[2] *Letters of R. B. and E. B. B.*, vol. i. p. 17.

CHAPTER IX

MARRIAGE

Early life of Elizabeth Barrett Barrett—Her disabling illness—Loss of her favourite brother—Work her only solace—Her Poems—Browning's approbation—Their first meeting—Their correspondence—Rapid growth of their attachment—Improvement in Miss Barrett's health—Arbitrary conduct of her father— It precipitates their engagement and, subsequently, their marriage—They set out for Italy—Their meeting in Paris with Mrs. Jameson—Their residence at Pisa—The Sonnets from the Portuguese.

THE year of the death of Wordsworth was the year of the publication of *In Memoriam* and the *Sonnets from the Portuguese*. Each commemorates an exceptionally beautiful and helpful love ; and each, singularly enough, is associated with Wimpole Street, "the long unlovely street" of Tennyson's poem, described by Miss Barrett, so close a prisoner there, as looking "like Newgate turned inside out." In one "dark house" dwelt Arthur Henry Hallam ; another was the home of Elizabeth Barrett during the twenty months of that courtship whose story she has enshrined in the *Sonnets from the Portuguese.*

Browning first met Miss Barrett on 20 May, 1845, and, as she herself expressed it, "there was nothing between the knowing and the loving." At the age of thirty-nine Miss Barrett was already "tired of living . . . unaffectedly tired," and felt that her life was practically ended. Seven years earlier she had broken a blood-vessel in the lungs, and since then had been continuously an invalid. She saw hardly any one but the members of her own family, and not even all of these together for more than a brief half-hour on Sundays. All the more remarkable, therefore, is the story of her restoration to activity and, in a measure, health, thanks to the influence of a great love and a supremely happy marriage.

Six years Robert Browning's senior, she was born at
Coxhoe Hall, near Durham, the home of Mr. Samuel Barrett,
her father's only brother, to whom she was much indebted ;
for she benefited by his will to an extent which enabled her
to take an independent line at the most critical moment of
her life. The eldest of eleven children, she was the first of
her family for generations to be born in England ; for her
father, Edward Moulton Barrett, was connected, as were
John Kenyon and the Brownings, with the West Indies.
Looking around him for a house of his own, Mr. Barrett
pitched his tent in Herefordshire. In that pleasant county,
four miles west of the Malvern Hills, he built himself a
many-domed house, which he named Hope End. Hither he
migrated when his daughter was three years old ; and here
she spent twenty-three years of her life, in a seclusion so
complete that she afterwards compared herself to a bird in a
cage. She was a singing-bird, however. She made rhymes
over her bread and milk, and copied them out in little
clasped volumes ; these she would fondle lovingly and take
with her for a change of air in holiday time. At nine she
began a series of epics, one of which, *The Battle of Marathon*,
survived, for her father had it printed.[1] At ten, in her "little
house under the sideboard," she busied herself with composing English and French tragedies for representation in
the nursery. She thought seriously of disguising herself as a
page, in order to enter the service of Lord Byron, whom she
adored ; at the same time she could, as she said afterwards,
"write of Virtue with a V." She had a healthy liking for
outdoor pleasures, too ; would scamper on Moses, her black
pony, through the Herefordshire lanes.

Moses, however, had a serious rival in Pope's *Homer ;* for
she dreamt more of Agamemnon, she told Horne, than of her
pony. At the age when Browning played at the siege of Troy
in the Camberwell drawing-room, Elizabeth Barrett was cutting
her garden-plot " into a great Hector of Troy, in relievo, with a

[1] She was then fourteen years of age. A presentation copy of this work,
inscribed " A birthday offering to dearest grandmama from her affectionate child,
Elizabeth, March 6, 1820," was sold at Sotheby's on 17 December, 1908, for £80.
Browning, as he wrote to Mr. Wise in 1888, was inclined to doubt its very
existence, having never seen a copy of it.

high heroic box nose and shoe-ties of columbine." The gods
and goddesses of Hellas became so real to her that she might
have been seen performing pagan rites to the grey-eyed
Athené with a pinafore-load of sticks and a match from the
housemaid's cupboard. But Pope's version was not enough ;
she must read Homer in the original. She set to work on
Greek, first by herself, then with her brother's tutor, and
then, which was best, with her friend Hugh Boyd, the blind
scholar at Malvern, to whom she loved to read aloud. She
"ate and drank" Greek, and made her head ache over Plato,
the dramatists, and the early Christian poets. Hebrew too
she studied, and read her Hebrew Bible from Genesis to
Malachi, not stopping even at the Chaldee. She was as
inveterate a reader as Browning himself ; Mr. Kenyon called
her his "omnivorous cousin." Her father warned her against
the books "on *this* side of the library," and she therefore
avoided the Scylla of Gibbon and *Tom Jones*, to fall into the
Charybdis of the other side in the shape of Tom Paine,
Voltaire, Hume's *Essays*, *Werther*, Rousseau, and Mary
Wollstonecraft, which, she remarked, did quite as well.
Throughout her life she remained a devotee of fiction,
devouring "all possible and impossible British and foreign
novels and romances," and playfully suggesting for her
epitaph, " *Ci-gît* the greatest novel reader in the world."

Miss Barrett would only allow her mother one fault, that
of being "too womanly "—in the sense that she was "one of
those women who can never resist." She herself inherited
no such failing. She would, if some childish whim were
crossed, send the books flying across the room and upset the
chairs and tables. In later life, when principle succeeded
whim, her passionate championship of any cause she deemed
right is manifest equally in her poems and in her correspondence ; while her besetting sin, she explained, was "an
impatience which makes people laugh when it does not
entangle their silks, pull their knots tighter, and tear their
books in cutting them open." Her mother died in 1828 ;
then came financial losses, and four years later Hope End
had to be sold. This was a great blow to Mr. Barrett. He
was enough a stoic to play cricket with his boys the night
before they left their home, but he could not bring himself to

say one word about his reverses. After living three years at Sidmouth, in the course of which Miss Barrett published a rapidly written translation of *Prometheus Bound*, the family moved in 1835 to London, occupying there a furnished house, 74, Gloucester Place, Baker Street.

The appearance of *The Romaunt of Margaret* in Colburn's *New Monthly Magazine*, in July, 1836, three months after Forster's laudatory article on *Paracelsus* in the same review, made Miss Barrett known to the reading public. Chorley's admiration has been mentioned. Miss Mitford, soon to become her close friend, sought her acquaintance, and took her for a drive with Wordsworth; she met Landor too, and from Talfourd, one of Miss Mitford's intimate friends, received a copy of the recently acted *Ion*. Early in 1838 Mr. Barrett bought 50, Wimpole Street; then came his daughter's serious illness, the publication of her *Seraphim* volume—just as Browning was visiting Italy for the first time—and her removal to Torquay in search of health. Here occurred the tragedy which bade fair to wreck her life entirely, the death by drowning of her eldest and favourite brother, Edward Barrett. He went out boating in Babbacombe Bay, one July day in 1840, and never returned. Two years her junior, he was the one being whom she then "loved best in the world beyond comparison"; and her grief was heightened by his having remained at Torquay to bear her company against his father's wish. Fifteen months wore away before the invalid, who could hardly be lifted to the sofa without fainting, dared undertake the return journey by road to London, despite the provision of an easy carriage "with a thousand springs." But she longed to attempt it. "The associations of this place," she wrote to Mr. Boyd, "lie upon me, struggle as I may, like the oppression of a perturbed nightmare." The attempt was made; and in the September of 1841 she reached the home which she was not to leave, except for a few hours at a time, until her marriage five years later.

Whatever Torquay had done for her lungs, her brother's death had shattered, for a time at any rate, her nervous system. Sleep would not easily come near her "except in a red hood of poppies." Her doctor could only combat the

L

intense restlessness and sense of weakness which oppressed her by prescribing opium. In her upper room, however, at the back of the house, brotherly hands had done their best to disguise all marks of invalidism, and to provide fit lodgment for her favourite authors. One shelf was occupied by Greek poets and the bust of Homer ; another by English poets and the bust of Chaucer. Flush, her devoted spaniel, Miss Mitford's gift, nestled beside his mistress on the sofa, and proved a valuable help in disposing of dinners and breakfasts which were beyond her appetite. Her only solace was "work, work, work," an anodyne which nowadays, by the way, would in the circumstances probably have been forbidden. Within six months of her return she had begun a series of articles in the *Athenæum* on the early Greek Christian poets, and it is in connection with these that we first begin to associate her name with that of Robert Browning.

As early as 1841 her cousin had desired to make the author of *Pippa Passes* known to her, but she felt unequal to looking on a new face. Next year we find her writing to Mr. Boyd that not only did R. H. Horne, with whom she had for some time corresponded, think well of her articles, but that "Mr. Browning the poet was not behind in approbation ; " moreover, this "Mr. Browning is said to be learned in Greek, especially in the dramatists." During the summer a second series of articles appeared, this time on the English poets, followed on 27 August by a review of Wordsworth's recent volume, at the end of which Browning found himself classed with Tennyson among those "high and gifted spirits," who, in spite of the low estate into which poetry seemed to have fallen, "would still work and wait." Early in 1843, when the critics were assailing *A Blot in the 'Scutcheon,* her private letters reveal her sympathy with the author ; a little later she confessed to having been made quite misanthropical by her valued *Athenæum's* review of the *Dramatic Lyrics,* and declared that "it is easier to find a more faultless writer than a poet of equal genius." Great, then, must have been her delight when the admired writer was found approving her poetry as heartily as he had approved her critical work. She had sent Kenyon the manuscript of her *Dead Pan,* a poem suggested by some lines of his own, and he thereupon "chaperoned it about wherever his kindness could reach." Of course it reached Browning— Kenyon often spoke to him of his cousin—and he expressed his approbation in such cordial terms that Kenyon sent the letter to Wimpole Street. Miss Barrett retained the note as an autograph, and soon afterwards forwarded it to Horne, who had criticized the *Dead Pan*, that he might see the appreciative opinion of a poet "whom they both admired." During the autumn Browning and Miss Barrett, though neither knew it, were co-workers; for both were occupied in helping Horne to choose mottoes for the sketches of those writers whom he was about to include in his *New Spirit of the Age*. When, in the February following, this work appeared, Horne sent Miss Barrett copies of the eight portraits it contained ; and she forthwith had framed for her room those of Carlyle, Wordsworth, Harriet Martineau, Tennyson, and Browning. She asked her cousin if Browning's portrait were a good one? "Rather like," was all that could conscientiously be said.

The next link to be forged in the invisible chain which was to bind these two together was the appearance of her *Poems* in the summer of 1844, just as Browning was starting on his second Italian journey. On his return in December the volumes fell into his hands, and he found mention of his own work, side by side with that of Tennyson and Wordsworth. "Or from Browning," run the lines,

"Or from Browning some pomegranate which, if cut deep down the middle,
  Shews a heart within blood-tinctured of a veined humanity."

He would have been less than human had he not been gratified. The *Poems* had a great reception. Readers, known and unknown to her, wrote to thank their author ; among others Mrs. Jameson, hitherto a stranger, who actually gained admittance to the invalid's room, Miss Martineau, Talfourd, Landor, and Carlyle. Should not Browning write too ? Kenyon said emphatically, "Yes." So it was that on the 10 January, 1845, Miss Barrett received her first letter from Robert Browning—the first letter of a wonderful and unparalleled correspondence, for in no other age were such a pair of poets lovers too. Browning begins with characteristic impetuosity :—" I love your verses with all my heart, dear Miss Barrett." We may trace their story for ourselves in the successive letters, not without a sense, as we do so, of intruding upon hallowed ground. But our emotions, as we read, are purified and ennobled ; for which cause, let us hope, our trespass is forgiven.

To Miss Barrett, Browning's praise outweighed the rest. " I had a letter from Browning the poet last night," she writes to a friend, "which threw me into ecstasies—Browning the author of *Paracelsus*, and king of the mystics." The intimacy, conducted on paper, grew apace. " I had rather hear from you," he wrote to her a month later, "than see anybody else." She promised to receive him when spring came—"winters shut me up as they do dormouse's eyes "— and they met for the first time towards the end of May. Over a score of letters had already passed between them, and Miss Barrett afterwards confessed that she had read and re-read each one that she received, and that when Browning came " he never went away again." For his part, his resolve was quickly taken. Though he supposed, when first he saw her, that she would never be able so much as to stand upon her feet before him, he determined to devote his life to hers. The letter which he wrote after their first meeting—the only one afterwards destroyed—was virtually the confession of a love which Miss Barrett did not then believe that it could be right for her to accept. Her youth was past, she felt, and her health broken ; she " had not strength, even of *heart*, for the ordinary duties of life." The subject, consequently, was forbidden ; but the friendship deepened. The visits continued once, occasionally even twice a week, while the letters "rained down more and more " ; and, as the months passed, events occurred by which the two friends were insensibly drawn nearer. Miss Barrett grew stronger. During July she was able to exchange the sofa for the armchair, to walk about the room with something of the uncertainty of a young child, and to drive out two or three times a week. She planned a visit to Kenyon in Regent's Park, and even hoped to reach Mr. Boyd's house in St. John's Wood. That this improvement might not be lost, her family

began to discuss the advisability of her wintering in Malta or
in Egypt; while her doctor recommended Pisa, then a
recognized resort for invalids.

Browning, who joined eagerly in the inquiries about
vessels and cabins, had hitherto only known Mr. Barrett
from the dedication of his daughter's recently published
Poems: he was now to discover something else in that
"beloved image" beside the parental smile and the tender
affection of which this dedication spoke. During the family
councils Mr. Barrett maintained a dead silence. From
such attitude disapproval might naturally be inferred; and,
presumably in order to remove all doubt upon the point,
he withdrew his countenance from his favourite daughter.
His little kindnesses and his daily visits to her room were
discontinued. October came, and Miss Barrett had by this
time decided to go to Pisa without her father's consent,
should it still be withheld. A last effort was made to obtain
it. Her brother George undertook to intercede for her, and
pressed the matter home. Then the oracle spoke: his
daughter might go, if she pleased, "but that going it would
be under his heaviest displeasure." This she might have
braved; but others were involved. She would not go alone,
and a brother and sister were ready to accompany her. She
rightly shrank from bringing Mr. Barrett's wrath upon their
heads also, and consequently the much-debated project was
finally renounced. "The bitterest part of all," she wrote to
Browning, "is that I believed Papa to have loved me more
than he obviously does." In proportion as the breach with
her father widened, it was almost inevitable that the bonds
between the friends should be drawn closer. By the end of
September Browning had become more than a friend, he was
an acknowledged lover. "Henceforward," wrote Miss Barrett,
"I am yours for everything but to do you harm. It rests
with God and with you—only in the meanwhile you are most
absolutely free, unentangled, as they call it, by the breadth of
a thread."

This avowal was one thing, the possibility of marriage
was another. Happily the winter proved abnormally mild,
and Miss Barrett steadily gained ground. The regular visits
went on, and Browning's flowers were continually upon her

table.   Her sisters, Henrietta and Arabel, now shared her
secret ; her brothers became discreetly suspicious.   Kenyon
periodically made her uncomfortable by staring at her
through his spectacles and asking pointed questions ; but he
knew Browning as "an incarnation of the good and true," and
he also knew what he termed the "monomania" of his cousin
and quondam college friend, Edward Moulton Barrett.   At
50, Wimpole Street marriage was a forbidden subject.
Browning, who detested underhand methods, had to be
convinced that it would be worse that useless to ask for Mr.
Barrett's consent.   "If a Prince of Eldorado should come,"
Miss Barrett once remarked to her sister, "with a pedigree of
lineal descent from some signory in the moon in one hand,
and a ticket of good behaviour from the nearest Independent
Chapel in the other——" (for Mr. Barrett was a staunch
Nonconformist)—"Why, even *then*," said Arabel, "it would
not *do*."   "You might as well think," Miss Barrett assured her
lover, "to sweep off a third of the stars of heaven with the
motion of your eyelashes.   He would rather see me dead at
his feet than yield the point ; he will say so and mean it, and
persist in the meaning."

It was obvious, therefore, that they must take the matter
into their own hands.   Thanks mainly to the substantial
manner in which her uncle's affection had expressed itself,
Miss Barrett did not depend on her father for support.   With
£8000 in the funds, yielding about £300 a year, besides other
sums, she could act for herself ; while both she and Browning
were confident that they could earn money, should they need
it.   Another mild winter could not reasonably be expected.
They determined to marry and set out for Italy before the
close of autumn.   As the summer of 1846 came on, Miss
Barrett began to make the best use of her increasing physical
powers.   In May she was in Regent's Park, standing on the
grass for the first time for years, plucking laburnum ; soon
she was in the Botanical gardens, rejoicing in the beauty of
"the green under the green—where the grass stretches under
trees" ; another day she was at Hampstead, gathering wild
roses from the hedges.   Or she would drive to Highgate, and
along the silent lanes near Harrow ; or to Finchley, to call
upon a son of Lamartine.   She paid visits to Kenyon and

Boyd; she accompanied Mrs. Jameson, now an intimate friend, to see Rogers' house in St. James's Place ; she went to hear the music at Westminster Abbey and attended service at Paddington Congregational Church; she contemplated a visit to the Brownings at Hatcham ; she tried her powers by occasional walks in Wimpole Street, with Flush at her heels, to rescue whom from the dog-stealers she drove through the noisy streets to Shoreditch. Early in August she could write, "I am as well at this moment as any one in the world—perfectly well, I am. At the same time, strong is different. But the health is unaffected."

The taking of the all-important step was unexpectedly precipitated. In September a sudden edict went forth that the house in Wimpole Street should be painted and repaired, and that George Barrett should set out next day to secure a house for a month at Dover, Reigate or Tonbridge. The risk to Miss Barrett's health of such a removal and of the return to a freshly painted house at the beginning of the cold season was obvious, and too great to take. The project, it appeared to Browning, would infallibly delay the marriage for another year. He at once wrote to Miss Barrett, "We must be *married directly* and go to Italy." He discussed the situation with his parents, and his father advanced him one hundred pounds for travelling expenses. Miss Barrett, for fear of compromising her brothers and sisters, told none of them what was impending ; not even Kenyon was taken into her confidence, and he proved grateful for the consideration shown him. Browning's decision had been taken on 10 September, and the marriage was fixed for two days later. Between ten and eleven on the morning of Saturday, 12 September, Miss Barrett left her home, accompanied by her faithful maid Wilson, in what state of perturbation may be imagined, and managed to reach St. Marylebone Church, though obliged to stop at a chemist's for *sal volatile* on the way. The only witnesses were Wilson and James Silverthorne, the bridegroom's cousin ; no wedding could have been quieter. "How necessity makes heroes—or heroines, at least," wrote the bride. After sending Wilson home to ask her sisters to follow her, she drove to Mr. Boyd's house ; there rested on the sofa and drank a little Cyprus wine ; then, when her anxious sisters arrived, drove with them out of bravado to Hampstead, but felt a mist come over her eyes as she passed St. Marylebone's on her way home.

Browning could no longer call at Wimpole Street and ask for his wife as " Miss Barrett," but events moved so quickly that his absence was not remarked. Five days after the marriage another decree went forth ; a house had been secured at Little Bookham, and the Barretts were to move on the following Monday. On the afternoon of Saturday, 19 September, Mrs. Browning and her maid, accompanied by Flush, who judiciously kept silence, quietly stole out of doors. Walking round the corner to Hodgson's, the bookseller's, in Great Marylebone Street, they found Browning waiting for them. A cab was called from the neighbouring and still existing cab rank. The quartet of fugitives drove to Nine Elms, Vauxhall, and left by the five o'clock train for Southampton, on the first stage of their momentous journey. Italy, freedom, and untrammelled happiness—at last the dream was to be realized.

Twenty-two and a half hours of travel at that time separated London from Paris, for the railway from Havre to Rouen was not completed ; but Mrs. Browning bore up wonderfully against the inevitable fatigue. At Paris her husband at once found out Mrs. Jameson, who had preceded them thither, and she welcomed with amazement the friends whom she described as " two celebrities who have run away and married under circumstances peculiarly interesting and such as render imprudence the height of prudence." Browning was thankful for the presence of a woman friend, for he naturally feared lest his wife should suffer from the effects of the long journey and from the grief of the separation from her family in such painful fashion, unavoidable though it was. Mrs. Jameson thought her "looking horribly ill " at first, and the Brownings were persuaded to rest a week in Paris, on the understanding that she would then accompany them to Pisa. Accordingly they joined her at the little Hotel de la Ville in the Rue d'Evêque, where she was staying with her niece, later her biographer, Miss Geraldine Bate ; from whence the whole party moved southward towards Italy.

From Paris to Orleans the high-road was, as the *Murray*

of those days remarked, " superseded by the railroad " ;
and from Orleans the way was made easy by steamers
on the Loire, the Saône and the Rhone.   After eleven
hours on the boat from Lyons they landed at Avignon
and drove to Vaucluse, where Petrarch sought seclusion, as
devotees of poetry should.   Here, when Browning seated
his wife on a rock in the middle of the stream, the anxious
Flush plunged from the bank, prepared to perish with his
loved mistress, and so was baptized, as she put it, in the name
of Petrarch !   From Marseilles they went by sea to Leghorn,
and Mrs. Browning sat spell-bound on deck as they coasted
along the Riviera, watching the mountains rising tier above tier.
At Genoa Browning was on familiar ground—France he had
not previously traversed—for it was but two years since he
had visited the last Italian home of Byron, the city whence
he had sailed to take part in the struggle for Hellenic freedom.
Thence they coasted southward, past the Gulf of Spezzia, in
the heart of which lies Lerici, Shelley's last home, and past
Viareggio, with its background of pine-woods and mountains,
where his body had been washed ashore.   So presently
Leghorn was reached ; and as they entered its harbour a
reminder of home appeared in the person of Father Prout,
that wandering man of letters whom most people know
to-day, if they know him at all, as the author of *The Bells
of Shandon*, now discerned standing upon a rock and gazing
out to sea.

Pisa was distant but a dozen miles by rail—" poor,
decrepit old Pisa," as Frances Power Cobbe termed it, " the
Bath of Italy," where people talked of their coughs and read
newspapers a week old.   *Pisa pesa a chi posa*,[1] says the pro-
verb ; but it was not so with one set of travellers.   To Mrs.
Browning everything was new and delightful ; Pisa seemed
the fit ending to a happy pilgrimage.   It was a delight and
a wonder to bask in warm December sunshine, to walk forth
and watch the lizards darting to and fro, and see the golden
oranges overhang the walls ; to think of their friend Horne
as they passed the statue of Cosimo de Medici in the little
piazza by the Tower of Famine ; of Byron as they passed the
Lanfranchi Palace on the Arno, where he and his motley

_____
[1] " Pisa weighs heavily on those who stop there."

household had dwelt, and where Leigh Hunt had been a sojourner ; or of Shelley and his *Epipsychidion*, as their gaze fell on the neighbouring Convent of Santa Anna, where Emilia Viviani had been " imprisoned." It was a joy to drive across the plain to the Mediterranean ; to visit the pine-woods where Shelley loved to wander, to look upon the Serchio stream where he had sailed in his boat ; or to drive to the neighbouring range of hills at whose foot the little Baths of San Giuliano nestled, where he heard the news of the death of Keats and wrote the *Adonais*. It was a delight to sit in the upper rooms of the large Collegio Ferdinando, their home for six months, and look out upon the adjoining Duomo with its many-pillared front, the Leaning Tower, the Baptistery with its famous pulpit, and the peaceful Campo Santo with its curious frescoes. To enjoy all this, and to enjoy it in the company of the chosen and tried friend of her heart, seemed to Mrs. Browning, after years of weakness and isolation, almost to transcend reality. Never before, she felt, had she truly known happiness. Her health also, as Mrs. Jameson declared, was not only " improved but transformed " ; the services of Flush were no longer needed for the disposal of dinners and suppers, although he remained a guest when the midday meal was sent in from the *Trattoria*, and when chestnuts and grapes made their appearance in the evening. At the end of six weeks Mrs. Jameson and her niece went away, and the Pisan life became " a perpetual *tête-à-tête*."

The prisoner of Chillon, we are told, " regained his freedom with a sigh." As much may be said, with a difference, of Mrs. Browning. Her sighs were all for her father's unrelenting temper. Neither then nor later did he forgive his daughter. She wrote repeatedly to him, but no reply was vouchsafed. Five years later, being on a visit to London with her husband and her child, she made a final and ineffectual appeal. Browning also wrote. To him a violent answer was returned, accompanied by all the letters which his wife had written, unopened and with the seals unbroken. There is no need to say more upon this painful topic. Mrs. Browning had counted the cost of her action, and was not unprepared for its results. What she gained was immeasurably greater than what she lost. " By to-morrow at this time," she had written to her husband, the night before they left London, " I shall have *you* only, to love me. . . . You *only !* As if one said *God only.* And we shall have *Him* beside, I pray of Him." Her choice was triumphantly vindicated ; and the letters which she wrote to her friends during the remainder of her life are the best and most illuminative comment on these impassioned and most touching words.

CHAPTER X

EARLY YEARS IN FLORENCE

The era of the *Risorgimento*—Pio Nono—English society in Florence
—American acquaintances: Powers, G. W. Curtis—Visit to Vallombrosa
—Mary Boyle—G. S. Hillard—Father Prout—The revolutionary year—
The Brownings' home at Casa Guidi—Visit to Fano and Ancona—
Guercino's " Guardian Angel "—Browning's illness—W. W. Story—Birth
of the Brownings' son—Revolution in Florence—Defeat of Charles Albert
at Novara—Consequent reaction—Death of Browning's mother—Visit to
the Baths of Lucca—Margaret Fuller Ossoli—Isa Blagden—*Christmas
Eve and Easter Day*—Illness of Mrs. Browning—Visit to Siena—Homeward journey—Meeting with Tennyson in Paris—Return to England.

IT had been the Brownings' original design simply to
winter in Italy; but as Mrs. Browning's father was
implacable, and her brothers, though later they became
fully reconciled to her marriage, at present disapproved it,
an early return to England promised little happiness. Consequently, they decided to remain abroad "for another year
if not longer." The early spring of 1847 found them still at
Pisa; but in April they set out by diligence for Florence,
the city which was destined to be their home, or at least
their head-quarters, for the next fourteen years.

When they first set foot in the Tuscan capital, they contemplated no such possibility. Indeed, Mrs. Browning had
been warned against its cold winter winds. But they were
under an engagement to spend some time there with Mrs.
Jameson, after which they intended to devote the summer to
wanderings in Northern Italy. A furnished apartment was
taken in the Via delle Belle Donne, close to the Piazza Santa
Maria Novella. Here, three days after their arrival, they
were joined by Mrs. Jameson, who had been staying in
Rome. She was, indeed, a day before her time; for she had

remembered that Shakespeare's birthday was at hand, and brought with her from Arezzo a bottle of wine "to drink to his memory with two other poets." She talked of recent visitants to Rome ; of Cobden, who was determined "to try to admire Michael Angelo" ; of O'Connell, seemingly come there to die ; of the artists, Gibson and Wyatt ; above all, of the new Pope, Pio Nono, who, as Father Prout expressed it,[1] seemed to have brought back the golden days of Haroun al Raschid.

The Brownings, indeed, could hardly have come to Italy at a more momentous period of her history. The Austrian flag still flew in Lombardy and Venetia ; Mazzini was an exile ; Ferdinand II., though he had not yet earned the odious sobriquet of Bomba, was the oppressor of the Two Sicilies ; but Cavour's pen was already being plied on behalf of Italian unity, and Charles Albert, King of Sardinia, who needed only more tenacity of purpose to make him an heroic as well as a pathetic figure, had already given unmistakable signs of hatred of Austria and of liberal inclinations. It was at this juncture that Giovanni Mastai Ferretti was called upon to fill the throne of Saint Peter, under the title of Pius IX., in succession to a Pope who for fifteen years had carried on the tradition of mis-government so long associated with the Papal States ; and from this most unexpected quarter came the first flash of light. Pio Nono was a kindly, well-meaning man, though his mental gifts were not on the same level as his good intentions. His first proceedings were admirable ; he granted a general amnesty to political prisoners, considered the possibility of allowing railways to be made in his dominions, and called laymen to his councils. This, as it afterwards appeared, was as far as he desired to go ; but during the first year of his rule he seemed to his countrymen the ideal pontiff of the Neo-Guelph party, the destined regenerator of Italy. Browning shared the general admiration. While still at Pisa, when it was thought that before the year was out England would send a minister to Rome, he had written to Monckton Milnes "that he would be glad and proud to be secretary to such an embassy and to work

---

[1] In one of his letters to the *Daily News*, subsequently reprinted under the title *Facts and Figures from Italy.*

like a horse " for it.[1]   No mission was sent ; but the offer is
illustrative of Browning's attitude towards the rising hopes of
Italy.   He and his wife were to witness the fall of those
large hopes, their resurrection, and, in part at least, their
triumph.   The cause of Italian liberty had their heartfelt
sympathy, as it had that of the majority of their countrymen.
But while it moved Mrs. Browning to the writing of much
verse, of which *Casa Guidi Windows* was the first instalment,
only occasional echoes of it are perceptible in Robert Browning's poetry.   There is, indeed, the earlier written *Italian in
England ;* and to have composed that heart-stirring monologue
is in itself a noble tribute to a great cause and a great people.
But outside of this it is impossible to name any poem, unless
it be *The Patriot,* which can have been directly inspired by
the events of the *risorgimento.*   A second time, therefore, we
are confronted with the fact that Browning abstained, on
principle, from making contemporary political events the
subject of his verse.   Mrs. Browning's way was different.
She could not watch in silence, as her husband could.   Her
emotions drove her into lyric utterances, not always judicious,
perhaps, but always sincere ; and thus she forged at fever
heat that

> " rare gold ring of verse (the poet praised)
> Linking our England to his Italy." [2]

Browning had an exalted opinion of his wife's poetic genius ;
he honestly believed her possessed of more of the divine
afflatus than had fallen to his own lot ; and in view of this
belief it is permissible, if another reason for his keeping
silence " even from good words " be needed, to suggest that
he deliberately chose not to intrude upon a field which she
was making peculiarly her own.   There are some lines from
Tennyson which do not seem too high-pitched to express
what he may have felt, both in these early days of wedded
happiness and later :

> " Thou from a throne
> Mounted in heaven wilt shoot into the dark
> Arrows of lightning.   I will stand and mark." [3]

[1] *Monckton Milnes, Lord Houghton,* by T. Wemyss Reid, vol. i. pp. 384-5.
[2] The concluding lines of *The Ring and the Book.*
[3] *Early Sonnets,* II., To J. M. K.

Tuscany was among the first of the Italian provinces to show enthusiasm for the new Pope's measures. The Brownings had early evidence of the feelings of the Florentines, who made Cobden's passing through their city an excuse for a liberal demonstration. Revolution was to come more gently than elsewhere, however, upon Florence, whose inhabitants were of an easy-going disposition, and had less substantial causes for complaint than many of their neighbours. The Grand Duke of Tuscany, Leopold II., though an autocrat, was a lenient one; a kindly if dull individual, whom his people liked well enough, though jokingly calling him their Gran Chinco, or "great donkey." He lacked, at any rate, the obstinacy commonly associated with that animal; for, observing the temper of his subjects, he mitigated the severity of the press censorship, with the immediate result of the freer spreading of liberal ideas in his capital and in Pisa and Leghorn. This was the chief political event during the early days of the Brownings' stay in Florence.

They lingered there, long after Mrs. Jameson's departure for England. Mrs. Browning had to see the wonders of the place gradually, as her health allowed. "I have seen the Venus," she writes, "I have seen the divine Raphaels. I have stood by Michael Angelo's tomb in Santa Croce. I have looked at the wonderful Duomo. . . . At Pisa we say, 'How beautiful!' here we say nothing; it is enough if we can breathe." Florence fascinated them, and they were in no haste to break its spell. They continued to lead the secluded life which they had begun at Pisa. The resident English were in the main " worth very little consideration," declared one of Mrs. Browning's friends; "frivolous, gay, giddy, and it must be owned for the most part not very intellectual," was the description of another. Charles Lever roundly declared that Florence was a city cursed by the presence of "a miserably mended class of small English." Their dances, their card parties, their private theatricals in the Cocomero theatre, and their picnics had little attraction for the Brownings, who courteously but resolutely held aloof—"struggled to keep out of it with hands and feet," as Mrs. Browning put it, till it came to be recognized that they desired to be left alone, and that "nothing could be made of us." They had not come abroad in search of society of this kind ; nor such as was to be found at the motley gatherings in the Pitti Palace, where the Grand Duke held every week what he called "the worst drawing-room in Europe."

"The tag-rag and bobtail of the men who mainly constituted that very pleasant but not very intellectual society," wrote Thomas Adolphus Trollope, "were not likely to be such as Mr. Browning would readily make intimates of. And I think I see in memory's tragic glass that the men used to be rather afraid of him. Not that I ever saw him rough or uncourteous to the most exasperating fool . . . but there was a quiet lurking smile, which, supported by very few words, used to seem to have the singular property of making utterers of platitudes and the mistakes of *non sequitur* for *sequitur* uncomfortably aware of the nature of their words within a very few minutes after they had uttered them." [1]

Nor was the lack of culture all. After four years in Florence Mrs. Browning described the society there as "worse than any coterie society in the world . . . people come together to gamble or dance, if there's an end, why, so much the better ; but there's *not* an end in most cases, by any manner of means and against every sort of innocence." Their chief associates, therefore, for some years at least, were mostly strangers, usually cultivated Americans, among whom Mrs. Browning's writings were exceedingly popular, and among whom also her husband was appreciated long before his poetry found general acceptance in England.

Within three weeks of their arrival one young American had found them out. This was Hiram Powers, then a rising sculptor, whose "Greek Slave" was presently to win him an international reputation. He had already lived ten years in Florence. Browning had visited his studio off the Via Romana, as was the manner of most English and American travellers, and a young American journalist, G. W. Curtis, happening to see his card, revealed to the sculptor that he had been entertaining angels unawares. Powers had much to recommend him besides his art. He was an unassuming man, but shrewd and quietly humorous ; something of a mystic too, with a devotion to Swedenborg which was later

[1] *What I Remember*, p. 190.

to be transferred to spiritualism. He professed a belief in phrenology, and declared that Mrs. Browning's organ of ideality was larger than her husband's. What he said about the latter's capacity for veneration has been already mentioned.[1]

Curtis, also, was a man worth knowing. He wrote and begged for Browning's acquaintance. In response Browning called upon him, advised him not to read *Sordello*, and invited him to tea. Three years earlier Curtis had been a member of that clever socialistic community at Brook Farm, where even "the weeds were scratched out of the ground to the music of Tennyson or Browning," a community visited by Emerson and by Margaret Fuller, who was something of a Sibyl. He had also belonged to a club at Concord, which used to meet in Emerson's library, and had known Nathaniel Hawthorne and Thoreau. With these credentials he was soon admitted to the Brownings' intimacy. When July came and they left Florence, "thoroughly burned out by the sun," intending to pass two or three months at the monastery of Vallombrosa, to whose abbot they had a letter of recommendation, he was also of the party. In that upland valley,

> " where the Etrurian shades
> High over-arched imbower,"

they counted upon finding both rest and coolness. Starting at four in the morning, they drove thirteen miles along the valley of the Arno to Pelago, and then Mrs. Browning had to endure five hours' jolting, as the white oxen slowly dragged her sledge-like, basket *troggia* up the four miles of steep and stony pathway to the convent. But the abbot disapproved of womankind, in the shape of Mrs. Browning and her maid. The fare, too, was so rough that they seemed likely to have to live upon the scenery. The abbot was the deciding factor, and after five days they had to leave. So they went back to Florence, "very merrily for disappointed people." Curtis long afterwards recalled how he had listened to Gregorian chants and a hymn by Pergolese, as Browning sat and played upon the organ of the monastery chapel, upon which it is believed that Milton played two hundred years before.

---

[1] *Supra*, p. 50.

M

Their old apartment now proving untenable owing to the heat, comparatively cool quarters were obtained on the first floor of Casa Guidi, south of the Arno, at the corner of the Via Maggio and the Via Mazetta. Here they were hunted up by Miss Mary Boyle, Lord Cork's niece, a vivacious lady, the friend of many authors and herself a writer.[1] She and her mother and sister were staying at the Villa Careggi, outside Florence, lent to them by Lord Holland, a noble dwelling whose wide gardens and wealth of marble were fit reminders of Lorenzo the Magnificent. Miss Boyle, of whom Landor declared that "Mary is more than clever, she is profound," was soon on intimate terms with the tenants of Casa Guidi. She was present with them at the next act of the Florentine political drama, when in September the whole party, Flush included, watched a great procession stream past their windows to the Pitti Palace opposite. The Grand Duke had granted a civic guard, and his people assembled in thousands to express their thanks. It was a scene of wild excitement, of shouting, tears, and embraces.

Increasingly satisfied with Florence, the Brownings determined to make the experiment of passing the winter there. In October they moved to other furnished rooms, in the Piazza Pitti, where the maximum of sunshine was to be had ; " small yellow rooms," Mrs. Browning calls them, " with sunshine from morning to evening." Here the weeks succeeded one another so rapidly that they were constrained to " wonder at the clock for galloping." They read, made music, talked much and wrote a little. On *festa* days the civic guard paraded in the Piazza in all the glory of their new helmets and epaulettes, till Browning caught himself asking, "Surely, after all this, they would *use* those muskets ? " In the daytime Flush was the companion of his walks, but not even a concert or the chance of seeing Alfieri acted could entice him from his home in the evening. There lay his happiness, a great and an increasing one. But Miss Boyle was a privileged intruder, coming constantly at night to join the poets over hot chestnuts and mulled wine, when talk was good and laughter plentiful.

---

[1] She embodied her reminiscences in a pleasant volume, *Mary Boyle, Her Book*, published in 1901.

It was in these rooms, too, that they received a visit from George Stillman Hillard, an American writer, who had reviewed Mrs. Browning's poems and wished to know their author. In his *Six Months in Italy* he has left a brief sketch of husband and wife, Browning "simple, natural, playful," Mrs. Browning all genius and sensibility. " Her tremulous voice," he writes,

" often flutters over her words like the flame of a dying candle over the wick. I have never seen a human frame which seemed so nearly a transparent veil for a celestial and immortal spirit."

Another passing visitor from the outside world was Father Prout, who had just completed his letters from Italy to the recently established *Daily News*. Meeting him accidentally, Browning had his latest impressions of Pio Nono, as well as news of Mrs. Jameson and her niece, and at the end of all was embraced " in the open street as the speaker was about to disappear in the diligence." Yet another visitor was a newly married cousin of Mrs. Browning, who exclaimed in amazement at her look of improved health. Being too happy, however, as she wrote to Miss Mitford, was not conducive to literary activity ; and whatever Browning meditated, he did not produce anything new, contenting himself during this winter with the revision of his already published poems.

From this occupation, perhaps, or from reading the *André* of George Sand, whose works they both admired, they were startled late one evening by the tramp of many feet and the sound of loud "evvivas," while "through the dark night a great flock of stars seemed sweeping up the piazza." The Grand Duke had made another concession to his people, nothing less important, this time, than the granting of a constitution. He had gone to the opera unattended, but was recognized, hailed with acclamations, and escorted home in torchlight procession by a multitude of his subjects. The revolutionary year had dawned. January, 1848, saw Sicily in revolt and Ferdinand II. granting a constitution ; Charles Albert, Leopold II. and Pio Nono shortly followed suit. Simultaneously the idea of an united Italy gathered strength. The Austrians were driven out of Milan after hard fighting ;

Venice was evacuated ; Charles Albert put himself at the head of the national movement ; and even Leopold urged his subjects to join "the holy cause of independence." From Paris came more sinister tidings ; the news that Louis Philippe had fled, and that a Republic was proclaimed, was whispered in Florentine ballrooms and cast a gloom over the dancers. A new acquaintance of the Brownings, Mademoiselle de Fauveau, a sculptor, had suffered exile for her legitimist opinions ; now she dreamt that " Henri Cinq " would come to his own. Among the English residents there was something like a panic ; a large proportion of them made haste to leave Florence, a circumstance which the more inclined the Brownings to remain. So it was that when in May an opportunity offered of securing the flat in Casa Guidi which they had already occupied, they decided, inclination and economy being for once on the same side, to take it, furnish it, and make it their definite abode.

Tuscany, however tumultuous, was at that time a little Goshen. Taxes were light and expenses so small that Florence was perhaps the cheapest place in Italy. Sixpence would purchase a goodly fowl or a flask—equivalent to three bottles—of capital Chianti. These were the days when "for three hundred a year," wrote Mrs. Browning, "one may live much like the Grand Duchess, and go to the opera in the evening at fivepence halfpenny." Her friends, Miss Blagden and Miss Frances Power Cobbe, who kept house together for a time, managed even more economically : their fourteen rooms in the Villa Brichieri, finely situated on the slopes of Bellosguardo—which suggested the villa described by Mrs. Browning in *Aurora Leigh* [1]—with a man-servant and a maid, and a carriage and pair when they drove into the city, cost them, all told, but £120 a year each. At Casa Guidi seven rooms, three of them "quite palace rooms and opening on a terrace," the favourite suite of the last Count Guidi, whose arms were on the *scagliola* in one of them, were rented at only twenty-five guineas a year ; and could be let furnished, should their occupants wish to travel, for some ten pounds a month.

The sale of their poems during the last two years—chiefly

---

[1] According to Miss F. P. Cobbe's statement in her *Italics*. "Not exactly Aurora Leigh's, mind," wrote Mrs. Browning to Mrs. Jameson.

Mrs. Browning's, it may be suggested—provided funds for furnishing. Browning was soon occupied in buying rococo chairs, old tapestries, and satin from cardinals' bedsteads ; a neighbouring convent yielded a large bookcase carved with heads of angels and demons. New English or French publications were scarce in Florence, and the Brownings had not burdened themselves with books when they left England ; but the empty bookcase was a provocation, and presently they sent home for their old favourites. Pictures, too, were added later, bargains one and all ; the great triumph being Browning's discovery in a corn-shop a mile outside the city of five paintings, in connexion with which the learned mentioned the names of Cimabue, Giottino, and Ghirlandaio—such works, in fact, as he afterwards described in *Old Pictures in Florence*. Much care, doubtless, went to the hanging of these treasures and the arrangement of other purchases ; after which their owners would sally forth to drive in the Cascine, the park of Florence, or on foot to look at the sunset on the Arno or watch Cellini's Perseus bathed in moonlight. In June took place the first elections to the Tuscan parliament ; the members walked through Florence in procession, and impressed Browning by the gravity and dignity of their demeanour. Tuscan soldiers, meanwhile, had borne their part in the earlier and successful conflicts with the Austrians, and at Curtalone and Montanara showed that they knew how to die.

This summer the Brownings attempted a more ambitious holiday. With Fano, a little seaport on the Adriatic, as their destination, they crossed the Apennines ; but the place was a disappointment in regard to climate, " the very air swooning in the sun." Ancona, whither they migrated after three days, " a striking sea city, holding up against the brown rocks and elbowing out the purple tides," was a little more endurable. Here they managed to remain a week, subsisting on fish and cold water ; and then went northward along the coast, through Pesaro and Rimini to Ravenna, where Dante, whose tomb they saw, had died an exile. Thence they re-crossed the Apennines by way of Forli, glad to breathe cool air once more, and spell-bound by the jagged and wooded splendour of the mountains. They had been away from Florence just three weeks, and the heat had been the only drawback. One picture at Fano, Domenichino's "David," made them feel that they could not agree with the estimate of that artist formed by the "graduate of Oxford," whose *Modern Painters* they had lately read; another, Guercino's "Guardian Angel," which hangs in the dim light of the church of San Agostino, charmed them even more, and inspired one of Browning's tenderest poems. The personality of Alfred Domett was brought vividly before him, whether by the memory of some other picture admired by them both, or by the sight of "the unplumbed, salt, estranging sea" which parted them. Domett must share with his friend, and that friend's wife, the glad emotion of the time :—

> "Guercino drew this angel I saw teach
>   (Alfred, dear friend!) that little child to pray,
>   Holding the little hands up, each to each
>   Pressed gently—with his own head turned away
>   Over the earth where so much lay before him
>   Of work to do, though heaven was opening o'er him,
>   And he was left at Fano by the beach.
>
> "We were at Fano, and three times we went
>   To sit and see him in his chapel there,
>   And drink his beauty to our soul's content—
>   My angel with me too." [1]

*　　*　　*　　*　　*

The lines end, as we have seen, with an expression of anxiety for his friend's welfare. *The Guardian Angel* is not, strictly speaking, a "dramatic lyric"; it is a fragment of auto-biography. The poet does not assume the mask of an imaginary person, as, for instance, in *Old Pictures in Florence*, but speaks unmistakably in his own. The poem appears to have been written at Ancona, during his stay there; and if that is the case it gives an intimate idea of the religious attitude of a mind already meditating, perhaps, the *Christmas Eve and Easter Day* of 1850.

Browning had now been two years in Italy, and it would seem that his constitution missed the more bracing air of

---

[1] *The Guardian Angel: a Picture at Fano.*

northern latitudes ; at any rate, soon after the return to
Florence from what had not been exactly an invigorating
holiday, although an enjoyable one, he fell ill, and was laid
aside for nearly a month with an ulcerated throat, accompanied by fever. He refused to see a doctor ; but happily
an amateur physician intervened. Father Prout, who was
passing through Florence on his way to Rome, burst in
breezily upon the dejected household. Recognizing that
weakness was the root of the trouble, he prescribed regular
potions of port wine and eggs, which proved a most successful
remedy ; and his cheerful society, for " he came to doctor
and remained to talk," completed the cure. Doubly welcome
must the Father's equable spirits have been at a time when
the new-born hopes of Italy seemed likely to perish. Milan
had capitulated to the Austrians, and Charles Albert, left in
the lurch by some of his allies and not reinforced by others,
agreed to an armistice. His motive in doing so was to
gather strength for a fresh attack, but it was not everywhere
appreciated. The Pope's abandonment of progressive principles was another disappointment. The Brownings must
have been glad, as the year closed, to have fresh matter of
interest in their personal affairs. The approaching publication of the second edition of Browning's poems, in the
preparation of which he had had the help of Forster, Talfourd,
and Procter, was at last notified in the *Athenæum ;* [1] and *A
Blot in the 'Scutcheon* was successfully revived by Phelps at
Sadler's Wells theatre. During this autumn, too, Browning
improved his acquaintance with the American sculptor,
William Wetmore Story, who is to be counted among his
half-dozen greatest friends. They were drawn together by
their common love of art and literature. Story had been
bred to the law, but his artistic instincts were stronger than
his legal aptitudes, though these were considerable. It was
after giving proof of both in his own country that he was
commissioned to execute a statue of his father, Judge
Story, to be erected in the memorial chapel of the cemetery
of Mount Auburn, near Boston. This commission was the
determining factor in his life ; for, aware that his education

---

[1] *Pauline* and *Sordello* were not included ; the latter was held over for
revision, and Browning had no desire to reprint *Pauline.*

in the sculptor's art was still embryonic, he sailed for Italy, to pursue his studies at the fountain-head ; and so congenial did they prove, and so successful was his first portrait-study in marble, that sculpture became his life's work and Italy his second and adopted country.   Arriving in Florence early in 1848, he called upon the Brownings, very probably at G. S. Hillard's suggestion.   Not long afterwards he left for Rome ; but returning in the autumn provided himself with a studio, and soon became their friend.

There is a gap, at this juncture, in Mrs. Browning's correspondence ; and when she resumes it Casa Guidi has another inmate.   Her child, Robert Wiedemann Barrett Browning, was born on 9 March, 1849.   He came upon Florence at a stormy period ; for within three days a revolution, mainly effected by the people of Leghorn and happily bloodless, drove out the Grand Duke ; and Browning from the windows of his house saw a tree of liberty planted close to his door, amid the booming of cannon and the ringing of bells.   This affair, the result rather of local jealousies than of patriotism, was destined to be advantageous neither to Tuscany nor to Italy.   Of a more serious and definitive cast was the news which presently arrived from Lombardy. Charles Albert had made his effort, and failed.   On the stricken field of Novara, where the bravery of the Italian troops and the enthusiasm of Garabaldi and his red-shirted volunteers, among whom Mazzini served, proved no match for the greater numbers of the Austrians and the superior skill of the veteran Radetsky, the King abdicated in favour of his son, Victor Emmanuel.   The cause of Italian unity was for the time overthrown, and another decade was to pass before its resuscitation.   In Florence the natural reaction followed. The Grand Duke returned, in an Austrian uniform, escorted by Austrian bayonets.   This time, unhappily, there was bloodshed, of which Browning was a witness.   The tree of liberty, planted seven weeks earlier, "came down with a crash"; the promoters of revolution subsided; and Browning, as he beheld the collapse of the short-lived Tuscan republic, may well have recalled his own cynically humorous Ogniben, in *A Soul's Tragedy*, who had "known three-and-twenty leaders of revolts."

No doubt the new joy of fatherhood largely mitigated his public disappointments. Grief, however, soon clouded this happiness; for shortly after his son's birth his mother died. He felt the blow as a man must who has had so good a mother, and loved her so devotedly. His subsequent depression made change of scene imperative, though he had little heart for it. Mrs. Browning, however, to whom the necessity was apparent, at last prevailed, and early in July they left Florence on a tour of exploration. Driving northwards along the coast, by the pinewoods and the marble mountains of Carrara, they passed through Lerici, on the bay of Spezzia, and Seravezza, a mountain village which attracted them; but as neither spot afforded suitable accommodation, they determined to see what the more sophisticated Baths of Lucca had to offer. The place had a bad name for gaming and scandal, but owing to the troubles of the time it was now comparatively deserted; and there was no denying the beauty of its surroundings. The Bagni di Lucca, now accessible by a railway which climbs up the mountain valley from the plain on which Lucca stands, four miles away, was then a favourite summer resort with the Florentine English. It consists of three villages; the first, called Ponte, from the fact that a bridge there spans the river Lima, was a kind of miniature Baden-Baden; the second, Alla Villa, where was the Duke of Lucca's summer abode, stands on higher ground; the third, Bagni Caldi, perched highest of all, had to be approached, on foot or donkey-back, by winding, stone-paved paths.

It is easy to imagine which of the three villages took the Brownings' fancy. They settled themselves for the summer in the highest house of Bagni Caldi, "a sort of eagle's nest," far from all reminders of Austrian occupation, and hearing only the cicale and the murmur of the mountain stream. Here, in the fine air and calming solitudes, Browning's health and spirits mended, the baby throve, and Mrs. Browning gained such an accession of strength as she had not known since girlhood. She was able to climb the hills and explore the forests with her husband. One day the whole party, Browning on horseback, Mrs. Browning, the child and nurse on donkeys, went on a

formidable expedition. Prato Fiorito was their objective, a
volcanic region rent with ravines, the watcher of many
mountains and of a distant sea, approached by a five miles'
steep ascent through the chestnut woods and along the bed
of dried-up torrents. When they reached home at six in the
evening they had been away ten hours. So their summer
passed, a period of isolation which pleased them well. A
belated *Galignani* brought them news of the outside world,
and occasionally they dropped down to Ponte, where a Mr.
Stuart lectured on Shakespeare and gratified them by citing
Mrs. Jameson as an authority. They had a visit too from
Charles Lever, who was living at Ponte, and was the pre-
siding genius of all amusements there. It was at Bagni
Caldi, too, that one morning after breakfast Mrs. Browning
stole quietly into the room where her husband was
working, thrust some manuscript into his pocket, and
then hastily withdrew. It contained the sonnets, hitherto
unseen by him, which she had written during their
courtship and engagement. He thought them " the finest
sonnets written in any language since Shakespeare's."
They were published next year as *Sonnets from the
Portuguese*, a disguise suggested to Browning by his wife's
poem *Caterina to Camoens*, of which he was particularly
fond.

The Brownings had more in common with another visitor
who sought them out on their return to Florence in October.
This was the Countess Ossoli, until lately Margaret Fuller.
She had been the first editor of the *Dial*, the organ of New
England Transcendentalism ; and had the distinction of
being succeeded in that post by no less a personage than
Emerson. She had written in the *New York Tribune* an
appreciative review of *Bells and Pomegranates*, but a better
passport to Browning's heart was that she had placed his
wife "above any female writer the world has yet known."
Signora Ossoli was fresh from the siege of Rome, where her
husband had fought in the ranks among the defenders of the
short-lived Roman Republic and she had nursed the wounded.
Now they were to remain six months in Florence ; and from
their rooms in the Piazza Santa Maria Novella she often
crossed the Arno to Casa Guidi. "I see the Brownings

often," she writes, "and love and admire them both more and more, as I know them better. Mr. Browning enriches every hour I pass with him, and is a most cordial, true and noble man."[1] She was deeply infected with socialistic opinions, of which then, as now, red was the symbolic and significant hue ; and these doctrines were abhorrent to her new friends. Mrs. Browning is explicit on this point: "I love liberty so intensely that I hate Socialism." And Browning says the same thing, by implication, in his sonnet *Why I am a Liberal.* Nevertheless, both husband and wife were attracted by Signora Ossoli's personality. She was certainly an interesting woman. She had seen and spoken with George Sand and fired Mrs. Browning with an ambition to do likewise ; she had been in touch with many of the leading minds in America ; and one feels that in the talks at Casa Guidi with one who had been so closely connected with the " Brook Farm experiment " the Englishwoman was unconsciously acquiring material for some of the views afterwards to be expressed in *Aurora Leigh.* Sad and full of forebodings, Signora Ossoli passed her last evening in Italy at the Brownings' home. She never reached her own country. The ship in which she sailed was dashed to pieces on the shores of America, and she perished with her husband and child. To Mrs. Browning the shock of her death was intensified by the manner of it, since it recalled to her the loss of her own dearly loved brother.

To these days, too, belongs the formation of another friendship, destined to be of a more intimate and permanent character. Miss Isa Blagden was described by Browning as a " bright, delicate, electric woman " ; she was also a woman of ready sympathy and active kindness. Other recommendations, had any been needed, were, that she lived by her pen, was a lover of flowers and dogs, and shared Mrs. Browning's growing admiration for Louis Napoleon. In this admiration Browning was no participant. The French President's protest against the misgovernment of the restored Pope was well enough ; but it seemed to him, as to others, somewhat inconsistent in one who had played so considerable a part in his restoration.

---

[1] *Memoirs of Margaret Fuller*, vol. ii. p. 311.

The spring of 1850 was marked by two events of signal interest to the Brownings. One was the marriage of Mrs. Browning's sister Henrietta to Captain Surtees Cook, in regard to which Mr. Barrett behaved precisely as he had done in his eldest daughter's case; the other, the appearance of *Christmas Eve and Easter Day*, Browning's first new publication since the last number of *Bells and Pomegranates*. This poem, though no doubt it had occupied his thoughts earlier, appears to have been composed after his return from Bagni di Lucca. The publishers were Chapman and Hall; two hundred copies were sold in the first fortnight, after which the demand flagged. Of its merits and its interpretation extremely divergent views were expressed. The *Athenæum*, while admitting the beauty of many isolated passages, deprecated the discussion of religious questions in what it termed "doggrel verse"; while the *Examiner*, no less friendly and appreciative than it had shown itself in the case of *Paracelsus*, gave unrestricted praise.

Those who would deduce from this poem, or rather pair of poems, a precise conclusion as to their author's religious belief are confronted by an initial difficulty. There is no apparent reason why the narrator in *Christmas Eve* should not have also seen the visions described by the chief speaker in *Easter Day*, but Browning is careful to point out that they are two distinct persons:

> "It chanced that I had cause to cross
> The common where the chapel was,
> Our friend spoke of, the other day."

There is also the third character—*Easter Day* being a dialogue—to be reckoned with; and he is by no means in accord with the seer of visions. The poems, therefore, are "dramatic," and it is consequently unsafe to identify Browning with any of his three characters. He would certainly have resented such identification. Short of it, however, the reader may naturally and reasonably desire to form some general notion of the poet's attitude towards the Protestant, the Roman Catholic and the rationalistic conceptions of Christianity, as set forth in *Christmas Eve*; and towards the question at issue in *Easter Day*, what it means "to be a

Christian." English thought was very much occupied with these topics towards the middle of the nineteenth century. On the one hand, the Tractarian movement might well appear to have a Romish tendency when its chief apostle joined the Church of Rome; on the other hand, the publication of Strauss's *Leben Jesu* seemed a no less formidable menace to the reformed faith. Browning is not the only Victorian poet whose verse is troubled by the controversies of the time. Tennyson, eight years earlier, made one of his characters lament

> " the general decay of faith
> Right through the world, at home was little left
> And none abroad." [1]

Clough has some lines suggestively named *Epi-Strauss-ium*, others in which he exhorts his generation to pause and "consider it again "; and he too, a few months earlier than Browning, composed in Naples an *Easter Day* of his own. Strauss's work had appeared in an English garb three months before Browning left England, and there is internal evidence in *Christmas Eve* that he had read it or heard it discussed ; as, for instance, when he makes his professor discourse on the "myth of Christ," and after examination of it bid his hearers

> " Go home and venerate the myth
> I thus have experimented with—
> This man, continue to adore him
> Rather than all who went before him,
> And all who ever followed after ! "

—exhorting them, in conclusion, to continue to call themselves Christians and to "abhor the deist's pravity." [2] But while Browning grappled with the German theologian, he was careful not to draw his portrait. The professor in the poem is a composite figure; his discourse embodies elements drawn from the teaching of Comte as well as that of Strauss. Browning, in short, took as wide a survey as he could of the rationalistic tendencies of the time.

---

[1] *The Epic*, being a preface to the *Morte d'Arthur*.

[2] See the preface to the *Life of Jesus* and Strauss's later work, *The Transitory and the Permanent in Christianity*, 1839.

The narrator in *Christmas Eve* finds the professor's lecture cold comfort. It neither touches his heart nor convinces his intellect. It wrings from him, at the most, a tribute half-sorrowful, half-contemptuous :—

> " Surely for this I may praise you, my brother !
> Will you take the praise in tears or laughter ? "

For the Roman Catholic standpoint there is, in his opinion, more to be said. Beholding in his vision midnight mass celebrated at St. Peter's in Rome, he recognizes that the heart of faith is beating strongly,

> "though her head swims
> Too giddily to guide her limbs.
> * * * *
> I see the error, but above
> The scope of error, see the love."

Where love is, there must love's embodiment be. But the same conclusion had been drawn in the ugly little chapel on the edge of the common, whose grotesque and sordid details take the reader's attention captive at the beginning of the poem. Protestantism, be it observed, is represented in its bleakest, Roman Catholicism in its most splendid form ; for all that, the narrator makes his choice without any hesitation.

> " I then, in ignorance and weakness,
> Taking God's help, have attained to think
> My heart does best to receive in meekness
> That mode of worship, as most to this mind,
> Where earthly aids being cast aside
> His All in All appears serene
> With the thinnest human veil between."

Thus far the narrator ; but what of the poet ? Taking his known opinions into consideration, we may deduce this much from *Christmas Eve :* that he had a sympathetic understanding of Roman Catholicism on its moral as distinct from its dogmatic side, a reasoned dislike of rationalism, and, as might be expected in one of Noncomformist upbringing, a preference for simplicity in the externals of worship. This preference he had, in fact, lately exhibited, by causing his son to be baptized in the church of the French Lutherans at Florence.

Passing now to *Easter Day*, we may tread more securely. Mrs. Browning writes to Mrs. Jameson about her husband's new book,

> " I have complained of the *asceticism* in the second part, but he said it was ' one side of the question.' Don't think that he has taken to the cilix—indeed he has not—but it is his way to *see* things as passionately as other people *feel* them."

With these words as commentary it is reasonable to conclude that Browning's intellectual sympathies are with the eager visionary rather than with his easy-going interlocutor. The former states his case passionately, at a white heat of thought ; no wonder, then, if he tends to overstate it. His is the instinct of the orator, who, in order to gain even a little, pleads for a great deal. He would not have his friend turn anchorite, but would save him from complete absorption in the things of sense ; would have him estimate the material world at its proper value, not rest in it supremely satisfied. Here is no call to asceticism. If God's saints were, while alive on earth

> "found grateful and content
> With the provision there, as thou,
> Yet knew he would not disallow
> Their spirit's hunger, felt as well—
> Unsated,—not unsatable,"

certainly his sinners are not called upon to abhor their temporal surroundings. Only, we infer, they are to use them meetly, not darkening the casements which open upon infinity. Lover of art and of all things beautiful, no wearer of the hair-shirt, Robert Browning is to be reckoned among those for whom the visible world served not to hide but to reveal the power and the love of God.

In spite of the description of St. Peter's, Mrs. Browning is not far wrong in saying that "there is nothing *Italian* in the book " ; that is to say, no Italian atmosphere. The rough humour which characterizes part of it is essentially British ; so too is the zest for hammering out abstruse arguments, and the occasional tenderness which is the more effective for its rugged setting.   This fruit shows no sign of having ripened under Italian skies.   But Browning's thoughts had lately been recalled by sorrow to his home in England, and to his mother's religious faith ; and it is perhaps not too fanciful to suppose that the tug at his heart-strings of all that England stands for to her exiled children was a factor in determining the scope and methods of his poem.   At any rate, it was only vexatious financial reasons which restrained him, in the summer of 1850, from turning his footsteps homeward.   From the same cause the family remained in Florence, Browning with grave anxiety for his wife's health.   For two months she was seriously ill, and it was not till September that they were able to get away.   A short railway journey took them to Siena and to that cooler air which an increase in altitude of over a thousand feet ensures.   They rented a small house about a mile and a half out of the town, "among a sea of little hills and wrapt up in vineyards and oliveyards."   After three weeks in this peaceful spot Mrs. Browning made a fair recovery.   Her child was ill for one day, overpowered by the sun ; but he was soon well again, his "singing voice" sounding joyfully about the house and garden.   They were destined to return in other summers to Siena ; now, when this visit closed, they parted regretfully from their villa and its many delights, Browning with a special memory of a wide prospect of undulating hills and distant plain.   A week was spent in Siena itself, that something might be seen of its pictures and its buildings ; and so, in October, back to Florence and home.   In the same month appeared Mrs. Browning's collected poems, to the revision of which she had devoted much time and care.   The volumes were made to correspond with those of her husband's collected works, which had been published by the same house, that of Chapman and Hall, the year before.

In December Mrs. Browning notes an interesting visitor at Casa Guidi : Goethe's grandson, who had come to Florence on purpose to discuss the character of Paracelsus with his English interpreter.   Now, too, Browning was persuaded by his wife to know Mrs. Trollope, whose son's impression of him has been quoted.   At first he resisted the idea strenuously, because this lady had written against Liberalism and the poetry of Victor Hugo; but in the end he gave way, and found no reason to regret his placability.

In the meanwhile neither husband nor wife could tolerate the idea of allowing another year to pass without seeing the familiar faces of their nearest and dearest. The spring of 1851 found them discussing schemes of travel. They let their rooms in Casa Guidi, and this was a material help. They talked of going southward first, to Rome and Naples; but this part of the plan was dropped, as being too ambitious. Venice should make up for Rome; and for Venice, which was to be the first halt on their homeward journey, they at last set out. They travelled by *vettura* in company with Mr. and Mrs. David Ogilvy, whose acquaintance they had made during their first year at Florence.

We may trace their progress in Mrs. Browning's letters, may see their gondola cutting its all but silent way to the Lido; may picture them in the Venetian opera-house, or at their coffee in the Piazza San Marco, in a setting of "music and the stars." To Mrs. Browning Venice was a veritable city of enchantment. Here they stayed a month, and might have stayed longer, had not the climate proved unsuitable to Browning, depriving him of sleep and appetite. They spent a night at Padua, that they might visit Arqua, the last abiding-place of Petrarch; thence through Brescia, "in a flood of moonlight," to Milan; thence to the lakes and across the St. Gothard to Flüelen, the snow-walls seeming to overhang the coach on either side as they crossed the pass, though it was midsummer. Beautiful as Como and Maggiore were, the lake of Lucerne delighted them even more. Paris was at last reached by way of Strasburg, the distance between the two places being traversed in four and twenty hours of almost unbroken travel. Here they accidentally met Tennyson, who was starting with his wife on that Italian journey which later formed the subject of his poem *The Daisy*. One may speculate whether they touched upon the laureateship, to which Tennyson had lately been appointed, while the *Athenæum* had canvassed Mrs. Browning's claims, and no one had advanced her husband's! He pressed them to occupy his house at Twickenham, and though this kind offer was not accepted, it formed another link in a true friendship between

N

the poets.[1]   The Brownings remained in Paris for several weeks, and late in July, after an absence of nearly five years, they stood on English ground once more.

---

[1] This meeting in Paris is the earliest recorded. "Mr. Browning," runs the account in *Tennyson, a Memoir*, vol. i. p. 341, "already my father's friend, was affectionate as ever." "The brother poets," states an unimpeachable authority, "were very fond of one another."

CHAPTER XI

WORK AND PLAY

London hospitalities—Winter in Paris—Carlyle as fellow-traveller—Louis Napoleon—Mrs. Browning's enthusiasm—George Sand—Joseph Milsand's article on Browning's poetry—Browning's preface to the Shelley letters—Milsand's influence perceptible—Occasion of Browning's first meeting with Milsand—Their great friendship—Visit to London—Return to Florence—" Hermit life " there—Frederick Tennyson—Robert Lytton —*Men and Women* foreshadowed—*Colombe's Birthday* at the Haymarket—With the Storys at the Baths of Lucca—and at Rome—The studios in Rome—Browning sits to Page and Fisher—Hatty Hosmer astonishes the Romans—The Kemble sisters—The Thackerays—Lockhart—Picnics on the Campagna—Return to Florence—Mrs. Browning seriously ill—*Men and Women* ready for publication—Homeward once more.

NOTHING could have been heartier than the welcome given by the London world of letters to the poet who had vanished from its midst so unexpectedly,

" Like a ghost at break of day."

It was natural that Browning's old friends should crowd about him, equally so that they should, desire to see and know that other poet whose life was now bound up in his, who to most of them had hitherto been a name and a voice. Invitations poured in upon the Brownings at 26, Devonshire Street, where they were lodged. Forster gave a dinner in their honour at Thames Ditton ; Rogers invited them to breakfast ; they spent an evening with Carlyle. Arnould wanted them to share his house ; " Barry Cornwall " called repeatedly, and Mrs. Jameson forsook her proofs for their company, though the printers clamoured. Miss Haworth, whose society at once proved congenial to the wife of her old friend, lent her books on mesmerism and Swedenborg. A couple of days were spent at Hatcham, that Mrs. Browning might make acquaintance with her husband's family and show them her son.   How a child, by the way, may soften literary judgments, is shown by a letter which Browning wrote about this time to William Cox Bennett, who sent him his *Poems* published the year before.   He had previously slighted Bennett's muse,[1] while recognizing his good-nature ; now his tone is altered.   " Your poems," he writes, " have abundant evidence of the right spirit, and some of the child-pictures go to our very hearts in their truth and beauty, now that we have a child of our own." [2]   As to Browning's father, child-lover that he was, his grandson went to *his* heart at once, where there was room for his new daughter too.   Browning, for his part, had to make acquaintance with his wife's brothers, whose umbrage now disappeared.

Arabel Barrett was a daily visitor, and Mrs. Surtees Cook came up for a week from Somersetshire to be near her sister. Browning found himself delighted with England, and would willingly have prolonged his stay ; but it soon became apparent that the climate was unsuitable to his wife, whose spirits, too, were depressed by the near neighbourhood yet estrangement of her father.   Already the possibility of wintering in Paris had been discussed ; and for Paris, on the twenty-fifth of September, they set out.

Whatever Browning's regrets on leaving London, it can hardly be denied that the Champs Elysées is a more agreeable locality than Devonshire Street.   They occupied an apartment at No. 138, on the sunshiny side of that avenue, for which, strange to say, they paid no more than they did for the very inferior accommodation in London.   Carlyle, who was bound for Paris on a visit to the Ashburtons, was their travelling companion, and it is worth remarking that the philosopher left the poet to struggle with porters and *douaniers ;* but his conversation, on several ensuing evenings, made full amends.   Nor was Browning, on Carlyle's departure, cut off from the kind of society which he enjoyed.   He had brought letters of introduction to the Elgins, where they

---

[1] *Letters of Robert Browning and Elizabeth Barrett Browning,* vol. ii. pp. 124, 330, 389.
[2] *Letters from Robert Browning to Various Correspondents,* edited by Thomas J. Wise, *Second Series,* vol. i. p. 12.

met Madame Mohl, to George Sand (this Mazzini gave), and to several leading Parisian journalists. At Madame Mohl's, no less than at Lady Elgin's, simplicity was the prevailing note. It was her ambition, which she realized, to carry on the tradition of the Salonières. A woman of character as well as cleverness, she received on Wednesday afternoons and Friday evenings, when her house in the Rue du Bac was thronged by eminent men and women, both native and from foreign capitals. The hostess made tea for her guests, herself boiling the water and making up the fire ; and she won Mrs. Browning's liking, though a pronounced opponent of Louis Napoleon.[1]

It was, indeed, hardly possible to be in Paris at this epoch without taking sides with or against the French President. Signs of reaction were certainly visible in the spring of 1851, and to a whole-hearted supporter of the democracy, such as Mrs. Browning was, Louis Napoleon, with his demand for the restoration of universal suffrage, which the Assembly had then revoked, might well appear the champion of the people's cause. On this account she was ready to forgive the rough treatment meted out to Thiers and Cavaignac, and even to overlook the bloodshed of the *coup d'état*, crime though Victor Hugo justly termed it. She overlooked it for the sake of the gift of universal suffrage, and because its author had, as the subsequent *plébiscite* showed, the approval of the vast majority of his countrymen. So, when on the fateful day he rode under the Brownings' window at the head of the troops, in avowed defiance of the Constitution, he had at least one English well-wisher there, for, so Mrs. Browning held, " he rode there in the name of the people, after all." Browning regarded him in a very different light. He mistrusted him from the first. It is, however, convenient for the present to defer consideration of his view of the third Napoleon's career, which was to be set forth twenty years later in *Prince Hohenstiel-Schwangau, Saviour of Society.*

In their admiration of the talents of George Sand, and their

---

[1] See *Madame Mohl : her Salon and her Friends,* by K. O'Meara. Of Lady Elgin, Mrs. Browning writes in 1858 :—" Her salon was one of the most agreeable in Paris, and she herself, with her mixture of learning and simplicity, one of the most interesting persons in it."

wish to know her, husband and wife were quite at one.   The
visit was at last accomplished, and afterwards repeated.
Browning also met the authoress on four other occasions.
There is no record of her conversation, but it seems to have
been oracular in nature, directed mostly to certain young
Frenchmen who hung upon her utterances, and was concerned
with topics of no special interest to her English visitors.
During their second call she said so little that Browning
observed that "if any other mistress of a house had behaved
so, he would have walked out of the room."   As it was, he
saw that no incivility was intended.   On the contrary, they
were informed that she "liked them very much."   Both, however, and Browning in particular, deplored the kind of society
—"the ragged Red diluted with the lower theatrical "[1]—in
which she moved ; and it is evident that they found her by
no means so attractive as her writings.

This was a mere episode ; more valuable, beyond all
comparison, and the happiest outcome of their first sojourn in
Paris, was their acquisition of the friendship of M. Joseph
Milsand.   With him of all men, it appears, Browning was in
the most complete moral and intellectual accord ; it was of
him that he wrote to Miss Blagden, twenty years later, "no
words can express the love I have for him, you know : he is
increasingly precious to me " ;[2] and it was to his memory that
he dedicated, in 1887, his penultimate volume of poems, with
the touching inscription, *Absens absentem auditque videtque*.[3]

Though Joseph Milsand's family had been settled at Dijon
for upwards of a century and a half, he had some dash of
British blood ; for his ancestor had migrated to Dijon from
New England in 1718.   His admiration for English literature
and institutions may conceivably be referred to his descent.
While studying Italian masterpieces, with the design of
becoming a painter, he made acquaintance with Ruskin's
works, and became more interested in the canons of art than
in its productions.   A born thinker, he gave up the brush
for the pen, and in a volume called *L'Esthétique Anglaise*
sought to familiarize his countrymen with Ruskin's theories.

---

[1] The words, it should be noted, are Mrs. Browning's ; see her *Letters*, vol. ii.
p. 63.

[2] Quoted in Mrs. Orr's *Life*, p. 293.   [3] Virgil, Aeneid IV, l. 83.

Concurrently he abandoned the Roman Catholicism in which he had been brought up, and became, says his son-in-law, M. Blanc, "engrossed with the problems of the soul and its relations to a Creator. Gradually and unawares he invented for himself Protestantism."[1] It is easy to see how much such a man and Browning would have in common. From Ruskin, Milsand passed on to contemporary English poets, and began to publish in the *Revue des Deux Mondes* a series of articles on English poetry since Byron. Tennyson was the subject of the first article, Browning of the second ; and it happened that the latter appeared in the *Revue* in August, 1851, the month before the Brownings went to Paris.[2]

The criticism of a foreigner, at once searching and sympathetic, could not but gratify a poet who had met with a very mixed reception from the reviewers of his own country. Browning found himself commended for originality, imagination and intellectual courage, as one capable above all other poets known to the writer of clothing the religious, ethical, and speculative ideas of the time in fit poetic raiment. His work was described as pervaded by an intense belief in the importance of the individual soul, by an aspiration as high as that of his own *Paracelsus*, and a determination (here we seem to be anticipating Brother Lippo's creed) to explore the higher possibilities of human life. Noteworthy as this appreciation is, and highly as Browning must have valued it, the paper contains other passages which, from an effect that they produced, are of even greater interest. At the very time of the *coup d'état* Browning was writing for Moxon a preface to a volume of Shelley's letters, hitherto unpublished. The letters turned out to be spurious and were withdrawn from circulation ; but Browning's preface remains, at once a tribute to the memory and the genius of Shelley and a statement of his own poetic faith. Now, if Milsand's article and Browning's essay be compared, it is almost impossible to doubt that the latter was in some degree inspired by the former.

[1] Quoted in *A French Friend of Browning*, by Th. Bentzon, from which these particulars are derived.

[2] His attention is said to have been in the first instance directed to Browning's poetry by Mrs. Fraser Corkran, a cultivated Englishwoman resident in Paris.

That one may absorb and at a later date unconsciously reproduce the thoughts of others is commonly admitted ; similarly, these may enable us, again without our realizing it, to formulate our own.   To suppose that Browning was thus influenced in the present case is not to belittle in the slightest degree his reasoning powers.   If the chemistry of another's thought enabled the ideas which were floating in his mind to crystallize, those ideas are not the less his own. It is surely one of the proper functions of the critical process that it should help the creative imagination to fructify, instead of hindering it, as brutality and ignorance, masquerading as criticism, have so often done.   That bastard criticism Browning evidently understood.   " The *E pur si muove* of the astronomer," he writes, "was as bitter a word as any uttered before or since by a poet over his rejected living work, in that depth of conviction which is so like despair."   But Milsand's was of a different order.   The theory of poetry which he shadowed forth was apprehended, amplified and defined by Browning.   Thus, in Milsand's estimate of Browning as primarily and most preciously an introspective poet, secondarily an artist or " maker," there lurks the germ of Browning's doctrine that there are two kinds of poetry, the subjective and the objective, of which the first is infinitely the higher. Again, " Browning's explorations," wrote his reviewer, " are adventures of the intellect ; his faculties expend themselves *within.*"   " The subjective poet," says Browning,

" digs in his own soul, as the nearest reflex of that absolute mind, according to the intuitions of which he desires to perceive and speak."

This is his central argument, upon which he proceeds to enlarge, applying it to Shelley's genius.

" His noblest characteristic," he says, " I call his simultaneous perception of Power and Love in the absolute, and of beauty and good in the concrete, while he throws, from his poet station between both, swifter, subtler and more numerous films for the connection of each with each than have been thrown by any modern artificer of whom I have knowledge.[1] . . . I would rather consider Shelley's poetry as a

[1] Here, again, is a curious similarity of phrase.   "C'est un jeu pour lui," Milsand wrote of Browning, "de distinguer les rapports qui unissent les choses

sublime fragmentary essay towards a presentment of the correspondency of the universe to Deity, of the natural to the spiritual, and of
the actual to the ideal than I would isolate and separately appraise
the worth of many detachable portions which might be acknowledged
as utterly perfect in a lower moral point of view, under the mere
conditions of art. . . . It would be easy to take my stand on successful instances of objectivity in Shelley, the unrivalled *Cenci*,
Julian and Maddolo, etc., but I prefer to look for the highest attainment, not simply the high, and seeing it I hold by it."

Here, then, is Browning's idea of what is loftiest in poetry.
Anything more unlike the doctrine of "art for art's sake" it
would be difficult to conceive. It was the "subjective" poet
that he revered in Shelley ; it was "subjectivity," we may
infer, to which he himself desired, as a poet, to attain.

Further, this highest kind of poetry, he argues, can only
issue from a pure source, being an effluence rather than a
production ; and we cannot love it without loving the source
from whence it came. Shelley the man, as well as Shelley
the poet, still retained the homage of his early worshipper.
We see this as late as the *Memorabilia* of 1855.[1] It was
therefore a real grief to Browning when he learnt, some three
years later, the facts as to Shelley's treatment of his first
wife. He had his information from Thomas Hookham, jun.,
a bookseller and friend of Shelley, who showed him letters
which he had himself received from Harriet Shelley.

These, in particular the one which she wrote in a state of
bewilderment, inquiring where her husband might be, satisfied him that the version of the affair hitherto accepted was
no longer tenable. It was apparent that husband and wife
had not parted by mutual consent, but that he had deserted
her. This discovery caused Browning deep regret. He
considered Shelley to have been, at that period of his life,
"half crazy and wholly inexcusable." He could not regard
him or, by consequence, his poetry, in the same light as

disseminées a tous les coins de l'infini, et qui vont de l'une à l'autre comme des
fils."

[1] Browning might, of course, have known many persons who had seen and
spoken with Shelley. Indeed, he was acquainted with several of his intimates,
Leigh Hunt and Trelawney among others. He saw Trelawney at Leghorn in
1844, in the course of his second Italian journey.

formerly.[1]   Yet Lucifer, Son of the Morning, lost not all his
brightness in his fall.   For Browning, Shelley's proud pre-
eminence was gone ; but he loved his poetry, and loved to
read it aloud, to the end of his days.

It was in January, 1852, when Paris was recovering her
normal serenity, that Browning first met Milsand.   The
occasion was as follows.   Miss Mitford, Mrs. Browning's
intimate friend, had just published her *Recollections of a
Literary Life*.   The book contained a chapter on the Brownings' poetry which would have given them pleasure, had not
the authoress seen fit to add an account of the accident
which robbed Mrs. Browning of her favourite brother.   To
this tragedy Mrs. Browning, to the end of her life, could
hardly bear the slightest reference ; when, therefore, she
accidentally heard of her friend's indiscretion, which had
made her sorrow public property, she was acutely distressed.
She did not disguise her feelings from Miss Mitford, who
hastened to express the deepest regret ; and it is creditable
to the two women that their friendship survived what might,
had either's nature been less generous, have wrecked it.
Meanwhile Milsand was writing an article on Mrs. Browning's
poetry ; and his editor furnished him with a copy of the
Athenæum containing, in the course of a review, the unlucky
passage.   The details, he thought, might be of service.   But
Milsand's finer nature felt instinctively that their inclusion
might be a source of pain, and he came to Browning to ask
for guidance.   The article appeared in due course, without—
need it be said ?—a single word which could offend.   The
sensibility and sympathy displayed in this matter by the
French critic was the straighest way to Robert Browning's
heart ; and the intimacy of the two men grew apace.

In the previous November Browning's father and sister
had paid him a visit of some weeks' duration.   In the April
of this year their lease of the Hatcham house expired, and
they decided to make a new home in Paris.   Browning had
the satisfaction of seeing them settled in an apartment before
his own stay in Paris ended.   There lived until recent years
those who recalled the kindness of the elder Browning to them

---

[1] See Wise, *ut supra*, vol. ii. pp. 25–26 and 49–50, and *Second Series*, vol. i.
pp. 86–89.

in their childhood, and how they were fascinated by the weird caricatures he drew ; who have written of his keen interest in crime and criminals, and of his delight in some old volume picked up at a bookstall for a few sous, absorbed in which he would become wholly oblivious of the lapse of time and the advent of the dinner-hour.[1]

The idea of returning to Florence before the ensuing winter set in now began to be canvassed ; but in the meanwhile the poet and his wife wished to see more of their English friends. Accordingly, they migrated to London at the end of June, and took up their quarters at 58, Welbeck Street. Mrs. Surtees Cook was lodging some twenty doors off, and Miss Arabel Barrett, in Wimpole Street, was a near neighbour. It is again a story of many social engagements. At Kenyon's house at Wimbledon they met Landor, who delighted Mrs. Browning by expressing a high opinion of Louis Napoleon's talents. Browning told Domett, long afterwards, that Landor wrote, though leaving it unpublished, an *Imaginary Conversation* in which she was one of the interlocutors. Was it at that meeting, one wonders, as her enthusiasm caught fire and she answered him in her low, impressive tones, that he conceived the idea ? Invitations to the country poured in upon the Brownings, but only one was accepted. It took them to Farnham, whither a year later Tennyson went house-hunting. Their visit was made memorable by a meeting with Charles Kingsley, whose " Christian Socialism " seemed to Mrs. Browning, with her strong individualist proclivities, " wild and theoretical " ; but the man himself they liked immensely. Another first meeting was with Mazzini, brought to their lodgings by Mrs. Carlyle ; another was with D. G. Rossetti, who came in William Allingham's company; another was with Ruskin ; yet another, on 5 September, with Hallam Tennyson, the poet laureate's son, who had come into the world some three weeks earlier. On the day of the christening Browning held the baby for some ten minutes. He tossed the child in his arms, so he told

---

[1] See Lady Ritchie's *Records of Tennyson*, etc.; and Miss H. Corkran's *Celebrities and I.* That love of the grotesque which so often is visible in the son's poetry was clearly an inheritance from the father.

Domett, and Tennyson, who was looking on, remarked, " Ah, that is as good as a glass of champagne to him ! " [1]

But the days were shortening, Mrs. Browning began to droop in the autumnal air and her husband consequently to be anxious. It was probably without reluctance that, early in November, they set out for Italy. A halt was called in Paris, and once more fortune favoured Mrs. Browning ; for from the balcony of Mr. Fraser Corkran, Paris correspondent of the *Morning Chronicle*, who had an apartment in the Rue Basse des Remparts, Boulevard des Italiens, they witnessed Louis Napoleon's progress through the city. This was almost immediately before he took the title of Emperor. He rode alone, ten paces in advance of his escort, thereby wringing from Miss Cushman, the American actress, who sat by Mrs. Browning, the reluctant admission, " That's fine, I must say." It may be added that Mrs. Browning's son showed himself no less enthusiastic for Napoleon than was his mother.

The route chosen for the passage of the Alps (from motives of economy) was the Mont Cenis. But the cold was excessive, and Mrs. Browning became so unwell that a week's stay at Genoa was imperative. At Turin it had been December, but in Genoa it was June ; warmth proved a restorative, and the party reached their journey's end in safety.

There was a delightful homeliness about Casa Guidi, where everything looked as if they had left it the day before. To Mrs. Browning there was no place like Florence ; and if to her husband it seemed dull at first, after the crowded sociability of London and the life and variety of Parisian boulevards, yet the old fascination was not slow to reassert itself. " You can't think," writes Mrs. Browning to Miss Blagden, " how we have caught up our ancient traditions just where we left them, and relapsed into our former soundless, stirless hermit life." [2] Certainly since they left Florence

---

[1] From Domett's *Diary*. The story is also told by a writer in the *Journal of Education*, 1 February, 1881, by way of commentary on Tennyson's dedication of his *Ballads and other Poems* (1880) to his grandson, where the child is described as " Crazy with laughter and babble and *earth's new wine.*"

[2] *Letters of E. B. B.*, vol. ii. p. 99.

sixteen months earlier the life they led had not been favourable to composition ; but now, with the recaptured quiet, the impetus returned. On 24 February, 1853, Browning writes a long letter to Milsand. "We live wholly alone here," he says. "I have not left the house one evening since our return. I am writing—a first step towards popularity for me—lyrics with more music and painting than before, so as to get people to hear and see . . . Something to follow, if I can compass it." These words foreshadow the *Men and Women* of 1855, which can yield precedence to none other of his works save *The Ring and the Book*. Some of his "fifty Men and Women" were already in existence. *Love among the Ruins, Women and Roses,* and *Childe Roland* are said to have been composed in Paris on three successive days, the 1st, 2nd, and 3rd January, 1852 ; and it is reasonable, as we have seen, to suppose a still earlier date for *The Guardian Angel. Old Pictures in Florence* may well have now been written. The Grand Duke had embarked on a course of repression, his subjects were in despair, and Browning, whose sympathies were entirely with them, has his fling at him in this poem ; for Leopold is to be identified with "a certain dotard" whom the writer would rejoice to see pitched "to the worse side of the Mont Saint Gothard." Meanwhile Mrs. Browning had begun to write *Aurora Leigh.*

The remark about loneliness is, of course, comparative, as this same letter to Milsand shows. "I have a new acquaintance here, much to my taste," it goes on, "Tennyson's elder brother, a very earnest, simple, and truthful man, with many admirable talents and acquirements. He is very shy. He sees next to no company, but comes here and we walk together."[1] This was Frederick Tennyson, poet and musician, who was humorously but with exaggeration reported to sit in the large hall of his villa in the Fiesole Road "in the midst of his forty fiddlers."[2] He, in his turn, has drawn Browning's portrait with a few happy strokes : "a man of infinite learning, jest, and bonhommie, and, moreover, a sterling heart that reverbs no hollowness."[3] These excellent gifts won also the

[1] Quoted in Lady Ritchie's *Records*, etc., p. 205.
[2] *Tennyson, A Memoir*, vol. i. p. 149.
[3] *Ibid.* p. 382.

regard of a young attaché of the Florentine Legation, Robert Lytton, the novelist's son, who shared with a colleague, Henry Drummond Wolff, a small house in the Via Larga (now the Via Cavour).[1] The intimacy with Lytton grew rapidly; he was himself preening his wings for a poetic flight, and dreaming of anything rather than of the viceregal glories which the future held for him.

In April *Colombe's Birthday* was produced at the Haymarket theatre, thus fulfilling the original purpose of its being, though its author was not financially interested in its appearance. Once more, as in the two earlier of his acted plays, the heroine's part was taken by Miss Helen Faucit, to whom the success achieved was largely due. The drama held the boards for a fortnight, and though doubts had been felt as to its power to keep the attention of a mixed audience, they proved unfounded. The *Literary Gazette* spoke of the "close and fascinated attention" of the house, the *Athenæum* recorded "an apparent perfect success on the first night," and the *Examiner* noticed that amid the general applause no jarring notes were to be heard. To the author and his wife, deep in the study of German mystics, or holding converse with the speculative Tennyson and the visionary Lytton, that applause must have sounded faintly, as sounds in the ears of upland harvesters the surf breaking on a distant shore.[2]

At the Baths of Lucca, during three summer months of this year, the same life of thought and composition was led, varied by the enjoyment of such society as was "pleasant, wise, and good." The Brownings did not return to the "eagle's nest" at Bagni Caldi of four years before, but occupied Casa Tolomei at Alla Villa, a house which boasted a spare room (occupied for a time by Robert Lytton), a row of plane trees, and a garden of its own, lit up at night by fireflies. At no great distance lived Mrs. Stisted, "Queen of the Baths," as she was called, whose harmless eccentricities have been chronicled by Trollope.[3] She was a collector of curiosities, and Browning mentions having seen and copied

---

[1] *Rambling Recollections*, by Sir Henry Drummond Wolff, vol. i. p. 149.

[2] The play was also produced, either this or the following year, at the Harvard Athenæum, Boston, U.S.A., with Miss Davenport as Colombe.

[3] *What I Remember*, by T. A. Trollope, vol. ii. ch. 8.

certain variations in one of Shelley's poems, from a manuscript in her possession.[1]

But the most constant associates of the Brownings at this time and place were the sculptor, Story, and his wife. With them they had "a grand donkey-excursion" to the mountain village of Benabbia, and repeated the Prato Fiorito expedition of the earlier year. Long evenings were spent at one another's houses, long days out-of-doors by the banks of Lima or in the chestnut woods, hours filled with reading, sketching, talk, and singing, in whose record there obtrudes only one complaint on Story's part, that Browning did not smoke![2] He found no friend like the poet, he has recorded, with whom to walk "the higher ranges of art and philosophy";[3] putting in prose something of what Lytton had a little earlier expressed in verse, that Browning was one

> " Than whom a mightier master never
>   Touch'd the deep chords of hidden things ;
> Nor error did from truth dissever
> With keener glance ; nor made endeavour
>   To rise on bolder wings
> In those high regions of the soul
>   Where thought itself grows dim with awe."[4]

This, it is arguable, is to claim too much ; but as an expression of contemporary opinion it is at least noteworthy.

It was presumably with reference to the departure of his friends, who had preceded him to Florence, that Browning in October wrote to Story, "This poor place has given up the ghost now, and we really want to get away."[5] At any rate, the Brownings were back in Florence before the month was out, but only for a brief sojourn. For their old ambition of seeing Rome together was now about to be realized.

They travelled by *vettura*, the journey taking eight days, past Assisi, " seeing the great monastery and triple church there," in Mrs. Browning's words, " and the wonderful

---

[1] Wise, *ut supra*, vol. i. p. 47.
[2] *William Wetmore Story*, by Henry James, vol. i. pp. 271–4.
[3] *Ibid*. vol. ii. p. 68.
[4] From the dedication of *The Wanderer*, by "Owen Meredith," 1859
[5] *W. W. Story, ut supra*, vol. i. p. 279.

Terni—that passion of the waters which makes the human heart seem so still." If the last stage of their progress may be taken as an index of the earlier ones, they were certainly a joyous trio, for, writes Mrs. Browning, "in the highest spirits we entered Rome, Robert and Penini [1] singing actually." As for her, we have it on her authority that the only sort of excitement and fatigue which did her no harm was travelling.[2] The Storys, choosing the sea-route from Leghorn to Civita Vecchia, were again the advanced guard, and had secured their friends an apartment at 43, Bocca di Leone, where lighted fires and familiar faces made the new arrivals welcome. But cheer soon gave place to sadness. The very next morning Story's eldest boy was taken ill and died before evening, and his little daughter sickened of gastric fever and was for some time in danger.[3] She recovered; but the sorrow of their friends could not but cast a shadow on the Brownings' earlier impressions of Rome. For Mrs. Browning, indeed, who had witnessed the bereaved mother's grief, and with her had visited the child's grave, the cloud never wholly lifted. "Rome is spoiled to me," she writes; "there's the truth." Besides, she was in an agony of apprehension for Penini; but as time passed and he continued well, the faculty of enjoyment, though its edge was blunted, gradually returned.

England and America were at this period handsomely represented in the artistic and literary life of Rome. There was Crawford, practically the first American sculptor to pitch his tent in Rome, who a few years earlier had borne arms in her defence; there was Gibson, then at the height of his fame, who was described as resembling rather an old Greek than a modern Christian;[4] there was Page, whose compatriots spoke of him as "the American Titian"; there was

---

[1] So their child was called. "Penini," afterwards shortened to Pen, arose from his attempt at pronouncing his second baptismal name, Wiedemann.

[2] *Letters of E. B. B.*, vol. ii. p. 75.

[3] It was to her, during her convalescence after this illness, that Thackeray read aloud "The Rose and the Ring." *Story, ut supra*, vol. i. p. 286.

[4] *Italics*, by F. P. Cobbe. Not the highest type of Greek sculptor, however, for he favoured the heresy of colouring statuary, as his "tinted Venus" proves. "Pity," Crawford's masterpiece, now watches over the grave of his son, F. Marion Crawford, the novelist.

Leighton—"young Leighton of Rome," as Mrs. Browning calls him—who at the age of twenty-three was painting the "Cimabue's Madonna carried in procession through the streets of Florence," which was to make him famous; and many lesser lights. The studios attracted Browning irresistibly. Presently he was sitting to two artists, Page and W. Fisher.[1] Page was unhappily possessed by a theory which time has falsified. Holding that the lapse of years did not tone a picture, he deliberately undertoned his in the first instance. His portrait of Browning, presented by him to the poet's wife and now in Venice, was "the wonder of everybody"; but within two years Browning is found expressing the fear that it is deteriorating. "So it fares," he writes to D. G. Rossetti, "with Page's pictures for the most part; but they are like Flatman the Poet's famous 'Kings' in a great line he wrote—'Kings do not die—they only disappear!'"[2] The words are prophetic; for the colour has not stood, blackness has stolen over the canvas, and the likeness can now barely be discerned.

Our list of artists does not pretend to be exhaustive, but Hatty Hosmer, who was something of a pioneer as well as a sculptor, must not be left out. The name of this young American lady figures repeatedly in the memoirs of the period. A pupil of Gibson, she occupied a studio close to his, and achieved considerable success in her profession. Her "Sleeping Fawn," probably her best work, was sold for £1000. She was clever, hard-working, ready-witted and independent; qualities which speedily won the Brownings' friendship. She has been described, moreover, as "the most bewitching sprite the world ever saw";[3] and she shocked the dignified Romans by insisting on her right to walk alone and ride her horse alone. The latter practice was, indeed, forbidden, on account of the excitement which it caused. "She is an immense favourite with us both," writes Mrs. Browning.

Even greater favourites, however, were the Kemble sisters, as typically English as was Miss Hosmer typically American.

---

[1] A reproduction of Fisher's portrait appears as frontispiece to the second volume of E. B. B.'s *Letters*.

[2] Wise, *ut supra*, vol. i. p. 19.

[3] By Miss F. P. Cobbe, in her *Life*.

o

"Thackeray is here," writes Fanny Kemble,[1] "and the Brownings, so it is not our fault if we are not both witty and poetical." To her "the outside of Rome," as she puts it, "was worth all the inside." She loved to ride or drive over the Campagna, and with a party of intimate friends, Leighton, Ampère (a member of the French Institute), the Brownings, Hatty Hosmer and others, to have luncheon "in the midst of all that was lovely in nature and picturesque in the ruined remains of Roman power," a description that brings to mind the setting of Browning's *Love among the Ruins*.

Thackeray's daughters, who were domiciled hard by in the Via delle Croce, spent many evenings with Mrs. Browning, when her husband was out paying visits. It is one of them, now Lady Ritchie, who has recounted an incident in which the other Kemble sister, Adelaide Sartoris, figures. Mrs. Sartoris, once a *prima donna* in grand opera, was artistic as well as musical, and an excellent hostess. To her house all the best elements of the Anglo-American colony in Rome gravitated. One afternoon she had been reading aloud to several friends from *Christmas Eve and Easter Day*. Upon the reading an eager discussion ensued, in the midst of which the author entered. The disputed passage was referred to him, but he evaded his questioners and turned the conversation. "He never much cared," the narrative ends, "to talk of his own poetry."[2]

To Lockhart, the veteran critic, who had come abroad in search of health, he probably talked, by preference, of any other subject. The two men liked and saw a good deal of one another. Once they spent a day at Frascati together, when, Browning owns, Lockhart's temper "got a pain in it" before the afternoon was over.[3] But allowance had to be made, for

---

[1] *Further Records*, vol. ii. p. 180. Fanny Kemble is described by Mrs. Browning as "looking magnificent still, with her black hair and radiant smile." She was then thirty-eight. Hers, it appears, was a beauty which bade defiance to time. On his way home from calling upon her, thirty-two years later, Browning met Domett; and on Domett's recalling her *Juliet*, and how handsome she used to look, with her great expressive black eyes, "Yes," said Browning, "and how handsome she is still."

[2] *Records of Tennyson, Ruskin, and Browning*, by Lady Ritchie, p. 195. With his intimates, however, he would occasionally do so. See *Robert Browning, Personalia*, by Edmund Gosse, p. 91.

[3] *W. W. Story, ut supra*, vol. i. p. 285.

Lockhart was anything but well. In April he went home to Abbotsford, and died before the year was out.

Old friends were met in Rome as well as new acquaintances made: Geraldine Bate, now become Mrs. Macpherson, and, seen again after half a score of years, M. de Ripert-Monclar, to whom *Paracelsus* was dedicated, who would admit no change in the appearance of his former comrade. Something must be allowed for Gallic complaisance, for Browning had shaved his beard on the morning of his arrival in Rome, and when it grew again it was tinged with grey.[1] The Marshalls claimed acquaintance as friends of Tennyson, Lady Oswald as Lady Elgin's sister-in-law; certainly there was no lack of sociability.

But Penini, to whose lot a goodly number of children's parties had fallen, became ill and lost his roses; and his need of change chimed in with Mrs. Browning's own preference for Florence. Thither, in the later days of May, 1854, they returned, again enjoying the *vettura* journey. They had intended to visit England this year, but the financial fates forbade, rendering impracticable even a summer flight to the mountains. But there were compensations. Penini recovered his roses, and there was " no place in the world like Florence, after all." At Rome their plan had been "to work and play by turns," but the social claims of the place proved exacting, and work hardly got its fair share. "I am trying," Browning writes to Story on the eleventh of June, "to make up for wasted time in Rome by setting my poetical house in order."[2] Once more, accordingly, the "hermit life" was resumed, upon which other hermits, Lytton and Frederick Tennyson in particular, were licensed to intrude. Not, we gather, in the mornings, for then husband and wife sat down regularly after breakfast, in different rooms, to write poetry.[3] As the winter drew on—the Crimean winter—Browning, like many another Englishman, was full of intense wrath at the mismanagement which condemned our troops to avoidable sufferings. With the new year he had a trouble that touched

---

[1] " It grew *white*," his wife writes. But in Fisher's portrait there appears the merest dash of grey.

[2] *W. W. Story, ut supra*, vol. i. p. 288.

[3] Lady Ritchie's *Records*, etc., *ut supra*.

him more nearly, for his wife fell ill with the worst chest attack she had so far experienced in Italy. Nursed devotedly by her husband, she weathered the storm; but her recovery found her the poorer by the loss of her great friend and constant correspondent, Miss Mitford, who died in January.

At the approach of summer the homeward journey was at last feasible. Browning had "set his poetical house in order" to some purpose, for his *Men and Women*, save only the *One Word More*, was finished. Good progress, also, had been made with *Aurora Leigh*. So, in the second week in June, 1855, they arrived in London once more, "bringing their sheaves with them."

CHAPTER XII
LATER MARRIED YEARS

Men and Women—Personal utterances—Sources of certain of the poems—Inadequate recognition—Spiritualism—Mrs. Browning a believer —Her husband's attitude—D. D. Home—Séance at Ealing—Browning's anger—Tennyson and *Maud*—Migration to Paris—Mrs. Browning's last stay in London—A family group at Ventnor—*Aurora Leigh*—Deaths of John Kenyon and Mr. Barrett—Mrs. Browning's sorrow—Her anxieties at Bagni di Lucca—Visit to Paris and Havre—A stormy passage— Alarmist rumours—Florence—Rome—High hopes for Italy—Napoleon's intervention—Victories of Magenta and Solferino—Armistice of Villafranca—Mrs. Browning's disappointment and illness—Browning undertakes the care of Landor—With the Storys at Siena—*Poems before Congress*—Death of Mrs. Browning's sister—Browning modelling in Story's studio—Declining health of Mrs. Browning—Her grief at Cavour's death—Her own death at Florence.

THE waning summer moon

" born late in Florence
Dying now impoverished here in London," [1]

found the Brownings settled at 13, Dorset Street, where *One Word More*, the Epilogue to *Men and Women*, was composed. There is no answering dimness in the devotion which illumines this poem with so uniform and clear a light. For once Browning speaks in his own " true person." Something of what his wife was to him is here manifested ; more, imagination aiding, is to be inferred. He has limned her outward semblance also ; for it is she who in *By the Fireside* sits

" Musing by firelight, that great brow
And the spirit-small hand propping it : "

[1] *One Word More*, Stanza 17.

and, slight as the sketch is, it is both in itself crowded with suggestion, and superlatively valuable because of its origin.

Men and Women, appearing in two volumes towards the close of this year 1855, must have been especially welcome to those readers whom the earlier *Dramatic Lyrics* and *Romances* had captivated.   To Fox, his first literary mentor, Browning read the proofs.   The new poems, both in subjects and treat-ment, are closely akin to the old.   It is a case rather of development than of difference ; the range has widened and the depth of thought is more consistent.   This kinship their author himself recognized ; for in the next issue of his collected works, that of 1863, the three series are intermingled and their contents redistributed, an arrangement maintained, with slight alterations, in all subsequent editions.

The clearly personal utterances of *The Guardian Angel* and *One Word More* need to be supplemented by the story told in *By the Fireside,* where the veil of disguise is of the slightest.   It is only natural to believe that the wonderful description of the coming of love therein contained was rooted in the poet's own experience ; though the scene has been shifted from London to a gorge in the Apennines.   Just such a ruined chapel as that of the poem lies beside the mountain path to Prato Fiorito ; and by it the Brownings had passed in pleasant company, two summers earlier.   Story's account of the expedition serves to identify the spot.   "After climbing an hour," he writes, "we arrived at a little old church near which the view was magnificent." [1]

Elsewhere in these volumes the poet prefers, as is his manner, to be "dramatic," to speak

"as Lippo, Roland or Andrea."

Cleon, the completed *Saul,* an *Epistle,* and *Bishop Blougram's Apology* may be regarded as offshoots of that deeper mood which had abundantly blossomed in *Christmas Eve and Easter Day,* though they are by no means charged with his latest thoughts on Christianity.   *Childe Roland* is, like *The Flight of the Duchess,* pure romance.   The story is quite in keeping with *Edgar's* whirling words, and is invested with no small measure of that horror which pervades *King Lear.   There,* it

[1] *W. W. Story, ut supra,* vol. i. p. 273.

may be submitted, lies the true inspiration of the poem.[1] *The Twins*, on the contrary, originated from sympathy with hard realities. Written with a charitable object, it had appeared in print a year earlier. It came out, between the same covers with Mrs. Browning's *Plea for the Ragged Schools of London*, in pamphlet form, and was sold at a bazaar promoted by Miss Arabel Barrett in aid of a refuge for young destitute girls which she had founded ; " the first of its kind, I believe," Browning wrote in 1882, "and still in existence."[2]

Many of the "Men and Women" are of no particular age or country ; but in those cases where an episode of some soul's history is given a local habitation, Italy easily predominates. There is but one glimpse, in *De Gustibus*, of scenery peculiarly English ; to modern Paris is allotted *Respectability*, to mediæval Paris *The Heretic's Tragedy ;* while at least thirteen poems have an Italian setting. Of these Venice claims one, *A Toccata of Galuppi's ;* Rome two, *Holy-Cross Day* and *Two in the Campagna ;* Florence four, *Fra Lippo Lippi, Andrea del Sarto, The Statue and the Bust*, and *Old Pictures ;* while three, *By the Fireside, Up at a Villa*, and *A Serenade at the Villa*, the two last in descending degrees of probability, may be ascribed to the Bagni di Lucca country. Fano and Ancona have, as we have seen, their tribute ; while the

> " castle, precipice-encurled,
> In a gash of the wind-grieved Apennine,"

and the

> " sea-side house to the farther South,
> Where the baked cicala dies of drouth,"

of *De Gustibus* are such recurrent types that it were rash to attempt to fix their identity. But it is at least curious to observe the proportion maintained in the distribution of these poems, where Florence, the author's chief abiding-place in Italy, gets the largest share, and the rest in their several

---

[1] This suggestion is offered not without knowledge of Mrs. Orr's comment (*Handbook*, p. 274), which mentions as contributory causes a tower seen in the Carrara mountains, a painting observed in Paris, and the figure of a horse in a piece of tapestry in the poet's own house.
[2] Wise, *ut supra*, vol. ii. p. 6.

degrees. It is mostly to the Italian poems, too, that belong certain fragments of literary history, which deserve remembrance. Of especial interest is the genesis of *Andrea del Sarto*. The facts upon which this poem is a commentary are beyond dispute. The "faultless painter," dragged backwards by weakness of character, strongly appealed to Browning's imagination ; but the match which fired the train was a portrait of Andrea and his wife, painted by the artist himself, which hangs in the Pitti palace. Kenyon had asked Browning to procure him a copy of this picture. None was to be had ; so Browning wrote his *Andrea del Sarto*, and sent it to his friend instead, who, it is to be hoped, this time found the poetry neither "muddy" nor "metaphysical"! Again, Lippo's "Coronation of the Virgin," which is in the Academia delle Belle Arti at Florence, cannot be dissociated from *Fra Lippo Lippi*, being, in fact, the very painting whose execution is foreshadowed at the close of that poem. Lippo figures in one of the *Imaginary Conversations* of Walter Savage Landor, of whose writings Browning was a consistent admirer ; " I know no finer reading than Landor," he once said.[1] But his treatment of the subject is all his own, and nowhere is one article of his artistic creed more cogently expressed :—

> " The world's no blot for us,
> Nor blank, it means intensely and means good ;
> To find its meaning is my meat and drink."[2]

A French critic (M. Etienne) questioned the poet's accuracy in making Fra Lippo the Master and Masaccio (called *Guidi* in the poem) the pupil, but Browning defended his opinion. The point, in fact, was and remains a moot one. Somewhat similarly a writer in the *Daily News* of 20 November, 1874, denied the existence of "the doctrine of the enclitic *De*" ; but him Browning easily overthrew on the authority of Curtius and Buttmann. On the other hand, a couple of minute errors escaped his notice. In *Transcendentalism* the celebrated mystic was accidentally described as " Swedish Boehme," " German " being substituted in later editions ;[3] and in *One*

[1] Lady Ritchie, *ut supra*, p. 239.

[2] Similarly in the *Introduction* to the Shelley letters, he had written: "The world is not to be learned and thrown aside, but to be reverted to and re-learned."

[3] Browning's attention was apparently not called to this error until 1866. He

Word More the name Karshook crept in where Karshish was intended. This mistake arose very naturally. In 1854 Browning wrote a couple of brief poems (twenty lines in all) called *Ben Karshook's Wisdom*, which appeared in *The Keepsake*—it was the era of "annuals" and "books of beauty"—two years afterwards, and the similarity of the two names begat confusion. "*Karshish* is the proper word," he wrote, in 1881, "referring as it does to him of the 'Epistle.'" Not only did he not include *Ben Karshook's Wisdom* in any edition of his works, but he seems to have disliked the lines, speaking of them as "the snarling verses I remember to have written, but forget for whom."[1]

Packed as they are with observation, thought, and humour, a pageant as vivid and as various as life itself, the two volumes of *Men and Women* failed to win anything like an adequate recognition from the public or the critics. There were, of course, exceptions, and the few who, like D. G. Rossetti, W. Bell Scott, and Robert Lytton, did admire them, felt the enthusiasm of devotees.[2] But Browning's conquests extended as yet over a very narrow territory. A generation which absorbed four editions of the poems of Alexander Smith, that light of the "spasmodic" school, in as many years, asked for no re-issue of *Men and Women*. To the end of Browning's Florentine days, we are assured, the society which surrounded him did not consider him a great poet, or the equal of his wife.[3]

Of published criticisms that of Milsand (*Revue Contemporaire*, September, 1856) was again the most appreciative and the most instructive. The sharp distinction between what is subjective and objective in poetry may more easily be maintained in theory than exemplified in practice. This Browning must himself have recognized, in any consideration

explained to a correspondent that he had been disturbed when at work on the poem by an accident to his wife's maid. Wise, *ut supra, Second Series*, vol. i. p. 17.

[1] Wise, *ut supra*, vol. i. p. 71. They are undeniably forcible, however. See Appendix A.

[2] "Blougram's Apology," wrote W. Bell Scott to W. M. Rossetti, "and the Syrian Doctor's letter are beyond all inventions he has yet done." *Ruskin, Rossetti, Preraphaelitism : Papers*, 1854–1862, p. 134 ; edited by W. M. Rossetti.

[3] *Life of F. P. Cobbe, by Herself*, ch. xiv. Miss Cobbe could not, she says, read his poetry.

of his *Men and Women* as a whole ; and his critic shrewdly offers a very probable explanation of the working, in this matter, of the poet's mind. "Mr. Browning," he writes, "sympathizes equally with both sources of inspiration, and I am inclined to think that his constant endeavour has been to reconcile and combine them, so as to be, not in turn, but simultaneously, lyrical and dramatic, subjective and objective. . . . His poetry would have us conceive of the inner significance of things by making us see their exteriors." Thus it appears, on comparing this passage with Milsand's earlier estimate, that the poet has developed, and the critic with him.

One other review of these volumes which appeared in the Roman Catholic *Rambler* of January, 1856, must be noticed. Browning admitted years afterwards to Gavan Duffy, his early admirer, that Bishop Blougram was intended to suggest Cardinal Wiseman, the first Roman Catholic Archbishop of Westminster.[1] He would not allow the validity of Duffy's contention that the Cardinal had been treated ungenerously ; nor need Wiseman himself be supposed to have felt any resentment, for the article in the *Rambler* is quite good-natured, and it is his. True there is something about its concluding words which reminds us of the position of the scorpion's sting. "If Mr. Browning is a man of will and action, and not a mere dreamer and talker, *we should never feel surprise at his conversion.*"

"Try, will our table turn ?" says the speaker in *A Lover's Quarrel.* It had refused to turn at Casa Guidi in 1853, when the Brownings and Lytton tried the experiment; but "we were impatient," writes Mrs. Browning, "and Robert was playing Mephistopheles, as Mr. Lytton says." Spiritualism crossed the Atlantic in the fifties, and became the rage in the chief cities of Europe. To Mrs. Browning and many of her friends in Florence the prospect of intercourse with departed spirits, whether expressing themselves by rapping upon tables or otherwise, was of supreme moment. Enthusiasm paralyzed, for a time at any rate, their critical faculty. With Browning

[1] *My Life in Two Hemispheres*, by Gavan Duffy, vol. ii. p. 258. Wiseman was a man of very varied intellectual interests. He wrote and lectured on social, literary, and artistic subjects, and always got a deservedly attentive hearing.

it was otherwise. He was a difficult subject, in fact, for any sort of "conversion"; nor was he the more amenable for the discovery, later on, that one of his Florentine friends, the artist Seymour Kirkup, whom he mentions in *Pacchiarotto*, one of the most simple-minded of learned men, had been grossly taken in by a supposed "medium." Sturdily, but with complete good-humour, he maintained an attitude of scepticism; as, for example, at Lytton's villa at Bellosguardo, whither the attaché had migrated after the marriage and departure from Florence of his house-mate, Drummond Wolff, when his host, Frederick Tennyson, Powers, Mrs. Browning, and others were all arrayed against him. He was, however, interested, if sceptical; and, when an opportunity for further investigation presented itself, he was not the man to decline it.

It happened that there arrived in England in 1855, a couple of months before the Brownings' return, one Daniel D. Home, the most noted of the American mediums. Home speedily became a lion. His séances were attended by such men as Lord Brougham, Sir David Brewster, the Lyttons, father and son, and, at a later date, the fourth Lord Dunraven. The Brownings, though certainly not from identical motives, determined to test his quality. Accordingly they were present, in July, at a séance which he held at the house of a Mr. Rymer at Ealing, where he was staying. The Rymer children had gathered some clematis, of which Home and Miss Rymer made a wreath; which wreath, opportunely enough, it must be admitted, since two poets were expected, was left upon a table in the room where the sitting was to be held. At any rate the hint, if such it was, was taken, for presently "spirit hands" lifted the wreath and placed it upon Mrs. Browning's head.

Browning firmly believed, as he told Nathaniel Hawthorne several years later, that the so-called "spirit hands" were fastened to the feet of the medium, who lay back in his chair with his legs stretched far under the table.[1] At the time he said nothing; but a couple of days later he wrote to Mrs. Rymer asking for a second séance, and for leave to bring his friend Miss Helen Faucit with him. The request was refused, on the plea of other engagements. Shortly afterwards Home,

---

[1] Nathaniel Hawthorne's *Note-Books*, ii. p. 10.

in company with Mrs. Rymer and her son, called on the Brownings in Dorset Street. Browning lost no time in informing Mrs. Rymer that he was profoundly dissatisfied with what he had seen at her house, and on Home's intervening gave him clearly to understand that he believed him guilty of a fraud. Home left the house rather precipitately.[1]

The " spirit-hands " had previously aroused the suspicions of a Mr. Merrifield and of Miss de Gaudrian, afterwards his wife ; and the latter, hearing of the Brownings' visit to Ealing, wrote to Mrs. Browning to ask her opinion. Both husband and wife replied, he at some length and in the third person. He is " hardly able to account for the fact," he writes,

" that there can be any other opinion than his own on the matter —that being that the whole display of ' hands,' ' spirit utterances,' etc., was a cheat and an imposture. He believes in the good faith of his host and hostess, and was sorry that they were taken in."

He goes on to lament the fact that " the best and rarest of natures " may be led eventually to

" a voluntary prostration of the whole intelligence before what is assumed to transcend all intelligence. Once arrived at this point no trick is too gross—absurdities are referred to ' low spirits,' falsehoods to ' personating spirits,' and the one terribly apparent spirit, the Father of Lies, has it all his own way. Mr. Browning had some difficulty in keeping from an offensive expression of his feelings at the Rymers; he has since seen Mr. Home and relieved himself."

In conclusion he does not advise any formal exposure, preferring " to leave the business to its natural termination." Mrs. Browning adds a covering note :

" I enclose to you in his handwriting an account of the impressions he received. Mine, I must frankly say, were entirely different."

These letters did not get into print until 28 November, 1902, when they appeared in the *Literary Supplement* of the *Times*. They evoked an interesting communication from Mr. Robert Barrett Browning, the " Penini " of old days.

After corroborating the story told to Hawthorne, with the addition that he had repeatedly heard his father describe

[1] *Incidents in My Life*, by D. D. Home, second series, ch. iv.

how he caught hold of Home's foot under the table, when
that member was nefariously at work, he proceeds :

" What I am more desirous of stating is that towards the end of her
life my mother's views on 'spirit manifestations' were much modified. The change was brought about, in a great measure, by the
discovery that she had been duped by a friend in whom she had
blind faith. The pain of the disillusion was great, but her eyes were
opened and she saw clearly." [1]

The language of Robert Browning's letter to Miss de
Gaudrian is that of indignation, afid from this time forward
it is plain that he had small patience with spiritualism ; [2]
while from his son's it is to be inferred that Mrs. Browning
continued, until the episode therein narrated, to hold a
divergent view. Nevertheless she displays a rather more
critical attitude. There is significance in her admission to
one of her correspondents that " Mediums cheat certainly,"
on occasion ; and in her request to Miss Haworth, who was
likely to attend a séance, to " *touch* the hands." She is less
positive than formerly, although anxious to be convinced.
The age was materialistic, and she, with her intense
spirituality, longed for witness to the reality of the unseen ;
less, in all probability, for her own satisfaction than that
others might be won from their materialism. This was an
aspiration which could not fail to have her husband's deepest
sympathy ; and their being thus far in agreement must have
enabled them to differ the more easily as to methods of
realizing it. Browning's mind was not naturally prone to
compromise, but he had too deep a respect for his wife's
genius and individuality to desire to coerce her opinions.

[1] The *Times, Literary Supplement*, 5 December, 1902.
[2] There is a consensus of testimony on this point. D. G. Rossetti, Rudolf
Lehmann, Miss Cobbe, Miss Corkran, and Lady Ritchie all tell the same tale.
Mrs. David Ogilvy (in a memoir prefixed to Messrs. F. Warne and Co.'s edition
of Mrs. Browning's poems) recalls a conversation on the subject in Dorset Street,
at which she was present. " And what does it all end in ? " said Browning. " In
your finding yourself in a locked room, and the keeper putting in his head, and
asking what you will be pleased to have for dinner ! " " What," he said, not long
afterwards in Paris to Mrs. Corkran, " a clever woman like you to be taken in
by such humbugs and charlatans ! " And Miss Cobbe writes (in her *Life*,
ch. xiv.) : " I have seen him stamping on the floor in a frenzy of rage at the way
some believers and mediums were deceiving Mrs. Browning." This would be in
1860.

They could and did agree to differ about spiritualism, as they agreed to differ about the character of Louis Napoleon. "Here is even Robert," writes Mrs. Browning on 16 June, 1860, "whose heart softens to the point of letting me have the *Spiritual Magazine* from England." Then follows a passage which admits a breath of fresh air into a rather hothouse atmosphere—the picture of Seymour Kirkup, who was as deaf as a post, trying to convert Landor to spiritualism, and of Landor, "his beautiful sea-foam of a beard all in a curl and white bubblement of beauty," laughing so loudly in reply that even Kirkup heard him.[1]

For Home, Browning did not choose to seek to expose him ; suspected by many, he remained unexposed to the end of his career.[2] But *Mr. Sludge, the "Medium,"* written in retrospect, after Browning's manner, and published in the *Dramatis Personæ* of 1864, is a merciless indictment of the man's character and pretensions, under the usual thin disguise of different circumstances and locality. Home himself, following the lead of the newspaper press, recognized that he was attacked ; for in his *Incidents in my Life* he has a chapter called "Sludge the Medium—Mr. Robert Browning—Fancy Portraits."[3] It is only fair to add that the poem is hardly less severe on those persons who wilfully encouraged "Mr. Sludge" to deceive them than on "Mr. Sludge" himself.

The house in Dorset Street, which witnessed the rather stormy interview with Home, was shortly afterwards the scene of an episode calculated to blot out all such unpleasant recollections. A first edition copy of *Maud*, the gift of Tennyson to Browning, is a memento of an evening which deserves to be reckoned among the great occasions of literary history. It is not often that four poets are gathered together

---

[1] *Letters of Elizabeth Barrett Browning*, vol. ii. p. 395.

[2] T. A. Trollope, with whom Home stayed a month at Florence, has recorded the growing doubt with which he and his friends regarded him (*What I remember*, p. 268). Sir Francis Burnand, who was present at one of his *séances* and had a long conversation with him afterwards, could not make up his mind "whether Home's 'spirits' were 'above' or 'below' proof," but appears to incline towards the latter view (*Records and Reminiscences*, one vol. edition, p. 331).

[3] *Incidents in my Life, Second Series*, ch. iv. There is a contemptuous reference in *Prince Hohenstiel-Schwangau* (1871) to "friend Home's stilts and tongs and medium-ware."

within the four walls of one room ; but so it was now, when,
to an audience that included the Brownings and D. G. Rossetti, Tennyson

> " read, mouthing out his hollow oes and aes,
>   Deep-chested music,"

his lately published monodrama.   Meanwhile Rossetti,
unobserved in his corner, made a rapid pen-and-ink sketch of
the reader, which he gave to his host ; who, when *Maud* was
finished, read aloud his own *Fra Lippo Lippi*.[1]   Verily, the
scene sends our thoughts backward to the "wit combats"
of the Mermaid Tavern.   " The *tête-à-tête* conversations
between Browning and my father," wrote the present Lord
Tennyson of their intercourse in later years, "when no one but
myself was with them, was the best talk I ever heard, so full of
repartee, quip, epigram, anecdote, depth and wisdom ; but it
is quite impossible to attempt to reproduce them owing to
their very brilliancy."[2]   A sigh for the limitations of humanity
escapes one.   In Dorset Street it was not all head work,
either.   " He [Tennyson] opened his heart to us," writes Mrs.
Browning ; and one can imagine how theirs leapt to meet it.

In other respects their London experiences closely resembled those of their last visit.   There was a renewal of
intercourse with Ruskin, Leighton, Carlyle, Kinglake, Forster,
the Kemble sisters, and the Procters.   There were invitations
to the country which again, owing to the care of their child
and the expense that would have been entailed, had to be
declined.   Together they visited Browning's old haunt, the
Dulwich Gallery, in company with a new acquaintance,
Russell Lowell ; to whom the poet pointed out, as they stood
before the "Jacob's Dream" of Rembrandt, that "some reeds
behind Jacob had evidently been scratched in with the handle
of the brush, showing how rapidly it had been painted."[3]
Many callers came to Dorset Street, and the pressure of social
engagements weighed heavily upon Mrs. Browning.   Browning sat to Rossetti for his portrait, corrected the proofs of

---

[1] Mr. W. M. Rossetti was also present : *Some Reminiscences of W. M. Rossetti*,
p. 236.   See also Wise, *ut supra*, *Second Series*, vol. i. p. 92.

[2] *Tennyson, A Memoir*, vol. ii. p. 229.

[3] J. R. Lowell, *Letters*, vol. i. p. 261.

Men and Women, and found he had too much to do. Both were glad to migrate to Paris in October, hoping, in the husband's words, for "blessed quietude after the London worry." But the expectation was not realized immediately. He writes in the same letter : "We are in little inconvenient rooms here"—102, Rue de Grenelle, Faubourg St. Germain, facing east—"and I have been in continual hot water, the landlady, a *Baronne*, profiting by the blunder of an over-zealous friend, who took the apartment against my direct orders. But the water is getting tepid now, and we shall do well enough in time, it is to be hoped. . . . I have lain perdu and seen nobody." [1] Perhaps the water grew hot again ; at any rate before Christmas they are found established in new quarters, 3, Rue du Colisée, off the Champs-Elysées, "as pleased as if we had never lived in a house before." Here there was no lack of room or sunshine. Mrs. Browning, on recovering from an attack of illness which had added to the discomforts of the Rue de Grenelle, worked hard at *Aurora Leigh*, and Browning set himself the task of remoulding *Sordello*, but could not achieve it to his satisfaction. Feeling, it may be, that his hand was out, he gave it new employment, taking to drawing in his spare time. He could not, on Mrs. Browning's testimony, find much relief from serious work in light literature ; "so," she writes, "while I lie on the sofa and rest in a novel, Robert has a resource in his drawing." Nothing much was stirring in the political or social life of Paris, and the winter passed quietly. Flush, the spaniel, it is pleasant to learn, was still in the land of the living.

Early in the year 1856 an heir was born to Louis Napoleon. Browning was among the spectators of the baptism of the infant prince in June, and on his way homeward,

> "Walking the heat and headache off,"

found himself confronted by the Morgue. It is to what he saw there that we owe *Apparent Failure*, a poem which was a favourite, its author told Domett, with Tennyson.

Since the spring the poet and his wife had been rendered anxious by the illness of their constant friend, John Kenyon.

[1] To D. G. Rossetti. Wise, *ut supra*, vol. i. pp. 20–21.

Late in June he put his house, 39, Devonshire Place, at their disposal, he himself being absent in the Isle of Wight. The measure of Mr. Barrett's continued resentment may be gauged by the fact that on learning of their arrival in London he promptly sent his family away to the seaside. To the not unpleasant exile of Ventnor the Brownings, at Arabel Barrett's entreaty, followed them in September, where Penini speedily won his way into his uncles' hearts. They encouraged him to stand up for his rights, *more Britannico*, and applauded when he confronted a child of twice his age, who had taken liberties with him. This family scene is vividly described by his mother :—

" Robert and I begged to suggest to the hero that the ' boy of twelve ' might have killed him if he had pleased. ' Never mind,' cried little Pen, ' there would have been somebody to think of *me*, who would have him hanged ' (great applause from the uncles). ' But *you* would still be dead,' said Robert, remorselessly. ' Well, I don't care for *that*. It was a beautiful place to die in—close to the sea.' " [1]

From Ventnor the Brownings joined Kenyon at West Cowes, where the kindness of their host, whose days were evidently numbered, touched them deeply. Under the roof of this dear "cousin" and "friend" the last pages of *Aurora Leigh* were written ; and when at the close of October, after a visit to Mrs. Surtees Cook at Taunton, they were preparing to start for the South, it was in his London home that Mrs. Browning dedicated to him this, the most considerable of her works. The painter, Ruskin has said, should give his picture, the poet his poem. Mrs. Browning had no truer, wiser friend than John Kenyon, and she gave him of her best.

The first news that reached her after the return to Florence was of the great and immediate success of her poem. The press was uniformly friendly, and private letters, among them a long one from Leigh Hunt, were enthusiastic. The book sold so well that a second edition was required within a fortnight. Browning, who had never paid much attention to what the critics said about his own work, was enraptured at his wife's triumph. Miss Cobbe, who travelled from Venice

---

[1] *Letters of Elizabeth Barrett Browning.* vol. ii. p. 238.

to Florence on purpose to present letters of introduction to the woman who could write *Aurora Leigh*, and joined forces, as has been said, with Miss Blagden, records that he came constantly to their villa, "glorying in his wife's fame, continually bringing up good reviews of her poem, and recounting the editions called for." [1] The career of Mrs. Browning as a writer was now unquestionably at its zenith. Unhappily sorrow followed closely upon the heels of success. The loss, in December, of the friend to whom *Aurora Leigh* was dedicated was a genuine grief, though devoid of all bitterness. John Kenyon proved himself consistent in generosity. Since the birth of the Brownings' son he had insisted, though Browning was unwilling to have it so, on allowing them £100 a year; now by his will he left them eleven thousand pounds. But the death of Mrs. Browning's father four months later, on 17 April, 1857, was a blow at the heart. She had given up all hope of reconciliation; yet her natural grief renewed and intensified every pang which her father's unnatural cruelty had cost her. The shock was one which could not fail to be detrimental to so frail an organism.

Alla Villa once more received the Brownings in its welcome coolness, when the July heat of 1857 made Florence untenable. Browning and his boy took delight in scouring the hills on mountain ponies, and bathed daily in the Lima. But anxiety marred the success of this holiday. Robert Lytton, who was repeating his earlier visit to the Brownings, fell ill with gastric fever. For some days his condition was serious, and Browning watched by his friend's bedside four nights out of five. Hardly had Lytton become convalescent and left for the Villa Bricchieri with Miss Blagden, when Penini was similarly attacked; and though his illness ran a favourable course, and was less severe than Lytton's, it was a further strain upon his mother's health and spirits, which, it now began to appear, where losing their former elastieity. Her energy as a correspondent flagged at this period, though later it was to revive in the stress of Italy's renewed struggles for unity. The care of her child's education absorbed her more active hours, while Browning supervised his music.

They had nourished schemes of visiting Egypt and the

---

[1] *Life of Frances Power Cobbe, by Herself,* ch. xiv.

Holy Land this winter; but recent anxieties had unfitted
Mrs. Browning for travel. To Florence, accordingly, they
returned in October, when the mountain air became too cold.
But Florence could be cold also. For the first time in ten
years there were fragments of ice upon the Arno's surface,
and "grippe" invaded Casa Guidi. Mrs. Browning escaped,
but was physically at a low ebb. Presently all Florence was
startled by the news of Orsini's attempt upon Napoleon's
life. To Mrs. Browning the Emperor had become "the only
great man of his age, speaking of public men"; already she
looked to him as the destined liberator of Italy,[1] and she was
proportionately indignant. But Italy had still to wait. No
other public event of moment disturbed Florence from its
wonted calm ; nor does any salient incident appear to have
varied, at this period, the quiet family life of Casa Guidi.

When the season for summer migration came, France was
their objective. "The scene changes," Mrs. Browning writes—

"No more cypresses, no more fireflies, no more dreaming repose
on burning hot evenings. Push out the churches, push in the
boulevards."

They chose the sea route to Marseilles, and there rested a
night : onward thence by express trains, breaking the journey
at Lyons and at Dijon. At Dijon an episode occurred which
illustrates Browning's deep affection for Milsand ; twice he
went and stood before his friend's house, "to muse and bless
the threshold." So Paris was reached and the Hôtel
Hyacinthe, Rue St. Honoré, where they passed a fortnight.
Browning, himself invigorated by the keener air, had the
comfort of finding his father, on whose birthday they arrived,
"looking ten years younger, and radiant with joy at seeing him
and Penini." There were meetings with Father Prout, whose
geniality was unfailing ; with Lady Elgin, robbed of speech
by paralysis, who could yet express by touch and motion her
affectionate regard ; and with Charles Sumner, the American
statesman, who was seeking in Europe for the renewal of
that health which the brutal assault of a fellow-Congressman
had undermined. Presently the three generations of Brownings set out for Normandy. A descent on Etretat proving

---

[1] *Letters of Elizabeth Barrett Browning*, vol. ii. p. 307.

ineffective, they found quarters in the outskirts of Havre. Mrs. Browning had been recommended sea-bathing, and in this respect they were well situated, their house, a large and airy one, being close to the sea-shore ; but for Havre and its neighbourhood they did not care at all. Mrs. Browning's health was benefited, however ; and it was here that the photograph was taken, pronounced by her husband to be good, which appears as frontispiece to the fourth and subsequent editions of *Aurora Leigh*. After eight weeks at Havre they spent another four in Paris, in a pleasant apartment close to the Tuileries Gardens—" small, but exquisitely comfortable and Parisian " ; ready enough, when October came, to turn their faces towards Italy again.

Preferring to avoid the long sea passage from Marseilles, they chose the Mont Cenis route. They travelled slowly, the journey occupying nine days. One of them was spent at Chambéry, that they might visit Les Charmettes, where Rousseau in his early days found a refuge with Mme. de Warens. Rousseau's romanticism, it may be supposed, the " resplendency " and " all-explosive eloquence " commended in *La Saisiaz*, attracted Browning ; of these he thought as he sat at the old harpsichord and played the " Dream " upon its cracked and faltering keys, and not of its author's pessimistic theories :—

"All that's good is gone and past ;
Bad and worse still grows the present, and the worst of all comes
   last."

After a night at Lanslebourg they crossed the Alps. Snow had not yet fallen, but the passage caused Mrs. Browning some suffering. At Genoa they took ship for Leghorn, and had a stormy voyage, of which she has left a graphic account.

"Half way over, the captain almost decided on returning to Genoa. We had whirlwinds, called by the Italians *burrasca*, and reeled about in the sea in our little old Neapolitan boat. The very male passengers were somewhat alarmed, and there was an English lady who called aloud on God to ' spare her a few more days ' ! "

After eighteen hours of wretchedness, the travellers were glad to rest a night at Leghorn. Meanwhile dismal rumours had preceded them to Florence. A friend in Paris, Mme. du Quaire, had notified a friend in Florence of the date of their departure, 12 October. As the days passed and they did not appear, all sorts of conjectures were afloat.

" Either we had perished by a railway accident on the Marseilles route (hinted at in a Galignani), or gone down in a steamer (one or two having gone down), or I had died on Mont Cenis and Robert had stopped to bury me at Turin. So that certain friends of ours were running about in a distracted way with pale faces—one confined to her room for four-and-twenty hours with fright. In fact, as I went upstairs the first time to our apartment in Casa Guidi I met an enquiring friend coming down who stared at me aghast, as at a ghost of an old inhabitant of the house haunting the ancient place ! "

But it was a joy to be at home again.

" Robert and I are delighted to feel here in a divine abstraction from civilized life. Florence looked like a city of the dead to us on our arrival. There was one man wandering along the quay (the fashionable Lung Arno !) and another man looking at him with intense interest. Still, we are acclimatized ; and we begin again to live our own lives, one day of which we have not lived for these four months." [1]

Yet, dear as Casa Guidi was, the winter climate of Rome was judged to be better for its mistress than that of Florence ; so that for this and the two following winters they are found in Rome.

The start was made within a bare month of their arrival. With favourable conditions, a comfortable carriage lent by American friends, the Eckleys, and fair weather, the journey was a good one. At one spot two oxen-drivers fell out, one of them attacking the other with a knife. Browning intervened, with the happy result that no blood was shed ; though at the journey's end a torn garment of his required mending. On Christmas Day Mrs. Browning was able to accompany him to St. Peter's to hear the silver trumpets ; but then cold weather came. Rome was very full, and he was soon carried away by the social stream.

---

[1] These extracts are from an unpublished letter.

"We are in a crowd," writes Mrs. Browning. "My husband is engaged two or three times deep at night for a fortnight together. I am saved by being imprisoned in the house by tramontana. The transition between the scorching sun and tomb-like draughts of air makes the danger of Italy, to say nothing of the exhalations peculiar to Rome."[1]

Her husband, however, defying these untoward conditions, kept his health and his appetite, thanks in great part to long walks with Eckley and to homœopathy. "No *Men and Women*," writes Mrs. Browning. "Men and women from without instead!" But indeed, the state of political affairs, quite apart from social distractions, was such as to monopolize the thoughts of those who had high hopes for Italy.

The decade which followed the battle of Novara had been to that country, outside the King of Sardinia's dominions, a period of constant repression, of dull pain, of acute and occasionally articulate suffering. In 1851 Mr. Gladstone wrote of "Bomba's" rule in the Two Sicilies that it was "the negation of God created into a system of government." At the Paris Congress of 1856 Lord Clarendon denounced the misgovernment of the Papal States as a scandal to Europe. These were the plague-spots, but the yoke of the foreigner weighed heavily upon Lombardy and Venetia, and upon the Duchies, while the worst offenders knew that they had the moral, and might have the material, force of Austria to support them. Nevertheless the oppressed Italians were learning in the school of adversity not only how to suffer, but how to be strong. In the words of Massimo d'Azeglio, the Piedmontese statesman, who called upon the Brownings about this time, it was '48 over again, but with matured actors. At last the moment came. Piedmont must make the attempt, but could not make it single-handed. Cavour had found an ally in Louis Napoleon. The Emperor of the French had a genuine desire to do something for Italy; he was equally bent on humbling Austria. He announced his intention of freeing Italy from the Alps to the Adriatic; and when, after various futile negotiations, culminating in a demand from Vienna that the forces of Piedmont should

---

[1] From an unpublished letter, dated Rome, 43 Bocca di Leone, January 9 [1859].

unconditionally disarm, Austrian troops crossed the Ticino, they had to reckon with French as well as with Italian resistance. Mrs. Browning's enthusiasm for the Emperor rose to fever height, and Browning himself was impressed. It was at Florence, whither they returned in May, a Florence whose Grand Duke had thought it wise to take his departure, that she and her husband, both, in'her own phrase, passionate sympathizers with Italy, heard with delight of the victories of Magenta and Solferino. They had begun, to write on the Italian question together, and designed to publish jointly. Triumph, however, soon gave place to bitter disappointment. Napoleon had fought enough to suit his purpose. He had humbled Austria, as he had humbled Russia. Far from desiring to incur her inveterate enmity, he schemed, as in the earlier case, to win her friendship by a show of generosity. Accordingly he concluded an armistice, and met the Emperor of Austria in conference at Villafranca. Then it was that Browning destroyed what he had written. But his wife's faith was more robust. For the moment she was stunned ; but presently concluded that her hero had done what he could, that the jealcusy of interested nations had prevented him from doing more. Lombardy was given up, if Venetia was retained. She even acquitted him later on, when it became known that Savoy and Nice were to be annexed by France as the price of his intervention. In one particular, however, her political instinct was sound. Napoleon "builded better than he knew." "The first battle in the north of Italy," she wrote, and wrote truly, "freed Italy *potentially* from North to South."

But as to the immediate effect of Villafranca : if, as we are assured, grown men in Florence fell ill in consequence of the peace, it is no wonder that Mrs. Browning's highly strung organization was strained almost to breaking. She became alarmingly unwell, with pains as of *angina* added to the usual chest troubles. Undoubtedly she had, by her own admission, talked too much, and excited herself too much, about the war ; but she could not help it.

"Women don't generally break their hearts on these exterior subjects," she writes, "but I am otherwise made. Whatever small worth may be in me (among my innumerable weaknesses and defalcations) arises exactly from the earnestness and thoroughness of thought and feeling upon subjects which don't personally touch me." [1]

The reed, to which she loved to compare herself, could only give forth its music after it had been "hacked and hewed." Thus was shaped the musical instrument; but

> " The true gods sigh for the cost and pain,—
> For the reed which grows nevermore again
> As a reed with the reeds in the river." [2]

Browning's hands were full during this July of 1859. For three weeks his night's rest was sacrificed to attendance on his sick wife. He took over, too, his son's lessons; and in the midst of his anxiety found himself faced with a fresh responsibility. Walter Savage Landor, now past eighty, had, after a long period of estrangement, rejoined his family at Fiesole. But the arrangement did not answer. He was ungoverned in speech and temper: to live at peace with him was not easy. The task, at any rate, proved too difficult for his family. Violent quarrels took place. Three times he flung himself out of the house, and was as many times brought back to it. On the fourth occasion he refused absolutely to return. His family, to whom he had made over his property, would make no provision for him outside their walls. He was now homeless, with nothing but the clothes he stood in and a few pauls in his pocket. In this plight he appeared at Casa Guidi. Browning at once took charge of his affairs, received him into his house, and after a few days got him an invitation to stop with the Storys at Siena, whither he himself was presently to follow. Meanwhile, he wrote to Forster, who after corresponding with Landor's brothers reported that funds would not be lacking to enable this second Lear to keep house independently. His was evidently a case where tact could do a great deal; for to those who now befriended him he showed himself gentle and affectionate. And indeed he might well do so.

---

[1] From an unpublished letter, dated Rome, 28 Via del Tritone, 31 December [1859].

[2] *A Musical Instrument*, written in Rome in the spring of 1860, first published in the July *Cornhill* of that year.

" I have never seen," says an observer, " anything of its kind
so chivalrous as the deference paid by Robert Browning to Landor.
It was loyal homage paid by a poet in all the glow of power and
impulsive magnetism to an old master." [1]

The Brownings reached Siena early in August, Mrs.
Browning in so weak a state that she had to be carried into
the house from the *vettura*. The Villa Alberti, their summer
house this and the next year, is a roomy house at Marciano,
two miles out of the city, separated from the road by a six-foot
wall and taller hedge. From its back windows the towers of
Siena are visible, and the chime of the bells of the Duomo
and San Dominico is within hearing. The front faces east,
and looks across a little valley to a corresponding slope,
where stand several other villas. One of these, the Misciatelli,
then called Belvedere, was the Storys' resting-place ; and
the path which leads through vines and olive-trees from one
house to the other was much frequented during the next two
months. The distance by road was longer, some three-
quarters of a mile ; a favourite gallop with Penini, when off
to join the Story children. For Browning here bought his
son a pony, which accompanied them to Rome and later to
England. Even nearer than the Storys was Landor, who
was now settled in a small house within a stone's cast of the
Villa Alberti. The experiment answered fairly well, though
Browning had often to smooth down the old lion when
enraged by imaginary grievances ; who found, otherwise, a
safety-valve in composing Latin Alcaics against his wife and
Louis Napoleon. Much of his time he spent with the Brownings and Storys at one or other villa ; appearing at the
Belvedere on little Edith Story's birthday in a wonderful
flowered waistcoat given him, years earlier, by Count D'Orsay.[2]
Mrs. Browning made him "laugh carnivorously" by telling

---

[1] *Last days of Walter Savage Landor*, by Kate Field, *Atlantic Monthly*, April,
1866. Landor was not behindhand in gratitude. He wrote to Forster of
Browning as "the kind friend whom I had seen only three or four times in my
life, yet who made me the voluntary offer of what money I wanted, and who
insists on managing my affairs here [Siena] and paying for my lodging and
sustenance." *Walter Savage Landor : a Biography*, by John Forster, vol. ii.
p. 562.

[2] *W. W. Story, ut supra*, vol. ii. p. 19, where there is added a very racy
account of his conversation, preserved by Mrs. Story.

him that one day, to please her, he would have to write an
ode in honour of the Emperor. Every evening the friends
would sit on the lawn under the ilexes and cypresses, talking
over their tea long after the cool night had fallen. It was
three or four weeks, indeed, before Mrs. Browning could share
this pleasure ; she had to content herself, at first, with the
sunsets visible from her upper room and the night winds
breathing through her open windows. In the rest and almost
absolute seclusion of the summer, with but two visitors from
the outside world, Odo Russell, afterwards Lord Ampthill, and
Mr. W. C. Cartwright, a Northamptonshire squire, Roman
friends, she regained a portion of her strength. Yet she
spoke later of this illness and of " the tendency it proved " as
making her "feel more than usually mortal." [1] It could not,
however, weaken her political enthusiasm ; and it was a great
joy to her, as it was to her husband and the Storys, when one
September day the cross of Savoy was uncovered in the
market place of Siena, in token of the formation of a northern
Italian kingdom under Victor Emmanuel.

They all left Siena regretfully ; and not remaining in
Florence much longer than to see Landor established in a
little house in the Via Nunziatina, with Wilson, now married
to an Italian, Ferdinando Romagnoli, to look after him, they
settled down in Rome for the winter.[2] Society then was
much restricted, disturbances being feared, and was mainly of
the diplomatic kind. " My husband," Mrs. Browning writes,[3]

" met yesterday at a dinner of seven the Neapolitan, Portugese and
English ambassadors, a chief of the Roman Liberals, and a brother-
in-law of the Princess Mathilde. We know a great deal more than
we can tell. But things are going beautifully, I thank God, things
political, that is."

As an outward sign of enthusiasm twenty thousand Romans
had combined in a lire subscription for two swords, designed
by the jeweller Castellani, to be presented to Victor Emmanuel
and Napoleon. The Pope banned this proceeding, and the

[1] From the unpublished letter last quoted.
[2] The street has changed its name, and Landor's house (where, in 1864, he
died) is now 93 Via della Chiesa. Wilson lived until 1902, when she died at
Asolo.
[3] From the unpublished letter last quoted.

swords had to disappear; but the Brownings were invited before that to come and see them.

"We were received at Castellani's most flatteringly as poets and lovers of Italy; were asked for our autographs; and returned in a blaze of glory and satisfaction."

Mrs. Browning paid for this expedition by an attack of illness, but happily a brief one. She was able to attend to the proofs of her *Poems before Congress*, which constituted her comment on the political crisis.

The little volume appeared early in the new year. It aroused, as its author had expected, considerable indignation in the English press. To her the very reasonable suspicion of Napoleon, which was a factor in our policy, and which had evoked in England a wave of enthusiasm for volunteering, was most repugnant. Browning also, it appears, though he had no confidence in the Emperor's disinterestedness, did not give their proper weight to these apprehensions. The "long poem" on which his wife mentions that he was occupied this winter was certainly a first draft of *Prince Hohenstiel-Schwangau*, as is shown by a letter written to Robert Buchanan in 1871.

"Why speak at all disparagingly," it runs, "of your poem [*Napoleon Fallen*], which I am sure is admirable in every way, full of power and music; besides, I see my fancies or fears that you might treat in your undoubted right the main actor after a fashion repugnant to my feelings were vain enough. I think more savagely *now* of the man, and should say so if needed. I wrote, myself, a monologue in his name twelve years ago, and never could bring the printing to my mind as yet. One day, perhaps." [1]

That his wife did not see the poem was in accordance with their habitual practice; for they only showed one another their completed work. But the transference of Savoy and Nice to France, officially announced in February, was a significant commentary on *Poems before Congress*. Italy, it was evident, must now achieve her own destiny unaided. On 14 May, Garibaldi and his thousand landed in Sicily, which thereupon became the centre of political interest. The

[1] Wise, *ut supra, Second Series*, vol. i. pp. 35-6. The poem appeared, in fact, at the close of the year 1871.

progress of his great adventure, upon which all eyes were bent, occupied the thoughts of the Brownings at Rome, at Florence, and at Siena.

Again the cool and quiet of the Villa Alberti, dreaming amidst its purple hills and vineyards, its olive-trees and fig-trees clothing it as with a forest solitude; again the Storys within hail, again the undertone of the old lion Landor's not ill-natured growl, as accompaniment to their lighter talk. There were long hours of rest and thought for Mrs. Browning, while her husband and son roamed over the country on horse-back; she had, too, the society of Isa Blagden, always a "perfect" friend to her. This should have been a happy and a renovating summer; but all was marred by the serious illness of Mrs. Surtees Cook. Mrs. Browning longed to go to her sister; but that, it was obvious, would have been the height of unwisdom. She could only sit still and endure, with what faith and hope she might; while Browning, in the kindness of his heart, did his best to reassure her. Her art, too, afforded her some solace; several of her last lyrics upon Italy being written during these anxious days.

In September they returned to Rome, to sunny rooms in the Via Felice. Here Mrs. Browning's worst anticipations were realized; for she had the news of her sister's death. She suffered dumbly; but this new sorrow served to aggravate her own debility. Mrs. Cook left three little girls, younger than Penini; and at thought of them Mrs. Browning could only see his face through a mist of tears.[1] In consequence of her trouble she led a very secluded life this winter, Browning shielding her from ordinary visitors. A few she saw, Sir John Bowring, for instance, an English liberal who was quite of her way of thinking about Italy, and Hans Andersen, no politician, but a king in his own sphere. The tale must be repeated of a children's party at the Palazzo Barberini, the Storys' home, where, after Andersen had read his *Ugly Duckling*, Browning followed with *The Pied Piper*; at the close of which reading Story, playing on his flute, which passed for bagpipes, headed a march of the delighted children.[2] Hans Andersen's simplicity and

[1] Mrs. David Ogilvy's *Memoir*, previously quoted.
[2] *W. W. Story, ut supra*, vol. i. p. 286.

earnestness won Mrs. Browning ; and he is the subject of
The North and the South, the last poem she ever wrote.

Browning had done hardly any writing since the previous
winter ; and as in Paris he took to drawing for a change, so
now he found a new and engrossing pursuit. He had made
some study of anatomy ; and now, in Story's studio, he
tried his hand at modelling in clay. He took great delight
in this occupation, employing as it did both mind and body,
and would work at it six hours a day. He copied such
masterpieces as the Young Augustus and the Psyche, and
the more he tired himself the better he was pleased.
" Nothing," he assured his wife, " ever made him so happy
before ! " A characteristic utterance ; for when one outlet
for his energy failed him, he must find another, or be
miserable. He does not seem to have been more than
usually apprehensive about Mrs. Browning's health. The
triumphant success of Garibaldi's enterprise, which gave
Sicily and Naples to the Italian crown, cheered her spirits,
and consequently raised her husband's hopes. Already
they began to discuss summer plans and journeys, and to
canvass the suitability of Fontainebleau as a place where they
might join forces with Arabel Barrett and Browning's father
and sister. But a few days before their return to Florence—
their last return—Mrs. Browning had a short but alarming
attack of illness. Browning had to fetch a doctor in the
night, who stayed with them till morning. " It really
seemed," he wrote to Story, " as if she would be strangled on
the spot, and that for six hours together." [1] This frightened
him, and he insisted on the idea of a journey to France being
abandoned. It was enough, for the present, to get safely
home to Casa Guidi.

Another cause of depression followed. Of all the great
Italians who had laboured for their country at this epoch,
Cavour appeared to Mrs. Browning to be the greatest. Only
fifty years of age, he had done the work and the thinking of
several men ; and at the moment when he saw the achievement of those great results which without his courage and
sagacity could hardly have been effected, his health collapsed,
and he died after a week's illness. " If tears or blood could

---

[1] *W. W. Story, ut supra*, vol. ii. p. 57.

have saved him to us," Mrs. Browning wrote, "he should have had mine." In truth, the life which she would cheerfully have given was nearing its close. Cavour died on 6 June. Her own last illness, or, to speak more exactly, its last stage, began on the 23rd. She was not considered to be in danger until the third or fourth night. Even then she rallied, left her bed for the sofa in the salon, and read the *Athenæum* and the *Nazione*. On the 28th she did not leave her room, but received a visit from Miss Blagden in the afternoon, and heard with pleasure of the new premier's intention to walk in Cavour's footsteps. Her friend left her without apprehension. She bade her son good-night, telling him she was much better. She had herself no presentiment and little pain; only her sleep was broken and troubled. At four o'clock she awoke, and assured her husband that she felt stronger. With no idea, it seems, that she was about to leave him, she gave expression to her love for him in the tenderest words. Supported in his arms, she became drowsy. Her head fell forward. He thought that she had fainted; but it was the end.

CHAPTER XIII

SORROW AND ACHIEVEMENT

Sorrow and resolution—Browning's farewell to Italy—His house in Warwick Crescent—His occupations—Neighbourhood of Arabel Barrett—His seclusion—His gradual return to social activities—First mention of "the Roman Murder Story"—Its protracted incubation—How the subject came to him—Mr. Cartwright's testimony—*Pompilia*—Mrs. Browning's prose writings—Proposals to write her *Life*—Her *Letters to R. H. Horne*—Summers at Sainte-Marie, near Pornic—Browning's house there—*Dramatis Personæ*—Browning at Oxford—He makes acquaintance with Jowett—Death of his father—His sister makes her home with him—Death of Arabel Barrett—Summer sojourns at Croisic—*The Ring and the Book* published—Unstinted praise—Travels in Scotland—At St. Aubin with Milsand—*Hervé Riel*—*Balaustion's Adventure*—Its popularity—*Prince Hohenstiel-Schwangau*—The reviewers mystified.

THAT robust optimism which characterized Browning's attitude towards life, as it does his writings, had caused him throughout to take a sanguine view of his wife's physical powers ; the shock which their failure caused him was consequently overwhelming. Only when she was gone did he realize the truth. "Looking back at these past years," he said to the Storys, who on receipt of the news hastened from Leghorn to Florence, "I see that we have been all the time walking over a torrent on a straw." His grief was lasting and profound, but there was no rebellion in it. He could express his thankfulness that she passed almost painlessly, and without consciousness of separation ; that her last words and looks were full of happiness. Our sorrow for the dead must be in proportion to the love we bear them ; something, therefore, of the depth of his may be imagined. But what requires to be emphasized is, that even when his bereavement was new, his intensely virile temperament made despair impossible. He had at once determined,

as he told Story, to begin life afresh ; "to break up everything, go to England and live and work and write." Brave
and admirable words, expressive of a purpose which ultimately triumphed ; yet, because he was human, there came a
moment when it seemed as if he had over-estimated his own
endurance. That was when the time came for him to leave
Florence. " The staying at Casa Guidi was not the worst of
it," he wrote to Story subsequently. " I kept in my place
there like a worm-eaten piece of old furniture, looking solid
enough ; but when I was *moved* I began to go to pieces."
The crisis passed, however, and his native vigour won the
day.[1]

Moreover, his wife had bequeathed to him a sacred trust,
though with no word spoken, the care of their child ; whose
up-bringing now became his chief personal preoccupation.[2]
In the hour of sorrow Miss Blagden showed herself a mother
to Penini ; when Mrs. Browning had been laid to rest in
Florence she looked after him until his father's preparations
for departure were completed ; and when on the first of
August they bade farewell to the city of so many happy
memories, which Browning was never again to behold, she
accompanied them to Paris. There they parted, but met
later on in England. Browning found Paris unbearable ; but
when with his father, sister, and son he reached St. Enogat,
near Dinard, he could breathe and live. The solitude of sea,
shore and open country was medicine to his spirit. Now, we
may suppose, was conceived that liking for the coasts of
France which in future summers brought him back to them
again and again. Yet in some moods he longed for action as
an antidote to sorrowful thoughts. Even before August was
out he felt, he wrote to Story, " impatient at doing nothing."
Still, he remained ; and knew, in spite of his impatience,

---

[1] See *W. W. Story, ut supra,* vol. ii. pp. 66 and 97. A letter from Story to
Norton contains a very full account of Mrs. Browning's last illness and death.
Other sources of information are Browning's own letters to Leighton and Miss
Haworth, given in full by Mrs. Orr, and Kate Field's article in the *Atlantic
Monthly* for September, 1861.

[2] Jowett, writing to a friend in 1865, shortly after making Browning's
acquaintance, says : "Of personal objects he seems to have none except the
education of his son, in which I hope in some degree to help him." *Life and
Letters of Benjamin Jowett,* vol. i. p. 401.

that to remain was salutary. "I am getting 'mended up' here," he writes in the same letter, "and shall no doubt last my proper time, for all the past." As to the future, his eyes were turned towards London, partly for his boy's education, partly that he might be near his wife's surviving sister, Arabel Barrett, who was established in a house in Delamere Terrace.

Father and son set out for London in October. A *contretemps* about the boy's pony delayed their start. Misinformed as to the proper train for its transport, Browning demanded its conveyance by the express. "No Briton's to be baulked," as he says half-seriously, half in irony. His dogged persistence, maintained through a two hours' controversy, wore down the polite resistance of the officials, and he carried his point. The incident is characteristic. Though he had lived abroad so much, though he was sometimes taken for an American, he was, as he himself put it, effectually rooted in his own garden. Another little episode of the journey shows that while he could assert his rights in his usual sturdy manner, he was still very vulnerable on the point of feeling. At Amiens he caught sight of Tennyson, who was travelling homewards with his wife and children. Browning pointed out the poet to his son ; but remembering a similar encounter, in earlier and happier days, he pulled his hat over his brows and so escaped notice. Recognition, just then, was more than he could have borne.[1]

He had put aside as intolerable the idea of housekeeping, and came to his first London anchorage in Chichester Road, off Westbourne Terrace. Miss Blagden had a lodging close at hand. Here he remained for some months. A tutor was engaged for Pen, who was to go to the University in due course, but not by the way of a Public School. Browning was also occupied in preparing for the press his wife's *Last Poems*, together with her *Translations*, the "advertisement" to which is dated London, February, 1862. Dedicated to "grateful Florence," the little book was published in March ; with what respective degrees of pride and pain to himself it would require a measure of his own analytical subtlety to determine. He also acted as Story's literary representative

---

[1] *W. W. Story, ut supra*, vol. ii. p. 100.

in England, finding hospitality in the columns of the *Daily News* for a series of three letters in which the sculptor put forth the claims of the North to English sympathy, the American Civil War being in progress, and attending to matters concerned with the production of his *Roba di Roma*, a kind of Roman sketchbook. Thus his life did not lack occupations; but it was, he told his friend, as grey as the winter sky of London.[1] Often, it is evident, he was, in thought, back again in Florence; or longing for the smell of the wet clay in Story's studio, where the singing of the birds came through the open door.

It must have been some relief, at any rate, when he exchanged the discomforts of life in lodgings for a more settled abode. When he first took No. 19, Warwick Crescent, which was to be his home for twenty-five years, he took it as a *pied-à-terre*, with no intention of a long sojourn. But he got used to it, found it convenient, and so remained. It had the attraction of being close to Miss Barrett's house, Warwick Crescent being practically a continuation of Delamere Terrace. The place, too, has a certain charm of its own, an element of the unusual denied to most localities in London. The houses face a balustrade and trees, with the Grand Junction Canal beyond them, which at this point widens to the dimensions of a minute lake, with a tree-clad islet in its midst. Westward the neighbourhood is decidedly squalid; but in the sixties, when Pen Browning used to row along the canal as far as Kensal Green, there were, beyond Delamere Terrace, no houses on its banks. Just beyond No. 19, a bridge spans the canal, to which, as Browning used to tell the story, Byron once dragged a reluctant John Murray, to show him the spot where a publisher had drowned himself!

It was Browning's habit to call upon his sister-in-law every afternoon; and with her he attended Bedford Chapel during the incumbency of the Revd. Thomas Jones, a gifted Welshman. On several occasions he conversed with him in the vestry after service, and once received a visit from him at his house. He wrote, in 1884, a preface to a posthumous volume of Jones' sermons, *The Divine Order*, in which he pays a tribute to his " liberal humanity " and his eloquence.

[1] *W. W. Story, ut supra*, vol. ii. p. 111.

"It was a fancy of mine," he wrote, "that, in certain respects and under certain moods, a younger Carlyle might, sharing the same convictions, have spoken so, even looked so."

For some time after his return to England, he shrank from society, seeing hardly any old friends even, except the Procters. Early in January he was twice at D. G. Rossetti's studio, who considered himself highly favoured, since the poet had "hardly seen any one as yet since his bereavement"; and a little later he made acquaintance with Millais. His reason assured him that seclusion availed him nothing; that the long solitary evenings, after Pen had gone to bed, tended to morbid introspection. The Storys urged him not to shut himself up; and as early as March, 1862, he is found acting on their advice, though at first with painful effort. Indeed, a year was to pass before he finally resolved that no suitable invitation which came to him should go unaccepted.[1] After this he moved freely in general society, and was a frequenter of the studios and concert rooms; of the theatres, too, when anything of serious interest was on hand.[2]

His first spring in England brought him an offer of the editorship of the *Cornhill Magazine*, from which Thackeray had retired; but the offer, after some consideration, was declined. For a summer holiday he took his boy to Saint Marie, a Breton coast village.

He was at present occupied in preparing a new three-volume edition of his works—the third—inclusive of all his published poems except *Pauline*. Some slight modifications were introduced in *Paracelsus*, and in *Sordello* various rhymes were changed and some new lines incorporated. He had also determined to reprint Mrs. Browning's early contributions to the *Athenæum*, which appeared, as did his own new edition, early in 1863, under the title of *The Greek Christian Poets and the English Poets*. His own volumes were dedicated to Forster, who about this time was making, with Procter's collaboration, a book of Selections from those poems of

[1] See Sir Edmund Gosse's article in the *Supplement* to the *Dictionary of National Biography*.

[2] An early fruit of his intercourse with the art world is found in the lines *Deaf and Dumb*, written in 1862 for a group of statuary by Woolner, but not published until 1868.

which he had been, in their author's own words, " the prompt-
est and staunchest helper from their first publication." [1]
The design, as a preface explains,

" originated with two friends, who, from the first appearance of
Paracelsus, have regarded its writer as among the few great poets
of the century ; who have seen this opinion, since, gain ground with
the best readers and critics ; and who believe that such a selection
as the present may go far to render it universal."

The book may be regarded as stronger and more representative than its successors in this kind, since it contains
not only lyrics and romances, but also extracts from all
the longer poems (*Pauline* again excepted), and from all the
dramas save only *A Soul's Tragedy*.   This tribute from the
friends who had believed in him from the first must have
been a source of true pleasure to the poet ; and indeed he
needed solace just now, being pestered by various persons
desirous of printing certain letters of his wife, which were not
in his keeping, and of writing her biography.   All such
proposals put him in a frenzy of indignation and pain ; he
met them with a point-blank refusal, and was prepared, in the
case of letters, to take legal action.   Nor is this attitude
surprising, when it is remembered what positive agony was
caused to his wife by any written, still more by any printed,
reference to her personal sorrows.   He somewhat modified it
later on, when in 1877 he sanctioned the publication of her
correspondence with R. H. Horne ; because, as he informed
a correspondent, this " was literary only, between persons
who had never seen each other, and before I could pretend to
any sort of guardianship." [2]   He agreed to the printing of
these letters, as he told Domett, without asking to see them ;
because he knew that there would not be contained in them
any narrow opinions or ill-natured criticisms of any one which
it might be objectionable to publish.   Further, he recognized,
many years later, the propriety of an account of his wife being
inserted in the *Dictionary of National Biography*, and consented to verify the dates in the manuscript of his friend Lady
Ritchie, to whom the task was entrusted.   But beyond this

---

[1] From the dedication to Forster.
[2] Wise, *ut supra*, *Second Series*, vol. i. p. 74.

he would not go. When Domett remarked that it was a pity her Life could not be written, " No," he said, " it could not, or should not, be done." It was attempted, however ; and when preparing a complete edition of her writings in 1887 he took occasion to point out certain errors of fact which had found their way into a biography, in the production of which he had declined to bear a part.

But to pass to his own fresh compositions ; when, in accordance with what now became his customary practice, he sought in the summer of 1863 for rest and seclusion in a remote village, some of the poems which were to form his next volume must have been already in existence, and others in the making. One, *May and Death*, had already appeared in the *Keepsake* for 1857. Certainly two of them, *James Lee* (later called *James Lee's Wife*) and *Gold Hair* are intimately and respectively connected with Sainte Marie, the tiny hamlet of Breton fisherfolk which was his retreat during this summer and again two years later and with Pornic, the little neighbouring seaport, in those days not the full-fledged watering-place it has since become. At Sainte Marie Browning occupied the mayor's house, " large enough, clean and bare," he tells Miss Blagden. It is a solid and severe structure, built of greyish rough-cast, with shutters of the same colour and slated roof, an unpretentious door, and two red-brick chimneys, which only by their colour can be said to vary the general monotony of effect. Hard by is an old church, with a neglected, since ruined, Norman porch ; and the winds sweep mournfully through the wild grasses which cover the adjacent graves. Truly, the spot was one to inspire such sorrowful reflections as might people the lonely hours of *James Lee's Wife*. The fig-tree, the writhen vines, the fields, the sun-dried turf, the beach and the wide expanse of sea which she beheld from the " doorway," made up the view from Browning's windows. Something of its undertone of melancholy may have harmonized, we may suppose, with his then prevailing mood. But the note of wide spaces of sea, sky and land is not one of unrestricted sadness. If the wind was mournful, the sea was soft, and rich with promises of healing ; and there was the

" good gigantic smile o' the brown old earth,"

with its message of hope and better cheer. The poet " rather liked it all." He could work undisturbed, and keep early hours, read a little with his son, and have his father with him.[1]

Gold Hair is a true story, and may be read in M. Carou's *Histoire de Pornic*. Browning has not diverged in any particular from the details there recorded. The discovery of the gold was made in 1782. " Pleasant little Pornic church," dedicated to St. Gilles, was pulled down during his third visit to Sainte Marie, to give place to a new one ; an unnecessary piece of vandalism which he regretted keenly. It was at the annual fair of St. Gilles that he saw the handsome gipsy-woman who suggested his *Fifine*.

James Lee and *Gold Hair* hold the first and second place in *Dramatis Personæ*, his next volume. Published in 1864, it has been well described as a continuation of *Men and Women*. Yet certain differences are to be noted. On the one hand, the seamy side of life is more often in evidence, as in *The Worst of it*, *Dis aliter visum*, *Too Late*, *Confessions*, and several more. On the other hand, in some of the poems, notably in *Abt Vogler*, *Rabbi Ben Ezra*, *Prospice*, and the *Epilogue*, the poet's spiritual fervour touches its high-water mark. It is as though, possessed with a deepened sense of the tragedy of human things, and less alive, for the time being, to their joy, he turned for relief to other planes of existence ; upon which he fixes a gaze direct, confident and fearless. Vestiges of his own sorrow, and of his conflict with it, are certainly to be discerned in *Dramatis Personæ* ; hardly, indeed, could it be otherwise. In *Prospice*, one of his rare autobiographical utterances, they are plain for all to see. To this year also belong the lines on Frederick Leighton's *Orpheus and Eurydice*, the expression of a wife's intense devotion ; which, with sublime ineptitude, those responsible for the Royal Academy Catalogue printed as prose.

The tendency to find a starting-point in actual personages, whether belonging to previous ages or his own, is a strongly-marked feature in *Dramatis Personæ*.

May and Death, as we have seen, commemorates his cousin, James Silverthorne ; *A Face* is that of the first Mrs.

---

[1] His father was certainly with him once at Sainte Marie, probably oftener. *Le Poète Browning à Ste. Marie de Pornic :* par l'Abbé J. Dominique.

Coventry Patmore, " the Angel in the House " ; and the
features of Home lurk behind the mask of *Mr. Sludge, the
" Medium."* As a student of Rabbinical lore, Browning knew
that Ben Ezra was an appropriate mouthpiece for the
sublimest spiritual musings. This learned Hebrew, who
flourished in the twelfth century of our era, was one of the
four great lights of the Jews in the middle ages. He
travelled widely, was the author of many scientific and
biblical treatises, and was a strong upholder of the doctrine
of the immortality of the soul. Question has been raised
why Browning did not choose a greater composer than the
Abbé Vogler, whose name is less familiar than those of
several of his pupils, Weber and Meyerbeer for instance, to
express his feelings as to those lofty ideas which music is
capable of inspiring. But he needed, in order to illustrate
his parable, not music that has survived, but that of an
extemporizer, the persistence of whose chords has to be taken
on trust ; and so the Bavarian Abbé serves his turn quite as
well as a greater master. Besides, account must be taken of
his liking for out-of-the-way characters and careers. The
Abbé Vogler's life was full of vicissitudes and much-travelled ;
his " orchestrion," defamed in Amsterdam, was a success in
London ; and of those who knew him, some held him to be
a genius, others (wrongly, be it said) a charlatan. These facts
were eminently calculated to awaken Browning's interest.
Vogler's countenance, if Zeller's portrait at Darmstadt does
it justice, is expressive of shrewdness and good-humour
rather than of any marked spirituality.

About one poem in this volume he received through
Sir Edmund Gosse a message from Dr. H. H. Furness, of
Philadelphia, eminent as a Shakespearian scholar, which
highly gratified him. " Tell him," it ran, " how deeply, how
fervently I bless him for writing *Prospice*." [1]

For a summer holiday, *Dramatis Personæ* published, he
had a fancy to see what Arcachon was like. Finding it noisy
and modern, he and his party pushed on to St. Jean-de-Luz,
and thence, there being no accommodation, to Cambo in the
Pyrenees. From this village he visited the *pas de Roland*,
which, as letters to Story and to Tennyson testify, impressed

---

[1] Wise, *ut supra, Second Series*, vol. ii. p. 21.

him greatly.   On his return to London in October he received from the latter a present of his newly published *Enoch Arden* volume.   *The Northern Farmer*, shrewdly analytic, after the fashion of many of his own character-studies, took him by storm ; and he terms the metre of *Boadicea* " a paladin's achievement."   " I am thinking," he writes, " of Roland's Pass in the Pyrenees, where he hollowed a rock that had hitherto blocked the road by one kick of his boot." [1]

It was after he left Cambo for a three weeks' stay at Biarritz that a well-known reference to the future *Ring and the Book* occurs, in a letter of September 19, 1864, to Miss Blagden.   " My new poem that is about to be, and of which the whole is pretty well in my head—the Roman murder story, you know."   To this task he was now free to devote himself.   During the four years which he gave to it his creative powers were certainly at their highest.   A shrewd observer's description of what he was at this period is consequently of especial interest.   In 1865, with a view to entering his son's name at Balliol, he made the acquaintance of Benjamin Jowett, then senior tutor at that college.

" It is impossible," writes Jowett, " to speak without enthusiasm of his open, generous nature and his great ability and knowledge.   I had no idea that there was a perfectly sensible poet in the world, entirely free from enmity, jealousy, or any other littleness, and thinking no more of himself than if he were an ordinary man.   His great energy is very remarkable, and his determination to make the most of the remainder of his life." [2]

It is noteworthy that about this time Browning expressed precisely the same resolve to Miss Blagden : " I certainly will do my utmost to make the most of my poor self before I die." [3] Truly, any reader of *The Ring and the Book* who knew nothing of its author might well picture him as gifted with

---

[1] *Tennyson, a Memoir*, vol. ii. p. 16.   It is not without interest to note a parallelism of dates in the production of some of the greatest works of the two poets.   *In Memoriam* and *Christmas Eve and Easter Day* both appeared in 1850, *Maud* and *Men and Women* in 1855, *Enoch Arden* and *Dramatis Personæ* in 1864, *The Holy Grail* and the last parts of *The Ring and the Book* in 1869.

[2] *Life and Letters of Benjamin Jowett*, by Evelyn Abbott and Lewis Campbell, vol. i. pp. 400–1.

[3] Mrs. Orr's *Life*, p. 270.

those very qualities and powers which Jowett enumerates.
On the principle that "in small proportions we just beauties see," it is open to any reader of Browning to prefer this, that, or the other of his shorter poems to *The Ring and the Book* ; yet that this " Roman murder story " is the greatest achievement of his art it would be difficult to deny. To one who desired to become acquainted with his poetry and asked what he should read first, he made answer, " *The Ring and the Book*, of course." It is therefore of interest to remark how protracted was the period of incubation of this masterpiece. It was a burning noontide of June, 1860, when, as he crossed the Square of San Lorenzo in Florence, Browning picked up the " square old yellow book," from amid a heap of " odds and ends of ravage " offered for sale,

> " Gave a lira for it, eightpence English just ; "

it was the winter of 1868 when the first instalment of *The Ring and the Book* appeared. For eight years, then, this true tale of wrong and pity was, though with varying degrees of concentration, the companion of his inner life. That such long and close companionship is the necessary basis or only begetter of a great poem it would be futile to affirm ; but it is certain that Browning never wrote better or with more point and vigour than in this case, and never after longer or profounder meditation. To the fact that he brooded over his theme so long and so deeply, that he read the documents at his disposal eight times, that by continual association with his characters he became almost, as it were, identified with each one of them in turn, the finished work owes that certainty of touch and that air of utter completeness which have never been disputed. Here are no ragged edges, no makeshift reasonings, no tentative portrayals. The poet has entire mastery over his materials, and he knows it ; he moves amid them with ease, with power, and with triumph.

He has told us, in his own inimitable fashion, how, as he walked homewards that day in Florence, he was wholly absorbed in his prize ; how he read on

> " from written title-page
> To written index, on, through street and street,
> At the Strozzi, at the Pillar, at the Bridge ; "

until by the time he reached the doorway of Casa Guidi he had acquainted himself with the whole story of the trial and execution of Guido Franceschini for the murder of his wife ; how that same night he stepped out on to the balcony, and looking over the roof of the Church of San Felice, lit up for festival, saw in imagination through the blackness all the scenes where the grim tragedy was played out—Arezzo, where Pompilia was at once wife and prisoner, the wayside inn at Castelnuovo, still unchanged to-day, where the furious husband came up with the fugitives at dawn, and Rome, where he glutted his revenge and paid the penalty. It all acted itself over again before him, as he stood there, breathing

" The beauty and the fearfulness of night."

Such were the experiences and impressions of " that memorable day ; " and, he being the poet that he was, there can be little doubt that on the vision there followed a desire to embody it in verse. But the next day, or the day after, or many days after—it is impossible to be precise—there came reaction, and he put away any such design. It is certain that he offered the story to one of his friends in Rome that winter, Miss Ogle, as subject for a novel ; equally certain that he seriously suggested to another friend, Mr. W. C. Cartwright, that he should write an account of it. He went so far as to say that he would give him the book. Mr. Cartwright is under the impression, though unable positively to affirm, that he had it not then with him, but had left it in Florence. If that be so, Browning's statement that he took the book with him to Rome in order to institute inquiries upon the matter must be regarded as a poetic figment. In any case it is fortunate that neither of his friends accepted his proposal. As time went on, the " murder story " captivated his imagination more and more, and his heart as well. The figure of Pompilia, so infinitely pathetic, so intensely spiritual, unquestionably owes something to his own dearest memories and his own bereavement. When Nathaniel Hawthorne visited the Bownings in 1858 he described Mrs. Browning as " a pale, small person, scarcely embodied at all ; " as elfin, rather than earthly ; yet " sweetly disposed towards the

human race, though only remotely akin to it." [1]   Many years
afterwards Browning characterized this description to Domett
as very good and correct.   Pompilia, it is true, was " tall " ;
yet she has much of that almost unearthly grace and graciousness which Hawthorne saw in Mrs. Browning.   Well, therefore, might it seem matter of " predestination " that
Browning, and no other, should relate her story.

Upon that story's actual composition he spent four years :
so at any rate his own words, in the last section of the poem,
lead us to suppose ; when, handling once more the old
vellum-covered quarto, he exclaims—

> " How will it be, my four years' intimate,
>   When thou and I part company anon ? "

Mr. Cartwright, who spent a night or two at Warwick
Crescent, about 1863 or '4, remembers that Browning then
told him that he was engaged upon a poem based on the
Franceschini affair, as to which, he added, he had procured
further information : this would be that contained, we
judge, in a contemporary manuscript pamphlet, sent him by
a friend, containing an account of the murder and of Guido's
trial and execution.[2]   The contents of the " square old yellow
book," now in the library of Balliol College, have been
described by the poet himself.   Three-fifths of it are print,
the remainder manuscript.   The larger part consists of an
account of the trial, with its pleadings and counter-pleadings ;
with which have been bound up, probably by their recipient,
three manuscript letters announcing and describing the
execution of the murderer to Cencini, a friend of his
house, and the printed " instrument of the Definitive
Sentence," by which the innocence of Guido's victim was
affirmed.

---

[1] *Italian Notebooks*, pp. 11–13. There is more true insight in this picture of
the Browning household than in any other.
[2] See *Letters of R. B. to Isa Blagden*, pp. 65 and 68.   The friend was a Mrs. Baker,
of Florence.   On September 19, 1862, he asks for the MS. to be sent to him, on
October 18 acknowledges its receipt.   " It contains," he writes, " a few notices
of the execution, etc., subsequent to my account that I can turn to good.   I am
going to make a regular poem out of it."   This is his earliest reference to the sources
of *The Ring and the Book*.

" The Book ! I turn its medicinable leaves
    In London now till, as in Florence erst,
    A spirit laughs and leaps through every limb,
    And lights my eye, and lifts me by the hair,
    Letting me have my will again with these."

Thus does the poet vouchsafe us a momentary glimpse of
the joy of his creative hours.   The Book was " pure, crude
fact " with which he had to fuse his own " live soul."   His
own fancy was the alloy ; and not until fact and fancy were
commingled could he hope to hammer out a perfect Ring.
And as an actual Book, so an actual Ring played its part in
his inspiration ; he had in mind a simple and modern
Castellani ring, which his wife had worn, and which he wore
later fastened to his watch-chain, with the letters A E I upon
its flattened upper surface.[1]

It gratified him, on his visit to Oxford, to find
among the undergraduates a growing interest in his work.
He knew that he was gaining ground, for *Dramatis Personæ*
had reached a second edition, and, as his publishers told him,
most of the new orders came from Oxford and Cambridge.
But the process was slow ; and the impression which long
neglect had made upon his mind could not readily be
obliterated.   Writing to Mrs. Millais as late as January, 1867,
he speaks of himself as " the most unpopular poet that ever
was." [2] But the welcome given in this same year to a
volume of essays on his poetry by J. T. Nettleship was an
agreeable assurance that, if the circle whom he addressed
was comparatively small, it did not lack appreciation.

Meanwhile, work upon the great poem went on steadily,
whether he was at home or abroad.   It occupied the lion's
share of the time he devoted to composition, which meant
some three hours in the earlier part of each day.   Certain
minor tasks, however, were fulfilled.   In 1865 he prepared a
selection from his wife's poems, and another nosegay from
his own for Moxon's " Miniature Poets."   In this series
Tennyson had led the way.   No verses chosen for the earlier

---

[1] Communicated by Mr. R. Barrett Browning. Mr. W. C. Cartwright is the
authority for the incidents with which his name is connected. He was on intimate
terms with the poet ; used, in Rome ,to be constantly in his company.
[2] *Life and Letters of Sir John E. Millais*, by J. C. Millais, vol. i. p. 440.

selection were included, nor any but the lightest of his pieces. He also attended to the revision of his works for the fourth, or third collected, edition, that of 1868[1] ; and *Hervé Riel*, which remained unpublished until 1871, is dated " Croisic, September 30, 1867." It is arguable, also, that the descriptions of locality in *The Two Poets of Croisic* (1878) are too graphic to be reminiscent. But with these exceptions *The Ring and the Book* engrossed him wholly. As he wrote to a correspondent, "the business of getting done with some twenty thousand lines [in fact, over twenty-one thousand] very effectually suppressed any impulse to whistle between-whiles."[2]

Before its completion he was to lose two persons very dear to him, his father and his sister-in-law. His father had almost completed his eighty-fifth year when he died in Paris after a short illness, retaining to the end all the clearness of his brain and all the unselfishness of his disposition, begging his son and daughter not to grieve for him, since he was entirely happy. When all was over, Browning took his sister back with him to London, and from this date (14 June, 1866) she shared his home and was his constant and congenial comrade. There was in Miss Sarianna Browning much of her brother. She was a woman of excellent understanding, good sense and good temper, and she devoted herself to her brother as she had previously devoted herself to her parents. The comparatively early death of Arabel Barrett, which took place just two years later, was in a sense a sharper grief, since it re-opened an old wound. There was much in her nature that resembled that of her sister Elizabeth. Browning felt her death keenly ; it was long before he could bring himself so much as to pass the house where she had lived.

Sainte Marie had served its turn for three years ; but the neighbourhood still charmed the Brownings, and Croisic was chosen as their summer retreat in 1866 and '7. Croisic, northward of the mouth of the Loire, was another Pornic, only rather wilder ; it lies on a small bay near the extremity

---

[1] In this edition *Pauline* was acknowledged and included.

[2] Wise, *ut supra*, vol. i. p. 24. The letter was written, about a month before the first volume of *The Ring and the Book* was published, to Mr. E. S. Dallas, author of *The Gay Science*, who had invited him to contribute something to the *Mirror*, a short-lived weekly journal.

of a sandy peninsula, whose shores are swept and often drenched by great rushing waves. A few miles inland is the ancient walled town of Guérande, and "wild Batz," whose inhabitants, supposed of Saxon race, and getting a hard livelihood out of the salt-marshes, attracted the poet's notice by their quaint attire, shirts and baggy breeches of white and large black flapping hats. Vestiges of druidical worship are in sight ; and the survival of pagan rites, which Catholic remonstrance could not wholly kill, interested him not a little. He was lodged handsomely, too; he had never occupied a more delightfully quaint old house, and seldom a more roomy one. For these amenities he made repayment, as his manner was, in verse. Croisic's forgotten worthy, Hervé Riel, lives again in the stirring lines which go by his name. Croisic's *Two Poets* are resuscitated ; René Gentilhomme, whose courtly sonneteering was all burnt up by the sudden lightning flash of, so he believed, a message from God ; and Paul Desforges-Maillard, whose

> " story furnished forth that famous play
> Of Piron's ' Métromanie,' "—

a very diverting story it is—and may consequently be read in French or in English, according to the reader's predilection.[1]

In 1867 the University of Oxford honoured Browning and itself by conferring on him by diploma the degree of M.A., a distinction only awarded for eminence in the field of learning. He must have recalled with pleasure that Dr. Johnson's merit had been similarly recognized. A little later he became, chiefly through Jowett's instrumentality, honorary fellow of Balliol, where in after years he was repeatedly his guest. Next year he might have been Lord Rector of St. Andrews ; but this, and all similar positions, he declined, shrinking, as Gosse has recorded, from the " vague but considerable extra expense " which they would have entailed.[2] About the same period he changed his publishers ; Messrs. Smith and Elder from this time produced his works.

---

[1] Browning had probably read the story of Hervé Riel in Caillo's *Notes sur le Croisic*.

[2] He refused in 1875, and again in 1884, the offer of the Lord Rectorship of Glasgow University.

The reason was that Browning formed a personal friendship with Mr. George Murray Smith, who practically was the firm, and this put business dealings on a pleasant footing. An example of Mr. Smith's sagacity was quickly furnished. On reading the manuscript of *The Ring and the Book*, he took so favourable a view of it that he believed it would bear printing in four monthly volumes, instead of two, as the author had proposed ; and this, accordingly, was done.[1]

With the end of his great undertaking in sight, Browning must have fully appreciated this year's summer holiday. Again Brittany was the choice. In company with his son and sister he visited a district rich in prehistoric monuments and full of memories of Balzac's *Chouans*—Rennes, Carnac, Locmariaquer, Ste. Anne d'Auray, where Breton pilgrims most do congregate, the quaint old-world Morlaix, St. Pol de Léon with its tapering spire, and Roscoff with its wide, rock-strewn sands. Thence, by way of Quimper, to the little fishing-town of Audierne, on the westernmost point of France, where they found rest for their feet and took their ease, this time, at an inn. Perfect weather, bathing, and interesting walks predisposed them to contentment.[2]

The *Athenæum* for 21 November, 1868, contained an announcement that the first volume of *The Ring and the Book* was ready ; and the remaining three followed at regular intervals of one month, as arranged. On the 20th Browning had read the first part aloud at James Knowles's house at Clapham, where Tennyson was staying. It seemed to

---

[1] Wise, *ut supra*, *Second Series*, vol. i. p. 27. Browning makes this statement in a letter to Messrs Fields, Osgood and Co., dated September 2, 1868. In another letter (*Second Series*, vol. ii. p. 13) dated 17 February, 1884, he says that for fifty years he had stipulated that his publishers should never read a line of the work they were to publish until it was in *corrected* proof. He adds that Mr. Smith "cheerfully accepted this condition from the very first; and on the very last of our transactions he good-naturedly remarked, 'Had you let me read *Jocoseria* I would have printed 500 additional copies at once.'" The discrepancy must be explained either by postulating a lapse of memory on Browning's part, or by supposing "manuscript" in the earlier letter to be a slip for "proofs."

[2] Mrs. Orr (*Life*, p. 279) implies that the inn was not very comfortable. This may mean an absence of carpets and easy-chairs, which obtained at St. Pol-de-Leon's one hotel when the present writer visited it fifty years ago. The fare, however, was good and plentiful, and the same may have been the case at Audierne.

Tennyson "full of strange vigour and remarkable in many ways," but he was " doubtful whether it can ever be popular." [1] Some later comments by individuals are of interest. Fitzgerald could make nothing of the poem, but then he "never could read Browning." [2]   Connop Thirlwall found it at once attractive and difficult, and deplored the undue and " Chinese-like" condensation of its style; [3] Carlyle spoke of it with surface sarcasm.   But these casual utterances are of small moment in comparison with the considered verdict of the weightier reviews.   They were practically unanimous in their approval—*Fortnightly, Quarterly, Edinburgh, London Quarterly, Revue des Deux Mondes, Athenæum.*   Never before had the poet won such general and unstinted praise.   Room must be found for two of the most striking commendations. Speaking of the Pope, Caponsacchi and Pompilia, the *Edinburgh Review* said : " In English literature the creative faculty of the poet has not produced three characters more beautiful or better to contemplate than these three " ; and the *Athenæum*, in summing up, remarked : " We must record at once our conviction, not merely that *The Ring and the Book* is beyond all parallel the supremest poetical achievement of our time, but that it is the most precious and profound spiritual treasure that England has produced since the days of Shakespeare."

Before we take our leave of this poem, an interesting discovery must be recorded.   In January, 1900, thirty-one years after its publication, Signor Giorgi, librarian of the Royal Casanatense Library in Rome, unearthed a manuscript volume of old trials, wherein is bound up, along with the examination of Beatrice Cenci and the account of the recantation, in 1686, of Miguel de Molinos, whose followers are so often mentioned in *The Ring and the Book*, a narrative of the trial and death of Guido Franceschini.   The manuscript has much in common with the information of the " square old yellow book," but supplements it in various ways, and is the fullest prose account of the whole case which is known to exist.   Towards the end of it a reflection occurs which

---

[1] *Tennyson, a Memoir*, vol. ii. p. 59.
[2] *Ibid*. vol. ii. p. 69.
[3] *Letters to a Friend*, vol. ii. p. 184.

curiously anticipates the three points of view adopted by Browning in *Half Rome*, *The Other Half Rome*, and *Tertium Quid.* "Some defended the Comparini, on the ground that they had received ill-usage ; others the Franceschini, on the point of honour ; but upon calm reflection both were adjudged equally guilty—except Pompilia "—it is permissible to linger for a moment on that fragrant name—"who, being totally ignorant of the truth, had committed no other fault than that of having consented to a marriage at the command of her mother without the knowledge of her father ; and who had fled from her husband's home under fear of death, with which she had been repeatedly and unjustly threatened." [1]

After the appearance of his *magnum opus* Browning rested for a while from the labours of composition. It is natural to conceive of poets as brooding lovingly over their completed works ; but to attribute such an attitude to him would be to misunderstand his temperament and the deliberate principle on which he worked. He had a facility for forgetting his own things when once they were done. A finished poem was put away and behind him ; not, as he explained, because he undervalued it, but because he held it " good husbandry of energy in an artist to forget what is behind and press onward to what is before." *The Ring and the Book* was no exception. Writing twelve years after its publication, he says : " I have not looked at the poem since it appeared in print. At present I have the faintest memory concerning any particular part or passage in it." There is something almost forbidding in this neglect ; an unreasoning desire surges up to reproach the poet for slighting his own offspring ! Surprising as the attitude is, however, it has to be accepted ; [2] but not, indeed, wholly without deductions. He would read from his poems when requested : we find him reading aloud, this summer of 1869, parts of *The Ring and the Book* at Naworth.

In any case, his leisure never took the form of inactivity.

---

[1] A translation of this version of Pompilia's story, done by W. Hall Griffin, appeared in the *Monthly Review*, November, 1900. See Appendix B.

[2] See Wise, *ut supra, Second Series*, pp. 13 and 14, a letter written to Professor Dowden about *Sordello ;* and another written to Lord Courtney of Penwith, published (in part) by him in the *Times Literary Supplement*, 25 February, 1909.

R

If he did not at once begin to meditate a new poem, he did not fail in his allegiance to the sister arts of painting and music, whose kinship with poetry he expresses so finely in *Balaustion's Adventure*, or neglect the claims of society. He made many new friends, but none who proved dearer than the old and tried ones. Constantly in the spring Milsand was his guest in London, and this summer saw a renewal of intercourse with the Storys. In July he was out of sorts. "I was unwell," he writes to Mrs. Frederick Lehmann, "having been so for some time—and feel the grasshopper a burden all day long in the house, from which I never stirred." In this mood northern latitudes attracted him. In company with the Storys and their daughter he set out for Scotland, staying first at a little inn on Loch Achnault, near Garve, where the old style of life was renewed—luncheon amid the heather, followed by chapters from *Rob Roy*—and afterwards at Loch Luichart Lodge, where Louisa, Lady Ashburton, a brilliant if somewhat overpowering personage, was their hostess. Lady Marian Alford, a friend in Roman days, was among those who listened to the readings from *The Ring and the Book*. For another friend, Lord Dufferin, who had built a tower at Clandeboye in honour of his mother's memory, Browning wrote a sonnet, as Tennyson a poem; but did not include his *Helen's Tower* in any edition of his works.[1]

The following summer found him and his sister at St. Aubin,

> "Meek, hitherto un-Murrayed bathing-place,
> Best loved of sea-coast-nook-ful Normandy."

The presence of Milsand was the attracting cause, the only drawback the war then raging between France and Germany. Browning would tramp along the beach, with Homer for companion, and he took his customary delight in sea-bathing; but Milsand's society was the crown of the feast. He has sketched for us this reserved, sensitive, understanding man, a Protestant physician of souls, whose nature was in many ways the complement of his own.

---

[1] This northern travel is recorded in Mr. James's *W. W. Story*, vol. ii. pp. 197-8, and 200. For the poem see Appendix A.

" There he stands, reads an English newspaper,
Stock-still, and now, again upon the move,
Paces the beach to taste the Spring.

. . . .

He knows more, and loves better, than the world
That never heard his name, and never may.
What hinders that my heart relieve itself,
Milsand, who makest warm my wintry world,
And wise my heaven, if there we consort too ? " [1]

To this close friend, it is worth remembering, and to none
other, Browning used to submit his manuscripts, for criticism
of their matter and even of their punctuation. Other visits to
St. Aubin were to follow ; but on this occasion the intercourse
of the two men was cut short by the vexatious incident of the
Englishman being taken for a German spy. Milsand therefore
insisted on the necessity of immediate retreat. The usual
passenger boats were no longer running, but he hurried his
friends to Honfleur, where they secured their passage on a
cattle-boat bound for Southampton. Browning did not
approve of the French cause, but he sympathized with the
sufferings of the distressed Parisians. One practical instance
may be recorded. Averse, as a rule, from his poems
appearing in the magazines, he offered the as yet unprinted
Hervé Riel to his publisher for insertion in the *Cornhill;*
and there, in the number for March, 1871, it found a
place. The cheque for £100 which he received from Mr.
Smith in payment he at once forwarded to Paris ; an act,
when the subject of the poem is considered, as graceful as it
was generous.

With the spring of this year his muse was again in flower.
Balaustion's Adventure, imposed on him as a task by Lady
Cowper, and proving "the most delightful of May-month
amusements," was the first outcome of an extensive study
of Euripides undertaken some years earlier. It came out in
August, when he was staying with friends, the Benzons, at
Little Milton, up in the hills above Loch Tummel. He was
full of a translator's eagerness, coming over to Tummel
Bridge, where Jowett was staying, to talk to him about a
new rendering of a phrase in the *Alcestis*, αὐχμηρὸν οὖδας,

[1] From *Red Cotton Night-Cap Country.*

which he preferred, with reasonable probability, to interpret
as—

> " the floor
> unsprinkled as when dwellers loved the cool."

This is prettier, at any rate, than to interpet αὐχμηρὸν as
" dusty " or " uncared-for."   Swinburne was with Jowett,
but, alas! there was no Boswell present.   Browning was also
at work on his Napoleon poem, which appeared before the
year was out.[1]   A greater contrast than that presented by
Balaustion's Adventure and *Prince Hohenstiel-Schwangau* it
would be difficult to conceive.   The former is among the
most lucid and direct of his poems, the latter among the most
perplexing.   No one could possibly misunderstand the one,
plenty of people did misunderstand the other.   An *Edinburgh*
reviewer described it as an " eulogium on the Second Empire,"
another critic called it "a scandalous attack on the old
constant friend of England."   Browning, as we have seen,
always distrusted Louis Napoleon.   He believed, however, in
the genuineness of his desire to do something for Italy ; a
desire maimed, when he came to put it in execution, by its
owner's calculating temperament.   The poem is neither an
attack nor an eulogy ; but the kind of sophistical defence
which an opportunist might offer for his opportunism.   In the
February of this same year 1871, at Chislehurst, the Empress
Engénie said to Colonel Brackenbury of her husband :—
" History will yet give him the credit of having maintained
order in France for twenty years." [2]   This is practically what
Hohenstiel-Schwangau is made to claim ; that he had been
for that period, at the cost of certain abandoned ideals, the
" Saviour of Society."

It must be accepted as an instance of Browning's versatility that he could pass directly from Balaustion's glad,
confident view of life, to that other dim, foggy atmosphere,
in which the very forms of right and wrong are difficult to
distinguish.

The germ of this vision of the Hellenic world is derived
from a passage in Plutarch's *Life of Nicias*, which tells how

---

[1] *Life and Letters of Benjamin Jowett*, vol. ii. pp. 12–13.

[2] *Memoirs of my Spare Time*, by General Sir Henry Brackenbury, *Blackwood's
Magazine*, February, 1909.

a ship of Caunus, being chased by a piratical vessel, sought to make the harbour of Syracuse, and was at first refused admittance; then, question being put whether those on board of her knew by heart any of the poems of Euripides, and such assurance given, was straightway suffered to come in. In this manner the Rhodian girl, Balaustion, who had by heart the *Alcestis*, "that strangest, saddest, sweetest song" of his, saves herself and her fellow-travellers. It is a curious fact that when Browning gave his Rhodian heroine that melodious name of hers, which signifies "wild pomegranate flower," he was unaware that this flower was actually the emblem of Rhodes; he only learnt that it was so later, from the repro- duction of a coin in the British Museum given him by a friend. Balaustion's plight is her poet's opportunity; he gives us, through her lips, his version of the *Alcestis*, a play whose theme must to him have been infinitely touching; and not only so, but he intersperses comments of his own, for which he asks indulgence in a passage of rare grace and charm.

"'Tis the poet speaks :
But if I, too, should try and speak at times,
Leading your love to where my love, perchance,
Climbed earlier, found a nest before you knew,
Why, bear with the poor climber, for love's sake !"

It is arguable that he has made Euripides mean more than he intended; that there is a touch of modernity in his reading of Heracles and of Admetus; but it can be maintained with equal cogency that he has made intelligible and beautiful to the modern mind much that was obscure and much that was repellent. And as the invocation, "O Lyric Love," expressly connects *The Ring and the Book* with his wife's memory, so is her name bound up with this transcript from Euripides, the poet whom she loved and hailed as pre-eminently human. It contains also a reference to one who had been her friend and was still his, who had designed her monument in Florence, Frederic Leighton. Leighton is the "great Kaunian painter" who "has made a picture of it all." It was now that his "Heracles struggling with death for the body of Alcestis," said to have been suggested to him by the restoration to health of a great friend whose life was in imminent peril, was exhibited at the Royal Academy. Browning was a frequenter of Leighton's studio ; he found more poetry in his pictures than in those of any contemporary artist ; and without doubt had watched the growth of this particular one, dealing as it did with a story which greatly attracted him, and which he was presently to make his own.

Balaustion's Adventure had an immediate success. Within five months 2500 copies were in circulation, and a second edition was in the press ; "a good sale for the likes of me." Miss Browning told Domett that she and her brother considered it the most popular of his works. Beautiful as the poem is, and worthy to be admired, it unquestionably owed some measure of its popularity to earlier triumphs, which had disposed the public to give its author a favourable hearing. For he had come into his kingdom, after a protracted minority, with *Dramatis Personæ* ; and *The Ring and the Book* had crowned him.

CHAPTER XIV

NOTES FROM A DIARY

Alfred Domett's return from New Zealand—His diary—His *Ranolf and Amohia*—Browning's description of *Fifine at the Fair*—He finds the subject for a new poem at St. Aubin—*Red Cotton Night-Cap Country*—R. H. Hutton's opinion of it—The limits of the horrible—*The Inn Album*—Browning and vivisection—Horne's pension—Miss Egerton Smith—*Aristophanes' Apology*—Unfair methods of criticism—Browning's vocation, according to Carlyle—His true province, according to Swinburne—The *Pacchiarrotto* volume—Browning turns upon his critics—Domett's remonstrance — Browning unrepentant — Reminiscences of Shelley and Keats—Browning's *Agamemnon*—Domett's strictures—Death of Miss Egerton Smith—*La Saisiaz*.

THE year 1872 brought loss to Browning by the death of one of his closest friends, Miss Blagden ; but it also restored to him the chosen companion of his earlier manhood. In February Alfred Domett returned from New Zealand after close on thirty years' absence. There he had risen to be premier, while not neglecting the pursuit of poetry. He came back, somewhat tired of politics, with a long poem and the purpose to find a publisher for it. From his return, until his death in 1885, he kept the diary from which quotation has already been made. In it Browning's name, as might be expected, repeatedly figures.

He had written to his friend on Mrs. Browning's death, and received no answer. He had felt the silence, and the thought of it was with him on his first call at Warwick Crescent. Browning was out, but next morning Domett received the following letter, whose explanation and welcome were surely all that he could desire. "How very happy I am," it runs, "that I shall see you again ! I never could bear to answer the letter you wrote me years ago, though I carried it always about with me abroad, in order to muster up

courage some day which never came; it was too hard to
begin and end with all that happened during the last thirty
years. But come and let us begin all over again. My sister
tells me how your coming may be managed most easily.
Ever affectionately yours, Robert Browning." The letter is
dated 1 March. Three days later, at Warwick Crescent,
where was Milsand also, the old intercourse was renewed.

At this, the first of many meetings, the talk was of
old and recent days, and when they passed to present
times and present social conditions the returned exile
could hardly have had a more entertaining commentator.
Browning, when they were in society together, pointed
out to him many persons who had hitherto been but names
to him, though most of them distinguished names; George
Lewes, for instance, "not strikingly intellectual looking,
however remarkable for his talents"; at the Athenæum
Coleridge, the Attorney-General, who expressed the wish that
he could have got "the Claimant" a good flogging, Aubrey
de Vere, Cartwright, and Herbert Spencer, with high-peaked
forehead, reading in the library. Often they talked of poetry,
Domett jealous for the inclusion of old favourites in the new
selection Browning was making from his works, Browning
pointing out that he must pick and choose. He went through
the business, he explained, with reference to the imaginary
life of a sort of man, beginning with one set of likings and
fancyings and ending with another.[1] Then, too, the fate of
Domett's New Zealand Epic, *Ranolf and Amohia*, was
discussed. It is a long poem, some 14,000 lines. Smith
declined it because it "would not pay"; Murray on the
ground that he "never had anything to do with poetry or
sermons." At Browning's advice its author published it with
Smith and Elder at his own risk; and the advice was good,
for handsome things were said of the poem, by Tennyson
among others, and Domett was not out of pocket by it in the
end.

In April Domett notes in his diary: "Browning tells me he
has just finished a poem, 'the most metaphysical and boldest
he had written since *Sordello*, and was very doubtful as to its

---

[1] The published preface says much the same: only that "a sort of man"
becomes "an imagined personality." A "second series" was added in 1880.

reception by the public.'" This was *Fifine at the Fair*; and Browning's anticipation proved well grounded. *Fifine* was as fertile a source of misapprehension as *Hohenstiel.* To understand the poem it is necessary to remember, once more, Browning's fondness for putting a case, and his proneness to write "dramatically." If some reviewers and readers, as did happen, attributed to the poet the opinions upon love which he has put into the mouth of the Don Juan of *Fifine*, the mistake arose from their ignoring these methods of his. He has chosen to imagine and to express the sort of justification for inconstancy which a subtle intelligence, with a bad heart behind it, might devise. It would be just as reasonable to saddle Browning with his *Caliban's* religious scheme as with his Don Juan's conception of the laxity of the marriage-tie. Yet the mistake was made; and this, too, though *Fifine* was introduced and closed by two short poems which breathe a passion of faithful remembrance, whose application, in the light of his own past history, cannot by any possibility be misconstrued.

To take up the cudgels in defence of Byron, as the *Times* did, was at least more reasonable. Browning's old devotion to Byron has been mentioned, nor had he ceased to admire his poetry; but one article of "the famous bard's" creed he found particularly unpalatable, his assertion of the soul's nothingness in comparison with the Ocean. This he attacks somewhat boisterously in *Fifine*, and again in *La Saisiaz*; and, when Domett expressed surprise, averred that he protested against it as a Christian. "I never heard him, I think," comments the diarist, "avow his Christianity distinctly in his own person, except on this occasion."

By the time that the critics were puzzling their heads over his *Fifine*, he was once more at St. Aubin, occupying with his sister a tiny cottage

" With right of pathway through the field in front,
    No prejudice to all its growth unsheaved
    Of emerald luzern bursting into blue,"

scrupulous, as he tells us, to

" Keep the path that hugs the wall,"

as he "padded" from door to gate, on the way to his early

morning bathe. Milsand was again his neighbour, and at Lion-sur-mer, five miles away, Miss Thackeray (now Lady Ritchie) was spending the summer. She it was who bestowed on this region the name of White-Cotton-Nightcap country, from the head-dress worn by its inhabitants, which seemed in harmony with the sleepiness of the land ; and it was to her that Browning, as they paced the sand together, told the story of Mellerio, the Paris jeweller, whose tragedy was played out in this quiet corner of Normandy, where a superficial glance would least expect tragedy to be found. On leaving St. Aubin he passed a month at Fontainebleau, when his chief reading was in Æschylus, the one book, perhaps, which Miss Thackeray saw in the St. Aubin cottage ; but he had at least one other with him, his friend's newly-published *Ranolf and Amohia.* From Fontainebleau, on 18 October, he wrote Domett a long letter in which he praises the poem highly.

"I hope," he writes, " I am no more surprised at the achievement than is consistent with my always having held to the belief that whenever 'Waring' reappeared some such effect would follow the phenomenon . . . . Whether people accept it now, or let it alone for a while, in the end appreciated it is certain to be."

When the friends met again in London, Browning reiterated his expressions of approval, suggested that a copy should be sent to Carlyle (which had been already done), and agreed to send one to Tennyson from the author. Domett received, in course of time, an appreciative note from Tennyson, which he showed to Browning, who considered it was a good deal for *him* to say. "When I sent him *Fifine at the Fair,* the only acknowledgment I got was, ' Received and welcomed.' " The diarist hastens to add : "I have, however, always heard him speak of Tennyson as most generous in his recognition of the claims and merits of others."

Browning had also poetical news of his own. He said enthusiastically, "I have got *such* a subject for a poem, if I can do justice to it." This was the Mellerio story, picked up in Normandy, where it still was common talk, which was presently to appear under the title of *Red Cotton Night-Cap Country.* Mellerio's tragedy explains the substitution of "red" for white. Browning meant to devote himself to it and not dine out for two months. In the end it occupied him only seven weeks, and was printed from the first manuscript as he wrote it off. "This," says Domett, "I think a great pity, though it may and does show his great facility and power of execution;" and he quotes Byron's remark about easy writing and hard reading.

An unexpected difficulty arose about publishing. All the incidents of the story being true to the letter, Mr. Smith got alarmed at the risk of an action for libel which might arise from certain passages reflecting upon the conduct of members of the "hero's" family and upon that of the bankrupt tailor who was the "heroine's" husband, disguised as the names and localities in some respects were. Could a Frenchman obtain damages for libel in this country, supposing the poem to be libellous? The first lawyer consulted left the point doubtful. Browning then applied to his friend the Attorney-General, who thought that unless fictitious names were in all cases substituted an action might lie. This was accordingly done, and the poem sent to press. Browning was a little vexed by the delay caused by the first lawyer's ambiguity, and jokingly remarked on the density of the legal intellect, declaring that "Poets were the clearest headed, after all."

Red Cotton Night-Cap Country appeared in May, 1873. Domett's diary affords a curious comment. "September 16. Called on R. H. Hutton [of the *Spectator*]. He did not think there was a single line of poetry in *Red Cotton Night-Cap Country*. Certainly wrong there. I mentioned the allusion to Napoleon. He admitted *this* was." [1]

> [1] "Some dead and gone
> Notice which, posted on the barn, repeats
> For truth what two years' passage made a lie :
>
> .   .   .   .
>
> And, woe's me, still placards the Emperor
> His confidence in war he means to wage,
> God aiding and the rural populace."

Some retrospective comment on this poem is furnished by a letter which its author wrote, in 1888, to Mr. J. T. Nettleship : "I heard, first of all, the merest sketch of the story, on the spot : Milsand told me that the owner of the house had destroyed himself from remorse at having behaved unfilially to his mother : in a subsequent visit he told me some other particulars—and they at once struck me as likely to have been occasioned by religious considerations as well as passionate women-love. I concluded that there was no intention of committing suicide,

What the reader of this poem and of *The Inn Album*, published two years later, will probably feel is, that they have more than their fair share of what is repellent and even horrible; yet their author had clear views as to the limits of the horrible in poetry. During Emerson's late visit to England, Browning had argued against his assertion that Shakespeare always avoided the horrible and the disgusting in his dramas. Browning did not believe that Shakespeare wrote *Titus Andronicus*, but he instanced the stamping out of eyes in *Lear*. He thought that it was Shakespeare's established pre-eminence of reputation that made the public accept murder scenes and revolting circumstances from him without disgust. Some one had submitted to him, as matter for a poem, the account of a very revolting episode in byegone days in Norfolk. He stopped in his reading of it to express his disgust at the subject. " Besides," he said to Domett, " it is very nearly the same as that of Horace Walpole's ' Mysterious Mother.'" He dwelt upon the bad taste of choosing such themes for works of art. " As if," he said, " a painter should choose no colours to work in but blood red and lampblack."

This conclusion is unimpeachable, but like other people Browning did not always practise what he preached. Gloucester's atrocious punishment in Lear is only tolerable because of Edgar's filial distress and care ; just as Regan and Goneril are endurable because of the contrasted nobleness of Cordelia. But in *Red Cotton Night-Cap Country* the sketch of Milsand is, so far as character is concerned, the sole relief in a desert of moral ugliness ; and in *The Inn Album* it is only a subordinate personage who lightens, for a moment, the prevailing atmosphere of gloom. Both narratives are unquestionably moral in their tendencies, in both the poet makes truth his main object: but he seeks truth so exclusively that beauty, an equally essential element of poetry, is neglected.

About this time Browning received a Trans-atlantic compliment as characteristic as it was, from a monetary point of view, unprofitable. The Chicago Railway Company began

---

and I said at once that I would myself treat the subject *just so*. Afterwards he procured me the legal documents, I collected the accounts current among the people of the neighbourhood, inspected the house and grounds, and convinced myself that I had guessed rightly enough in every respect."

to publish his works, part by part, as an appendix to their periodical time-tables, of which 10,000 copies circulated monthly. They began with *Paracelsus*. Taking up this edition at Warwick Crescent, Domett began to read aloud a passage which he considered for beauty of imagery and fervour of diction its author had never surpassed. It is that which ends :—

> " To me, who have seen them bloom in their own soil,
> They are scarce lovely : plait and wear them, you !
> And guess, from what they are, the springs that fed them,
> The stars that sparkled o'er them night by night,
> The snakes that travelled far to sip their dew ! "

Browning listened attentively, and then remarked : " If I had written those lines nowadays, I wouldn't have left such a defect in them as those rhyming endings 'you' and 'dew' in blank verse." Domett, who had known them by heart for nigh on forty years, and had never noticed the rhyme, thought this comment hypercritical.

Browning had now (July, 1873) returned to Euripides. As the friends crossed the Park one afternoon he repeated the whole plot of the *Hercules Furens* which he had just been translating, collating four editions as he went along. " I think," writes Domett,

"he made the story more affecting than it is either in the original or in his own subsequent version . . . He was full of the pathos of the scenes in Euripides, particularly of that in which Hercules becomes conscious of what he has done and comments upon it passionately to Theseus."

He gave Domett a copy of each of his new books as they were published, also the Tauchnitz edition of his poems so far as it had appeared—it began in 1872—and that of the *Selections* from Mrs. Browning's poetry and of her *Aurora Leigh*. He said of *Ranolf and Amohia*, " My appreciating your book is only like appreciating myself." Talking of critics, he said there was not a single one living whose opinion he valued " a snuff."

He again this year passed the early autumn at St. Aubin. During the winter his son, encouraged thereto by Millais, determined to take seriously to painting as a profession.

Nothing could have pleased Browning better. He had himself, as he repeated to Domett, "always envied the life of a painter." He took the keenest interest in his son's artistic studies, which were pursued at Antwerp, and the greatest delight and pride in the success which in course of time attended them. The new year found him in capital spirits, as Domett testifies.

"Feb. 3, 1874. Dined at the Miss Swanwicks, Regent's Park. Browning there, Miss Frances Power Cobbe, a young poet named Gosse, and others. Miss Cobbe very animated, clever and jovial, looking rather like a Dan O'Connell in petticoats, her dress a loose kind of purple satin jerkin, her face square and ruddy. She and Browning got into a lively discussion as to good or evil preponderating in human life generally, Browning taking the optimistic view of the matter and ending, 'Well, I can only speak of it as I have found it myself'; which did not satisfy Miss Cobbe. He told me he had dined with the Chief Justice, Sir A. Cockburn, a fortnight since; and had been present during the whole of his summing up on the Tichborne Case."

Upon one subject, vivisection, Miss Cobbe and he were quite agreed. "I would rather," he had said to her in Florence, "submit to the worst of deaths, so far as pain goes, than have a single dog or cat tortured on pretence of sparing me a twinge or two." To this opinion he adhered consistently, as is shown by the *Tray* of 1879, and a letter written in 1883, in the course of which he says: "If I were not committed by an inveterate habit of abstention from all public or quasi-public meetings . . . I would be present at yours; but whoever cares to know does by this time know how much I despise and abhor the pleas on behalf of that infamous practise—Vivisection." The *Arcades Ambo* of his final volume expresses precisely the same view.

His old acquaintance, R. H. Horne, who, besides being a poet, had done some public service in Victoria, had fallen on evil days, and found it necesary to apply for a Civil List pension. Browning, with many other leading literary men, signed the petition. Happening to meet Gladstone at Alton Towers, he pressed the point upon him, backed up by Lady Marion Alford. Gladstone thanked them, and made a memorandum, but nothing came of it. It was reserved for his successor in the Premiership to grant the pension in the June of this year. "Gladstone ought not to have let slip this piece of graceful justice," comments Browning, in the course of a congratulatory letter to Horne, " but the gods are against him just now."[1]

During the summer holiday of this and the three following years (1874–1877) Browning and his sister joined forces with Miss Anne Egerton Smith. The acquaintance had begun in Florence. Miss Smith, who now lived in London, had considerable private means, being part proprietor of the *Liverpool Mercury*. She went little into society, but was a great lover of music. This was the main bond of union between her and Browning ; every important concert found them together in the audience ; but she was also the possessor of sterling qualities, behind a reserved exterior, as readers of *La Saisiaz* know. Mers, a sea village on the outskirts of Tréport, was the trio's choice this year ; followed in turn by Villers-sur-Mer, the Isle of Arran, and the Salève district, near Geneva. Browning published nothing during 1874 ; but he finished his Greek play, and at Mers, where nine weeks were spent, worked hard at *Aristophanes' Apology*, in which it is introduced.

The following spring his portrait was painted by Rudolf Lehmann, at the request of Frederick Lehmann, his brother, and exhibited at the Academy. A little later his *Aristophanes' Apology* appeared, a work remarkable for the extensive knowledge it displays, both of the plays of Aristophanes and of what the scholiasts said about them. Of the manner of its reception let the diary speak :—

" Called on Browning, found him and his sister at home. We talked about his new book, and how some of the critics had abused it. The most virulent of these, he said, had written attacks upon it in three different periodicals—misquoting passages and designedly leaving out words or lines so as to make absolute nonsense of them. It was the old story, ' Folly loves the martyrdom of Fame.' I remarked, however, upon the large demands Browning makes in this book on his readers' knowledge, and said that I believed no one would be able to understand all the allusions without referring over and over again to the Comedies : and that he thus wilfully restricted the number of his readers to comparatively few. He would not hear of explanatory notes ; said it could not be helped, but that he was not likely to try anything of the kind again. This reminds me of the way in which he dismissed his ' experiment' in play-writing in *Bells and Pomegranates* in 1845 or '6."

He had a further grievance against the critics. In the *Athenæum* it was suggested that *Aristophanes' Apology* was "probably written after one of Mr. Browning's Oxford symposia with Jowett." Upon this several other reviewers reported the poem to be "the transcript of the talk of the Master of Balliol "—"whom," he assures a correspondent, " I have not set eyes on these four years, and with whom I never had a conversation about Aristophanes in my life. Such a love of a lie have the verminous tribe! " [1]

Nor is the praise awarded to a poet always happy. Seated on the hearthrug at Cheyne Row, with a screen between his face and the fire, and smoking his pipe as he talked, Carlyle told Browning that he liked *Aristophanes' Apology* much, but asked why he did not tell it all in plain, straightforward statement ?   " As if," Browning exclaimed, in describing his visit, "this did not make all the difference between a poet's treatment of a subject and a historian's or a rhetorician's! " It must have been a bit of Carlyle's banter, Domett thought. At any rate, Carlyle appreciated Browning's transcripts from Euripides, for he said to him not very long after, " Ye won't mind me, though it's the last advice I may give ye ; but ye ought to translate the whole of the Greek tragedians—that's your vocation." Browning did mind him, however, to the extent of translating one play, to gratify his venerable mentor, as his *Agamemnon* and its preface show.

Aristophanes' Apology, memorable for the reappearance of the delightful Rhodian girl, Balaustion, and for the justice done to two great exponents of the tragic and the comic muse, was speedily replaced in its author's mind by another and this time a modern subject. Of this, and of other matters which were engaging his attention, his friend's diary gives us an idea.

" July 24.   Met Browning in Westbourne Terrace. Walked with him.   He had seen Tennyson the day before.   He had

[1] Wise, *ut supra*, vol. i. p. 34.

expressed an opinion strongly in favour of Tennyson's play of *Queen Mary.* . . . He had received in acknowledgment of this what he called a 'charming letter,' which he shortly described.   He expatiated on Tennyson's hearty appreciation of the merits of brother poets. . . . He had received a picture from Pen, 'his first composition,' an old man contemplating a skull. . . . He complained of being bilious ; had been hard at work.   'Why don't you rest ?' said I.   'We shall have time enough to rest by-and-bye.' . . . He had finished nine-tenths of a new poem already."

This was the *Inn Album,* which came out in November, 1875, and of which the diary (9 December) has more to say :—

"Calling on Browning found him confined to the house by a bad cold. . . . He looked rather paler than usual, but was as animated as ever.

"He seemed to have seen all the critiques on *The Inn Album,* laughed at some abuse in the *Guardian* on the style, confessed to a slip in grammar noticed by the *Saturday Review.*   Talking of the plot he maintained that there was sufficient motive for the young man killing the old one, who had attempted to make him the instrument of degrading the woman he was in love with under threat of ruining her.   He said the nucleus of the story was actual fact : he had heard it told thirty odd years ago of Lord de Ros.   He wrote the poem in two months.   Smith and Elder told him that 1100 copies out of an edition of 2000 had already been sold.   He had intended originally to write a tragedy upon the subject, but hearing Tennyson was engaged upon one (*Queen Mary*) gave up the idea.

"He congratulated himself on having got rid of his American publishers, who had neglected to send the money they had agreed to pay for his last work for a considerable time after it was due. He had now had the pleasure of telling them that the *New York Times* had paid him double the money they offered him for the new poem, and he could do without them.   It appears accordingly in that paper, seven columns of it at a time.

"He did not much admire Rossetti's poetry, 'hated all affectation.'   He laughed at the cant about the 'delicate harmony' of his rhymes about the Haymarket.   He quoted Buchanan's parody of them, adding a line or two of his own, similarly rhymed :

'But grog would be sweeter
And stronger and warmer,' etc.

"I was mentioning the absurdity of the praise some one had bestowed on the idea in Rossetti's *Blessed Damozel* of the Damozel's arm resting on the bar of Heaven and making it warm, a fancy after all originally and infinitely better given in *Sordello*, where Palma throws her scarf upon Sordello 'her neck's warmth and all.' He said he was afraid I was going to quiz the notion with a similar case a lady had told him of the other day ; how, she having a bad cough in church, an old gentleman sitting next her pulled a lozenge out of his waistcoat pocket and offered it to her, 'quite warm, and redolent of old churchwarden.'

"We were interrupted by a great screeching at the back of the house. 'Ah, there are my pets,' said Browning. They were two geese. 'They are such affectionate creatures, and I am sure it is not for what one gives them.'"

Although the *Athenæum*, strange to say, rated the *Inn Album* higher than *The Ring and the Book*, as a whole Browning had lost ground in general estimation since the publication of his great poem. The series of psychological studies beginning with *Fifine at the Fair* had perplexed and alienated many minds ; nor is it likely that posterity will put any one of them on a level with the best of his earlier work. More remarkable is it, therefore, that it was these very studies which captivated Swinburne, who took no pleasure in Browning's plays or lyrics. Of *Fifine* he said, "This is far better than anything Browning has yet written. Here is his true province." One fruit of this development of taste in Swinburne was the enthusiastic appreciation of Browning's poetry which finds a place in his essay prefixed to R. H. Shepherd's edition of the poems of Chapman, published in this year. It amazed, we are told, some of Swinburne's friends, and bewildered Browning as much as it gratified him. Copies of *Pacchiarotto*, *Agamemnon* and *La Saisiaz*, presented to Swinburne by their author, attest his grateful recognition of a brother-poet's glowing tribute. But the temperaments of the two men were inharmonious, and their acquaintance never ripened into friendship. It may be added that in 1879 Browning, all unwittingly, gave great offence to Swinburne by accepting the presidency of the New Shakespeare Society, of which Swinburne was the sworn enemy.[1]

[1] *Swinburne : Personal Recollections.* By Edmund Gosse, *Fortnightly Review,*

Pleasant as the praise of a fellow-craftsman was, it could not altogether atone for the hasty and unfair criticism which had assailed him from other quarters. It is no wonder that he grew tired of "slaps in the face" apparently dealt him "in order," as he puts it, "to keep some fellow's critical hands warm."[1] Later on he grew indifferent to such treatment. When, in 1887, a correspondent forwarded to him a so-called criticism from the pages of a provincial newspaper, he replied, with praiseworthy equanimity,

"I am quite sure you mean very kindly, but I have had too long an experience of the inability of the human goose to do other than cackle when benevolent, and hiss when malicious; and no amount of goose criticism shall make me lift a heel at what waddles behind it."[2]

But in 1876 his mood was not so peaceable. Nor is it apparent why a man may not defend his literary repute from unfair attacks, as he would his moral character. Browning determined, as Byron did before him, to trounce his detractors handsomely; and trounce them he did.

The unsuspecting reviewer who turned the pages of *Pacchiarotto*, making notes by the way upon the jerkiness of its metre and the crudity of its phraseology, must have undergone painful emotions of surprise when he found, without a moment's warning, himself and his pretensions gibbeted.

> "I have told with simplicity
> My tale, dropped those harsh analytics

(those, that is, of *Fifine* and its successors)

> And tried to content you, my critics,
> Who greeted my early uprising!"

And then follows an audacious apologue. It is May morning, the critic-sweeps are assembled in their wonted

June, 1909. When Browning died, the younger poet wrote a noble set of appreciative sonnets. "But this," added Gosse, "was a late literary exercise, and part of the extraordinary 'funereal' taste of Swinburne, who had a passion for delivering imperious demands for the immortality of persons recently deceased. And of course he knew that Browning was a great poet; and probably he felt that in his lifetime he had not consistently done him justice."

[1] Wise, *ut supra*, vol. i. p. 90.
[2] Wise, *ut supra*, Second Series, vol. ii. p. 52.

disguise, trampling on the flower-beds in the poet's garden and pressing upon him their uninvited services.   He appears at his window and lets loose upon them a torrent of boisterous ridicule and invective, half jest, half earnest, good-natured in the main, but rather savage at the close.   Who could stand up under such a cataract ?   We actually see the unwelcome visitors, buffeted, belaboured, deafened, making off as quickly as they can from so tempestuous a neighbourhood.

Combative methods of this nature are obviously liable to be regarded differently by different people.   Domett, in deprecating them, probably voiced the feelings of many other readers of the *Pacchiarotto* volume.   He thought them hardly worthy of the poet ;   contemptible attacks were, in his opinion, better unnoticed.   But Browning stuck to his guns ; he declared that the allusion to a particular critic, with which the tirade closes, was a mere piece of fun, indulged in once in a way.

" He has been flea-biting me," he wrote, " for many years past in whatever rag of a newspaper he could hop into—which I should never have turned on my side to escape ; but there was talk of ' administering castigation to poor Mr. Browning,' which I have never brought myself to acquiesce in, even in metaphor. . . .   I don't mind leaving on record that I had just that fancy about the people who ' forty years long in the wilderness ' criticized my works."

After this onslaught upon his critics he proceeds, in two other poems of the *Pacchiarotto* volume, to apologetics of a less militant character.   In *At the " Mermaid "* he enters a just protest against the fallacy of identifying a dramatic writer with the children of his fancy, in *House* claims that respect for the privacy of his inner life which is the right of every human being.   The *Epilogue*, with its contention that the wine of poetry cannot at once be sweet and strong, is less convincing ;   since it is easy, without going further afield, to refute the doctrine out of Browning's own writings.   The *Epilogue* is his last printed word to his critics, save for the brief and good-humoured postscript to the controversy in the *Pambo* of 1883, from which quotation has been already made.[1]

---

[1] Or was it ?   Mr. T. L. Hood's search in the *Examiner* has brought to light (1) a disclaimer by Alfred Austin, (2) further stanzas of invective signed R—— B——

The volume has the further interest of being the first collection of miscellaneous poetry which he had published since *Dramatis Personæ* ; and of the pieces which it contains several are up to his highest lyrical and dramatic standards ; notably the beautiful *Prologue, Appearances, A Forgiveness,* and *Numpholeptos.* The description of the " arms of Eastern workmanship " in *A Forgiveness* was suggested by a collection of such weapons bequeathed to him by his friend Ernest Benzon—" daggers of various kinds," so Domett describes it, " Italian, Portuguese, Malay creases, a long silver-chased Turkish pistol, etc. The hilt of one sword had been set with valuable jewels." Such " horror coquetting with voluptuousness " pleased Browning well, both on the score of rarity and suggestiveness.

In *Filippo Baldinucci on the Privilege of Burial,* a masterpiece in its kind—he always wrote admirably when he wrote of Jews—the narrator describes the old spokesman Jew as High Priest, whereas Rabbi should be the term used. In a discussion on the poem the error was pointed out and attributed to Browning, whereupon he took up his parable :—

" This comes of forgetting that one writes dramatically. The speaker, Baldinucci, is a typically ignorant Tuscan, and makes the gross mistake already noted in Arbuthnot's *Martinus Scriblerus*— of whom it is said, at the very beginning, ' Those who had never seen a Jesuit took him for one, while others thought him to be rather some High Priest of the Jews.' Somebody," he continues, " objected to a Jewish burying-ground being in the neighbourhood of any habitation, but Baldinucci tells the story, and describes the locality as he knew it—and I follow him, of course." [1]

Of the origin of *Cenciaja* he writes :—

" I got the facts from a contemporaneous account I found in a MS. volume containing the ' Relation ' of the Cenci affair—with other memorials of Italian crime—lent me by Sir J. Simeon, who

(3) a leading article summing up the controversy. However, the verses, " To my critics ; written since my late publication," are such shocking doggerel that it is hard to believe that Browning wrote them. Can the Editor of the *Examiner* have been taken in ?

[1] Wise, *ut supra, Second Series,* vol. ii. p. 61. Baldinucci wrote a History of Art, and the story told by the poet as " a reminiscence of 1676 " appears there in a notice of the life of the painter Buti. The episode of the intervention of the Rabbi's brawny son is Browning's own.

published the Cenci Narrative, with notes, in the series of the Philobiblion Society. It was a better copy of the ' Relation ' than that used by Shelley, differing at least in a few particulars." [1]

To Shelley his thoughts recurred at this period owing to an interchange of letters with Mr. Buxton Forman, who was preparing his library edition of that poet's works. It will be remembered that a copy of Keats' *Lamia* was found in the drowned Shelley's hand.

" Leigh Hunt told me," Browning writes, " that the *Lamia* was the only copy procurable in Italy. That he lent it to Shelley with due injunctions to be careful of the loan on that account, and that Shelley replied emphatically : ' I will return it to you with my own hands.' He told me also of the consolation there was to him in the circumstances that the book had been found in Shelley's bosom, together with the right hand—evidently thrust there, as his custom was, when, having been struck by any passage in whatever book he might be reading with a friend, he paused to enjoy and pronounce upon it. This circumstance Leigh Hunt considered decisive as to the suddenness and comparative painlessness of the death. It is altogether incompatible with the truth of the silly story put into circulation recently. [That is, that he was murdered.] On my asking Leigh Hunt if the book still existed, he replied : ' No, I threw it into the burning pile ; Shelley said he would return it with his own hands into mine, and so he *shall* return it.' I confess to having felt the grotesqueness of a spirit of a duodecimo as well as that of a man. I remember Leigh Hunt was standing by a piano when he told me this. He had been singing to his own accompaniment the old *Stanco di pascolar le pecorelle*. I observed : ' Do you know Shelley has mentioned that air ? ' He did not, though he said it had been a great favourite with Shelley." [2]

Of the last days of the author of *Lamia* he had heard much from Joseph Severn, whom he knew in Italy. One day Severn found Keats, who was studying Italian, deep in Ariosto. " Fine, isn't it ? " he said. " Yes," answered Keats, sadly ; then, tapping his own forehead, " but there's something here that could equal it, if they would give me but a chance." Domett, to whom Browning repeated this inci-

[1] Wise, *ut supra*, vol. i. p. 43.

[2] Wise, *ut supra*, vol. i. pp. 48-9. Shelley *alludes* to the air in the *Triumph of Life*; where Mary Shelley added a note in explanation.

dent, believed that he would have made good the assertion, had he lived. " I believe it too," said Browning ; and then expressed a very high opinion of his extraordinary powers of imagination and of the beauty of his diction. Horne, Domett remarked, remembered Keats at Edmonton, when apprenticed to a surgeon there ; and how he used to wait for his employer outside the houses where he visited, " sitting in his gig, holding the reins, and looking half asleep."

Browning's own contribution to verse in 1877 was his translation of the *Agamemnon*, largely undertaken from a wish to please Carlyle, who was gratified at the manner in which he is mentioned in the preface.[1] One who approaches the *Agamemnon* with a determination " to be literal at every cost, save that of absolute violence to our language " can hardly expect to please widely ; moreover, the metre chosen to represent the iambic trimeters of Æschylus must strike any reader of the original as curiously infelicitous. It would seem that Domett was among those who were a little restive.

" I asked him, supposing on his own theory that the English version ought to be as difficult to English readers as the Greek original was to the Greek ones, and the Greek avowedly required the Greek notes of the Scholiast to render it intelligible—whether it was not reasonable to give English notes to his translation, that English readers might understand it. He agreed that notes might be necessary, and said he had no objection to any one else making them. This, however, should have been done in the first instance. He mentioned that, while engaged upon his work, he met one of the first Greek scholars in England, who asked him if it were true that he was translating the *Agamemnon*. Browning answering in the affirmative, the other said, ' And can you understand it ? For I have known it these twenty years, and I can't.' "

His summer holiday this year had closed very tragically. Together with his sister and Miss Egerton Smith he was staying at a little villa, La Saisiaz (the sun), at the foot of the Salève, four or five miles S.W. of Geneva. An ascent of the mountain by carriage had been arranged. The friends had parted over night in the best of spirits, and, seemingly,

[1] The task was, says the preface, " commanded of me by my venerated friend, Thomas Carlyle, and rewarded will it indeed become if I am permitted to dignify it by the prefatory insertion of his dear and noble name."

of health.   What followed may be told in Miss Browning's version, as Domett reports it.

" Browning had been for his usual bathe in a pool among trees down the mountain-side, and on returning found Miss Smith had not made her appearance.   ' All right,' he thought, ' she is saving herself for the journey.'   Miss Browning going into her room to look for her, found the poor lady lying with her face downwards upon the floor.   She put her arm round her, saying, ' Are you ill, dear ? ' then saw that she was insensible.   It was three hours before a doctor could be procured, they having to send to Geneva for one."

He could have done nothing, however, had he been close at hand, for Miss Smith was dead.   After her burial at the neighbouring village of Collonge, the brother and sister returned to England, in no mood for further holiday.   It was some time, his friends remarked, before Browning recovered his usual spirits.   The sad experience through which he had passed bore fruit presently in the tender and beautiful poem called *La Saisiaz*.   The " travelled friend," who was to have gone with them on the expedition that fatal morning, was a Frenchman, M. Gustave Dourlans.   The poem has many facets ; it is autobiographical, elegiac, and reflective. It abounds in glowing description of Alpine scenery, in intimate personal touches, and in splendid rhetorical passages. It must, to those who welcomed its appearance in 1878, have seemed a return to all the poet's finer characteristics.   The debate on the soul's immortality, subtle as it is, is yet suffused with emotion.   And this is doubly natural, not only because of Miss Smith's death, but because she and Browning had a few days before been discussing this very subject, which from June to October had formed the theme of a " symposium " in the *Nineteenth Century*.   Among those who took part in it were Mr. Frederic Harrison, R. H. Hutton, Huxley, Lord Blachford, Roden Noel, and W. G. Ward.   The later pages of *La Saisiaz* may be regarded as charged with Browning's contribution to this

                                " fence-play—strife,
Certain minds of mark engaged in ' On the Soul and Future
    Life.' " [1]

---

[1] The *Epilogue* to the La Saisiaz volume, it may be noted, can be traced to the *Anthology*, where there occur two versions of the Cicada story, one under the name of Paulus Silentiarius (6.54), the other (9.584) anonymous.

CHAPTER XV

THE LAST DECADE

Italy once more—Intermediate halting places—The Splügen—Gressoney—St. Pierre de Chartreuse—Browning revisits Asolo—and Venice —*Dramatic Idylls*, first and second series—A note on *Clive*—Death of Carlyle—The Browning Society—How Browning viewed it—He visits Oxford and receives the D.C.L.—Impressions of an eye-witness—*Punch's* shrewd lines—*Jocoseria*—A growl from Domett—Mrs. Arthur Bronson— Browning's Venetian days—*Ferishtah's Fancies*—Visit to Edinburgh— At Llangollen—Death of Domett—and of Milsand—*Parleyings with Certain People of Importance in their Day*—A subject for verse declined —Browning's health gives cause for anxiety—The Rezzonico palace— His last visit to Oxford—and to Cambridge—Third and last sojourn at Asolo—At Venice—Catches cold on the Lido—Brief illness—Death —*Asolando* published—Impressive ceremonial in Venice—Burial in Westminster Abbey.

I N the year of the publication of *La Saisiaz* Browning had the satisfaction of seeing his son's status as a painter recognized. Already, two years earlier, Frederick Lehmann had given a handsome price for a study of a monk reading a book; now "The Armourer" was hung in the Academy and found a purchaser in Mr. Fielden, a member of parliament, with whom neither the artist nor his father was acquainted. The private view of "Pen's" pictures at a house in Queen's Gate Gardens, where a room was lent for the purpose, became an annual event, to which Browning was wont to bid all his friends. It was on one of these occasions that he failed at first to recognize in a well-dressed visitor his own cook; and on discovering her identity did the honours of the exhibition without the least embarrassment and with, if anything, an added touch of cordiality.

He had now been self-exiled from Italy for seventeen years. The intention to return had been only dormant; and the year 1878 saw it at last fulfilled. At the Splügen, where he broke his journey, the keen air and wild scenery found him in the vein : he there wrote, as has been mentioned, *Ivàn Ivànovitch,* and also *Ned Bratts,* having in his mind, in connexion with the latter, the story of " Old Tod," as told in Bunyan's *Life and Death of Mr. Badman.*[1] He never went further south than Venice ; but Venice, from this time forward, drew him with a sure attraction each successive autumn. Only thrice was he an absentee, when circumstances were too strong for him ; a flooded country in 1882, and his sister's illness in 1884 and 1886. The first halt on the Splügen proved so restorative that it became his habit to spend five or six weeks in the mountains, amid whose solitudes he breathed in new life and refreshment after the social exigencies of the London season, before descending to the plain.

"Six weeks in this delightful solitude, with one day only to prevent our leaving the house ! On every other morning and afternoon we have walked right and left, never less and often more than five hours a day—and the good to us both, I hope, certainly to myself, is in proportion. At Venice we shall be social, however, and I cannot expect to return with as florid a pair of cheeks as I occasionally get glimpses of in the glass." [2]

Thus he wrote from Gressoney St. Jean in 1883, the " delightful Gressoney " of the prologue to *Ferishtah's Fancies,* rich in those country products on which he loved to fare when on his travels. In another letter he describes it as—

" a beautiful place indeed, a paradise of coolness and quiet, shut in by the Alps ; just under Monte Rosa with its glaciers."

The difficulty of attaining to this paradise added zest to the endeavour.

" From Jura to Pont St. Martin by two hours' carriage-drive, and thence seven continued hours of clambering and crawling on muleback. And just so shall we have to descend when time comes and snow falls." [3]

But whether on mule-back or afoot, Miss Browning was as constant and tireless a companion to her poet-brother as

[1] Wise, *ut supra,* vol. ii. p. 7.   [2] *Ibid.* p. 24.
[3] Wise, *Second Series,* vol. i. p. 84.

was Dorothy Wordsworth to hers; and cheerfully accepted such primitive accommodation as happened to satisfy his taste. Thus at St. Pierre de Chartreuse, their place of sojourn in 1881 and 1882, the "hotel" was "the roughest inn, and its arrangements the most primitive, I have yet chanced upon —but my sister bears them bravely"; a roughness, no doubt, which was a small matter in comparison with "the extraordinary picturesqueness and beauty of the wild little clump of cottages on a mountain amid loftier mountains."[1] Another attraction was the neighbourhood of the Grande Chartreuse, where Browning would stay the night in order to hear Midnight Mass. This, privilege, however, was denied to his sister. Another of their summer haunts was St. Moritz. There they were the guests, in 1884, of an American friend, Mrs. Bloomfield Moore, at the Villa Berry. "We have walked every day," writes Browning, "morning and evening —afternoon, I should say—two or three hours each excursion, the delicious mountain air surpassing any I was ever privileged to breathe."[2] And from the same place, three years later, describing an August snowstorm:—

" we are ' snowed up ' here this morning; cannot leave our house to go to the hotel opposite, close by, where we get our meals! Our amends is in the magnificence of the mountain, and its firs black against the universal white . . . exactly such a snow-storm as I happened to read of in the *Iliad* this morning, the only book I brought with me. . . . The days slide away uneventfully, *nearly*, and I breathe in the pleasant idleness at every pore. I have no new acquaintances here—nay, some old friends—but my intimates are the firs on the hill-side, and the myriad butterflies all about it, every bright wing of them under snow to-day, which ought not to have been for a fortnight yet."[3]

Such were his halting-places on his way to Venice, invigorating alike to mind and body. But before Venice, Asolo. He trod the streets of Asolo in 1878 after an absence of over forty years. From the ruined castle on its hill-top he sought and found a remembered echo; with such echoes,

[1] Wise, *ut supra*, vol. i. p. 69. Both Gressoney and St. Pierre were recommended by M. Dourlans, the "travelled friend " of *La Saisiaz*.

[2] Wise, *ut supra*, vol. ii. p. 37.

[3] *Ibid.* p. 71.

be sure, of his poetic youth as do not faint into nothingness, but "grow for ever and for ever."

After a short sojourn here he removed to Venice, putting up at a quiet hostelry, the Albergo dell Universo, where he again lodged in the three ensuing years. He was not slow to determine that Venice should always in future be the goal of his autumnal pilgrimage. No other place seemed half as satisfying.

The *Dramatic Idylls* of 1879, a worthy successor to *Dramatis Personæ*, showed that increasing years had not undermined his vigour or diminished his poetic faculty. The wine is as strong as ever and, in *Pheidippides* at least, as sweet. As much can hardly be said for the *Dramatic Idylls : Second Series*, of the ensuing year, though *Clive* is great enough to atone for much inferior work. Of the origin of this poem Domett's diary has the following account :—

" Referring to that most vivid and thoroughly realistic narrative of Lord Clive and his duel, Browning told me he heard it first from Mrs. Jameson, soon after his marriage. Mrs. Jameson said she had it from Lord Lansdowne, to whom it had been told by Macaulay. The idea of what Clive would have done [viz. blown his own brains out] had his antagonist (after Clive's pistol was accidentally discharged, leaving Clive at his mercy) generously given him his life, at the same time reiterating his innocence of the cheating Clive had charged him with, instead of throwing down his pistol and confessing it—all this, he said, was merely his own invention, which he had no authority for, or for attributing it to Clive himself. ' But what else,' said he, ' could such a man as Clive have done ? He could not have reasserted the charge, unless as a calumniator, for no one would have believed a man so magnanimous could have been capable of cheating at cards.' He added that he had only very recently read Lord Macaulay's article on Clive, and had looked up other authorities, but had not found the duel anecdote recorded anywhere. One would like to know how Macaulay got hold of it." [1]

A little later (February, 1881) death severed his long acquaintance with Carlyle. A fortnight or so earlier Browning had called at his house, and had seen him lying

---

[1] Macaulay, however, while giving no details, does mention "a desperate duel with a military bully who was the terror of Fort St. David."

on the sofa in "a comatose state," so would not let him be
disturbed. Carlyle, he told Domett, was anxious to die.
Froude's subsequent "disclosures" awoke Browning's strong
resentment. He refused to believe that Carlyle was other
than the most tender-hearted of men. He was fond of
telling how when once he was walking with him they were
passed by a butcher-boy "savagely leathering his horse,"
and how Carlyle exclaimed with passion, "Ah! if I could
only get at that brute!"

It was in this year that Browning received one of the
greatest compliments ever paid to an author: the foundation,
in his lifetime, of a Society for the study and discussion of
his works and for the wider diffusion of the knowledge of
them. The Browning Society of London, which had presently
allied branches in other parts of the United Kingdom and in
America, was the joint creation of Dr. F. J. Furnivall and
Miss Emily Hickey. What Browning thought of the movement is explicitly stated in several letters which, happily,
have survived. The first of these, written to Miss West
(later Mrs. Dowden), and dated 12 November, 1881, has the
following passage :—

"I will tell you how I feel about the Society. It was instituted
without my knowledge, and when knowledge was, I do not think
acquiescence had need of being asked for. I write poems that they
may be read, and—fifty years now—people said they were unintelligible. If other people, in the fullness of days, reply ' we understand them, and will show that you may, if you will be at the pains,'
I should think it ungracious indeed to open my mouth for the first
time on the matter with ' Pray let the other people alone in their
protested ignorance.' I see a paragraph in *The World* to the effect
that none of my personal friends figure in the list of members. Had
I persuaded them to do so, the objection would have been more
cogent, ' only a clique—the man's personal following !'

"Exactly what has touched me is the sudden assemblage of
men and women to whose names, for the most part, I am a stranger,
who choose to incur the ridicule sure to come readily to the critics
who dispose of my works by the easy word 'unintelligible,' instead
of saying safely to themselves ' *I* understand it—or something of it—
anyhow !' That there would be exaggeration in the approval was
to be looked for ; they react against a good deal.

"As for Dr. Furnivall, I am altogether astonished at his caring about me at all. I suspect it is a late discovery with him—like that of Fontenelle when, chancing upon some out-of-the-way literature, he went about asking everybody, ' Do you know Habbakuk ? He's a genius ! ' I think him most warmhearted, whatever may be the mistakes about me of which his head is guilty ; and as Lear's last instance of ingratitude is that of the mouth biting the hand for lifting food to it—so, it seems to me, would as signal an one be the writer of books that are commonly pronounced unintelligible, objecting to the folk who propose to try that question." [1]

To Dr. Furnivall, in 1882, when certain journals affected to sympathize with him on being made ridiculous by the Society, he wrote :—

" Pray don't imagine I can't understand the mock compliments to myself pretended to be involved in the censure of those who make so thoroughly appreciated a person ' ridiculous ': the *ridiculus mus* is the inveterate nibbler at, and spoiler of a man's whole life's labour, which might otherwise go to the bakehouse and prove tolerable ship-biscuit." [2]

And about the same date he gave Edmund Yates the memorable assurance,

" As Wilkes was no Wilkeite, I am quite other than a Browningite. But," he adds, " I cannot wish harm to a society of, with a few exceptions, names unknown to me, who are busied about my books so disinterestedly. . . . That there is a grotesque side to the thing is certain ; but I have been surprised and touched by what cannot but have been well-intentioned, I think." [3]

Finally, that the debates of the Society, and its performances of several of the plays, not only spread a knowledge of Browning's poetry, but had a substantial effect on the sale of his works, is attested by a letter written in the last year of his life to J. T. Nettleship.

" When all is done," it runs, " I cannot but be very grateful for the institution of the Society ; for to what else but the eight years' persistent calling attention to my works can one attribute the present demand for them ?

" If Johnson showed his good sense in telling somebody who

---

[1] Wise, *ut supra*, *Second Series*, vol. i. p. 64.
[2] Wise, *ut supra*, vol. i. p. 97.
[3] Wise, *ut supra*, *Second Series*, vol. i. p. 81.

deprecated the appearance of an adverse criticism on something he had just brought out, 'Sir, if the critics did not notice me, I should starve'—well, I am justified in fancying that, but for what was done by Furnivall and his colleagues, I should have no more readers than ten years ago." [1]

Such an effectual helper to the poet was the Society which existed to do him honour and service.

On the completion of his seventieth year another distinction awaited him, the University of Oxford conferring upon him the honorary degree of D.C.L. In the course of the ceremony an undergraduate jester let down from the gallery a red cotton nightcap, and dangled it above the new doctor's head. He was like to pay severely for his prank, but Browning interceded with the Vice-Chancellor, and the culprit was forgiven. An observer who watched the procession to the Sheldonian remarked how lightly Browning carried his seventy years, how briskly he stepped along, in his new red gown, with head thrown back and eyes on the buildings, roofs, and sky. The same observer (Mrs. Arthur Sidgwick) had met him at Balliol the previous evening.

" He took me down to dinner," she writes, " and on the stairs I discovered the kind, blue-eyed man to be friendly and not formidable. He talked on any subject; we selected the Cherwell water-rats, which interested us both; but I was all the time trying to get him to talk of his wife, and, as far as I remember, we spoke of Florence and of Venice. He gave one the feeling of being never to be old; [2] and the gentlest, dearest of men ! "

Punch, which always " treated him gently," as he said, took occasion to publish his " fancy portrait," a clever sketch by Sambourne, as " Robert Browning, D.C.L., The Ring and

---

[1] Wise, *ut supra, Second Series,* vol. ii. p. 74. One indirect benefit should be mentioned : the writing of Mrs. Sutherland Orr's valuable handbook to Robert Browning's works. The poet himself wrote of it :—" I should say that Mrs. Orr's Handbook is anything but a hindrance, rather the best of helps to anyone in need of such when reading—or about to read—my works. It is done far better than I could hope to do it myself." Letter to Mr. R. M. Leonard, 21 January, 1889.

[2] So also Lady Ritchie in her *Records,* etc. : " He was always young, as his father had been before him." The epithet " blue-eyed " will be remarked ; it should be " gray-eyed," but it is not always easy to distinguish between grayish-blue and bluish-gray. Mrs. Browning, oddly enough, described Athene as the blue-eyed (γλαυκῶπις) goddess, a rendering not usually accepted.

Book-maker from Red Cotton Night-Cap Country." Many a true word is spoken in jest, and two stanzas of the verse which accompanied the portrait are interesting as a contemporary estimate of his position. The parody of his own *At the " Mermaid"* is at once apparent.

> " Though the world may cry out, frowning,
>   ' Hard is he to understand ! '
> See societies called ' Browning '
>   Flourish largely in the land.
> I'm too crabb'd, confus'd, and mystic
>   So brays out each kindly ass,
> Sounds his trumpet eulogistic,
>   'Ορείχαλκος—made of brass.

> " Let the world wag on, these letters
>   Show one poet's got his due ;
> I've received them like my betters,
>   Smaller men have gained them too.
> But, in spite of all the stir made,
>   Put the robes upon the shelf :
> I 've my corner at ' the Mermaid '
>   With ' rare Ben ' and Shakespeare's self."

He had been for some time guardian, so to say, of the memory of an earlier poet, Thomas Lovell Beddoes (1803–49), all whose papers, together with correspondence referring to him, had been bequeathed to him by Kelsall, Beddoes' executor. Beddoes' life was an unhappy one, and Browning felt great difficulty in dealing with these memorials of it. The time, indeed, was not ripe for such an adequate account of the dead poet's career as a study of them indicated. Edmund Gosse, Browning's near neighbour in London, might well, he conceived, undertake the responsibility. It was Gosse's habit to pay him an early visit on his way to his work ; and on one of these visits the contents of "that dismal box," as Browning called it, were unreservedly handed over to his custody and discretion.

"A collection of things grav*ish* and gay*ish*—hence the title *Jocoseria*—which is Batavian Latin, I think."[1] Such is Browning's own description, in 1883, of his new volume of

---

[1] Wise, *ut supra*, vol. ii. p. 12.

miscellaneous verse. Its longest piece, *Jochanan Hakkadosh*, was misunderstood in certain quarters. It will be remembered that Jochanan's days are prolonged by the self-sacrifice of some of his disciples. But no physical process is supposed to be entailed. It was here that misapprehension arose.

" I got an American paper last night," wrote Browning, " wherein there is repeated that Jochanan revived by ' a transfusion of blood.' There is not a word about such a thing ; on the contrary, the account in the poem makes it impossible. How could the ' transfusion' bring experiences with it ? Or how could the boy's gift, ' which he threw and it stuck,' be taken in that manner ? This comes of the critics reading attentively the criticisms of their brethren, and paying no attention at all to the text criticized. The writer of the article in the *Times* made the mistake first, and even the *Academy* article must needs follow him. The whole story is a fiction of my own, with just this foundation, that the old Rabbins fancied that *earnest wishing* might add to a valued life." [1]

The rebuke is just. The poem in question, however, is by no means one of its author's clearest ; and it is worth remarking that Domett's comment on the volume, in his diary, is a prolonged growl. After criticizing the " defect of perversity in the use of words," he concludes, glancing at the phraseology of the introductory lines,

" It is questionable whether the poet would not have gained more admiration as well as given more pleasure had he condescended to attract the vast numbers his obscurity repels, by ' completing his incompletion ' and letting his meaning ' pant through ' the beauty of his poem a little more decidedly and distinctly."

One poem, which would certainly have graced its pages, *Jocoseria* did not include ; a translation of a German lyric, made about this time for a friend, Mrs. R. Courtenay Bell, for inclusion in her English version of von Hillern's novel, *The Hour will come.*[2]

The pleasure of the Brownings' annual visit to Venice had latterly been enhanced by their acquaintance, which ripened into friendship, with an American lady, Mrs. Arthur Bronson. When, in 1882, financial ruin came upon their Albergo, she

[1] Wise, *ut supra*, vol. ii. p. 16.
[2] See Appendix A.

T

put at their disposal a suite of rooms in the Palazzo
Giustiniani Recanati, which, says Mrs. Orr, formed a supplement to her own dwelling, and would take no refusal.   Here
the brother and sister kept house, only dining and passing the
evening with their friend ; but during later sojourns they
occupied an apartment under her own roof.   Mrs. Bronson
has left an account of Browning's Venetian days ;[1] of his
explorations of the byways of the city, his repeated visits to
the Public Gardens, where his friends were the wild creatures
in captivity there, his delight in hunting the curiosity shops
for bargains, and his joy in walking on the Lido, "even in
wind and rain."   There he would take the keenest pleasure in
the magnificent sunsets, and, as he writes to a friend, in "the
break of sea on the strip of sand, as much as Shelley did in
those old days."[2]   Venice, whether in its work-a-day or its
holiday garb, equally fascinated him ; he would comment on
the beauty of the street children, and, remarking on a workman's well-cut features, would pronounce them worthy of one
of Tintoret's senators.   And Venice, for her part, was not
careless of his presence.   When, in 1883, a statue of Goldoni,
the dramatist, was erected, he was asked to write a word or
two for insertion in an album to which the principal men of
letters in Italy had contributed.   "I made a sonnet," he says,
"which they please to think so well of that they preface the
work with it."[3]   It was written rapidly, but bears no mark of
haste.   Published in the *Pall Mall Gazette* of 8 December, it
has been reproduced in no edition of his works, but deserves
to be remembered both on account of its excellence, and in
testimony of his appreciation of the sound and colour of
Venetian life.

> "Goldoni—good, gay, sunniest of souls—
>   Glassing half Venice in that verse of thine—
>   What though it just reflect the shade and shine
> Of common life, nor render, as it rolls,
> Grandeur and gloom ?   Sufficient for thy shoals
>   Was Carnival : Parini's depths enshrine
>   Secrets unsuited to that opaline
> Surface of things which laughs along thy scrolls.

[1] Published in the *Century Magazine*, vol. 63, pp. 578-9.
[2] Wise, *ut supra*, vol. i. p. 85.
[3] Wise, *ut supra*, vol. ii. p. 35.

There throng the people : how they come and go,
  Lisp the soft language, flaunt the bright garb—see—
On Piazza, Calle, under Portico
  And over Bridge ! Dear king of Comedy,
Be honoured ! Thou that didst love Venice so,
  Venice, and we who love her, all love thee !"

There was, indeed, another side to the picture. His love
for Venice made him the more indignant with the vandalism
of some of her citizens.

" Everybody who can block up a window, brick over a moulding,
or other apparently useless ornament, does so ; or, better, disposes of
it—a balcony, well, or such like fixture—to the Jew antiquity-
mongers. It is really an argument against the throwing open
museums and galleries to the people on Sundays that here, where
the works which glorify such institutions were originally produced,
and where similar excellences may be still seen every day, the
inhabitants have the worst taste in the whole world." [1]

Something may be allowed here for a touch of the spleen ;
at any rate, " though much is taken, much remains " ; Venice
was still Venice, and unrivalled.

Ferishtah's Fancies, its author's matured speculations on
some of the deepest things of life, appeared in 1884. In this
year Edinburgh University, on the occasion of its tercen-
tenary, followed the example of Oxford and Cambridge, and
conferred upon him an honorary degree. He was the guest
of Professor Masson, whose daughter has since published her
impressions of the visit, and remained in Edinburgh nearly
a week, charming everyone by his accessibility, good-humour,
and unflagging spirits. Once Miss Masson observed him

" standing silent, facing and looking down upon a shorter man, who
looked up at him and spoke eagerly and excitedly. Mr. Browning's
expression was one of mild and benevolent kindliness, with a hint
of humour behind the smile. And the words of the shorter man, as a
passer-by overheard them, were : ' The *best* thing I ever wrote—— ' "

The shorter man's name has, mercifully, not been preserved.
Another afternoon, at a conversazione held in the Museum
of Science and Art, when he and a companion, a little
embarrassed by the attentions of the crowd, found themselves

---

[1] Wise, *ut supra*, vol. ii. p. 27.

face to face with a large glass case containing a stuffed lion, his friend was fain to whisper, "Mr. Browning, it seems as if you would be safer if *you* were in that case instead of that other lion!" But when, a little later, his hostess asked him apologetically, "Do you object to all this adulation?" he answered, anxious, no doubt, to set her apprehensions at rest, "Object to it! No; I have waited forty years for it, and now—I like it!" But what he liked best of all was the tremendous reception which the students gave him. Indeed, it so moved and touched him, that for once he broke through his invariable rule. He, who alike at a lord mayor's dinner and in hall at Balliol—though in the latter place R. L. Nettleship tried to tempt him by describing him as "one who had touched nothing which he had not struck fire out of"—had refused to answer for "literature," on this solitary occasion was persuaded to reply—for himself. In a very few words—the only "public speech" with which he is to be credited—he thanked them.[1]

In the following year his son, who had not visited Venice since his childhood, was with him there. Ambitious plans were the sequel of this sojourn.

"I have been kept thus long here," Browning writes (17 November, 1885), "by the business of buying a Venice Palace, the Manzoni Palazzo, of which you may see an account in the guide books. I think, with many or most of them, that it is the most beautiful house —not the biggest nor most majestic—in Venice. I buy it solely for Pen, who is in love with the city beyond anything I could expect, and had set his heart on this particular acquisition before I joined him, quite unaware that I had entertained a similar preference for it years ago. Don't think I mean to give up London till it warns me away; when the hospitalities and innumerable delights grow a burden, even as we are assured the grasshopper will eventually do in the case of the stoutest of us. Pen will have sunshine and beauty about him, and every help to profit by these, while I and my sister have secured a shelter when the fogs of life grow too troublesome."

A hitch occurred, however, in the negotiations. The vendor drew back, believing he could get a better offer. Browning

[1] *Robert Browning in Edinburgh*, by Rosaline Masson, published in *Cornhill*, February, 1909.

went to law with him, to make him carry out his contract ; but afterwards, on learning that the main walls, hidden by tapestry when he saw them, were cracked and the foundations shaky, he gave up, paid his costs, and withdrew from the action.[1]

Next summer his sister was ill, and they did not go abroad ; but spent eight or ten weeks at the Hand Hotel, Llangollen, where Miss Browning's health was happily restored. They had old friends as neighbours, Sir Theodore and Lady Martin. Each Sunday afternoon Browning was to be seen in the little old church at Llantisilio, and after service he would accompany the Vicar to the Martins' house, there to spend the evening.

" A term of delightful weeks," he called it in retrospect, " each tipped with a sweet, starry Sunday at the little church, leading to the House Beautiful, where we took our rest of an evening spent always memorably." [2]

Yet a shadow was cast upon these quiet days by the death of Milsand, whose health had for some time been failing ; a loss the heavier to Browning in that a bare twelvemonth earlier his oldest friend, Alfred Domett, had passed away.

There are several important landmarks in 1887. In the spring appeared *Parleyings with Certain People of Importance in their Day*, his penultimate volume, the reminiscent character of which has already been discussed.[3] It need only be added that in *Francis Furini* the handling of the ever-recurrent subject of the nude in art was suggested to him by some objections raised to a picture which his son had lately painted of Joan of Arc standing beside a pool, where she is about to bathe.

In June he left Warwick Crescent for a much better and roomier house in De Vere Gardens ; and in October occurred the marriage of his son, an event which he welcomed with the utmost satisfaction. At St. Moritz, in August, he was well and in good spirits, after slight indisposition, as several letters prove. To Dr. Furnivall, who had suggested as a subject for poetic treatment the incident of a fisherman promising to take the pledge if the lady who pressed him

---

[1] Wise, *ut supra*, vol. ii. p. 46.   [2] Mrs. Orr, *Life*, p. 406.
[3] Of this work he characteristically wrote to Mr. Laurence Barrett, " it ought to be my best."

to do it would strip like Godiva and swim to him, he replied, as wittily as decisively—

"Oh, for your subject—really it is not versifiable—sufficient to the deed is the prose treatment thereof. Besides, since she could swim a mile with ease, the reward of the feat was surely in itself during the hot weather of last month :

> Accoutred as she was not, plunging in,
> She watered, so to speak, the boatman's gin."

Of the achievement itself he adds :—

"Is it so wonderful ? I think I could have managed it once upon a time, but I gave up swimming because of a peculiar affection of the throat—real strangulation—if the salt water got into it ; and I rather aimed at long continuance in the sea, than going away from shore. Pen could have performed the feat with ease. But I thought your approbation went to the fact that she stripped and swam to win over a sottish fellow to leave his bestiality, and I hold that if he were unamenable to the ordinary reasons why he should cease to make a beast of himself, his life was not worth saving at any price ; and I, for my part, would have refused, 'accoutred as I was, to plunge in'—unless I bade him follow, sure that he would go to the bottom. Such a fellow, after exacting such a sacrifice, would be sure to get drunk the next day on the strength of his having made a fool of her." [1]

In the winter his health for the first time gave serious apprehension to his friends. One severe cold followed another ; but he made light of them, and in the intervals went about his ordinary avocations. The spring of 1888 found him stronger, and occupied with a final revision of his poems. They appeared in monthly volumes, and the series was completed in July, 1889. The mountain halting-place chosen for the summer was Primiero, in the Dolomite Alps. Thither he set out in August, though, as he was suffering from an affection of the liver, the journey proved a very trying one. At Primiero, however, which seemed to him even more beautiful than its predecessors, he recovered in a few days, pronouncing himself "absolutely well" ; and his subsequent Venetian sojourn was prolonged beyond its usual limit. His son had bought the Rezzonico palace, which was

---

[1] Wise, *ut supra*, vol. ii. pp. 73 *et seq.*

an additional source of interest.   It was February, 1889, before he was again in London.

Looking back on the completed life of man or woman, it often seems that their later actions were, all unwittingly to themselves, in the nature of farewells.   In this, his last summer, Browning made the circuit of his favourite haunts. It had become his custom to visit Oxford in Commemoration week.   Mr. A. L. Smith recalled that on one such occasion, in 1879, he came to a ball at Balliol and sat on the dais beside Jowett, the two looking "like a pair of sphinxes," as some one said ; and that he said it interested him to see the dancing.   He used often to say how much he regarded himself as an intimate friend of the College, and he was particularly eager to hear about everything that concerned Jowett or illustrated his character.   Now, at the same season, he was at Balliol once more, and much in the society of the Master. His last words to a friend on leaving Oxford were : "Jowett knows how I love him."   A little later he was at Cambridge. Mr. Gosse, who sat with him in a secluded corner of the Fellows' Garden at Trinity, recalls that he was in a quiet, retrospective mood, talking principally of old Italian days ; and then, some episode instinct with latent drama cropping up, the "shaping spirit of imagination" asserted itself, and he was showing, with his usual animation, how he would from these materials build up a poem.   The 18th June, Mrs. Orr records, found him paying his customary visit to Lord Albemarle, the last surviving officer who fought at Waterloo. And one of the last letters he wrote before leaving England was to congratulate Tennyson on reaching his eightieth birthday.   It is the summing-up of the love and admiration of many a year.

Another letter, written a little earlier, shows that he still did not shrink from social engagements, and that he had not lost his sympathy with youth and charm.   It is to Frederick Lehmann's daughter, and tells how he met the Shah at dinner, and how the monarch asked him for a volume of his poems.

" I have been accordingly this morning to town, where the thing is procurable, and as I chose a volume of which I judged the binding might take the imperial eye, I said to myself, 'Here do I present my poetry to a personage for whom I do not care three straws; why should I not venture to do as much for a young lady I love dearly, who, for the author's sake, will not impossibly care rather for the inside than the outside of the volume?' So I was bold enough to take one and offer it to you for your kind acceptance, begging you to remember in days to come that the author, whether a good poet or no, was always, my Alma, your affectionate friend,

"ROBERT BROWNING"

There is one other note, a very brief one, which may here fittingly find a place in further witness of the graciousness of old age. A schoolgirl, an entire stranger to the poet, was set, as a task, to write an explanation of *Prospice*. Dissatisfied with her attempt, she ventured to send it for his inspection. He returned it with sundry corrections and the following comment :—

"There, my dear young lady, I have done the little that was necessary, and hope it may suffice. Affectionately yours,

"ROBERT BROWNING"

When the season for migration came he was disinclined for long travel, and thought of letting Scotland take the place of Italy; but pressing invitations, from Mrs. Bronson at Asolo, and from his son, now installed in the Palazzo Rezzonico, turned the scale. The journey was accomplished safely and without discomfort.

Round the minute, ancient city of Asolo there creeps and winds an almost ruined wall; and niched in one of its eighteen towers, resting partly upon the wall, half found in existence, and half constructed, stands "La Mura," Mrs. Bronson's summer refuge from the heat of the plains. The apartment provided for her guests, consisting of a couple of bedrooms and a little sitting-room where the poet wrote, is just the other side of the way. On the outside of the building is a tablet, thus inscribed: "In questa casa abito Roberto Browning summo poeta inglese, vi scrisse Asolando, 1889." La Mura opens on the street; but its most delightful feature is the loggia on its outer side, with walls of sliding window-frames, commanding those near and distant prospects which had captured Browning's imagination on his first visit, and which on his last proved equally enthralling. Immediately to the north is the palace of Queen Catherine Cornaro ("Kate the Queen"). To its right rises the campanile of the former Duomo, now a Capuchin church, and near it a four-storyed house which is certainly the "Palace by the Duomo," supposed the residence of the Bishop's brother in *Pippa Passes*. On one side are the Alps, all around are the Asolan mountains, and westward, beyond rippling hills, the vast plain of Lombardy. In the words of Shelley :—

> "Beneath is spread like a green sea
> The waveless plain of Lombardy,
> Bounded by a vaporous air
> Islanded by cities fair."

And before the distance melts into that "vaporous air" there is discernible many an old stronghold, each familiar to the poet's memory.

The place teemed for him with recollections of the old chronicles which he had studied for *Sordello*, even their Italian phraseology coming back to him across the intervening years ; and *Pippa* was not forgotten, as he wandered amid the scenes which her passing by has rendered memorable. He took delight in everything ; in the performances of a company of strolling players, in the basking lizards, in walking—although tried at times by a difficulty of breathing —and in his afternoon drive ; but above all in the sunsets viewed from the Loggia, which he would never miss. The Loggia was, indeed, his favourite resort. Here were his evening hours passed ; in one corner of it stood an old spinet, on which he would play ; or he would read aloud from Shakespeare, Shelley, or his own *Pompilia*. His talk was as copious as ever ; yet he seemed, his hostess remarked, purposely to avoid deep and serious topics. "If such were broached in his presence, he dismissed them with one strong, convincing sentence, and adroitly turned the current of conversation into shallower channels." So charmed was he with Asolo that he entered into negotiations for the purchase of such another site, with the shell of a building upon it, as Mrs. Bronson's ; which, by a strange fatality, were only concluded, and favourably, upon the day of his death. One more element of pleasure in his stay at Asolo was that

Story was there, to whom his parting words, as he left for Venice, were : " We have been friends for forty years." [1]

He reached Venice on 1 November, and was full of satisfaction in his son's new home. There the proofs of his last volume, *Asolando*, reached him. The title, derived from a fanciful word whose invention he imputed to Queen Cornaro's secretary, *asolare*, "to disport in the open air, amuse oneself at random," connects it also with a place where several of its numbers had been lately written. Browning continued apparently in health, and assured a physician whom he met at dinner that such was the case. Half jokingly he held out his wrist to this new acquaintance, who, on feeling his pulse, knew that this confidence was ill-founded. Late in the month he returned from his customary walk on the Lido with a cold, which speedily became bronchitis. On 1 December he consented to see his son's doctor. The bronchial trouble was largely overcome, but symptoms of heart failure followed. He had looked forward to years more of activity ; but on the last evening he was aware of his condition. That very day, in London, *Asolando*, with its strikingly appropriate *Epilogue*, was published. A message came across the wires of its very favourable reception, evinced both by reviews and the demand for copies of the book. The sick man was able to receive the news, and to take pleasure in it. At ten o'clock, on the night of 12 December, "without," in his son's words, "pain or suffering other than that of weakness or weariness," he passed away.

When all was over, the question as to the place of burial had to be decided. Florence seemed to his family most appropriate, but further interment in the English cemetery there had lately been forbidden. Thereupon Venice might have been chosen ; but the matter was decided by a proposal from Dean Bradley that he should be laid to rest in Westminster Abbey. On Sunday, 15 December, after a private service in the Rezzonico, the body, in accordance with Venetian requirements, was taken to the mortuary island of San Michele. The ceremony was of a public character and in the highest degree impressive ; a flotilla of gondolas

[1] Several of the above details are derived from Mrs. Arthur Bronson's *Browning in Asolo, Century Magazine*, April, 1900.

following in the rear of the funeral barge. Two days later its burden was removed from the island chapel, by night and privately, to the railway station at Venice, and so to London. On the last day of the year, amid a great and reverent assemblage of Robert Browning's countrymen, with the spiritual presence of his wife suggested by the chaunting of her beautiful stanzas, "He giveth his beloved sleep," Poets' Corner received one poet more.

Thus Venice restored to London her distinguished son ; but, for reminder to future generations of what had been, she caused a tablet to be affixed to the outer wall of the Palazzo Rezzonico, stating that he died there, with this most significant couplet added :—

> " Open my heart and you will see
> Graved inside of it, Italy."

CHAPTER XVI

THE MAN AND THE POET

A consistent character—Tenacity of Browning's affections—His talk
—Horror of affectation—Depth of feeling—Love of music—Modesty—
Appreciation of others' work—His wide reading—His exactness in money
matters—An old-fashioned liberal—Subject to passionate outbursts—A
dinner-party incident—Breach with Forster—The FitzGerald episode—
Devotion to his wife's memory—Religious opinions—Spiritual optimism
—Appearance in younger and in later days—The question of his obscurity
considered—Accesible to friendly criticism—On his own poetry—His
great period—His extensive range—His place in literature.

IF a man's traits do not continually assert their presence
throughout the pages of his biography, that biography
is naught. The reader of the foregoing narrative has,
it is hoped, received upon the retina of his mind an impression of its central figure which at least approaches clearness.
Perhaps it would be more accurate to say a series of impressions; for only at the close is it possible to gather into one
harmonious whole those several characteristics, displayed at
different times and on different occasions, which go to the
making of a personality. A more finished portrait is now
to be attempted, towards the completion of which sundry
episodes will contribute whose earlier introduction would have
delayed the course of the story.

An impartial student of the character of Robert Browning
can hardly fail to be struck with its consistency. With him,
emphatically, the child was "father of the man." The
tendencies of his boyhood are all found developed in his
maturity. For this the manner of his education (in the
widest sense of the term) is largely accountable. He was
allowed to grow; no effort was put forth to make of him
something other than he was by nature.

His affections, according to universal testimony, were

remarkably tenacious, equally within the four corners of his own family and the large circle of his friends. Those who lost his regard were very few, and the severance was their fault, not his. In social intercourse he was direct, cordial, and sincere. Not jealous in limiting his acquaintance, he regarded every new-comer as a possible friend. He disliked foolish people as much as another ; indeed, the expression, "What a lot of fools there are in the world!" was not un-common in his mouth ; but mere foolishness did not incur his resentment. Those who were introduced to him as admirers of his works he would welcome, literally and figuratively, with both hands outstretched. To women he was invariably courteous. To the young and to the "lesser people" he was always kind and never condescending. He sought to put every one at his ease and to give every one his due. But he knew also what was due to himself, and resented any approach to familiarity.

His talk was clear enough, whatever may be said of his writings ; and he talked copiously. He would converse freely on all general topics, but with regard to the deeper problems of life he had a great deal of reserve. He was intensely interested in the texture of life, in the progress of the world, in anything and everything that his friends were doing. He would give a fillip to the dullest party. He liked to offer advice about affairs, and his advice was commonly worth having. There was about him a brave optimism of spirit, which infected those he met. People felt the better and the stronger for his presence. "After talking with him," says one who had a heavy burden to bear, "I used to feel that I could at any rate hold up my head for the rest of the day." "It was always," writes Mr. Comyns Carr, "a spiritual re-freshment to meet him. . . . By means hardly definable he contrived to keep his converse, even with the most common-place of his acquaintance, on a certain high spiritual level." This is to exercise a great power. Again, his talk owed much to his wide reading and fine memory ; and he had an unfailing fund of good stories which he told with point and spirit. Lord Leighton spoke of him as "a never-failing fountain of quaint stories and funny sayings."[1] Miss

[1] *Life*, vol. i. p. 146.

Cobbe remarked the same thing at Florence.   Mr. Sidney
Colvin remembers him at Cambridge keeping an undergraduate breakfast-party in a roar of laughter with doggerel
rhymes and good stories; he also recalls the elbow-nudge
which to an individual listener emphatically pointed the
anecdote.   His repartees were ready and effective.   When
Theophrastus Such was under discussion, and he was asked
for some account of the literary methods of the Greek writer
after whom George Eliot's philosopher was named, "To give
an example," he said, turning to a girl who had just before
greeted him with a compliment on his looks, "Theophrastus
would say, 'A flatterer is such an one as, meeting an old
man of seventy, congratulates him on looking young and
well.'" [1]

In all this there is nothing peculiarly characteristic of the
poet; and indeed the sister arts of painting and music
probably usurped a larger share of his conversation than did
poetry.   It would, however, be a mistake to suppose that he
never spoke of it; indeed, we have seen the contrary; but he
reserved its discussion for his intimates.   He had a horror,
carried almost to excess, of assuming anything like a bardic
pose; indeed he seemed, in general society, anxious not to be
reminded, or to remind others, that he was a poet.   But in
moments of noble enthusiasm of which a few were witnesses,
when he would move a listening group to tears by his reading
of *Andrea del Sarto*, or would recite with fire Smart's *Song to
David* or his own *Thamuris Marching*, then, indeed, the
disguise or armour of daily life fell from him, and the true
poet was revealed.[2]   There were great depths of emotion
underneath the polished surface.   As he sat with friends, who
still remember it, in a box at Covent Garden, listening to
Salvini in *Lear*, his face grew gradually paler, till at last tears,
of which he seemed unconscious, ran down his cheeks.   "I
almost think," he said afterwards, "that the actor is as great
as the poet." [3]

---

[1] Mr. Wilfrid Meynell in the *Athenæum*, 4 January, 1890.

[2] The fine lyric, *Thamuris Marching*, is embedded in *Aristophanes' Apology*.
For the story, see Iliad ii. 594-600.

[3] His admiration of Salvini was unbounded.   He told Mr. W. M. Rossetti that
he had seen the actor in *Œdipus*, and that it was absolutely the finest effort of art he
had ever beheld ; not only the finest in the art of acting, but in any art whatsoever.

Of his lifelong love of music much has been already said, but one or two further illustrations may be added. When, in the autumn of 1860, Mr. W. M. Rossetti called upon the Brownings at Siena, in company with Vernon Lushington, whom Browning had not met previously, the talk fell upon the compositions of Ferdinard Hiller, which Lushington commended. "Ah, now I understand who you are," said Browning. "When I find a man who shares with me a liking for Hiller's music, I can see into him at once ; he ceases to be a stranger." "I don't know whether you care for music, Mr. Browning," said a new acquaintance of later days—a young lady—"but if you do, my mother is having some on Monday." "Why, my dear," he answered, perhaps half believing what he said, "I care for nothing else." [1]

As his manner was absolutely devoid of affectation, so he was never unduly elevated by his own achievements. When success came to him, with admiration not always judicious in its train, it did not turn his head. "Invariably," writes Domett, "without a single exception to the contrary that I have ever heard or seen, he expressed the same modest estimate of himself and his doings—though he cannot but be aware of his own superiority." The corollary of this attitude was a generous appreciation of the work of other poets. He never wavered in his assertion of Tennyson's supremacy. Mr. Carr, who remarked his "constant expression of loyal admiration of the genius of Tennyson," adds, "I have heard him bear witness to it again and again, and always with entire sincerity." [2] Mr. Marcus Huish once witnessed a meeting between the two poets, when the younger man advanced to greet the elder, bent low, and addressed him as "Magister meus." [3] And he was ready with appreciation elsewhere. When William Morris's *Defence of Guenevere* appeared in 1857, Browning wrote enthusiastically of it to Mr. W. M. Rossetti : "I shall hardly be able to tell Morris

"I do not say," adds Mr. Rossetti, " that this statement of Browning's was a perfectly reasonable one ; but certain it is that he made it to me, and this in a tone of entire conviction." *Some Reminiscences*, p. 189.

[1] *Athenæum* article, *ut supra.*
[2] *Some Eminent Victorians*, p. 204.
[3] *Happy England*, p. 44.

what I think and rethink of his admirable poems, the only new poems, to my mind, since there's no telling when."[1] His recognition of Mr. Edmund Gosse's poetic faculty was, in his own words, "from the first complete and immediate."[2] And he was always eager to encourage new practitioners, where he could discern promise. *Verses by E. D. W.* (Miss West, afterwards Mrs. Edward Dowden), printed for private circulation in 1879, had his warm commendation ; and among the last of his letters which have been preserved is one addressed to a lady who had submitted to him her verses in manuscript, in which he assures her, in words borrowed from one of her own poems, that "There is room in the blue for a new song-bird."[3]

Of the width and variety of his reading much has been already said. Mr. Gosse speaks of him as "steeping himself"—particularly between the years 1837 and 1840—"in all literature, modern and ancient, English and exotic." Rabbinical lore was particularly congenial to him. During this period he made some study of Hebrew, though afterwards, as he wrote to Miss Barrett in 1845, he "let it slip." Among the Greek poets Homer and Euripides were his favourites, and often his travelling companions. He was probably a wide rather than an exact scholar, nevertheless his version of the *Agamemnon* shows that he could be exact when he chose. He liked the later Latin writers, such as Claudian and Apuleius. He was certainly familiar with philosophic theory ; but it is questionable whether he ever had the patience to study systematically the writings of a Hegel or a Herbert Spencer.

In financial matters he was exact to a nicety. As a young man he had neither desired nor had control of much money ; and during most of his married life he was obliged to be extremely careful. His wife records that it was pain and grief to him to be in debt even to the amount of five shillings. When he undertook to be steward of the £200 a year allowed to Landor by his brothers he insisted, though they deprecated this, in rendering an account of every penny

---

[1] *Ruskin, Rossetti, Preraphaelitism: Papers,* 1854-1862, p. 119.
[2] Wise, *ut supra, Second Series,* vol. ii. p. 6.
[3] Wise, *ut supra, Second Series,* vol. i. p. 94.

of it. This extreme carefulness became a fixed habit, and pervaded his own expenditure after it had ceased to be necessary. He habitually rode in omnibuses and practised various small economies. But he knew how to be generous ; witness his liberality to the beleagured Parisians ; and that he was not set on the acquisition of money there is interesting proof available. He could not bring himself to write for periodicals. " If I publish a book, and people choose to buy it, that proves they want to read my work. But to have them turn over the pages of a magazine and find me—that is to be an uninvited guest. My wife liked it. She liked to be with the others ; but I have steadfastly refused that kind of thing from first to last." So he wrote, about 1886, to the editor of a Boston magazine, who had offered him £400 for a short poem. And he had declined even handsomer offers from an English one. The English editor named a large price, which was declined, and then a still larger, which was again refused ; finally, sent a blank cheque for the poet to fill out to his own satisfaction, which he forthwith returned. This is hardly a course which one actuated by the love of money would pursue.[1]

An equal consistency characterized his political opinions. He developed, but he did not change. He began as a liberal and ended as a liberal unionist. But his liberalism was of a diffused and general rather than of a restricted or partisan character. When he said of himself in *Pauline* that he was " vowed to liberty," he meant precisely what he said. What he instinctively demanded, as his sonnet *Why I am a Liberal* shows, was liberty for the individual to achieve his own destiny, hampered by no more restrictions than are necessary to be imposed for the maintenance of a similar liberty for other individuals. He was suspicious of State interference. The late Master of Balliol, who as an

---

[1] Wise, *ut supra*, *Second Series*, vol. ii. p. 25. A proposition emanating from another American magazine, that he should *submit poems for approval*, had been already rejected with contumely. In the course of his reply he wrote—

> " The air one breathes with Smith may be the sharper ;
> But—save me from Scirocco's heat in *Harper!* "

His reasons for making an exception in the case of *Hervé Riel* have already been explained.

U

undergraduate met Browning at dinner at Jowett's on his first visit to Oxford, remembered that he expressed much approval of the English method of leaving hospitals and other works of public beneficence to the energy of individuals rather than to State control. Browning would have heartily sympathized with the complaint of Tennyson, written more than twenty years before this meeting, that

" The individual withers, and the world is more and more."

Holding, as he did, that nothing in life was so interesting or important as the history of an individual soul, he could not approve of any political system which tended to retard its development; and he was convinced that socialism would have this effect. And he was no mere theorist. His undergraduate fellow-guest in Jowett's rooms, who was surprised by the absence of poetry from the conversation, remembers that he talked like a man of the world and a student of affairs. His extraordinary knowledge of all that related to the *Times* newspaper was also subject of remark at Balliol, and his great admiration for Delane, its editor in the sixties. He approved also, in a rather different fashion, of the *Pall Mall Gazette* in the first stage of its career, calling it "the perfection of a paper for people who wanted to know what was going on in the world, as a man might learn it at a club or over a dinner-table." [1] As the sonnet above mentioned may be taken as Browning's profession of political faith, and as it is not included in any edition of his works, it is here appended.

Why I am a Liberal.

" 'Why?'   Because all I haply can and do,
    All that I am now, all I hope to be,—
      Whence comes it save from fortune setting free
    Body and soul the purpose to pursue
God traced for both?   If fetters not a few
    Of prejudice, convention fall from me
      These shall I bid men—each in his degree
Also God-guided—bear, and gladly too?
But little do or can the best of us:
    That little is achieved through Liberty.

---

[1] *My Life in Two Hemispheres*, by Gavan Duffy, vol. ii. pp. 355-6.

> Who then dares hold—emancipated thus—
> His fellow shall continue bound?   Not I
> Who live, love, labour freely, nor discuss
> A brother's right to freedom.   That is ' Why.' " [1]

Thus far we seem to have been contemplating the demeanour and disposition of an admirable but in many respects not very unusual type ; a man kindly, benevolent, cultured, and precise ; but Browning was a great deal more than this. Vesuvius with a light wreath of vapour curling from its summit is by no means the same as Vesuvius in eruption. It was not for nothing that Browning was born " supremely passionate." The fairest fruit of this attribute was his intense devotion to the poet-soul that was united with his own. But other outcomes of it were manifested in his life from time to time. He was subject to violent explosions of wrath, for which there was not invariably adequate justification. But who would desire to eliminate wrath from the world ? There is a just anger which clears the atmosphere, a moral indignation which is a sweetener of society ; but it is too much to expect a flawless discretion from those capable of this passion.

Browning in his younger days was the guest at dinner of a man who had Oriental ideas about the subjection of women. This person in the course of the meal reduced his wife to tears and dismissed her from the room. The attitude of the remaining guests, save one, was complaisant. The host followed his wife, and the pair were discovered in the drawing-room, she all meekness, he all magnanimity. Browning stood by and waited his opportunity. It soon came.

" I listened *arrectis auribus*, and in a minute he said he did not know somebody I mentioned. I told him, *that* I easily conceived— such a person would never condescend to know *him*, etc., and treated him to every consequence ingenuity could draw from that text—and at the end marched out of the room ; and the valorous man, who had sate like a post, got up, took a candle, followed me to the door, and only said in unfeigned wonder, ' What *can* have possessed you, my *dear* Browning ? ' " [2]

---

[1] Written in 1885.

[2] *Letters of Robert Browning and Elizabeth Barrett Barrett*, vol. i. p. 413.

For the consequences of another of the explosions only regret can be felt, whatever be thought of the dispute, inasmuch as it resulted in the dissolution of an ancient friendship. Browning owed a great deal to John Forster, as he himself willingly and explicitly acknowledged.[1]   Forster was a man of genuine kindness, and helpful to his friends to an uncommon degree ; but he was heavy-handed and dictatorial, and apt to assume the proprietary airs of the showman towards those whom he had "discovered."   On Browning's return to England the intimacy between the two men was renewed ; it became the custom for Browning to lunch with Forster on most Sundays.   But he grew restive under Forster's patronizing airs.   At a dinner-party at the Benzons' the two men began, in the words of an eye-witness, "to nag at one another."   On Browning citing, in support of some story he had told, the authority of a lady of his acquaintance, Forster expressed a doubt of her veracity.   Browning, in a sudden rage, seized a decanter and threatened to throw it at his head if he said another word.   Before his opponent could recover from his astonishment, friends intervened, and the situation was saved ; but neither on that evening nor subsequently was a reconciliation effected.[2]

There remains yet another episode, to ignore which, painful as it is, would be misleading.   In the last year of Browning's life appeared the *Letters of Edward FitzGerald*. By an editorial oversight, for which deep regret was afterwards expressed, the following passage was allowed to appear in print :—

"Mrs. Browning's death is rather a relief to me, I must say : no more Aurora Leighs, thank God !   A woman of real genius, I know ; but what is the upshot of it all ?   She and her sex had better mind the kitchen and the children," etc., etc.

Opening the volume at his club, and unhappily at this very passage, Browning was overcome with indignation.   He wrote in hot haste a savage denunciatory sonnet, and sent it

---

[1] See the dedication to Forster of the third edition of his works, 1863.

[2] The story of this episode is narrated at length in Mr. R. C. Lehmann's *Memories of Half a Century*, chap. 8.   See also *John Forster : by one of his Friends*, p. 38.   "In those days," writes Mr. Percy Fitzgerald, "there were tempestuous spirits abroad.   Forster could be violent enough."

to the *Athenæum*. A little later he would have withdrawn it, but this proved impossible. His own subsequent comment on the matter is contained in a letter to a friend, which he wrote a few days afterwards.

"As to my own utterance after receiving unexpectedly an out-rage, why, like all impulsive actions, once the impulse over, I believe I might preferably have left the thing to its proper contempt. But there was something too shocking in a man, whom my wife never even heard of, 'feeling relieved at her death, he must say'—and I too said what I must. The people who tell you 'his opinion was really on the woman question' talk nonsense. He might have uttered any amount of impertinence about women's work in general, and that of my wife in particular, without getting a word out of me—but, 'to be relieved at the *death* which would stop the work, thank God'!

"How editor and publisher could let this passage remain in the letter which a pen-scratch would have left unobjectionable, passes my power of understanding." [1]

It is superfluous to dilate upon this unhappy affair, which serves, however, to emphasize the poet's passionate devotion to the memory of his wife. The depth of this devotion was well known to his intimates, to whom he often spoke of her. She was his muse, his source of inspiration, as his readers know. He loved to show his friends her Hebrew Bible, profusely annotated in her own minute handwriting. "See what a scholar she was!" he would say.

"I had happened to remark," writes Domett, who had never seen her, "as I looked at her portrait, 'she looks all intellect.' 'Ah, she was more than *that*,' he said, musingly and with feeling. I should rather have said (what I suppose I meant) all *spirit* or soul."

"He shewed me," says the diarist in another place, "her Hebrew Bible with Greek notes in her handwriting in the margins, and said Jowett and Blomfield (late Bishop of London) had both expressed surprise at the learning they evinced. Also several other relics and mementos of her, particularly the little reddish-leathered Pembroke table at which she wrote her poems. He always mentions her, though with few words and in a low tone, with the deepest admiration and regard; and if possible more often for her beauty of character

---

[1] Wise, *ut supra*, vol. i. p. 97.

than brightness of intellect. Miss Browning, too, was strong in praise of her total freedom from assumption, or the slightest apparent consciousness of being a 'genius.' I suppose they know the world has abundant proofs of the qualities of her *head*, so insist more on what they have more exclusive knowledge of, those of her heart."

To such as had but a superficial sight of the poet who "went everywhere," who enjoyed the comforts and luxuries of life, who was often the centre of a group of admiring ladies, his devotion to this sacred memory was naturally not apparent. There was nothing new, however, in the feminine adulation which attended him. His own wife had written, "The women adore him everywhere far too much for decency."[1] But he did not take the proffered incense seriously; though it is possible that his expansive manner was occasionally misconstrued. He might very certainly have married again, had he chosen to do so. But "the memory of what had been" remaining with him, though unperceived by the world, was probably the most potent factor of his life, and kept him as he was.

It is always a delicate matter to speak of a man's religious beliefs; but to ignore them in the case of one in whose poetry they play so prominent a part is impossible. Except for the brief period of his "growing pains" Browning was through life an ardent and consistent theist. There is no need to labour this point, so far as his poems are concerned, for it is apparent to every reader of them. It is also manifest in his correspondence. "The rest is with God—whose finger I see every minute of my life." "I am not without fear of some things in this world—but 'the wrath of men,' all the men living put together, I fear as I fear the fly I have just put out of the window; but I fear *God*—and am ready, He knows, to die this moment in taking His part against any piece of injustice or oppression, *so* I aspire to die!" These passages are taken from his letters to his future wife.[2] His intense conviction of the immortality of the soul, a doctrine on which he so constantly insists, is not less familiar to his readers. "As to immortality," Professor

---

[1] *Letters of Elizabeth Barrett Browning*, vol. ii. p. 434 [to Miss Browning].
[2] Vol. i. p. 133; vol. ii. p. 229.

Knight reports him saying, "I don't need arguments, I know it by intuition, which is superior to proof." [1] These are postulates in whose acceptance, be it observed, there is nothing unphilosophical, unless we are to say that Kant (for example) was no philosopher ; yet, presumably because he held them, it got abroad that Browning was "strongly against Darwin, rejecting the truths of science and regretting its advance." These imputations he was at some pains—for letter-writing had become very distasteful to him—to refute at length.

"It came, I suppose," he writes (11 October, 1881), "of Hohenstiel-Schwangau's expressing the notion which was the popular one at the appearance of Darwin's book—and you might as well charge Shakespeare with holding that there were men whose heads grew beneath their shoulders, because Othello told Desdemona that he had seen such. In reality, all that seems *proved* in Darwin's scheme was a conception familiar to me from the beginning : see in *Paracelsus* the progressive development from senseless matter to organized, until man's appearance (Part V). Also in *Cleon*, see the order of ' life's mechanics '—and I daresay in many passages of my poetry : for how can one look at Nature as a whole and doubt that, whenever there is a gap, a ' link ' must be ' missing '—through the limited power and opportunity of the looker? But go back and back, as you please, *at* the back, as Mr. Sludge is made to insist, you find (*my* faith is as constant) creative intelligence, acting as matter but not resulting from it. Once set the balls rolling, and ball may hit ball and send any number in any direction over the table; but I believe in the cue pushed by a hand. When one is taunted (as I notice is often fancied an easy method with the un-Darwinized)—taunted with thinking successive acts of creation credible, metaphysics have been stopped short at, however physics may fare : time and space being purely conceptions of our own, wholly inapplicable to intelligence of another kind —with whom, as I made Luria say, there is an everlasting moment of creation, if one at all—past, present, and future, one and the same state. This consideration does not effect Darwinism proper to any degree. But I do not consider his case as to the changes in organization, brought about by desire and will in the creature, proved." [2]

A further consideration arises. Holding firmly two doctrines which Christianity enjoins, does Browning accept

---

[1] *Reminiscences*, 1904.
[2] Wise, *ut supra*, vol. i. p. 82-84. *Cf.* the sermon on evolution in *Francis Furini* (1887).

the other tenets of that faith ?   He is unquestionably a religious teacher, but is he also a Christian teacher ?   It would perhaps have been unnecessary to raise this question, had he not been explicitly reported, by Robert Buchanan, to have affirmed the contrary.   " I well remember," writes that author in the " Letter Dedicatory " to his *Outcast*,

" the amazement and concern of the late Mr. Browning when I informed him on one occasion that he was an advocate of Christian theology, nay, an essentially Christian teacher and preacher.   In the very face of his masterly books, which certainly support the opinion then advanced, I hereby affirm and attest that the writer regarded that expression of opinion as an impeachment and a slight.   I therefore put the question categorically, ' Are you not, then, a Christian ? '   He immediately thundered, ' No.' "

It is to be regretted that this statement was not made in Browning's lifetime, that he might have dealt with it himself. Domett, it will be remembered, records an exactly opposite assertion.   If there were nothing else to go upon, it would be necessary to put Domett's authority in one scale and Buchanan's in the other ; but there is, of course, a very great deal.   The more the data are examined, the more astonishing does Buchanan's story appear.   These must now be briefly reviewed.   Browning was brought up a Christian ; his earliest poem contains a passionate address to Christ ; he nowhere makes an attack on Christianity ; *Christmas Eve and Easter Day* is in its general drift a defence of the reformed faith ; in the introduction to the Shelley letters he describes Christ as " a Divine Being ; " the gospel narrative fascinates him as a subject for verse ; he returns to it again and again. Then, take his practice as to religious observances.   In London, with one exception already mentioned, he was not a church-goer, but he was when visiting the universities ; in Normandy he attended a French reformed service with Milsand, during his Llangollen visit he never missed Sunday afternoon church, and in Venice he often went to a chapel of the Waldenseans. But something much more convincing remains.   In 1876 he received a letter from a lady who, believing herself to be dying, wrote to thank him for the help she had derived from his poems, mentioning particularly *Rabbi Ben Ezra* and *Abt Vogler*.   He replied as follows :—

" It would ill become me to waste a word on my own feelings except inasmuch as they can be common to us both, in such a situation as you describe yours to be, and which, by sympathy, I can make mine by the anticipation of a few years at most. It is a great thing, the greatest, that a human being should have passed the probation of life, and sum up its experience in a witness to the power and love of God. I dare congratulate you. All the help I can offer, in my poor degree, is the assurance that I see ever *more* reason to hold by the same hope—and that by no means in ignorance of what has been advanced to the contrary ; and for your sake I could wish it to be true that I had so much of ' genius ' as to permit the testimony of an especially privileged insight to come in aid of the ordinary argument. For I know I, myself, have been aware of the communication of something more subtle than a ratiocinative process, when the convictions of ' genius ' have thrilled my soul to its depths, as when Napoleon, shutting up the New Testament, said of Christ : ' Do you know that I am an understander of men ? Well, He was no man ! ' Or when Charles Lamb, in a gay fancy with some friends as to how he and they would feel if the greatest of the dead were to appear suddenly in flesh and blood once more, on the final suggestion, ' And if Christ entered this room ? ' changed his manner at once, and stuttered out, as his manner was when moved, ' You see, if Shakespeare entered, we should all rise ; if *He* appeared we must kneel.' Or, not to multiply instances, as when Dante wrote what I will transcribe from my wife's Testament wherein I recorded it fourteen years ago, ' Thus I believe, thus I affirm, thus I am certain it is, that from this life I shall pass to another, there, where that lady lives of whom my soul was enamoured.' [1] Dear friend, I may have wearied you in spite of your good will. God bless you, sustain, and receive you ! "

That thunderous " No " becomes more perplexing than ever. But Browning was eclectic in his beliefs ; and the

[1] That ' the solemn Tuscan's ' phrase haunted him *La Saisiaz* shows—

" Is it fact to which I cleave,
Is it fancy I but cherish, when I take upon my lips
Phrase the solemn Tuscan fashioned, and declare the soul's eclipse,
Not the soul's extinction ? take his ' I believe and I declare—
Certain am I—from this life I pass into a better, there
Where that lady lives of whom enamoured was my soul.' "

Above all, there is what he said to Mrs. Orr of the last stanza of the ' Epilogue ' to *Dramatis Personæ*—" ' That one Face ' is the face of Christ. That is how I feel him."—*The Religious Opinions of Robert Browning, Contemporary Review*, December 1891.

doctrine which makes a system of rewards and punishments the sole motive to right living was no part of his creed.   The idea of vindictive punishment in another world is repeatedly attacked in his poems : in *The Inn Album*, in *Ixion*, and in *A Camel Driver* (*Ferishtah's Fancies*).   Now, if Buchanan chose to put this doctrine in the forefront of Christianity, and as an essential part of it, Browning very probably lost his temper and asserted that if *that* were Christianity, he was no Christian.   Otherwise, there seems no alternative but to regard the anecdote as apocryphal.[1]

In any case, when a poet deals with religion, it is unreasonable to expect exact definitions and precise statements.   It is not his business to provide them.   But by suggestion and insight he may cast a light upon dark places, and he may write verses instinct with Christian feeling though without a word of dogma in them.   It is well to remember this in reading, for instance, such a poem as *La Saisiaz*.   The main constituents of theology, as Browning saw it, were Power and Love ; and it would be rash to deny that their union is perceptible in any worthy conception of Christianity. He never pretended to have solved in its entirety " the riddle of the painful earth."

" I do not ask," he wrote in the last year of his life, " a full disclosure of Truth, which would be a concession contrary to the law of things, which applies equally to the body and the soul, that it is only by striving to attain strength (in the one case) and truth (in the other) that body and soul do so—the effort (common to both) being productive, in each instance, of the necessary initiation into all the satisfactions which result from partial success : absolute success being only attainable for the body in full manhood—for the soul, in its full apprehension of Truth—which will be, not *here*, at all events."

Life, in Browning's view, was a period of probation ; throughout which it was man's happiness and duty to

" Hold on, hope hard in the subtle thing
That's spirit ; though cloistered fast soar free."

---

[1] An *obiter dictum* from Browning's Shelley preface is worth quoting in this connexion. " In religion one earnest and unextorted assertion of belief should outweigh, as a matter of testimony, many assertions of unbelief."

[2] Wise, *ut supra*, vol. ii. p. 90.

The unconquerable spiritual optimism which dominates his poetry was also his most salient characteristic as a man.

The pictures of the poet by Lehmann and Watts which hang in the National Portrait Gallery, to say nothing of the art of the camera, render an impression of his appearance in his later days accessible to all.   The portrait of him as a young man published in the *Spirit of the Age* was pronounced by Domett "a very poor representation indeed."

" Browning," says this authority, " in young days and in middle life (according to Gordigiani's portrait) was decidedly *good*-looking, as well as intellectual-looking.   His full face when young—with pale, very clear complexion, long flowing fine black hair, and bright grey eyes—when animated or excited by conversation or otherwise was indeed very handsome."

He and his sister both inherited their mother's pale complexion, but there was nothing in their features to suggest the admixture of Semitic or alien blood.   Their grandmother, Margaret Tittle, was a Creole only in the sense that she was born in the West Indies.[1]

Except that in his early manhood he was subject to severe neuralgia, he was throughout life remarkably free from illness.   " He says," wrote Domett, " that he was much subject to headaches when young, but now never has one, nor has had for years, and would think himself ill indeed if he had." " He was," his son writes, " the healthiest man I ever knew." In his old age he was the picture of health and strength, with none of the signs of delicacy which Domett noticed in the time of their earlier acquaintance.   His appearance was robust, manly and impressive ; his abundant white hair, expressive glance and alert demeanour made him a noticeable figure in any assemblage ; but there was nothing in his look which distinctly proclaimed the poet.

It is no part of the intention of the present work to add to that already considerable mass of writing devoted to the detailed criticism and exposition of Browning's poetry ; but a brief attempt to estimate his poetic stature and his place in literature will not be superfluous.   There was a time when

---

[1] This is the proper connotation of the word Creole, often mistakenly supposed to imply an admixture of black blood.

to charge him with obscurity was regarded as the mark of a Philistine. But had enthusiasts considered the matter historically, they would have found that the Philistines were reinforced by some highly reputable names. Landor's recognition of a brother-poet has been recorded, but this is how he writes with reference to *Sordello*. " I only wish he would atticize a little. Few of the Athenians had such a quarry on their property, but they constructed better roads for the conveyance of the material." Tennyson and Miss Martineau were repelled by the complexities of this poem. Domett was not blinded by friendship to its harshness. Arnould, who returned so constantly to *Paracelsus*, wrote as late as 1847, " I would to God he would purge his style of obscurities."

Another well-wisher and admirer, Leighton, went so far as to accuse him of, at times, "writing wilfully in cypher." This charge is absolutely groundless ; but, admitting the unduly condensed style of *Sordello*, a fault which though exorcized for a time recurs at intervals, and re-asserts itself unpleasantly in certain of the longer philosophic monologues, to what cause or causes may it be attributed ? It had its origin to some extent in the supposed needs of the drama, and had already permeated *Strafford*. It was a reaction from the verbosity of the school of Sheridan Knowles, with reference to which a critic inquired, " Which of our smartest dramatic poets nowadays can ask, ' How d'ye do ? ' in less than three verses ?"—a reaction so extreme that the *Edinburgh Review* in an article on *Strafford* went so far as to compare the manner of its dialogue to the staccato speech of Mr. Alfred Jingle. This warning, however, was unheeded, as *Sordello* shows. For there was another cause at work. Browning was a very rapid thinker. " He never thinks but at full speed ; and the rate of his thought is to that of another man's as the speed of a railway to that of a waggon, or the speed of a telegraph to that of a railway." Such was Swinburne's judgment. Browning's gift of expression, great as it was, could not always keep up with the rapid flow of his ideas. Language, as a medium, was apt to baulk him, as soon as he put pen to paper ; a phenomenon noticeable, also, in his letters. He wrote, in general, very fast indeed, and shrank from the labour of revision ; not because it was

arduous, but because he found it distasteful. That contemporary readers found *Sordello* so difficult certainly came
upon him as a painful surprise, though, as he said, he " wrote
it for only a few " ; but he had too much good sense to shut
his eyes to the moral deducible from the manner of its
reception. After discussing with his friend, some thirty
years later, the meaning of a passage in *A Toccata of
Galuppi's*, Domett made the following entry in his diary :—

"Browning, I saw, had not lost the good-humoured patience with
which he could listen to friendly criticism on any of his works.
I have proof of this in a copy of the original edition of *Sordello*,
which he sent me when it appeared. The poem is undoubtedly
somewhat obscure, though, curiously enough, much more so in the
mere objective (so to speak) incidents of the story than in its subjective phases, that is in the narrative of the hero's varying moods of
mind or the philosophical reflections of the poet. Accordingly I
had scribbled in pencil on the book two or three impatient remarks,
such as ' Who says this ? ' ' What does this mean ? ' etc. Some time
after he asked me to let him see my copy, which I lent him. He
returned it with two or three pencil notes of his own, answering my
questions. But I was amused many years afterwards, in New
Zealand (in 1863), on the appearance of a second edition of *Sordello*,
to find he had altered, I think, all the passages I had hinted objection
to, or questioned the meaning of."

This poem, which its author designed, as the 1863 dedication tells us, to turn into something which the many might
like, but which he eventually decided to leave as he found it,
remained, nevertheless, something of a sore subject. " Ah ! "
he said, with a grimace, on seeing a copy of it on a friend's
table ; " the entirely unintelligible *Sordello* ! " But, in general,
he did not in the least mind the monitions of intimate friends,
such as Domett or Tennyson, on the obscurity or length of
his poems. His answer was invariably the same : " I did my
best." It is, however, noteworthy that, at any rate from the
publication of *Men and Women* onwards, his finest work is
contained in those volumes whose contents were not written
at high pressure and top speed.

Something of his own attitude towards his poetry is to be
gathered from an interesting letter which he wrote, in 1868,

to Mr. W. G. Kingsland, afterwards the author of *Robert Browning, Chief Poet of the Age.*

"Intelligence, by itself, is scarcely the thing with respect to a new book—as Wordsworth says (a little altered) 'You must like it before it be worthy of your liking.' In spite of your intelligence and sympathy, I can have but little doubt but that my writing has been, in the main, too hard for many I should have been pleased to communicate with; but I never designedly tried to puzzle people, as some of my critics have supposed. On the other hand, I never pretended to offer such literature as should be a substitute for a cigar, or a game of dominoes, to an idle man. So perhaps, on the whole, I get my deserts and something over—not a crowd, but a few I value more."[1]

He is, in short, no "idle singer of an empty day." His is no garden of Proserpine where men may fold their hands and be lulled to an indifferent calm by soulless melodies. He is strenuous, virile, restless, even combative. But no one who approaches his work with those two qualifications— intelligence and sympathy—need go empty away.

To make a bogey of his obscurity would be as foolish as it is to ignore it. After *Sordello* he *did* "atticize"; not a little, merely, but a great deal. In what may be called his best period—from *Pippa Passes* to *Balaustion's Adventure*— there is little in the way of difficulty with which intelligence and sympathy need fear to cope. The high level at which he kept his productions during those thirty years is certainly one of the most notable achievements of English poetry. The wide circle of interests over which his genius played gives cause for admiration; and not less remarkable is the instinct which guided him to invest each interest with its appropriate poetic garb. So extensive is his range that it is difficult to believe that the same man wrote, for instance, *Love Among the Ruins* and *Shop*. Yet see how admirably the metre and phraseology of each poem are suited to the effect they are intended to produce. In the first are noble words and harmonies, creating in succession the atmosphere of departed greatness and of triumphant love. In the second are such expressions as "City Chaps" and "Hampstead Villa's kind

---

[1] Wise, *ut supra*, vol. i. p. 25.

defence "—calculated, it might be thought, to frighten away
the shy muse. But read *Shop* from beginning to end, and
you find that all its queer phrases are a part of the picture ;
and that the concluding stanza, with its impassioned cry,
victoriously lifts the whole piece from the realm of doggerel
(to which it seemed perilously near) to the domain of poetry.
Or, contrast the rapid measure and torrential flow of words in
Waring—making us, as it were, participants of the speaker's
aching self-reproach and noble longing—with the designedly
mean structure of *Confessions*, fit vehicle for its unhappy,
squalid story. Above all, how magnificently Browning's
blank verse at its best—as in the finest parts of *The Ring
and the Book*—subserves the display of passions which at
once lacerate and purify the human heart. Browning is
supreme in his mastery of metre ; and if language occasionally got the upper hand of him, he amply avenged himself,
a hundred times over, in his best period. For then language
was his servant—the servant of a great creative intelligence.

Of course he did not always maintain so high a level ;
he fell, in later days, into metaphysical quagmires, whither
already, it is probable, few care to follow him. He was not
a good judge of his own work, and appeared to lose, at times,
his sense of beauty. His very facility of rhyming, in which
he took great delight, sometimes proved a pitfall, as (to take
the very worst example) in *Pietro of Abano*. But his best work
has undoubtedly won him a place in the van of English poetry.
Such poems as *Prince Hohenstiel-Schwangau* and *Red Cotton
Night-Cap Country* will in future ages probably attract the
attention of none but those whom Hazlitt called "eaters of
olives and readers of black letter." But the great gallery of
Men and Women—extended so as to include the protagonists
of *The Ring and the Book*, and many another figure from
Bells and Pomegranates, *Dramatis Personæ*, and elsewhere—
will continue to echo with a host of footfalls, so long as the
love of poetry endures.

CHAPTER XVII

SUPPLEMENTARY

(WRITTEN IN 1938)

Readers of Mrs. Orr's *Life and Letters of Robert Browning* will recall that in discussing *Fifine at the Fair*, which appeared in June, 1872, " that piece of perplexing cynicism " she called it, she concluded that " some leaven of bitterness must have been working in the poet's mind when he wrote it."

This conclusion was correct. Mrs. Orr probably had a shrewd idea of the source of the leaven, but she left it unspecified. Its influence may be traced not in *Fifine* only but in several of the poet's subsequent works, even, some hold, in his penultimate volume. The emotional crisis through which he passed between 1869 and 1872 made a deep incision in his nature, could not easily be forgotten, and for years thrust itself upon his consciousness with painful iteration. Signs of this are visible in the *Correspondence with Isa Blagden*, and in Hood's *Letters of Robert Browning*, which were published, it should be noted, with the consent of the poet's daughter-in-law. In one of them, written to Edith Story, whom he had known from her childhood, Browning tells the whole discomfortable tale.

Handsome, rich, and talented, Louisa, Lady Ashburton, had been left a widow in 1864. Browning appears to have made her acquaintance a year earlier, and by 1869 she is " an old friend." About that time, when his son was an undergraduate at Christ Church, he began to contemplate the possibility of a second marriage. The advantages, from a worldly point of view, of a union with Lady Ashburton were obvious. They were mutually attracted. But in Browning's mind prudence and sentiment were at variance. He proposed to her, seemingly in 1871, but, in utmost frankness, thought it right to tell her, in his own words to Miss

Story, " two simple facts " ; that his heart was buried in
Florence, and that the attractiveness of the marriage lay in
its advantages to his son. It does not appear to have
occurred to him that such reservations could have detracted
from the value of his offer. " I had never," he writes, " left
her in ignorance of them for a moment, though that I ever
paraded them in a gross form to anybody is simply false."
The lady, however, viewed the matter in a different light,
and considered herself aggrieved. The upshot was a violent
quarrel, followed by a complete and lasting estrangement.

It is impossible not to feel regret for this angry breach
between two high-spirited, impulsive, great-hearted people.
Not the slightest fleck of anything dishonourable attaches
to either, but each was made unhappy. Moreover, apart
from the pain and vexation of the episode, Browning seems
to have reproached himself for a lapse from fidelity to his
wife's memory. The calls of life and of the present had come
between him and his sacred past. Professors Raymond and
De Vane independently reached the conclusion that the
experience is darkly and psychologically shadowed forth, not,
of course, literally, in *Fifine*. Their arguments are too subtle
for abbreviation here, and must be studied in their own pages.
There certainly does seem an echo of the affair in the *St.
Martin's Summer* of 1876 ; and Professor De Vane discerns
its reappearance in the *Parleying with Daniel Bartoli* of 1887.

I do not know that this has been remarked. Most portraits of the poet give him just that confident, untroubled
expression that one would expect such a man to have. But
there is a photograph taken by Fradelle and Young about
1872 which conveys a very different impression. The face
is anxious, almost haggard, the eyes seem charged with
remorse and suffering. The distress he had undergone had
left its mark.

But when I saw him, once and once only, in a street in
Oxford ten years later, that strained look had disappeared.
There was in his countenance, I like to remember, nothing
but peace, serenity, benevolence—and intellectual power.

H. C. M.

x

APPENDIX A

A FOREST THOUGHT

I N far Esthonian solitudes
   The parent-firs of future woods
   Gracefully, airily spire at first
   Up to the sky, by the soft sand nurst;
Self-sufficient are they, and strong
With outspread arms, broad level and long;
But soon in the sunshine and the storm
They darken, changing fast their form—
Low boughs fall off, and in the bole
Each tree spends all its strenuous soul—
Till the builder gazes wistfully
Such noble ship-mast wood to see,
And cares not for its soberer hue,
Its rougher bark and leaves more few.

But just when beauty passes away
And you half regret it could not stay,
For all their sap and vigourous life,—
Under the shade, secured from strife
A seedling springs—the forest-tree
In miniature, and again we see
The delicate leaves that will fade one day,
The fan-like shoots that will drop away,
The taper stem a breath could strain—
Which shall foil one day the hurricane:
We turn from this infant of the copse
To the parent-firs,—in their waving tops
To find some trace of the light green tuft
A breath could stir,—in the bole aloft

Column-like set against the sky,
The spire that flourished airily
And the marten bent as she rustled by.
So shall it be, dear Friends, when days
Pass, and in this fair child we trace
Goodness, full-formed in you, tho' dim
. Faint-budding, just astir in him :
When rudiments of generous worth
And frankest love in him have birth,
We'll turn to love and worth full-grown,
And learn their fortune from your own.
Nor shall we vainly search to see
His gentleness—simplicity—
Not lost in your maturer grace—
Perfected, but not changing place.

May this grove be a charmed retreat . . .
May northern winds and savage sleet
Leave the good trees untouched, unshorn
A crowning pride of woods unborn :
And gracefully beneath their shield
May the seedling grow ! All pleasures yield
Peace below and peace above,
The glancing squirrels' summer love,
And the brood-song of the cushat-dove !

These lines were addressed to friends on the occasion of the christening of their eldest son, to whom the poet stood godfather. On returning to the house after the christening, Browning went into a room by himself and there wrote the poem and handed it to the parents. The dedication runs : "Written and inscribed to W. A. and A. D. by their Sincere Friend, Robert Browning, 13, Nelson Sq., November 4, 1837."

SONNET

Eyes calm beside thee (Lady, could'st thou know !)
    May turn away thick with fast-gathering tears :
I glance not where all gaze : thrilling and low
    Their passionate praises reach thee—my cheek wears
Alone no wonder when thou passest by ;
Thy tremulous lids bent and suffused reply
To the irrepressible homage which doth glow
    On every lip but mine : if in thine ears

888888

888

Their accents linger—and thou dost recall
Me as I stood, still, guarded, very pale,
Beside each votarist whose lighted brow
Wore worship like an aureole, "O'er them all
My beauty," thou wilt murmur, "did prevail
Save that one only :"—Lady, could'st thou know!

Printed in the *Monthly Repository*, 1834, New Series, vol. viii. p. 712. It is (chronologically) possible that this sonnet was addressed to Eliza Flower.

BEN KARSHOOK'S WISDOM

I

"Would a man 'scape the rod?"
  Rabbi Ben Karshook saith,
"See that he turn to God
  The day before his death."

"Ay, could a man inquire
  When it shall come!" I say.
The Rabbi's eye shoots fire—
  "Then let him turn to-day!"

II

Quoth a young Sadducee:
  "Reader of many rolls,
Is it so certain we
  Have, as they tell us, souls?"

"Son, there is no reply!"
  The Rabbi bit his beard;
"Certain, a soul have *I*—
  We may have none," he sneer'd.

*   *   *   *   *   *

Thus Karshook, the Hiram's-Hammer,
  The Right-hand Temple-column,
Taught babes in grace their grammar,
  And struck the simple, solemn.

Dated Rome, April 27, 1854, printed in the *Keepsake*, 1856.

HELEN'S TOWER

(Written at the request of the Marquis of Dufferin)

Who hears of Helen's Tower, may dream perchance
How the Greek beauty from the Scaean gate
Gazed on old friends unanimous in hate,
Death-doom'd because of her fair countenance.
Hearts would leap otherwise at thy advance,
  Lady, to whom this tower is consecrate !
  Like hers, thy face once made all eyes elate,
Yet, unlike hers, was bless'd by every glance.
The Tower of Hate is outworn, far and strange :
  A transitory shame of long ago,
  It dies into the sand from which it sprang ;
But thine, Love's rock-built Tower, shalt fear no change :
  God's self laid stable earth's foundations so,
  When all the morning stars together sang.

Dated April 26, 1870.

VERSES FROM *THE HOUR WILL COME*

The blind man to the maiden said,
  " O thou of hearts the truest,
Thy countenance is hid from me ;
Let not my question anger thee !
  Speak, though in words the fewest.

" Tell me, what kind of eyes are thine ?
  Dark eyes, or light ones rather ? "
" My eyes are a decided brown—
So much at least, by looking down,
  From the brook's glass I gather."

" And is it red—thy little mouth ?
  That too the blind must care for."
" Ah ! I would tell it soon to thee,
  Only—none yet has told it me,
I cannot answer, therefore.

" But dost thou ask what heart I have—
  There hesitate I never.
In thine own breast 'tis borne, and so
'Tis thine in weal, and thine in woe,
  For life, for death—thine ever ! "

1883.

APPENDIX B

THE MURDER OF POMPILIA

(Reprinted from the *Monthly Review*, Nov., 1900, with Mr. John Murray's sanction)

For the discovery, last January, of the Italian manuscript, of which the following is a translation, I am indebted to Signor Dottore Ignazio Giorgi, Librarian of the Royal Casanatense Library in Rome. The volume from which it is taken [Misc. MS. 2037] is entitled " *Varii successi curiosi e degni di esser considerati*," and also contains an account of the trial of Beatrice Cenci, and of the recantation, in 1686, of Miguel de Molinos, whose followers are so often mentioned in *The Ring and the Book*.

The baptismal dates of the Franceschini and of Caponsacchi are taken from the Archives of Arezzo, which have yielded many other interesting details. Several of the footnotes are based upon the evidence adduced in the trial of Guido Franceschini in January–February, 1698, as contained in the actual source of Browning's poem, his "square old yellow book." The manuscript here printed for the first time has much in common with the information in that book, but supplements it in various ways, and is the best prose account of the whole case which is known to exist.—W. HALL GRIFFIN.

THE TRIAL AND DEATH OF FRANCESCHINI AND HIS COMPANIONS FOR MURDER AND ASSASSINATION COMMITTED ON THE PERSONS OF PIETRO COMPARINI, HIS WIFE AND DAUGHTER, WHICH TOOK PLACE IN THE TIME OF INNOCENT XII.

ABATE PAOLO FRANCESCHINI, born in Arezzo, Tuscany, was of noble family, although he had inherited but a small patrimony; yet, being possessed of sufficient talent to push his fortunes, he moved to the city of Rome, where he was admitted by Cardinal Lauria[1] to his household

[1] Cardinal Lorenzo Brancati di Lauria, born 1612, made Cardinal 1681, died 30 November, 1693. He would be an excellent patron, being widely known for

as Secretary of the Embassy. A natural fitness of mind gained him the favour of this Cardinal, who stood so high in the esteem of the Sacred College for his learning that it seemed by no means improbable that he might be raised to the Pontificate.

Under these favourable auspices, Paolo, who was desirous of making the most of his opportunities, thought of arranging a marriage for his brother Guido, so that he might, by means of a substantial dowry, re-establish the family fortunes. Guido had also found employment in Rome as Secretary of the Embassy to a Cardinal—Cardinal Nerli [1]—but, either because he had not the opportunities or the skill of his brother, he had quitted this service. Now, although Paolo knew that the fact of his brother being out of employment would damage his chances of forming a good alliance, yet he did not cease to try and make an advantageous match, for he hoped that the reflection of his own importance might atone for the shortcomings of his brother.

Guido was now getting towards middle life, of delicate constitution, mediocre appearance, a disposition gloomy rather than pleasing—above all, with very little means, so that his matrimonial expectations would be but slight unless he could profit by his brother's position.

After having sought a number of alliances with people of good position, Paolo finally decided upon Francesca Pompilia, daughter of Pietro and Violante Comparini, because, as she was an only child, and, on account of the age of her parents there was no possibility of other offspring, she would succeed to 12,000 scudi held in trust; and Paolo hoped to make the match without difficulty, as the Comparini were rather beneath him than his equals by birth.

There was a female hairdresser [2] who used to visit the Comparini with that freedom with which such women are admitted by those who desire to appear to their husbands more beautiful than they are, and are tolerated by those men who hold too high an opinion of the

---

his learning, modesty, and liberality. I find Paolo, then aged thirty-three, dedicating a poem to him in 1683—doubtless the first step toward securing the Cardinal's favour. Cardinal Lauria secured fifteen votes at the Conclave which in 1689 elected Alexander VIII, the predecessor of the " Pope " of Browning's poem.

[1] Guido seems indeed to have missed his opportunity. Nerli was literary, very wealthy, and, like the Franceschini, a Tuscan—from Florence. Born 1636, made Cardinal 1673, he died, aged seventy-two, in 1708. Browning was not aware of the *names* of either Lauria or Nerli.

[2] This " woman-dealer in perukes " figures in *Tertium Quid* (430-51), where the bribe promised her is put at the modest sum of 20 zecchines, *i.e.* £10, as against the 200 scudi—nearly £200 of modern money—mentioned here.

fidelity of their wives. Paolo considered this woman the most likely means of forwarding his matrimonial schemes. Guido, therefore, repeatedly went to the woman's shop in the [Piazzo Colonna] on various pretexts, and, having won his way into her confidence, he occasionally turned the conversation upon the subject of his marrying, whereupon she told him, one day, that he might easily approach the daughter of the Comparini, who had a dowry worthy of him, as she had the expectation of inheriting the trust-money, and also had few kinsfolk, these being the conditions of which he was in search. It was agreed, therefore, that, if she should succeed in bringing about the match, he would pay her 200 scudi.

The hairdresser lost no time in opening the subject to Violante, who, being anxious that her daughter should succeed to the property, and also that she should be advantageously settled, agreed to speak to her husband, whose consent she felt disposed to obtain, should the facts be as they were represented. Violante spoke of the matter to Pietro, and he consented to entertain the proposal on condition of the verification of the wealth boasted of by the Franceschini, who, said he, must furnish a written statement attested by well-known people.

The hairdresser informed the Franceschini of this, and they sent for an account of their real estate in Arezzo, amounting to an annual income of 1700 scudi, this statement being certified by people known to the Comparini, and also confirmed by them by word of mouth.

Abate Paolo, fearing lest the fortune should slip through his fingers, did not wish to allow the Comparini time to change their minds; on the contrary, in order to make sure of things, he desired to strengthen his position by the influence of Cardinal Lauria, his patron, by whom he had a marriage contract drawn up, his Eminence being pleased to show his interest in the welfare of a man whom he regarded with a certain degree of favour.

Meanwhile Pietro Comparini, having made inquiries as to the social condition and the property of the Franceschini, found a state of affairs very different from that represented, both in regard to their rank and their possessions. Thereupon he had warm disputes with his wife, who persisted in urging the marriage, and said that he had taken the advice of people who were envious of the welfare of both families, and wished to hinder the good fortune of the two households; and that therefore they ought not to depart from their first intention, for she was quite sure, from several truthful witnesses, that the Franceschini were of the first nobility in Arezzo, and not of the second, as was stated, and that the wealth mentioned in the written statement was exactly as declared. But the warmer her interest became, the more that of Pietro cooled down; for, having an eye to his own interest, if he could not gain, at least he did not wish to lose by the marriage of his daughter. But what does not a man lose when he allows himself to be ruled by women! He loved his wife so tenderly, that from the first day of his union with her he had made her the arbitress of his will: notwithstanding this, however, Violante, fearing that, in a matter of such importance, Pietro might rather be guided by good advice than yield to her flattery, and not being able to endure any delay in making sure of the trust-money—which would go to another family if the Comparini lacked descendants—she resolved to complete the marriage without the knowledge of Pietro. So, having obtained the consent of her daughter, who was always amenable to her commands, and having arranged matters with Guido, one morning she took Pompilia, suitably dressed, to San Lorenzo in Lucina, their parish church, and gave her in marriage.[1]

This was a heavy blow to Pietro, but, realizing that there was no remedy for it, he concealed his wrath by pretending that he had only been displeased at not having been at the marriage, and that this was forgotten in the pleasure of the wedding feast which was held at his house (in the Via Vittoria). For dowry, he made over to his daughter twenty-six bonds, with the ultimate succession to them all: and that very day, as they were talking of the advantages which would result to both households from the union of their interests, it was arranged that the Comparini should go to Arezzo; and this took place a few days later,[2] the administration of all the property being left absolutely in the hands of Guido. On their arrival in Arezzo the Comparini were received by the mother and the relations of the Franceschini with all those marks of affection which are usual on such occasions; but very speedily, as they saw more of one another, they passed into quarrels, and from these to acts of open hostility. The mother of Guido,[3] a proud, niggardly woman, who kept house in a penurious style, and despotically limited even the bare necessities of life, provoked the Comparini to complain, and their remonstrances were answered at first by words of contempt

[1] The real date of the marriage is August or September, 1693. Browning, for artistic reasons, places it in December—"one dim end of a December day"—on account of the gloom associated with it.

[2] This would be in November, 1693, early in the month.

[3] Guido's mother was Beatrice Romani, a woman of sixty-two in 1693, as she was born in 1631. She died, aged seventy, in 1701, three years after her son's execution.

and then by threats. Violante, being a woman with her own share of natural pride, could not endure this, and therefore began to worry Pietro, and curse the day on which he had decided to go to Arezzo, laying upon him the whole blame for that for which she herself was responsible! Pietro, who was one of those men who are beside themselves if a woman sheds a couple of tears, instead of reproaching her as the cause of the trouble, in that she had, against his will and without his knowledge, concluded the marriage, begged her with caresses to bear this ill-usage with patience, as it would perhaps cease when the Franceschini saw that their daughter sided with them.

At this time Cardinal Lauria died [30 November, 1693], a Cardinal whose merits were beyond all praise, and Abate Paolo was appointed Secretary in Rome of the Order of the Knights of St. John of Malta,[1] and this increased the proud bearing of the Franceschini to such a degree that they now considered that the Comparini should deem themselves fortunate to be among their friends, much more their relations.

Violante, who could not endure to live any longer under the proud sway of another woman, when she had been accustomed to command, had now quite regained the upper hand with her husband, and so worried him that she induced him to go back to Rome once more, and to this end the Franceschini supplied them with money sufficient for the journey, and for the furniture necessary for the house.[2]

But scarcely were they arrived in Rome than, to the amazement of everybody, it was reported that Pietro had issued a judicial monition, in which he declared that Francesca Pompilia was not really his daughter, and that therefore he was not bound to pay the dowry. This document was certified by Violante, his wife, who deposed that, in order to keep off her husband's creditors in regard to the deed of trust, and to enjoy the interest of the bonds, she had feigned to be with child, and, that her deception should not be perceived by her husband, she had agreed with him that if ever this should happen they should have rooms apart until the birth of the child. She took the opportunity of the absence of Pietro, when busy over

---

[1] This was a good appointment. The headquarters of the Knights in Rome was in the still existing building in the Via Condotti, close to the Piazza di Spagna. The home of the Comparini was close by.

[2] The Comparini returned in March, 1694, to their former home in the Via Vittoria. Browning represents them as going to another house in the Via Paolina, erroneously associated with the road at the south of Rome leading to the church of S. Paolo *fuori le mura.*

his lawsuits one day, to bring about the appearance of the child. All passed off successfully owing to the sagacity of a nurse with whom she had arranged to provide all that was needful. Accordingly, in order that the man-servant should have no suspicion as to the fraud, they sent him off to the chemist's to have some prescriptions made up, and, during his absence, away went the nurse to fetch a child which she had brought into the world the day before for a neighbour, with whom she had made previous arrangements to this effect. Having got back to the house, she called through the open window to an acquaintance of the Comparini, everything being so neatly arranged that when the neighbour arrived there remained nothing to be done but to make her believe what was not really the fact.[1]

This unexpected act of Pietro's was noised abroad in Rome like wildfire, and was listened to with no less amazement than displeasure, and the Franceschini, who were justly indignant, would have taken fitting vengeance had not their anger been tempered by the hope that, if Pompilia were not really and legitimately the child of Pietro and Violante, the marriage might be annulled, and their injured reputation thus reinstated. But, having taken the advice of a number of lawyers, and finding that their opinions differed, they did not wish to stake their chances upon an issue so doubtful; for, if they instituted legal proceedings, they must inevitably acknowledge and presuppose the illegitimacy, and by such a confession they would themselves remain prejudiced in their claims upon the dowry. They therefore opposed the judicial notice of Violante and obtained a decision to the effect that Pompilia was so far to be regarded as the Comparini's daughter that the bonds promised in the marriage settlement were to be transferred to her. But Pietro appealed from this decision to the Signatura di Giustizia [the Court of Appeal].

The chief sufferer from this hatred between the two families was the unfortunate Pompilia, who remained by herself at Arezzo, exposed to the arbitrary treatment of her husband, her mother-in-law, and the Franceschini kindred, all of whom were mortally offended with her parents, so that not an hour passed without her being threatened with death. In a situation so desperate the heart of any woman, even of one more experienced, would have sunk

---

[1] These events took place on 17 July, 1680, as the baptismal entry in S. Lorenzo in Lucina proves. It runs as follows : " Die 23 Julii 1680 Ego Bartholomæus Minius Curatus baptizavi infantem natam 17 hujus ex D. Petro Comparini et ex D. Violante Peruzzi conjugibus degentibus in hac Parocchia, cui nomen impositum fuit Francisca Camilla Vittoria Angela Pompilia." (*Cf.* the opening lines of *Pompilia.*)

within her, much more that of a girl of sixteen who had no share in the deceit of her mother nor in the wiles of her father, and who, by reason of her good qualities, was worthy of caresses and not of cruelty. The unfortunate girl bore up as long as she could under their tyrannies, which daily became worse and worse, but, seeing that all prospect of peace was hopeless, she fled several times to the Governor of Arezzo [1] to seek the interposition of his authority with the Franceschini; and, as he gave her no help, she cast herself at the feet of the Bishop,[2] who summoned Guido to his presence and reconciled them. But, as Guido's anger was increased by reason of such public appeals, he threatened her with certain death if ever she should do such a thing again.

The wretched girl, seeing every avenue of peace closed, implored the help of Canon Conti,[3] brother-in-law of the Franceschini, who was perfectly familiar with what she had had to suffer, as he used to visit the house; and she begged him to save her life, which was in continual peril. He was moved to pity, and, knowing that there was no remedy but flight—in which, however, he could personally take no part, lest he should bring upon himself the hatred of the whole family connexion—he suggested that the only person for such an enterprise was Canon Caponsacchi,[4] his personal friend, and in a remote degree related to him—a man whose spirit was no less apt to incur danger than to overcome it.

Pompilia having accepted the advice of Conti, he lost no time in opening the subject to Caponsacchi, who, when the matter was first broached, manifested repugnance towards aiding a wife to flee from her husband, even though the only object in view was to accompany her to the home of her parents. But, on being fully informed as to the unbearable ill-treatment of Guido and his family, pity overcame every other feeling, and he accepted the undertaking. Pompilia, who now longed for this result, kept urging it upon him by means of

[1] This, as the poem mentions, was Vincenzo Marzi-Medici, governor from 1693–95. Pompilia went to him in 1694, and he wrote a letter to Abate Paolo in Rome, giving him an account of the Comparini and their doings in Arezzo, dated 2 August, 1694. Marzi-Medici, was not, however, as the poem says, a relative of the Grand Duke; he was the son of a Florentine lawyer.

[2] This Bishop—*Arch*bishop the poem calls him—was Giovanni Matteo Marchetti, Bishop for thirteen years, from 1691–1704. He was of a well-known Pistoian family, and had a splendid collection of drawings by old masters, which came to England after his death.

[3] Guido's only sister Porzia married Count Aldobrandini, Conti's brother.

[4] Caponsacchi was aged twenty-four at this time (1697), having been baptized 22 March, 1673.

letters [1] and endearing incitements, always, however, preserving her fidelity as a wife, as may be gathered from her letters, in some of which she praises the modesty of Caponsacchi, and in others reproves him for having sent her some rather unbecoming verses, and begs him to preserve unsullied that good character which she has praised.

The day of the flight having been arranged,[2] these two, with the assistance of Conti, got into a carriage, and, travelling as fast as possible—never stopping except when needful to change horses— they arrived, the second morning at dawn, at Castelnuovo. Here, although the landlord got ready one bed for both, Pompilia rested in a chair and Caponsacchi rushed down to the stable to hurry up the driver.

Guido waked up some hours after Pompilia had departed, and, finding that she was not in bed, got up in a passion ; and seeing her jewel-case open and the jewels gone, together with some money which was kept there, he divined what had taken place. So he tore along the road to Rome on a good horse, and overtook the fugitives at the inn at Castelnuovo [3] one hour after they had arrived.

When she saw him appear, Pompilia, with a boldness such as despair frequently produces even in a sluggish nature, seized the sword of Caponsacchi, which was lying on a table, and, having drawn it, rushed out to meet Guido ; and calling him a traitor and a tyrant, threatened his life ; but he, fearing that her boldness no less than the valour of Caponsacchi—whom he had not previously known to be her protector—might result rather in his own death than in his taking vengeance, turned his horse's head, and, rushing off to the magistrate, had them arrested and soon afterwards taken off to the New Prisons [in Rome, sixteen miles distant], where they were accused of the flight and then of adultery.

Abate Paolo, who, as has been said, was Secretary in Rome for the Knights of Malta, made urgent representations to the Pope concerning the injury to his honour, and besought the Governor of Rome, Monsignor Pallavicino,[4] protesting that he ought to give judgment against Caponsacchi for having eloped with his sister-in-law,

---

[1] Twenty-two such letters, or fragments of them, were said to have been found by Guido, and were produced in the evidence at his trial. They are of slight interest.

[2] They fled on Sunday, 28 April, "seven hours after sunset "—*i.e.* about 2 a.m. Browning artistically alters this to 23 April—St. George's Day.

[3] The inn still exists unchanged, with the very room in which the scene here described took place.

[4] Marc Antonio Venturini, mentioned as Governor in the poem, was in fact a Deputy-Governor for criminal cases—*Locum tenens in criminalibus.*

and declare them both guilty of adultery, and that on this account his brother Guido ought to obtain possession of the whole dowry.

Legal proceedings were instituted with all the rigour of the law, but there appeared no evidence of guilt against Pompilia and Caponsacchi except the letters indicating an affectionate intercourse, and written while the flight was being planned, the flight itself, and the depositions of the driver,[1] who said that he had several times seen them, as he turned round while driving, face to face together— *i.e.* cheek against cheek—a thing which is no proof of wrongdoing, while the roughness of the roads, and the speed at which they were driving, by shaking them, might have been the cause. Wherefore the Court prudently sentenced Caponsacchi to three years' relegation in Civita Vecchia for his rash act in running away with a wife from the home of her husband, even though he had been actuated by motives of pity.[2]

Meanwhile the proceedings against Pompilia continued, and with the consent of the Franceschini she was sent under restraint to the monastery of the Scalette in the Lungara,[3] Guido giving a bond that he would pay for her board. After some time it became evident that she was *enceinte*, and as the rules of the place did not allow of her remaining any longer there, the Governor of Rome, with the approval of Abate Paolo, who held a power of attorney for his brother, issued an order that Pompilia should be removed to the house of the Comparini, her parents, under security of 300 scudi, declaring at the same time that the obligation on Guido's part to pay for her board should cease the very day on which Pompilia should leave the monastery.[4]

This suit, in which the Franceschini represented themselves as being solely actuated by a desire to repair their honour, was recognized as having for its chief motive their greed for money, so that there was not a single club in which the conduct of both sides was not criticized. For this reason the Knights of St. John quietly hinted to Abate Paolo that he had better resign his position as Secretary. The loss of so honourable a position gave free course to the malice of the tongues of his enemies, and reduced the mind

[1] This was Francesco Borsi, called "Venerino," a servant of the landlord of the still existing *Canale* Inn at Arezzo. He drove them to Camoscia, that is, for the first night only.

[2] This decree is dated 24 September, 1697.

[3] The Scalette—so called from the steps in front of it—still exists, under the name of the "Buon Pastore." Browning chose to speak of the Convertite, who also had a home in the Lungara.

[4] This order is dated 12 October, 1697.

of Paolo to such a state of anxiety that he felt ashamed to face even his dearest friends. He therefore decided to quit Rome and to pass to a land whither there should never come news of the dishonour which had so deeply afflicted him.[1]

Guido being informed of his departure and of the obligation now resting upon himself of repairing the honour of their house, reflected that if he, like his brother, should voluntarily exile himself, it would be regarded as a confirmation of that cowardliness of spirit with which he had been justly charged when he had overtaken his wife in her flight, and had not then and there taken that vengeance which was expected at his hands.

Her time having arrived, Pompilia gave birth to a male child,[2] whom the Comparini sent out to nurse. Everybody thought, and in particular Violante, that this event would dispose Guido, by the very force of nature, to a reconciliation with his wife, while the minds of the Comparini, in spite of their declaration that Pompilia was not their child, might also be inclined to re-establish peace. The thought of Guido, however, was wholly different, for he was ceaselessly urged on by Paolo, who, even though absent, kept plotting to blot out of the world every memory of his own dishonour by the death of Pompilia, Pietro, and Violante.

Guido had a field labourer, a bold man of evil life, to whom he repeatedly told exaggerated tales about the disgrace which his wife and the Comparini had brought upon his house; and he confided to this man that, if he would aid him, he would be able to wipe out with their blood the stains upon his honour. The assassin at once agreed, and himself suggested that, if other help were needed, he had three or four friends for whom he could vouch. Guido's answer was that he should select three bold and trusty ones for the sake of security, in case of meeting with resistance, and that he should be particularly careful to engage them at as low a rate as he possibly could.

This being all arranged, and the weapons suitable for such a deed made ready, Guido with his four companions, disguised, and with changed garments, took the road to Rome, and arrived[3] at the house of the Comparini[4] two hours after sunset. One of them

---

[1] I have traced him to Prague, where he published a poem in 1699.

[2] A boy, Gaetano, born 18 December, 1697.

[3] They arrived at Rome 24 December, 1697. The murders took place on Thursday, 2 January, 1698.

[4] Browning places this outside Rome beyond the Porta S. Paolo; the murders actually took place in a house—since rebuilt—which stood at the corner of the Via Vittoria and the Via Babuino, formerly called Via Paolina.

knocked at the door, and when Pietro answered, the assassin said that he had a letter to deliver from Civita Vecchia from Caponsacchi. When the women heard this, they told Pietro that he must tell the man to come back in the morning, and objected to his opening the door; but Pietro being curious about the news from Caponsacchi, and the assassin making reply that he could not call again next morning, as he had to depart that very night, Pietro opened the fatal door through which entered death for himself, for Violante, and for Pompilia.

Beside himself with passion, Guido was the first to rush in with two companions [1]—the other two remaining to keep guard—and, having repeatedly stabbed the poor old man, they deprived him of life before he could utter a word. Scarcely had the unfortunate women beheld this than they were thrust through in a similar manner and experienced the same fate; the blows of Guido being directed against the unhappy Pompilia, and being accompanied with innumerable insults. After having trampled her under foot several times and repeated his blows, Guido, not sure that his fury had accomplished its purpose, told his companions to see if she were really dead, and one of them lifting her up by the hair and then letting her suddenly fall, made sure that she was no longer alive.

The barbarous slaughter over, and Guido having paid the cut-throats the money agreed upon,[2] he wished to separate from them, but they would not allow either him or any of the others to depart, fearing lest one should kill the other, as not infrequently happens in such crimes. Or, perchance, the cut-throats had arranged with their leader, if they kept together, to kill Guido, supposing that he would have upon him a large sum of money, and therefore, it is said, they would not consent to his going away. Accordingly they took the road to Arezzo together, being obliged to travel on foot on account of not having been able to procure post-horses.

Life was totally extinct in Pietro and Violante by reason of their numerous wounds, but Pompilia was still living, although her wounds were even more numerous,[3] for in her innocence, and aided by Divine mercy, she had been able to feign death so well that she deceived the assassins. When, therefore, she could see that they were gone, collecting her dying breath, she had still sufficient strength of voice to make the neighbours hear her cries for help.

---

[1] These two were Francesco Pasquino and Alessandro Giovanni Baldeschi. Those who kept guard were Biaggio Agostinelli and Domenico Gambassini.

[2] This account differs on this point from that used by Browning, who says the assassins were *not* paid, and therefore were about to kill Guido.

[3] Twenty-two dagger wounds, five deadly.

Being found in a dying state, the needs of the soul were first eagerly attended to, and afterwards those of her body. Her wounds were so many in number, and of such a character, that, although they did not immediately deprive her of life, yet they rendered her death inevitable; an event which, to the universal sorrow of those who attended her, and of as many as had information about so lamentable a case, took place a few days later.[1]

The constancy with which she endured the sufferings of her medical treatment was no less amazing than the love excited by her resignation to the Divine will; while not only did she not blame the cruelty of her husband, but with fervent prayers she implored God to pardon him.

As evidence of the compassion of those who ministered to her soul and to her body, I quote the following sworn testimonies, not only as to her innocence, but also as to the happy passage of her pure soul to heaven.

TESTIMONIES AS TO THE AFORESAID STATEMENT

" I, the undersigned Barefoot Augustinian, solemnly testify that, having ministered to Signora Pompilia from the first moment of the woful case until the last minute of her life, I state and swear, as I am a priest in the presence of that God who shall be my Judge, that I have remarked and have been amazed at the innocent and pure conscience of this ever-blessed girl; and in the four days [2-6 January] which she survived, she, having been exhorted by me to pardon [her husband], replied with tears in her eyes, and with calm and compassionate voice, ' May Jesus pardon him as I have already done with all my heart.' But what was most wonderful was that, although she suffered great pain from her injuries, I never heard her utter an offensive or an impatient word, or even give any sign of such, either against God or her fellow-beings; but with uniform submission to the Divine will she would say, ' The Lord have mercy on me '; a fact, in truth, which is incompatible with a spirit not closely united to God; and such union does not take place in a single moment, but truly is due to long-continued habit. Moreover, I declare that I have uniformly noticed her to be most modest; and in particular on those occasions in which the doctors attended to her, so that, if she had not been of good habits, on such occasions she would not have given evidence of modesty in regard to certain little

---

[1] Pompilia died on Monday, 6 January, 1698, the day on which she is supposed to speak in the poem.

details carefully noticed by me, and much wondered at, that a young girl should be able to bear herself in the presence of so many men with such modesty and composure as did this saintly girl, even though half dead. And if we are to believe what the Holy Spirit, speaking by the mouth of the Evangelist, says, in the 7th chapter of St. Matthew, *arbor mala non potest bonos fructus facere*, noticing that he says, "non potest [*i.e. can* not], and not non facit," [*i.e. does* not] :—that is, he pronounces it impossible to translate our powers into acts of perfection when these forces are themselves imperfect and tainted with evil—we must perforce say that this girl was full of goodness and modesty, since with all ease and perfection she behaved virtuously and modestly during the close of her life. Moreover, she died full of faith in God, her heart filled with Divine grace, and with all the sacraments of the Church, so that all who were in her presence were filled with wonder and pronounced her a saint. I say no more for fear that I may be taxed with being partial. I know full well that *Solus Deus est scrutator cordium :* but I know also that *ex abundantia cordis os loquitur*, and that my own Augustine declares, *Talis vita, finis ita :* wherefore, having remarked in this ever-blessed girl devout words, virtuous deeds and most modest acts, and a death in the fear of God, for the satisfaction of my own conscience I am obliged, and can do no other than declare that it must needs be that she has ever been a young girl good, modest, and honourable.

The above is my testimony, whereof in my own hand-writing, this 10th day of January——.

[Signed]   FRA CELESTINE DI S. ANNA [1]

Barefoot Augustinian

AFFIDAVIT SIGNED BY SEVERAL WITNESSES

We, the undersigned, having been asked to state the truth, give full and incontrovertible testimony under oath, that on the occasion on which we were present and rendered assistance in the last illness from which Francesca Pompilia died, she having been several times questioned by priests and others as to whether she had committed

---

[1] From this name Browning has constructed a wholly imaginary "Hospital of St. Anna," in which Pompilia is supposed to die after Fra Celestine—who is often mentioned in the poem—has confessed her. These depositions supplied the poet with the suggestion for his conception of an idealized Pompilia, and it was mainly in allusion to them that he is reported to have said, " I assure you that I found her, just as she speaks and acts in my poem, in that old book."

any offence against Guido her husband, which would have afforded him reason to ill-treat her in the manner we saw, and cause her to be done to death; she uniformly replied that she had not at any time committed any such fault whatever, and had always lived in all chastity and purity. And this we know through having been present during her sufferings ; and from having heard all the said questions and answers; and also from having treated her medically and aided her; and from having heard her replies to the aforesaid questions during the four days that she survived while suffering from her wounds, and from having seen her, and heard her, and witnessed her die like a saint.

In evidence whereof, etc.

This 10th day of January,

I, NICOLO CONSTANTIO, who took part in the medical treatment.

I, PLACIDO SARDI, priest, with my own hand confirm what Fra Celestine has said above, having been present as above.

I, MICHELE NICOLO GREGORIO, confirm the above.

I, GIUSEPPE D'ANDILLI, with my own hand, etc.

I, DOMENICO GODYN, etc.

I, LUCA CORSI, etc.

I, GIO. BATTISTA GUITEUS.[1]

I, GIO. BATTISTA MUCHA.

I, Abate Liberato Barberito, Doctor of Theology, hereby give full and indubitable evidence that, having been summoned to attend the death-bed of the late Signora Francesca Pompilia Comparini, I repeatedly noticed, and in particular during one entire night, how she bore with Christian resignation the pains of her wounds, and with more than human generosity pardoned the wrongs done her by him who had so cruelly caused her death. Thus, during the whole of the aforesaid night I observed the tenderness of her conscience, the time having passed in affording me evidence that her everyday life had been full of heroic Christian perfection. And I can testify from the experience which I have had, during the four years in which I was Judge of the Ecclesiastical Court of the late Archbishop of Monopoli, that I have never seen any one meet death in such a state of mind, especially when this had been due to violence.

Wherefore, in evidence, etc.,

This 10th day of January, 1698,

I, ABATE LIBERATO BARBERITO

---

[1] Guiteus was an apothecary who administered medicine and helped in the medical treatment. Mucha was his assistant.

All these sworn testimonies form part of the evidence in the suit against Guido, and are signed and confirmed by the above-mentioned witnesses who took part in ministering to the bodily and spiritual needs of Pompilia until her death.

Divine justice, which will not suffer so atrocious a crime to pass unpunished, brought it about that the evil-doers were overtaken at dawn by the police at the New [Merluzza][2] Inn [at Baccano], some few miles from Rome; where, after a scanty meal, overcome with the fatigue of their journey and with sleep, they had lain down to rest by the fire. The police suddenly rushed in, and pointing their carbines at the heads of the offenders, they were seized and bound.

They were removed at once to the New Prisons [in the Via Giulia, Rome], and the Governor of Rome informed the Pope of the barbarous murder and of the arrest of the guilty; he issued orders that there should be no delay in proceeding against them with all the rigour of the law, this being the case which, by reason of the consequences that might ensue, the Court was bound to examine with the most scrupulous attention.

Far less than had been imagined, however, was it found needful to apply torture to ensure the confession of the assassins and of Guido, who more emphatically than the others persisted in denying his guilt. Notwithstanding this, simply at the sight of the torture his heart failed him and he made a full confession, although he declared that he had been actuated in his crime by no other motive than the desire to make reparation for his honour, which had been so publicly injured—a thing which any man, even if of ignoble birth, would undertake, much more one like himself, who was of good family; and that, if in his first examination he had denied the truth of this, he had done it solely so as not to prejudice his companions who had helped him in a deed worthy of all indulgence, because their only motive had been honour.

With the confession of Guido and its ratification by the others the trial was at an end, and sentence was given,[3] the assassins being condemned to the gallows and Guido to the *mannaia* [a kind of guillotine], an instrument of death conceded to him rather out of

[1] All three, together with some additional matter, are printed in "the book" which the poet bought.

[2] The name is omitted in the Roman MS. I supply it from another source.

[3] The Court gave sentence on Tuesday, 18 February. The lawyers for the defence, however, appealed to the Pope, who signed the death-warrant on Friday, 21 February—the day on which Innocent XII is supposed, in the poem, to utter his noble monologue.

respect to his having taken minor religious orders than for other reasons.

The written arguments of [Desiderius Spreti] the Advocate, and [Hyacinthus de Arcangelis] the Procurator of the Poor, in their defence on the plea of honour were so able that there is no mention of more learned pleadings;[1] but the charges against the accused were so numerous, and each of them punishable by death, that they were overpowered no less by the character than by the number of these. The bearing of deadly arms of prohibited shape; the killing of Pietro and Violante, who had not been accomplices in the flight of Pompilia; the fact of the murders having taken place *in lite pendente*, in the home of the Comparini, which, with the consent of Guido, the Court had assigned to Pompilia as a secure place of confinement; and many other accusations of weight, brought into prominence the profound learning of the counsel for the defence and the justice of the condemnation of the guilty.

Although, with the usual hope of all who know themselves guilty of a crime punishable with death, Guido had flattered himself that he should be able to save his life on the plea of honour; yet, when the unexpected condemnation was pronounced, he did not yield himself up to such ill-regulated manifestations as for the most part occur among those who pass through so terrible an experience. He remained like one dazed; then, after some moments, he heaved a deep sigh, accompanied by a few tears, which by their extraordinary size indicated mortal symptoms, and exclaimed: " Verily I feared a heavy sentence, but not that of death. My offence is great, but my love of honour has never allowed me to see it in its true light until now, when it has been adjudged by justice, for which I have so profound a veneration that I do not wish to appeal even to God, to whom alone I turn as the sole source of mercy. Except by the will of God, I should never have come to this awful pass, and this I desire should be a source of comfort to me, and not of pain, so that, by my utter resignation to His will, I may acquire some claim to Divine pardon." And hereupon he cast himself into the arms of the Frati and showed such signs of lively contrition that his prayers were accompanied by their tears rather than by their exhortations.

The four accomplices did not by any means dispose themselves

---

[1] The pleadings here alluded to are those contained in the poet's " square old yellow book." The two pleas by Spreti were especially commended for their learning. As *Advocate of the Poor* he was the leading lawyer for the defence ; Arcangeli, who wrote three pleas, being one of his *Procurators.* The poet, for reasons of his own, has chosen to make Spreti the " junior " of Arcangeli. The eleven pleas in the trial are all in Latin.

for death with the same resignation; for, as their mental capacity was in keeping with their viler nature, they could not be persuaded of the justice of their condemnation. The oldest and the youngest [1] were the most firm in their obstinacy; the former because his heart had been hardened by so many years of evil life, the latter because he felt so bitterly the dreadful punishment for this first crime, committed in the flower of his youth, he having also shed not a drop of blood, his only offence being that he had been induced to keep guard at a door by which Guido had to pass that he might wipe away with the blood of his enemies the stains upon his honour.

The nearer the hour of execution approached, the more the obstinacy of these two unfortunate men increased, so that the Frati were, so to say, in despair about their repentance; when Divine mercy, which accomplishes wonders even when they are least expected, penetrated their hearts, and thus gave glorious evidence of its omnipotence. Finally, they yielded to God, and the memory of their offences, which had hitherto rendered them obstinate, became, under the illumination of Divine grace, the means of disposing them to repentance and of fitting them for absolution.

These souls being secured to God after so prolonged a struggle, the procession started from the New Prisons of Tor di Nonna to the scaffold, which was set up in the Piazza del Popolo in view of the city gate and the Corso. In the middle was the block on a high platform, made much broader than usual, and having carefully arranged steps leading up to it; the gallows being placed, one on each side, at equal distances. Vast as is the area of the Piazza, there was not a single foot which was not occupied with raised stands, and these, being draped with tapestry and other decorations, formed a theatre suited rather for festive games than for a solemn tragedy.

His four companions preceded Guido, each in a separate cart, attended, as usual, by the pious Frati, and followed by a huge crowd of people, who prayed that they might have a blessed end, of which, to judge by their contrite resignation, there seemed a sure and certain hope.

Guido Franceschini hardly ever took his eyes from the crucifix, except when nature became faint from his continued gaze, and then he turned away his head, but not his heart, which being wholly given to his Creator, there remained no portion for himself. Arriving at the Piazza di Pasquino, the tumbrels halted before the church of the Agonizzanti, where it is customary to expose the Host and to bestow

[1] This, as far as I can discover, was Biaggio Gambassini.

the Benediction upon condemned criminals on the day of their execution. Guido here fell upon his knees and recited, in a voice clearly audible to the bystanders, several verses of the *Miserere*, among them this : " Hide thy face from my sins and blot out all my iniquities " [Psalm li. 9], accompanying his words with such demonstrations of sorrow and repentance that the people, in tears, manifested as much grief as the condemned man. Guido's companions received the Benediction with similar devotion ; but the behaviour of the youngest was unprecedented : beside himself with love to God, his words were like those of one inspired, so that the priests, with all their learning, were filled with humility.

Thence, through the most inhabited streets, they continued their way to the Piazza del Popolo, where all suffered death, Guido being the last.[1] They exhibited the same signs of contrition as they had shown while being prepared for death; and just as the youngest had given special tokens during life, so it pleased God that these should again appear at his death ; for as the hangman was casting him off, he clasped to his bosom the crucifix—that emblem of mercy by which they had just been assured of Divine pardon. This made the populace all the more certain of his salvation, just as it filled them with compassion for his untimely death.

Never was there a greater concourse of people at an execution in Rome, nor is there recollection of a case which formed so universal a subject of conversation. Some defended the Comparini, on the ground that they had received ill-usage ; others, the Franceschini, on the point of honour ; but upon calm reflection, both were adjudged equally guilty—except Pompilia, who, being totally ignorant of the truth, had committed no other fault than that of

---

[1] This was on Saturday, 22 February, 1698. The Guido of the poem was then aged fifty : the Guido of history was a man of forty, who had married at thirty-five. Abate Paolo, the " second son " of the poem, was really the eldest son and Guido's senior by some eight years ; while

> " The boy of the brood, the young Girolamo,
> Priest, Canon,"

was born four years after Paolo. The dates in the baptismal register of the Pieve church are : 28 October, 1650, Paolo ; 2 January, 1653, Porzia ; 5 August, 1654, Girolamo ; and on 14 January, 1657 [1658 N.S.], Guido di Tommaso di Girolamo Franceschini e di Beatrice di Guido Romani sua consorte. The Guido of history was therefore not the " Head of the House," nor was he a Count. The family seems at that date to have belonged to the *fourth* of the eight " degrees of nobility " distinguished in Arezzo. A certain Count Giacomo—Jacobus Comes Franceschini—died there on 26 January, 1399, and is the first of the name mentioned. The title, it would appear, had gone to another branch of the family.

having consented to a marriage at the command of her mother without the knowledge of her father; and who had fled from her husband's home, under fear of death, with which she had been repeatedly and unjustly threatened.

The union of these two families had its origin in deception: on the part of the Franceschini, in the fraud as to the property which they did not possess; and on the part of the Comparini as to the birth of Pompilia, who either was not their child, or had been said not to be when she really was. The deceit of the Franceschini sprang from their greed to secure the trust-money; that of the Comparini from a desire to add to their comforts; so that everything was done contrary to what is right by both human laws and divine. Wherefore there justly followed from a bad beginning a worse end, as has been described above.

INDEX

A

z

INDEX